D1328384

*Eight Days in May*

"Gripping, immaculately researched. . . . In Volker Ullrich's account, the murderous behavior of the Reich's last-ditch loyalists was not a reaction born of rage or of stubbornness in the face of defeat—common enough in war—but of something that had long ago tipped over into the pathological."

—Andrew Stuttaford, *Wall Street Journal*

"Vivid, fast-paced. . . . Superbly researched, *Eight Days in May* communicates the pity of Hitler's war and its aftermath with sympathy and an impressive narrative verve."

—Ian Thomson, *The Spectator* (UK)

*Hitler: Downfall, 1939–1945*

"Skillfully conceived and utterly engrossing."

—Peter Fritzsche, *New York Times Book Review*

*Hitler: Ascent, 1889–1939*

"A fascinating Shakespearean parable about how the confluence of circumstance, chance, a ruthless individual and the willful blindness of others can transform a country—and, in Hitler's case, lead to an unimaginable nightmare for the world."

—Michiko Kakutani, *New York Times*

"A major achievement."

—Nicholas Stargardt, *Literary Review*

GERMANY 1923

ALSO BY VOLKER ULLRICH

*Hitler:*
*Ascent 1889–1939*

*Hitler:*
*Downfall 1939–1945*

*Eight Days in May:*
*The Final Collapse of the Third Reich*

# GERMANY
# 1923

---

## HYPERINFLATION, HITLER'S PUTSCH, AND DEMOCRACY IN CRISIS

## VOLKER ULLRICH

*Translated by Jefferson Chase*

**Liveright Publishing Corporation**

*A Division of W. W. Norton & Company*
*Celebrating a Century of Independent Publishing*

Copyright by Verlag C.H. Beck oHG, München 2022
Translation copyright © 2023 by W. W. Norton & Company, Inc.

Originally published in German as *Deutschland 1923*

For information about permission to reproduce selections from this book,
write to Permissions, Liveright Publishing Corporation, a division of
W. W. Norton & Company, Inc., 500 Fifth Avenue, New York, NY 10110

For information about special discounts for bulk purchases,
please contact W. W. Norton Special Sales at
specialsales@wwnorton.com or 800-233-4830

Manufacturing by Lake Book Manufacturing
Book design by Lovedog Studio
Production manager: Julia Druskin

ISBN 978-1-324-09346-6

Liveright Publishing Corporation, 500 Fifth Avenue, New York, N.Y. 10110
www.wwnorton.com

W. W. Norton & Company Ltd., 15 Carlisle Street, London W1D 3BS

1 2 3 4 5 6 7 8 9 0

# CONTENTS

CHAPTER 8
CULTURE IN A TIME OF CRISIS

CHAPTER 9
AFTER 1923
*A New Period in German History?*

# PREFACE

"MAY 1923 BE BETTER THAN 1922, THE WORST year ever in every respect—Amen!" That was how Thomas Mann's mother-in-law Hedwig Pringsheim ended her diary entry on December 31, 1922.[1] Pringsheim had no idea how much worse things would in fact get. The year 1923 would provide the most serious test yet for the still-young Weimar Republic. "No other nation has experienced anything comparable to the events of 1923 in Germany," journalist Sebastian Haffner would write from English exile in 1939,[2] while author Stefan Zweig confided in his autobiography *The World of Yesterday*, likewise written in exile, "I have a pretty thorough knowledge of history, but never, to my recollection, has it produced such madness in such gigantic proportions."[3]

*Germany 1923* is about this "time of lunacy," a year when the mark lost its value at a dizzying pace, a temporary state of emergency was applied with no set end, a political system verged on collapse, radicals on the Left and the Right planned assaults on the Republic, and various separatist movements threatened the territorial integrity of the German nation. Meanwhile, external pressure was exacerbating the domestic situation, as the occupation of Germany's industrial Ruhr Valley by French and Belgian troops in January 1923 caused ongoing conflict and greatly increased tensions. By autumn 1923, the country was teetering on the brink of an abyss. People at the time found it almost miraculous that the first German democracy was able to survive.

Historian Gerald D. Feldman titled his monumental study of the inflationary decade from 1914 to 1924 *The Great Disorder*.[4] War, military defeat, and revolution had swept away the seemingly unshakable monarchist system of the Wilhelmine Empire, but the democracy that was subsequently created in 1918 and 1919 never escaped postrevolutionary crisis mode. Even after the signing of the Treaty of Versailles and the ratification of the Weimar Constitution, the situation remained precarious. The old Wilhelmine elites from industry, big agriculture, the military, and the civil service remained fundamentally opposed to the "Weimar system," as the Republic was often disparagingly known. Attempted coups by the Left and Right rocked the country, and assassinations by right-wingers of representatives of the fledgling democracy were commonplace. "There is less security for political *personae non gratae* in today's Germany than in the most disreputable South American banana republics or the Borgias' Rome," remarked the diplomat and keen political and cultural observer Count Harry Kessler in May 1920.[5]

The serial crises reached their surreal zenith with the hyperinflation of 1923. All of Germany seemed to suffer from feverish delusion. "Time has come unglued," complained the Jewish German linguist and diarist Victor Klemperer in late May 1923, adding in early September, "Everyone senses something threatening at hand, but no one knows what's coming."[6] Everything was shaky, nothing was certain, and there was no counting on anything: these were the fundamental sentiments of the frenzied months of 1923. Not only did German currency lose its value as a means of exchange; in the turmoil of hyperinflation, social values and norms fell apart, too. Novelist Elias Canetti aptly called this a "double devaluation."[7] The disintegration went hand in hand with a basic loss of trust in the functioning of political institutions. The result was "a kind of everyday anarchy," a struggle of all against all.[8]

The sense in autumn 1923 that Germany was plummeting into a bottomless pit didn't allow for rational explanation. People were dumbfounded. "Often everything I saw and experienced back then seems like a fantastical dream," artist George Grosz recalled. "But strangely enough, the more prices rose, the greater our lust for life. Boy, was life ever grand!"[9] Such euphoria reflected the reverse side of the misery of broad segments of the populace after suddenly losing their life savings. People were seized by an irrepressible desire for intoxications of all sorts, and the German entertainment industry experienced an unprecedented boom. "The frenetic demand for amusement reached levels that made the panic-driven revelries of the medieval plagues look like sober performances of well-heeled glee clubs," historian Wolfgang Ruge has written.[10]

Historians who examine the madness of this time are inevitably struck by its breathless pace. Events and developments came not one after the other but as a deluge in which individual occurrences overlapped and augmented one another. That chaos must be reflected in any depiction of this period. The history of a year of extremes like 1923 cannot be told purely chronologically. In the interests of comprehensibility, I have tried to untangle the knots of crises and reorder the various strands thematically. The result is a nonchronological sequence of chapters.

The first examines the French and Belgian occupation of the Ruhr Valley at the start of 1923 and describes the ruinous effects of the German government's policy of passive resistance, which ultimately led to the fall of Chancellor Wilhelm Cuno in August.

The second chapter looks at the causes of inflation and hyperinflation and asks who profited and who got left behind. The focus is on how German society experienced the furious devaluation of the mark and how people's everyday lives changed as a result.

The third chapter revolves around the formation of a broad-based, "grand coalition" government—composed of the Social Democrats (SPD), the predominantly Catholic Center Party, the liberal-centrist German Democratic Party (DDP), and the center-right German People's Party (DVP)—under Chancellor Gustav Stresemann. It delves into his attempts to find a way out of the crisis, including such efforts as the end of the policy of "passive resistance" to the French occupation in September and the initiation of a currency reform with the founding of the *Rentenbank* (annuity bank) the following month.

The fourth chapter concerns the plans of the Bolsheviks in Moscow to exploit the chaos of hyperinflation and unleash revolution in Germany. The initial spark was supposed to be the German Communist Party (KPD) joining the Social Democratic–led regional governments in Saxony and Thuringia. The "German October" may never have materialized, and a Communist-led rebellion in Hamburg was quickly crushed. But the failed coup still had grave consequences. The hard line taken by the German military, the Reichswehr, in Saxony and Thuringia, especially in contrast to the leeway shown to separatists in Bavaria, led the SPD to quit the national government, dooming the grand coalition.

The fifth chapter shifts the focus back to the Right and the plans by extremists to establish a "national dictatorship" around the head of the Reichswehr, Hans von Seeckt. To illuminate the overall context, intense attention is devoted to the period before, during, and after Hitler's "Beer Hall Putsch" in Munich on November 8 and 9. This attempted coup, as we will see, was anything but an isolated undertaking. On the contrary, it was one of numerous efforts by influential industrial, military, and right-wing political circles to bring down the Weimar political system and institute an authoritarian regime.

The sixth chapter deals with the French-backed separatist movements in the Rhineland and Pfalz regions, culminating in the proclamation of autonomous republics there in the fall of 1923. Although short-lived, these rebellions symbolized the fraying of governmental authority in western Germany.

The seventh chapter focuses on the currency stability achieved by the "miraculous" introduction of the *Rentenmark* (mortgage mark) on November 15. Stresemann's centrist successor, Wilhelm Marx, decisively continued the steps that had been taken to reform the country's finances. A survey of commentaries appearing at year's end shows the degree to which people at the time felt the worst was over.

The eighth chapter is something of a departure in that it concentrates not on the crises dominating the economy, society, and politics but rather on the remarkable flourishing of Weimar culture. Examples from film, theater, literature, fine arts, and architecture illustrate the great achievements of creators of culture amid the difficult inflationary times—and the resistance from culturally conservative, nationalist circles that had to be overcome.

The ninth and final chapter looks ahead to 1924 and the Dawes Plan, which would lead to a preliminary mutual agreement on the issue of German reparations for its role in starting the First World War and pave the way for international deescalation. The agreement marked the definitive end of the immediate postwar period. Of particular interest is the question of how permanent the domestic and international consolidation of the Weimar Republic could have been or whether new trouble was already brewing behind the façade of a seemingly reinforced parliamentary democracy.

The classic histories of the Weimar Republic highlighted the question of why the first German democracy failed after only fourteen years, giving way to the criminal Nazi dictatorship.[11] But since the 1990s, historians have tended not to examine and evaluate the Weimar Republic from the perspective of its demise, instead treating it as a discrete period with its own legitimacy. Rather than reducing the epoch between 1918 and 1933 to a mere prelude to the Third Reich, scholars have increasingly examined its promising as well as its foreboding elements.[12] Particularly in this dual sense, 1923 was a critical year, a measure of both the extent of the right-wing threat and the potential for stabilization. In any case, the fact that the Weimar Republic survived the most exacting stress test is a compelling argument that it was in fact not condemned to failure from its onset.[13]

The extreme situation caused by hyperinflation burned itself into Germans' collective memory. Rising prices stripped broad segments of the population of everything they had—a process socialist and historian Arthur Rosenberg called "one of the biggest robberies in world history"—and left people unfathomably bitter.[14] The sudden devaluation of their assets and savings traumatized many Germans, who would never recover, and the fear of a new round of hyperinflation was passed down to following generations. Even today, anxieties of this sort remain much greater in Germany than in other European nations.[15] Among Germans, the rising prices precipitated by the contemporary coronavirus pandemic unleashed nightmarish memories of the hyper-inflation of 1923, although there are huge differences between today's economic and political situation and the constellation of crises that defined 1923. This book aims to sharpen readers' awareness of such distinctions, even as it reclaims the experiences and perceptions of the people who endured those crises a century ago.

# GERMANY 1923

# CHAPTER 1

# THE BATTLE FOR
# THE RUHR VALLEY

*A French armored vehicle on the streets of Essen shortly
after the occupation of the Ruhr Valley.*

T HE YEAR 1923 STARTED WITH A BANG. ON JANU-
ary 11, French and Belgian troops marched into the industrial
Ruhr Valley. The justification was that Germany was purposely delaying agreed-on deliveries of material to compensate for the destruction
in France and Belgium during the First World War. The spectacular
invasion didn't come out of nowhere. The victors in the war had previously threatened sanctions if the German government neglected to
live up to its reparation commitments.[1] Those threats included occupying territory on both sides of the Rhine River, which according to
the Treaty of Versailles was to remain demilitarized for fifteen years.
After negotiations in Paris on January 4, 1923, failed to achieve a

breakthrough, the conflict quickly came to a head. "The political situation is again something that weighs upon even dulled nerves," wrote Victor Klemperer in his diary on January 5. "French invasion is imminent after the failed reparations summit."[2]

Reparations placed the largest strain on the difficult relations between Germany and the Entente powers following the First World War. The armistice of November 11, 1918, had required Germany to hand over 5,000 locomotives, 150,000 railway cars, and 5,000 trucks. Article 231 of the Treaty of Versailles, which the German delegation was forced to sign in the Hall of Mirrors, assigned sole responsibility for the war to the Wilhelmine Empire and its allies. They were made responsible for all losses and damage caused by the war. But the exact sum Germany would be required to repay was left unspecified. Article 233 of the treaty mandated the naming of a committee that would determine the final amount of German reparations by May 1, 1921. But by that date, regardless of the ultimate ruling, Germany was to hand over 20 billion gold marks in currency and assets.[3]

The open questions of reparations remained the defining foreign policy issue of the immediate postwar era. The situation was complicated by the fact that France, Belgium, and Britain had incurred major war debts to the United States. As long as the United States insisted these debts be repaid, its European allies had a vested interest in extracting the maximum amount of reparations from Germany.[4] The French and Belgian governments faced even more pressure because German troops had maliciously caused widespread destruction in the territories from which they retreated—a fact that all postwar German governments and broad swaths of the German populace refused to fully acknowledge. Even four years after the war, in August 1922, Count Harry Kessler despaired over what he saw when he traveled through northern France:

> Large areas of uncultivated land overgrown with flourishing weeds, and a conspicuous number of untilled fields in between the cultivated patches. Bullet-riddled homes, collapsed roofs, col-

onies of barracks the size of small villages, and new rural buildings of horrible ugliness. St. Quentin isn't completely destroyed,
as people said, but the street to the train station and many houses
still lie in rubble . . . and the cathedral looms without windows,
topped with a provisional tin roof. It's a noble ruin, visible at
some distance, of a bombarded city. Chauny and Noyon are in
similar condition. The Noyon Cathedral makes a particularly
devastating and overwhelming impression with its two massive,
bullet-riddled towers covered in scaffolding.[5]

Exacerbating the situation was the fear of German revenge felt by
the French government and French society as a whole. The result was a
pronounced need for security that could not be satisfied even by occupying territory on the left bank of the Rhine. In the eyes of French
politicians and military leaders, reparations were a suitable instrument
not only for preventing Germany from regaining its former strength.
It also meant the French could claim a reason to march into Germany
should the deliveries and payments not be met.

By contrast, the British government under Prime Minister David
Lloyd George was faced with increasing difficulties in maintaining its
empire and thus was more interested in Central European stability.
Germany was not to be so weakened that it would affect the recovery
of the European economy as a whole. As a result, London was inclined
to compromise with the German government on reparations, even if
doing so created tension with Britain's main ally, France. Postwar British foreign policy faced the double challenge of preventing a rift within
the Entente while ensuring that France didn't grow too powerful.[6]

IN A SERIES OF CONFERENCES, the Entente nations tried to
agree on a common policy regarding Germany. At a July 1920 meeting in Spa, Belgium, the issue of reparations wasn't yet on the agenda.
Instead, the focus was on deliveries of coal from Germany. Ultimately,
Lloyd George succeeded in getting the French to reduce their demands

from 2.4 million to 2 million tons for the following six months—
with the value of deliveries to be credited at the going domestic price
toward Germany's reparations balance. It was the first negotiated—not
dictated—settlement between the Entente and Germany after the war.[7]

It wasn't until a conference of the Allied Supreme Council in Paris
in late January 1921 that Britain and France agreed on a reparations
plan. The plan required Germany to hand over a total of 226 billion
gold marks over forty-two years, with annual payments beginning
at 2 billion and gradually rising to 6 billion. In addition, Germany
was to pay a levy of 12 percent of the total value of its exports.[8] Such
demands came as a rude awakening to the German populace. "To
pay countless billions for forty-two years," wrote Klemperer, "it's like
something from the Congo, so bitter and fantastical, when you think
about what we were in 1914, that I can only try—successfully—not
to think about it."[9] In a February 1921 letter, German president Friedrich Ebert confided in former Prussian war minister Walther Reinhardt that only "fools" could believe that "the worst is behind us."
He added, "They must be all the more shocked by the most recent
events. The situation is very grave. It's very doubtful a solution will
be found."[10]

At a conference in London in early March 1921, German foreign
minister Walter Simons rejected the payment plan proposed by Paris
as impossible, arguing that it dramatically exceeded Germany's economic capacity. His proposed alternative was that the German government would pay 50 billion marks, with the 20 million in assets
already handed over included in that sum. The Entente powers dismissed this offer as utterly insufficient, and when Berlin missed a
deadline for accepting the reparations plan, they made good on their
threat to occupy Düsseldorf, Duisburg, and Ruhrort. The Inter-Allied
Rhineland High Commission assumed responsibility for customs in
those occupied cities.[11]

In late April 1921, the Allied Reparations Commission presented
Germany with a bill for 132 billion gold marks—a significant reduction from the 226 billion originally demanded by France. Nonetheless,

Germans were outraged, with many fearing that future generations would be yoked to an indentured servitude of debt. On May 5, Lloyd George summoned the German ambassador in London to give him an ultimatum: if Germany didn't cooperate, the Allies would occupy the Ruhr Valley in a week's time.

The new schedule of payments divided German debt into three series of bonds: payments on the principal and interest of A and B bonds totaling 50 billion marks would begin in 1921, while payments on the remaining 82 billion in C bonds would be indefinitely postponed. In addition, 26 percent of the value of Germany's exports was to be transferred. All told, that meant Germany would be liable for around 3 billion gold marks a year. Without doubt, this was a burden, but the sum wasn't far from the offer the German government had itself made in late March and would likely have been manageable had the German economy recovered normally.[12]


THE DAY BEFORE THE LONDON ultimatum, the German government under centrist chancellor Constantin Fehrenbach—whose coalition of the Center Party, the German Democratic Party (DDP), and the German People's Party (DVP) had only been in power since June 1920—stepped down after failing to convince the United States to mediate on the reparations issue. President Ebert named the former finance minister, Joseph Wirth of the Center Party, the country's new chancellor, and he formed a cabinet consisting of members of his own party, the DDP, and the Social Democrats. This was essentially another edition of the coalition that had drawn up the Weimar Constitution in 1919 and 1920, with the significant difference that it no longer enjoyed a parliamentary majority. Nonetheless, the Reichstag accepted the London ultimatum with the help of votes from the Independent Social Democratic Party (USPD) and the DVP. The Wirth government had passed its first test.[13] "The acceptance of the ultimatum is not a defeat," the journalist, pacifist, and pro-democracy activist Carl von Ossietzky wrote in the *Berliner Volks-Zeitung*.

It can be the start of a new and better era in which we stop the helpless drifting, which has unfortunately predominated since Versailles, and become active agents in our own right. This past year, we have been all too contented with the false hope that we would be able to get around this or that imposed obligation. The action came solely from the other side. We let ourselves be pushed and pressured, and ever sensitive to the fist at our backs, all we could do was complain. That was ignoble behavior, unworthy of a great people who should be able to produce enough clear heads capable of recognizing the consequences from a lost war.[14]

This was precisely what Wirth was trying to do. His idea was for Germany to show good faith by trying its best to meet its reparations obligations—but the ultimate goal was to show that those obligations were unmanageable, thus forcing the Entente powers back to the negotiating table to agree to another reduction. His aim, as he told the Reichstag, was "not to pursue a policy of fulfillment for its own sake, but to show the world, practically, by fulfilling what we can, where our limits are and that those lines cannot be crossed."[15]

Wirth and his political allies' strategy also aimed at resolving the still open status of Upper Silesia in Germany's favor. Although a large majority of the populace in the region (today part of Poland, near the Czech border) had voted in a March 1921 plebiscite to remain part of Germany, the Allied Conference of Ambassadors decided on October 20 to follow the recommendation of the League of Nations and divide the territory. Nearly one-quarter of this industrialized region was given to Poland. Dismayed by the decision, Wirth resigned on October 22 but was immediately charged by Ebert with forming a new government. But this time around, the DDP refused to cooperate, so Wirth's second governing cabinet had even less parliamentary backing than his first.[16]

Another seemingly insurmountable hurdle for Wirth's "fulfillment policy" was the rapid fall of the German mark. Foreign capital continued to flee the country, making it harder and harder to raise the money needed to make the payments. The German government already had considerable trouble paying the first installment of one billion marks on August 31, 1921, and it was apparent it would also struggle to cobble together the resources to make the payments due in January and February 1922.[17]

Germany wasn't able to borrow large sums on the international currency markets because of dwindling confidence that the country would be able to repay its loans. An attempt to convince German industry to take out foreign loans failed because representatives of German industry, particularly the entrepreneur and cofounder of the conservative DVP, Hugo Stinnes, made untenable demands, including the privatization of the German rail system, in return for their support. Thus, by December 1921, the second Wirth government had to request an extension of the payment deadline.[18]

At a meeting in Cannes in January 1922, the Conference of Ambassadors did offer a temporary moratorium on the January and February payments on the condition that the German government present a plan for reforming its state finances. The Wirth government complied. But a subsequent dispatch from the Reparations Commission on March 21 was a disappointment. Although the commission did approve a partial deferment for 1922, with Germany only required to hand over 720 million marks plus additional material goods, this concession came with a number of strings attached, including demands for comprehensive measures to combat the flight of capital from the country, independence for the Reichsbank from the government, and oversight of the German budget by the commission. The German government rejected these demands in its response on April 7.[19]

SINCE THE FIRST DAYS of 1922, the prospects for a consensus reparations treaty had been deteriorating. French premier Aristide Briand resigned in the middle of the Cannes conference, after the nationalist camp in France accused him of being too conciliatory toward Germany, and he was succeeded by the reparations hard-liner

Raymond Poincaré. In 1870, as a ten-year-old boy, Poincaré had witnessed Prussian troops invade his hometown of Bar-le-Duc in the
department of Meuse—a trauma that would follow him his whole
life. After a brilliant career as a lawyer, he had turned to politics and
had served as education and finance minister in several governing cabinets. Before 1914, as French premier and foreign minister, he played
a major role in securing France's alliance with Russia. Having been
elected French president in January 1913, he traveled to St. Petersburg during the July crisis of 1914 and offered the Russian government French support in its conflicts with Austria-Hungary and the
German Empire. During the war itself, Poincaré's great rival Georges
Clemenceau pushed him to the margins. Nonetheless, he was chosen
to give the opening address at the Paris Peace Conference on January
18, 1919, an occasion he used to lay blame for the war on Germany,
emphasize France's special sacrifice, and advance the latter's case for
demanding comprehensive compensation for its losses.[20]

Poincaré insisted that the Treaty of Versailles, including provisions
forced on Germany, had to be fulfilled to the letter. He suspected the
German government was intentionally allowing the devaluation of
the mark as a way of avoiding its obligations. In the belief that Germans were really unwilling to pay their debts, he advocated the idea
of "productive seizures," and he would only consider granting payment deferments if France received sufficient guarantees and reassurances in return. His main focus was the Ruhr Valley's coal reserves.
Ultimately, Poincaré wanted to permanently weaken the economy of
France's potentially threatening eastern neighbor and shift the long-
term balance of power on the European continent in France's favor.[21]
There was a contradiction, though, between trying to extract hefty
reparations from Germany and simultaneously radically restricting
Germany's ability to make the payments demanded.

Thus, from its very inception, the Genoa Conference, which was
convened at British request in April 1922, was ill-fated. It was the first
time the German delegation, headed by Wirth and industrialist Walther Rathenau, who had been Germany's foreign minister since the

end of January, took part as a full-fledged participant. No progress was made on the issue of reparations, as Poincaré had ordered the French delegation, led by former French premier Louis Barthou, to dig in its heels. More important than any result from the conference was something achieved on its margins. On April 16, in the nearby Mediterranean resort of Rapallo, Rathenau and the Soviet people's commissar for foreign affairs, Georgy V. Chicherin, concluded a treaty in which the former enemies formally renounced any claims to reparations and agreed to restore diplomatic relations and work together more closely on economic matters.[22]

This surprising agreement caused considerable consternation in western Europe. Lloyd George, who had traveled to Genoa with high hopes, felt as though he had been tricked, while the French government saw their fundamental mistrust of Germany confirmed. In a speech in Bar-le-Duc on April 24, Poincaré described the Treaty of Rapallo as a hostile act and refused to rule out the possibility of French military intervention should Germany continue to fall short of its contractual obligations. There was no reason for the Wirth government to hope for any substantial concessions. Kessler, who was at the conference as an observer, noted to his disappointment that those responsible for the Treaty of Rapallo had "dropped the precious vase of European trust, which had been painstakingly glued back together, causing it to shatter anew."[23] German president Ebert had feared this would be the result of any such deal, and Wirth had neglected to inform him in advance about the imminent treaty with the Soviets, leaving Ebert to learn about it from the newspapers. He never forgave the chancellor for the affront. After Rapallo, the two men's relationship was toxic.[24]

THE FAR RIGHT IN GERMANY, meanwhile, had rolled out a vitriolic publicity campaign attacking "fulfillment politicians," making Rathenau because of his Jewish background a particular target. By the spring of 1922, the public hounding had led to death threats against the German foreign minister. "Gun down Walther Rathenau, the god-damned Jewish sow," were the final lines of an antisemitic song popular in radical right-wing bars and taverns.[25] Rathenau was aware that his life was in danger. The demands of his office could hardly be borne physically at the best of times, Kessler recorded him saying. "But the worst thing was the hateful animosity in Germany itself. Every day he said that he received not only death threats but serious complaints lodged against him with the police."[26] Still, Rathenau refused to submit to special security measures, and on June 24, 1922, while on his way to the German Foreign Ministry, he was assassinated by the Organisation Consul. This secret society was also responsible for the killing on August 26, 1921, of centrist and former finance minister Matthias Erzberger and for an attack on June 4, 1922, that involved use of prussic acid on the Social Democrat Philipp Scheidemann, the mayor of Kassel and the man who had proclaimed the start of the Weimar Republic. "Rathenau was disparaged and defamed in the most boundlessly vulgar terms at ultranationalist and racist events and in most of the publications of that ilk," wrote the editor in chief of the pro-democratic *Berliner Tageblatt*. "Such intellectual groundwork made this crime possible, indeed inevitable."[27]

Rathenau's murder immediately caused the German currency, the Reichsmark, to fall even more swiftly in value. The German government was no longer capable of paying the sums agreed in the moratorium and was compelled to beg in two diplomatic dispatches on July 12 and 14, 1922, to be released from all payments, with the exception of those in material goods, until the end of 1924. Poincaré saw this as a chance to push for his "productive seizures." Although the Allies did grant another six-month deferment in late August 1922, the French government increased pressure on Germany to reform its public finances, with the threat of occupying the Ruhr Valley always hovering in the background.[28] Clearheaded observers like the British ambassador in Berlin, Edgar Vincent D'Abernon, knew that there was no way Germany's disastrous financial situation would allow the country to pay its debts. Before brakes were applied to the printing of money and the currency stabilized, D'Abernon argued, there would be

*German foreign minister Walther Rathenau on his way to the Reichstag. On June 24, 1922, he was murdered by members of the right-wing extremist Organisation Consul, which loathed him because of his Jewish background.*

no legitimate basis for any promises concerning payments. In conversation with Wirth in late August 1922, the chancellor confessed his doubts as to whether, given the catastrophic decline in the value of the mark, Germany could even keep its people fed in the winter to come. "He must put food before reparations: he had already said this, and he would stick to it," D'Abernon reported the German leader telling him. "He was convinced that Germany could not continue payments in kind through the winter: she must have a complete moratorium or breathing-space."[29]

In a dispatch to the reparations conference on November 14, 1922, the Wirth government requested a moratorium on all payments in currency and material goods for three to four years and a reduction of the amounts set in the London ultimatum to a level with which Germany could cope. For its part, his government would immediately move to prop up the Reichsbank in the interest of stabilizing the currency and restoring some balance to the budget.[30]

THE DISPATCH WAS WIRTH'S final act in office. He stepped down that same day after failing to expand his government's parliamentary basis. In September, the SPD merged with the remnants of the USPD—the majority of USPD members had left to join the Communist KPD in October 1920—and as a result the party lurched to the left. In the short term, there was no way the "United Social Democratic Party" would work together with Stresemann's DVP, which primarily represented the interests of big industry. Wirth had hitched his political future to the formation of a grand coalition, and Ebert, still smarting from the Treaty of Rapallo, did nothing to keep the chancellor in office.[31]

On November 22, 1922, Ebert selected businessman Wilhelm Cuno, the director general of the large Hamburg shipping company Hapag, as Germany's next chancellor. Born in 1876 in the eastern German town of Suhl and holding a doctorate of law, Cuno had been in charge of the German Grain Office during the war before quitting his post as privy superior government counsel in late 1917 to work in the private sector and joining Hapag's board of directors at the behest of the company's powerful owner, Albert Ballin. When Ballin committed suicide in November 1918, Cuno took over the leadership of the firm, earning respect for helping to rebuild Germany's commercial fleet. He was not a member of any party, but he did have connections to the DVP and was hardly a political unknown. D'Abernon was wrong when he characterized Cuno as "not at all a politician, rather a Lohengrin," who had appeared out of nowhere.[32] He had been considered on numerous occasions for ministerial posts and had taken part in the Genoa Conference as an economic expert. At the time, correctly sensing the businessman's political ambitions, Kessler had sarcastically compared Cuno to a "thick cigar that will have to be smoked at some point because its band is so appealing."[33]

"Cuno, tall as a tree, youthful, almost feminine, seems to consist of nothing but grace—blonde to the point of lacking pigmentation"—

that was how Kessler described the new chancellor.[34] The new head of Hapag could call upon excellent business connections in the United States and Britain. Ebert hoped that his skill as a negotiator and reputation as a public figure would help Germany make progress on the reparations issue. Moreover, a politically independent economic expert must have seemed particularly well-suited to play the role of a man of compromise and to win over the German business community—with its skeptical-to-hostile attitude toward the Weimar Republic—to the cause of democracy.[35]

But Cuno, too, failed to engineer a grand coalition that included the DVP and the reunited SPD. As a result, he formed something that had never been tried in the brief history of the Republic: a "business cabinet," which in addition to himself included four independent specialists as ministers. Former German envoy to Denmark Frederic von Rosenberg became Germany's foreign minister; Essen mayor Hans Luther, food and agriculture minister; ex-general quartermaster Wilhelm Gröner, transportation minister, a post he had previously held under Fehrenbach and Wirth; and former Reich Chancellery state secretary Heinrich Albert, treasury minister. The remaining ministries were divided up among the parties of the bourgeois center: from the DVP came Economics Minister Johann Becker and Justice Minister Rudolf Heinze; from the Center Party, Finance Minister Andreas Hermes and Labor Minister Heinrich Brauns; from the DDP, Reichswehr Minister Otto Gessler and Interior Minister Rudolf Oeser; and from the Bavarian People's Party (BVP), Postal Minister Karl Stingl. Cuno also handed the important office of state secretary in the Chancellery to Eduard Hamm of the DDP. But this "cabinet of leading personalities" remained a narrow bourgeois minority government put together without a formal coalition agreement and dependent on being tolerated by either the SPD or the ultranationalist German National People's Party (DNVP).[36]

In his governmental address of November 24, 1922, Cuno endorsed the German dispatch of November 14 "without reservation" and asked the Reparations Commission to approve as soon as possible Germany's request for a three- to four-year deferral in light of the country's poor economic and financial situation.[37] The reaction from Paris followed promptly. On November 27, the French government issued a press declaration rejecting the German request in no uncertain terms and openly threatening to occupy two-thirds of the Ruhr Valley, including the major cities of Essen and Bochum.[38]

The die had essentially been cast. Poincaré and his advisers were convinced that the Cuno government, like its predecessors, was playing for time and was fundamentally unwilling to fulfill Germany's reparations commitments. On November 27, the Council of Ministers under French president Alexandre Millerand already approved in principle the occupation of the Ruhr Valley.[39] New British prime minister Andrew Bonar Law, who had taken over for Lloyd George the month before, made it abundantly clear to Poincaré at a meeting that he would consider an actual occupation a mistake, but like earlier British leaders, he was unwilling to stay France's hand. In conversation with D'Abernon in December, he expressed his conviction that energetic action on the part of the United States could persuade Poincaré to change course.[40]

In fact, in late 1922, American secretary of state Charles Hughes did speak out on the issue. At a speech to the American Historical Association in New Haven, Connecticut, he rejected the French policy of threatening sanctions and suggested convening an independent international commission of experts to review Germany's economic capacity and redefine the total amount of reparations. But his suggestion fell on deaf ears in Paris,[41] and the situation escalated. The two sides were "now entering the most difficult period on the reparations question," Germany's ambassador in Paris, Wilhelm Mayer, wrote to Kessler on January 2, 1923, prophesying, "France won't be able to accept its massive disappointment over reparations without an explosion."[42]

STILL, POINCARÉ NEEDED an excuse to send in troops. It was provided by the Reparations Commission. On December 26, that body, over the objections of British representative John Bradbury, had officially registered insufficient German deliveries of timber and telegraph poles. On January 9, 1923, the commission officially censured Germany, again against Bradbury's wishes, for failing to deliver the agreed amounts of coal. Two days later, French and Belgian troops began occupying the Ruhr Valley.[43]

The official explanation Poincaré transmitted to Mayer on January 10 didn't call the deployment of troops a military operation. Instead, it claimed that French forces were only protecting a delegation of French and Belgian engineers. The Mission Interallié de Controle des Usines et de Mines (Allied Commission for the Supervision of Factories and Mines—MICUM) was charged with ensuring the strict delivery of the reparations stipulated by the Treaty of Versailles.[44] In reality, the invasion had the character of an act of war. A correspondent from *Berliner Tageblatt* reported from Essen on the afternoon of January 11: "At around 2:00 p.m., the French marched into the city. They were led by some cyclists, followed by infantrymen and several thousand cavalrymen. Three armored vehicles clattered through the streets, to their rear were infantry and artillery, and machine guns were also seen. At the very back were several trucks full of units of men. Guards with bayonets affixed to their rifles occupied all the public buildings and the train station and took up positions at every street crossing."[45]

That very day, the commander of the French occupation force, General Jean-Marie Joseph Degoutte, declared the city under siege.[46] Within a few days, the French also occupied Gelsenkirchen, Bochum, Recklinghausen, Hattingen, Dortmund, and other places between the Ruhr River to the north and the Lippe River in the south. By March 1923, between seventy thousand and a hundred thousand occupying soldiers were stationed in this area. A relatively small Belgian contingent of eight thousand men was also under Degoutte's command.[47]


THE GERMAN PUBLIC WAS OUTRAGED. "The Rubicon has been crossed," wrote the furious *Vossische Zeitung*, adding that the dispatch justifying the French action betrayed "the insecurity of a policy that can neither retreat nor move forward" and that Poincaré gave the "impression of a man who knows that he and his country are sliding toward the most enormous stupidity."[48] The commentary from *Berliner Tageblatt* was similar in tone. The French and Belgians, the paper wrote, had added a new phrase to the language of diplomacy—"military occupation with peaceful intent." In one fell swoop, the incursion had ripped apart "like spider's webs all judicial shrouds with which the lawyer at the head of France had tried to mask this brutal act of violence."[49] The *Deutsche Allgemeine Zeitung*, the mouthpiece of industrialist Hugo Stinnes, complained that the invasion had "created a completely altered political situation for Germany and Europe." The task for Germans now was to "keep their nerve and stand unbowed with their people and fatherland." The entire nation, urged the paper, had to come together in the "sacred conviction that the just cause will win the day."[50]

Such exhortations were more than just words. The occupation of the Ruhr Valley did in fact unleash a wave of German solidarity. Many observers were reminded of August 1914 when previously warring interests had concluded a "truce" on behalf of the nation. "The French, by their invasion of the Ruhr . . . have done more to bring together all parties and classes in Germany than it was possible to effect by any other means," wrote D'Abernon. "For the moment all class hostilities of the workmen against the owner have been submerged by the patriotic wave. The whole country appears to be united."[51]

Typical of the anti-French rage that boiled over during the early days of 1923 was a talk held by Gerhard Ritter, a historian and volunteer in the First World War, on the anniversary of the founding of the German Empire. Ritter—at the time a lecturer in Heidelberg—began his address by admitting there was little cause for celebration: "We don't want to celebrate. We want to act, to take the saber and the old wartime pistol down from the wall, put on the pith helmet and throw out the cowardly gang of thieves that is having its way in our house."[52]

From his cell in the Bavarian fortress of Niederschönenfeld, where he had been imprisoned since November 1920 as part of a fifteen-year sentence for taking part in the 1919 Munich revolution, the anarchist writer Erich Mühsam noted, "All of Germany is once again being tossed by giant waves of nationalism."[53] Still, the public mood wasn't unanimous. Some people at the time were appalled by the excessive chauvinism that sought to summon the anti-French fury of the 1813 German "wars of liberation" from Napoleon and the 1840 "Rhine crisis." Diarist Thea Sternheim, the wife of playwright Carl Sternheim, remarked after going to the cinema in Dresden, "The French occupation of the Ruhr Valley has caused patriotic Germany to vent its hatred wherever it can. In a film that depicted the Rhine, past and present, there were incendiary, sentimental interludes of singing to thunderous applause, and a nymph recited a prologue of vengeance aimed at young people. When [Prussian field marshal Gebhard von] Blücher appeared on screen, the cinema was completely beside itself."[54] The Austrian poet Rainer Maria Rilke, who had been living in a chateau in the Swiss canton of Valais since June 1921, complained that many German newspapers had lapsed back into the tone of the war years: "Their pages rustle, as soon as you open them, with the sound of enemies being hounded."[55]

Victor Klemperer had trouble making up his mind. As a patriotic German, he rejected Poincaré's reckless Ruhr Valley gambit, but as a professor of Romance languages with a deep affinity for French language and culture, he viewed the "inciting of a mood of revenge" with decidedly mixed feelings: "I cannot imagine when and how we are supposed to wage a war of liberation. . . . The issue of the Ruhr and the entire situation right now is too horrible."[56]

Thomas Mann in Munich felt much the same. The French seemed "to have gotten it into their heads to ruin the basic idea of everyone who tries to encourage good in Germany," he wrote to his brother and fellow author Heinrich Mann in mid-February 1923. The "rage" about the French action was "terrible—more profound and unanimous than that which brought down Napoleon." There was no telling where it would end, Mann bemoaned. The worst possibility was "that a French fiasco, as welcome as that scenario would [otherwise] be, would mean the triumph of nationalism domestically."[57]

In a letter to the French expert on German literature Félix Bertaux, Heinrich Mann predicted a "sharp radicalizing of domestic politics," although he didn't believe that the nationalism that was bubbling up possessed "the terribleness of 1914." Instead, Heinrich contended, it seemed "insecure, overwrought, pitiable." The best thing to do was wait patiently "until this bane had worn itself out." In any case, the idea of reconciliation between France and Germany remained an "unqualified necessity for existence."[58]

The French had brought about a "poisoning of Europe for a hundred years," complained *Das Tage-Buch*, a Berlin weekly edited by leftist journalists Stefan Grossmann and Leopold Schwarzschild.[59] And another leftist Berlin publication, the *Weltbühne*, also offered a vigorous condemnation of the French action: "Four years after what was at least a peace agreement, foreign soldiers have entered our country in the manner of a military offensive, with artillery and all the means of modern warfare, and waging, if not full-fledged war, than a step in that direction. This is and will remain an outrage." At the same time, the newspaper asked whether obstructionism by the German government had contributed to the disaster: "Was it truly necessary to protest against all deliveries, request deferrals, and fall behind in fulfilling commitments? . . . Was the strategy of constant troublemaking . . . really the right one?"[60]


THE STEP TAKEN BY FRANCE struck him as "extremely misguided," German foreign minister Frederic von Rosenberg told D'Abernon, but he was "fairly tranquil because it is not only Germany which is in question but the whole of Europe, and indeed all the world."[61] The Cuno government had been largely caught off guard by the occupation despite all the threats Poincaré had made. It wasn't until the evening of January 9, 1923, with the French incursion imminent, that Ebert summoned the governing cabinet to his offices, telling them the time had come to "face the coming events with clarity, strength of will, cool heads and complete unity." To that end, the German president had issued an address that afternoon to the population of the Ruhr Valley, and he now shared it with the ministers. As an initial reaction, Chancellor Cuno announced that Germany's ambassador, Wilhelm Mayer, would be recalled from Paris. But he didn't want to sever diplomatic relations entirely. Instead, they would be managed by the embassy counsel, Leopold von Hoesch. Both Ebert and Cuno were convinced that if the French made good on their threats, the result would be a "strong nationalist wave" that would have to be harnessed "to serve the [German] state."[62]

A preview of what that would entail was given on January 11 by the joint proclamation of the German president and German government, titled "To the German people!" In no uncertain terms, the statement's authors criticized the French "act of violence" as a "deed born of blindness" directed against the "defenseless livelihood of the German economy." No mention was made of the passive resistance that would determine German government policies in the weeks and months to come. But the proclamation did call upon the populace to show "iron self-discipline" and refrain from anything that could damage Germany's "just cause."[63] The German government's official letter of protest the following day was even more explicit, characterizing the French incursion as the "worst violation imaginable of German sovereignty." Admittedly, Germany was unable to defend itself militarily against what it saw as a contravention of international law. But on the other hand, the country was unwilling to submit to this violation of international law and to assist the French in carrying out their plans. As long as the illegal occupation continued, Berlin insisted, the government saw itself as incapable of making any further reparations payments.[64]

On January 13, the Reichstag, with flags flying at half-mast, convened for a special session. Cuno's ministers and state secretaries took their places on the governmental bench. The spectators' gallery was filled to capacity. The president of the German parliament, the Social Democrat Paul Löbe, spoke briefly, then turned the podium over to

Cuno. France's act of aggression, he asserted, was not aimed at exacting reparations but at realizing an "age-old goal" that French politics had pursued since the days of Louis XIV and Napoleon and that had lain at the heart of the Treaty of Versailles: extending French power to Germany's detriment. Germany would have to counter this attempt decisively but rationally. "Let us devote all the strength of our hearts and our hands to our people and our fatherland and bury all unnecessary quarrels," Cuno implored his audience.[65] Although the chancellor had read his speech without any great emotion from sheets of paper, his words were greeted by storms of applause. A resolution introduced by the Center Party assuring the government of full parliamentary support passed with 283 votes in favor, 12 votes against from the KPD, and 6 abstentions from the SPD. But the appearance of near complete unity was deceptive. Forty-nine members of the Social Democratic parliamentary group, mostly former members of the USPD, expressed their disapproval by not appearing for the vote at all.[66]

The government called for nationwide protests on Sunday, January 14. "Just as the Reichstag got behind the government, the masses backed the stance of parliament," wrote the *Vossische Zeitung*. "It has been a long time since much vocal support for the government has been articulated and recorded as it was yesterday.... If there is any consolation in what we've been through in the past days, it's the renewed solidarity prompted from the outside, despite all the depressing and divisive events of the past years."[67] Hundreds of thousands of Germans congregated in Berlin's Königsplatz square alone. "Anyone who saw this cohesive mass of people with bare heads standing, swearing loyalty and praying in front of the steps to the Reichstag and around the Bismarck Memorial and the Victory Column will never forget it," wrote a euphoric reporter for the *Deutsche Allgemeine Zeitung*. In front of the Brandenburg Gate, an entire police division had to be deployed to protect the French embassy located on Pariser Platz from being attacked by demonstrators.[68]

PASSIVE RESISTANCE TO THE Ruhr occupation was only possible if the unions cooperated. On January 8, 1923, Ebert and Cuno had asked leaders of the General German Trade Union Federation (ADGB) to tell them how those organizations planned to respond if the French marched in. Union leaders rejected the idea of a general strike as counterproductive because "under some circumstances the French might even welcome it." Germany's two top political leaders were told, "Without doubt, economic chaos will arise from an invasion, and the French will logically try to transfer the blame to the working classes if they go on strike." On the other hand, everyone agreed that the occupation of the Ruhr couldn't go unanswered. One of the ideas discussed was a short, symbolic strike, but no concrete decision was made.[69]

In a joint January 11 declaration, the ADGB, the General Federation of Free Employees (AfA-Bund), and the German Federation of Civil Servants condemned the French occupation of the Ruhr as an "expression of the worst sort of imperial policies of violence, the sort always resisted by the organized German labor." The declaration also called upon blue-collar workers, white-collar employees, and civil servants to "put everything that divides them on the back burner and to close ranks and fight together against insatiable, warmongering imperialism."[70] At a meeting of its national committee on January 24, ADGB chairman Theodor Leipart described in detail how this battle was to be waged. The guiding idea was to achieve the greatest possible effect with the "least possible effort." Independent labor unions would adopt the concept of passive resistance while reaffirming their goodwill to make reparations payments and distancing themselves from radical nationalism. The minutes of the meeting read, "Passive resistance alone should be employed while maintaining the willingness to fulfill obligations and the rejection of any sort of nationalist agitation."[71]

The early days of the occupation saw rare harmony between unions and businesses. On January 9, the industrialist Hugo Stinnes informed ADGB representatives about plans to move the Rhenish-Westphalian Coal Syndicate, the economic center of the Ruhr mining industry, from Essen to Hamburg in northern Germany. This deprived the occupiers of access to documents concerning mining conditions, mining facilities, and sales amounts, which they needed in order to get their hands on German coal. As the *Deutsche Allgemeine Zeitung* saw it, this step had massive economic as well as political and psychological significance: "By flouting our invaders' most avaricious expectations, it will energize Germany's entire political atmosphere."[72]

Stinnes had seen the occupation of the Ruhr coming for quite some time, but when it actually happened, he was as surprised as the German government and allowed himself to be swept along by the wave of anti-French sentiment. In a January 17 letter to Emil Kirdorf, the director general of the incorporated Gelsenkirchen Mining Company (Gelsenkirchener Bergwerks-AG), he described the French incursion as a "blessing for our country." He continued, "Just like one hundred years ago, the people are beginning to join together in common suffering and common hatred."[73] The passive resistance agreed to by the Cuno government and the unions also elicited the enthusiastic approval of most of the other companies in the Rhine and Ruhr Valleys. "I am happy that our government has remained steadfast and is putting up resistance," wrote Carl Duisburg, the director general and supervisory board chairman of the Friedrich Bayer and Company paint manufacturers. "Finally, deeds instead of just words, even at the risk of creating turmoil in our economy."[74]

One of the most passionate supporters of passive resistance among the Ruhr industrialists was Paul Reusch, the director general of Gutehofnungshütte machine company in Oberhausen. Right before the French occupied the city on January 11, he moved his company to Nuremberg to prevent it from falling into the hands of the occupiers. And in the weeks that followed, Reusch crisscrossed Germany, encouraging anti-French sentiment and whipping up resistance.[75]

*German president Friedrich Ebert speaks to a German delegation
from the French-occupied Ruhr Valley on March 18, 1923.
He assured them of the support of the national government.*

As with unions and business, German political parties also largely came together for a brief moment. In its message to the rank and file on January 11, the SPD leadership stopped short of calling on members to participate in the general protests scheduled for three days later, instead hoping that discontent would be expressed at closed events. But the tone of their appeals hardly differed from that used by parties of middle-class and affluent Germans. All of them excoriated the French incursion into the Ruhr Valley as a major violation of international law, one which showed that "even for years after the war, French militarism—supported by Belgian troops in reserve—is still wielding the means of war."[76] In front of the Reichstag on January 13, SPD party board member Hermann Müller, who had served as chancellor of Germany from May to June 1920, described the course of action chosen by Poincaré as an "imperialistic adventure" and the expression of a brutal power politics completely unsuitable to rectifying France's shaky state finances. "Bayonets," he remarked, "are not divining rods that show where gold is buried."[77]

That same day in the German parliament, speaking on behalf of the "bourgeois parties"—the DDP, DVP, BVP, and DNVP—Stresemann read out a declaration protesting in the sharpest of terms "the rape of the German people." There was no external threat, he added, giving France a "reason for this attack and larcenous raid on German territory." Ultimately Poincaré's policies were aimed at nothing less than "the destruction of Germany." In response, Germans would have to stand together as one and put aside all domestic conflicts: "Any hope for German disunity must collide with and shatter against unified German will and desire." In the weeks that followed, using his position as the head of the Reichstag's foreign affairs committee, the DVP chairman would advocate for a hard-line stance toward France.[78] Still, cracks in the façade of unity appeared only a few days after January 13, when a prominent DNVP deputy, Karl Helfferich, attacked the Cuno government for not severing diplomatic relations with France and voiding the Treaty of Versailles. With its illegal occupation of German territory, Helfferich argued, France itself had "torn the so-called peace treaty to shreds."[79]

From the very beginning, the ambitious local hero of the racist Right in Munich and chairman of the National Socialist German Workers' Party (NSDAP), Adolf Hitler, had no time for the "unified national front" against the occupation of the Ruhr. On the evening of January 11, 1923, he gave a speech in Zirkus Krone, an eight-thousand-seat venue used not only for circuses but for political events. In his address, he excoriated not France but the "November criminals" in Germany— that is, democrats and Jews. By "stabbing the German army in the back," Hitler claimed, they had left Germany defenseless, handing over the country to "total enslavement." There could only be an "outward German rebirth," the Nazi leader added, if the "criminals" were "held responsible and delivered up to their deserved fate." The "foolish talk of a unity front" served only to distract the populace from this task.[80] Hewing to this line, Hitler rejected any Nazi participation in an event directed against the "archenemy" that various "patriotic associations" had scheduled for January 14 in the Bavarian capital.

For Theodor Wolff, the editor in chief of the *Berliner Tageblatt*, the watchwords of the hour were "calm, order, unity, and discipline . . . until the moment French imperialism gives back what it has stolen." To his mind, radical sentiment on both the Right and the Left flew in the face of this imperative: "Whereas a populist demagogue on the extreme Right is allowed to declare at such a time, without any objection from his own ranks, that our struggle is not against France but against German November revolutionaries, the Communists have no scruples at all about declaring the bourgeoisie to be the enemy— although at least they include the French bourgeoisie."[81]

In fact, German Communists were convinced that the struggle would have to be fought on two fronts, against both the French and the German bourgeoisie. For that reason, in a call to the German proletariat on January 22, the Central Committee of the KPD countered the appeals for passive resistance with a rhyming slogan that mentioned Berlin's main river: "Defeat Cuno and Poincaré—in the Ruhr and on the Spree!" For Communists, French capitalists were "not one whit better than German ones, and the bayonets of French occupation troops are no less sharp than those of the Reichswehr." Consequently, working people in the Ruhr Valley first had a duty to "wage the defensive struggle against the French occupation authorities with full energy" where workers' rights were at issue. Only if the working classes acted as an "autonomous force," separate from the German bourgeoisie, would they avoid the danger of succumbing to the "nationalist intoxication," and only then could they win the support of the international, and particularly French, working classes.[82]

But the solidarity between the French Communist Party and its German comrades left much to be desired. French workers never came together in any effective action against the Ruhr occupation. And soon, German Communists were forced to acknowledge that their calls for a revolutionary battle on two fronts had largely fallen on deaf ears among the working classes in the occupied parts of Germany. As a result, the KPD would quickly redirect the primary thrust of their propaganda against the foreign occupiers.[83]

MANY OBSERVERS CONSIDERED the first weeks of the occupation to be the opening salvo in a new war between France and Germany, and the head of the Reichswehr, General Hans von Seeckt, willingly poured oil on the fire. France's "impudent invasion," he declared in a January 15 statement in the weekly military publication *Militärwochenblatt*, had "torn up the dictated articles of peace and forced us into a war of liberation."[84] Naturally Seeckt knew only too well that he couldn't risk a military conflict against Germany's western neighbor, given that his nation's military had been reduced to only a hundred thousand men. *Vossische Zeitung* editor in chief Georg Bernhard urged moderation. No one doubted, he wrote, that if the German people were called to arms, "a rush of enthusiasm would bring millions of men of all ages to the military recruitment centers." But no German government should be that rash. "How are the disarmed and financially battered German people," Bernhard asked, "supposed to wage a war against its enemies' intact fighting machine?"[85]

While an open military response in the west was unthinkable, Germany's eastern border was a different story. German political leaders and shapers of public opinion were quick to warn that Germany would defend itself militarily should Poland try to exploit the Ruhr occupation and seize German territory in the east. "Just because the Reich cannot put up resistance in the west, that doesn't mean we would abandon the east to an invasion without a fight," Cuno told the premiers of Germany's regional states on January 12.[86] Seeckt issued similar assurances to Germany's ambassador to Poland, Ulrich von Rauscher: if France were to pressure Poland to attack East Prussia and Upper Silesia, that act of aggression would be repulsed by all means at Germany's disposal.[87]

The German military leadership was dedicated to covertly building up an illicit "black Reichswehr" by recruiting temporary volunteers and working together with the right-wing militias that, while formally disbanded, still existed in many parts of the country. On January 30, 1923, the Reichswehr Ministry reached a formal agreement with the Prussian interior minister, the Social Democrat Carl Severing, that the Prussian administration would offer support on matters of "national defense." Severing hoped that the pact would prevent the Reichswehr from further alliances with right-wing paramilitary units, but he was sorely disappointed.[88] In addition, German military leaders began looking toward the Soviet Union. In February 1923, a delegation from the Reichswehr Ministry went to Moscow to explore the possibilities for closer cooperation on military and economic matters. Initial results were hardly promising, but the meeting did open a new chapter in military relations between the two countries.[89]

ALTHOUGH THE CUNO GOVERNMENT had ruled out a military response to the Ruhr occupation, the policy of passive resistance did have real effects on the French. On the very day of the incursion, German commissar for coal distribution Ernst Stutz instructed mine owners to cease deliveries to France and Belgium. When ordered by General Degoutte and MICUM president Émile Coste to resume shipments, mine representatives answered on January 17 that no one could be compelled to "work against his fatherland and commit acts of dishonor."[90] Two days later, the German government prohibited civil servants, including rail and telegraph personnel, from following occupation authorities' commands.[91] The aim of these measures, as made clear at a German cabinet meeting on January 22, was to cause the occupation force difficulties "wherever and however possible."[92]

Initially, the strategy was quite successful. In the first weeks of the Ruhr occupation, it looked as though France's attempt to carry out "productive seizures" of German coal pits would be a mistake. The iron- and steelworks in Lorraine and Longwy-Nancy were most dependent on Ruhr coal and thus hardest hit by the suspension of German deliveries.[93] "The first month ended with a heavy deficit for the French government," concluded Friedrich Stampfer, the editor in chief of the Social Democratic newspaper *Vorwärts*. "In contrast to

before the occupation, when France had effortlessly generated reve-
nue from the receipt of reparation coal, there were no profits extracted
from the Ruhr region in the first months of the occupation adventure.
On the contrary, unknown expenditures were required for the military operations." But even greater than the financial losses, Stampfer argued, were the moral ones since the occupation had cost France
goodwill around the world: "Riding whips, bayonets, and revolvers
aren't the tools for making people love you."[94]

The question was how long Germany could maintain its passive
resistance. In early February 1923, Cuno visited the Ruhr Valley
incognito to inspect the situation. In conversations with industry and
labor representatives, he made it clear that it was not yet time for negotiations. On the contrary, resistance would continue until the French
themselves comprehended "that they have produced a fiasco with this
whole enterprise."[95] After returning to Berlin, he pronounced himself
satisfied. "Things are good at the front," he said. "He had received the
same assurances that the resistance would persist. In particular, the
working classes had spoken in this way." Cuno stressed the special
importance of providing the occupied population with sufficient food
since that was "the main key to the resistance being a success."[96]

IN THE EARLY DAYS of struggle for the Ruhr, Cuno enjoyed
broad popular support. Working-class Germans gave him credit for
traveling personally to the occupied region, a journey not without
risk.[97] The chancellor was showered with ovations when he visited
Munich and Stuttgart in March, and he reiterated on those occasions
that negotiations with France would only be possible when the French
"unconditionally" left the occupied region.[98] But some questioned
Cuno's position. For instance, in conversation with Kessler in early
February, Gustav Krupp von Bohlen und Halbach, the head of the
mighty Krupp steelworks in Essen, complained that the government
hadn't made a new offer to France on the issue of reparations. Passive
resistance was needed and deserved to be energetically pursued, Krupp

von Bohlen und Halbach agreed, but at the same time, the government should have been doing the utmost to look for room to negotiate.[99] In a conversation later that month, Theodor Leipart, the head of the ADGB, pushed the chancellor to publicly declare his willingness to talk, rejecting Cuno's objections that he "couldn't negotiate under the pressure of bayonets."[100]

Calls for negotiations were based on the acknowledged reality that France had more leverage and the better means for applying pressure. The Berlin correspondent of the Barcelona newspaper *La veu de Catalunya*, Eugeni Xammar, who traveled through the Ruhr Valley in February and March, was impressed by the population's defiance toward their occupiers. After returning to Berlin, he reported that the spirit of resistance was "unbroken." But he also predicted that Germany would lose the Ruhr conflict, arguing that the battle "had been lost from day one."[101]

The French government had underestimated the steeliness of the German defense, but when its mere threat of intervention turned out to be a failure, the occupation of the Ruhr became a matter of French national prestige. There could be no backing down. "Without any thoughts of conquest or annexation but determined to seize the securities and reparations in line with the peace treaty, France will not be moved from its standpoint," French president Millerand announced on February 22.[102] Occupation forces devised a series of more or less draconian sanctions to break the passive resistance. On January 26, at France's request, the Reparations Commission concluded that Germany had violated the Treaty of Versailles by suspending reparation deliveries and that the petition for a moratorium was null and void. Instead, the London schedule of payments drawn up in May 1921, including the total demand for 132 billion gold marks, came back into force.[103]

On January 29, as the supreme commander of the occupation troops, General Degoutte, declared an "enhanced state of siege." That meant that violence would be used against any attempts at sabotage, and public rallies of all kinds would be rigorously suppressed.[104]

Businesses that refused to obey French commands faced severe penalties. A particularly spectacular case was the arrest of the industrialist Fritz Thyssen and five other mining company managers on January 20 for refusing to deliver coal to occupation forces. A court-martial in Mainz sentenced them to pay heavy fines.[105] After the verdict was announced, there were spontaneous demonstrations of solidarity by largely younger people who marched through the streets singing war songs like "Victoriously we will defeat France" and throwing stones at French soldiers.[106]

Many civil servants who refused to cooperate with the occupiers were arrested and deported from the occupied region. By October 1923, some 140,000 people, including 37,000 state employees, were evicted from their homes, often with their families—a measure that caused huge resentment.[107] "This is how vagabonds, illegitimate encroachers, dangerous political agents of foreign countries and their ilk are treated," protested the *Vossische Zeitung* in an article entitled "The Terror in the Ruhr Valley." But the French were foolish if they thought they could "wear down the civil servants who remained behind by removing a number of rebels from their midst."[108] During a meeting at the Reich Chancellery on January 24, representatives of government employees' organizations avowed that the "civil service was closing ranks behind the government and the people." The struggle for the Ruhr was the "last phase of the world war, a war waged by alternate economic means," in which "he who is defeated has lost for good."[109]

In February, after Cuno and Severing visited the occupied region, Degoutte banned all national and regional German ministers from the area.[110] Amid legal uncertainty, Stresemann—then only the chairman of the DVP—took the special precaution of procuring fake papers that identified him as the "insurance inspector Friedrich Erlenkamp" when he visited Dortmund on February 21. In one of his speeches, he declared, "Whosoever would try to take Rhineland and Westphalia from us would take our heart. Woe to him who does not know that the future of Germany is now at stake."[111]

The occupying forces gradually ratcheted up pressure on the German government and the German people. Particularly injurious was the erection of a customs border around the occupied region. In late January 1923, a ban was issued on exporting Ruhr coal to the rest of Germany. "This is the second act of the French 'sanctions,' as the violent measures are called, using a mellifluous Latin-derived term," huffed the *Vossische Zeitung*. "If they successfully prevent coal from being delivered from the Ruhr, Germany will struggle to find replacements and keep economic life going at least to some extent."[112] One immediate consequence of the economic isolation of the Ruhr Valley were the first supply bottlenecks for national industrial production.

Because German railway personnel refused to work for the occupiers, French authorities took matters into their own hands and recruited replacements, primarily from Alsace-Lorraine, which France had reclaimed after the war. These men were familiar with German machinery and could communicate with the local populace. The move allowed the coal reserves that had accumulated to be transported to France, punching a major hole in the initially successful strategy of passive resistance.[113] Increasingly, occupation authorities began to seize control of companies and lock out employees. Foreign replacements, including Polish miners, were brought in to restart the idle mines. Time was clearly on France's side. Week by week, it became more and more obvious that Poincaré's "productive seizures" were indeed producing results.

CONVERSELY, PASSIVE RESISTANCE in the Ruhr was increasingly proving to be a "bottomless pit."[114] Civil servants and white-collar employees who had been expelled from the occupied region had to be provided for at public expense. The national government took over the wages of people left unemployed by the shutdown of businesses—acid-tongued Berliners referred to them as "Cuno pensioners"—and offered generous lines of credit to compensate heavy industry for declines in production and profits, even though tax revenues from the occupied

region were spiraling downward. The ban on coal exports to the rest
of Germany was especially damaging. To avoid the complete collapse
of the German economy, the government in Berlin was forced to rely
on expensive imports from Britain, eating up part of its already low
currency reserves.

Skyrocketing deficits were covered by simply printing more money.
German debt increased exponentially, accelerating the devaluation of
the German currency in April 1923.[115] Clear-eyed observers recognized that the costs could not be covered in the long term. "We have
to reckon that we will arrive at the point where the resistance cannot
be continued," Prussian state premier Otto Braun confided to State
Secretary in the Chancellery Eduard Hamm.[116]

AS IF THE VARIOUS restrictions and regulations weren't hard
enough for the Ruhr Valley population to tolerate, the presence of
French troops was a constant source of friction. "Anyone who spends
time in the Ruhr Valley will encounter the French army wherever he
takes a step," wrote Xammar. "Sometimes it's a French watchman who
prevents you from passing through a narrow street. Sometimes a general ceremoniously prancing by, accompanied by his adjutant and an
armed guard.... Tanks dominate the streets. In Essen and the country roads in the Ruhr, people are treated to the same spectacle as those
they saw on the Somme and in Amiens in the summer of 1916."[117]

Occupation troops punished disobedience very harshly. According
to the Germans, 109 people were killed in violent clashes in the Ruhr
between January and December 1923.[118] The worst incident took
place on March 31, the day before Easter, on Krupp company grounds
in Essen.[119] At 7:00 a.m., a group of eleven French soldiers under the
command of a Lieutenant Durieux entered the Krupp factory motor
pool to requisition vehicles. News of what was afoot spread like wildfire among Krupp workers, causing an uproar. Two members of the
works council tried to convince Durieux to call off the operation—
without success. At 9:00 a.m., the factory siren sounded. Workers left

their stations and congregated in the motor pool in the middle of the cast-steel foundry across from the main administrative building. The works council members tried to keep the peace, but the mood turned increasingly hostile. Patriotic German songs were sung, and the impromptu demonstrators brandished their tools. Several hot-heads climbed atop the motor pool's glass roof and threw objects to the ground below. Hot steam was diverted in through a broken window. The French soldiers felt surrounded and feared for their lives. When the crowd threatened to push in the entrance gate to the main hall, Durieux ordered his men to fire warning shots. Shortly thereafter, around 11:00 a.m., he instructed his men to open fire on the demonstrators. The lamentable result was thirteen dead and many wounded.

How could the situation have so tragically escalated? *Berliner Tageblatt* reporter Paul Scheffer found a plausible explanation:

An event like what happened today in the vehicle pool of the Krupp company was only to be expected since the French marched in. Things may have worked out in the end ninety-nine times out of a hundred, but they were bound to blow up at some point. . . . It's always the same story. The French appear in a factory district, the workers gather, and the French try . . . either to get them back to work or, as in this case, to confiscate something of value. But it's much harder to retreat through the workers, pressed side by side, surrounding them, than it is to encroach upon the factory. Every one of these French expeditions only barely avoided an explosion sparked by both sides. To a man, the workers regard the presence of the French as a massive, monstrous injustice. But they see the presence of Frenchmen at their place of labor as the worst insult imaginable to their working men's pride, reinforced by bayonets and uniforms, and as a direct threat to their economic existence.[120]

What became known as "Bloody Sunday in Essen" unleashed a flood of outrage. In a dispatch on April 4, the German government formally protested the "heinous crime of blood" and held not only the French troops but the French government responsible.[121] Ebert expressed his horror at the "bloodbath French militarism unleashed upon peaceful, defenseless workers."[122] German unions considered the massacre only "the latest and most terrible but by no means only case in which unarmed workers were butchered by French militarism."[123] Even a level-headed, liberal journalist like Theodor Wolff articulated his thorough disgust. "The spirit of militaristic violence has stained the temple of the Easter festival with the blood of human victims," he wrote, adding that someday a memorial to the dead would be erected with the words, "For the fighters for the Ruhr—the German Republic."[124] Days after the massacre, Essen was still seething. The Communists hastened to exploit the tragic event. No one bandied about the slogan "Defeat Cuno and Poincaré—in the Ruhr and on the Spree" anymore. Instead, even the KPD central committee directed its anger at French militarism.[125]

The victims were buried in Essen on April 10. Businesses remained closed, and hundreds of thousands of people lined the streets. "Never has German soil seen such a funeral of mourning," wrote the *Kölnische Zeitung*. "Bosses and workers, civil servants and white-collar employees, and all political parties carrying everything from black, white, and red wreaths to the colors of Moscow marched solemnly behind the dead."[126]

On Easter Sunday, the French occupation authorities had arrested four Krupp board members, and the head of the company, Gustav Krupp, traveled from Berlin to Essen to be interrogated. He too was detained and charged with defying the French. After a trial, which took place from May 4 to May 8 in the town of Werden, the court-martial sentenced all the defendants to jail terms of ten to twenty years. Krupp himself received fifteen years and was also ordered to pay a hefty fine. The verdict only stirred up further public outrage, with the German government protesting that French justice had "shamelessly made itself into a harlot of French militarism."[127] Reusch sent a telegram to Krupp's brother-in-law, Baron Tilo von Wilmowsky, that his thoughts were "with the men ... who have had to endure grave injustice in the interest of their fatherland."[128] Unions and Social Democrats also declared their solidarity with the convicted prisoners. *Vorwärts* proclaimed that whatever quarrels the Social Democratic workers of the Ruhr Valley "may still have with the representatives of capital," they are completely one in their rejection of French policies of violence and their will to put up passive resistance."[129] *Das Tage-Buch* asked, "Are the French trying to drive us to acts of lunacy?" If so, the paper argued, Germans should not allow themselves to be provoked but rather should "draw the mask of cold indifference more tightly across our faces" since "even the scandalous verdict of May 8 should plunge Germany into heedlessness."[130] At any event, Gustav Krupp didn't unduly suffer during his incarceration. In his prison in Düsseldorf, he enjoyed all sorts of privileges to ease his situation, and after seven months, he would again be a free man.[131]

The encounters between French soldiers and German civilians were accompanied by an increase and intensification of propaganda. A deluge of brochures, flyers, postcards, and caricatures pilloried the occupiers' brutality. "Anti-French propaganda on notes and posters is omnipresent," reported Xammar from Essen. "The walls are all full of it. Every morning, French patrols have to go through the streets and tear down with their bayonets the fresh posters put up the previous night. Flyers of all sorts can be found everywhere: on shop counters, on the seats of taxis, and in the drawers of hotel night tables."[132] Satirical publications like Munich's *Simplicissimus* and Berlin's *Kladderadatsch* also got involved in the propaganda battle. For instance, in February 1923, the latter published a caricature entitled "Le jour de Gloire" that depicted a French soldier in a tank gunning down a boy playing in the street. Under the image was a quotation from the French newspaper *Matin*: "The glorious French army has fulfilled to the letter the difficult task it was given."[133]

Alleged mass rapes of German women and girls by "Black" French soldiers was another inexhaustible motif of German propaganda. "It speaks volumes about the ever-present racism of German society after the First World War that the image of the African *tirailleur* [light infantryman] raping a young German woman could become the symbol of the occupation of the Ruhr as a whole," writes historian Stanislas Jeannesson. The reality was quite different. There were twenty-two documented rapes in the Ruhr Valley in 1923, and they were by no means committed exclusively by Algerian and Moroccan soldiers.[134]

THE MORE VIOLENT THE CRACKDOWN in the Ruhr, the more encouragement was derived by those forces in Germany that wanted to see the country move from passive to active resistance. In the spring and early summer of 1923, the Organisation Heinz under the command of former paramilitary leader Heinz Oskar Hauenstein and the Zentrale Nord in Münster engaged in guerrilla warfare in the occupied region. They blew up train tracks and bridges to prevent the transport of coal, attacked occupation authority facilities, and assaulted individual occupying soldiers.[135] One Organisation Heinz activist was Albert Leo Schlageter, the twenty-eight-year-old son of a farmer from the southwestern German town of Schönau, who had volunteered for the military in 1914 after receiving his emergency high school degree and who had returned from the war as a lieutenant. Soon, he quit the university where he was studying economics to take part in the postwar battles against the Bolsheviks in the Baltics and against Polish rebels in Upper Silesia. After the French and Belgian incursion, he went to the Ruhr, where as the commander of three combat units he was responsible for several bombings, including the destruction of the train tracks and the Haarbach Bridge in Kalkum on March 15, 1923, which disrupted rail connections between Düsseldorf and Duisburg.[136]

On April 7, French military police arrested Schlageter in an Essen hotel, where he had checked in under his real name. On May 9, the French military court in Düsseldorf sentenced him to death. Two and a half weeks later, after multiple appeals for mercy were rejected, a French commando executed him in the Golzheim Heath near Düsseldorf. His body was exhumed from Düsseldorf's Northern Cemetery in early June and laid to rest in the village cemetery in Schönau.[137]

In a sharply worded dispatch on May 29, the German government protested French courts presuming "to decide over the liberty or even the lives or deaths of Germans." The crimes Schlageter had allegedly committed, on which the verdict was based, were known "only from press reports" and thus "could not be examined" by Berlin.[138] That was only half true. The Organisation Heinz had carried out its acts of sabotage with the blessing and full knowledge of the Reichswehr Ministry and the Directing Operational Railway Office in Elberfeld, part of the national Transport Ministry. The group also had connections to heavy industry, including Krupp factory management.[139]

The Cuno government dragged its feet on combating sabotage organizations because, as Foreign Minister Rosenberg told Kessler, it was dependent on "the goodwill of right-wing circles" as well as more moderate segments of society: "If they go after the saboteurs too vigorously or abandon them completely, they would lose this trust. It's only by constantly vacillating between Left and Right that the current government can keep the German people united in coordinated resistance."[140] Government tolerance directly encouraged former paramilitaries and members of nationalist defense associations to continue their activities—to the great detriment of Germany's global reputation.

The entire political Right, from German ultranationalists to the fascist Nazis, celebrated Schlageter as a national martyr, and his grave in Schönau became a pilgrimage site. In 1931, a large memorial was erected at the place of his execution in the Golzheim Heath. It was partially financed by the industrialists Paul Reusch and Fritz Thyssen.[141] Playwright Hanns Johst, later the president of the Nazi Writers' Chamber, dedicated a play to Schlageter that romanticized him as "the first soldier of the Third Reich." It premiered on April 20, 1933, Hitler's first birthday as German chancellor, in Berlin's Staatliches Schauspielhaus with Joseph Goebbels in attendance. "At the end, after the execution scene, there was no applause—following a brief silence, the audience stood up to sing the first verse of the German national anthem and then the Nazis' 'Horst Wessel Song,'" wrote theater critic Paul Fechter in the *Deutsche Allgemeine Zeitung*. "Only afterward did the applause commence, full of genuine enthusiasm, as Johst and the cast took their curtain calls. It was a great success. The new German drama is on its way."[142]

But right-wingers weren't the only ones who styled Schlageter as an icon of resistance. In a speech to the Extended Executive Committee of the Communist International (Comintern) on June 21, 1923, Karl Radek, a member of the Russian Communist Party leadership and a Germany expert, also paid tribute to Schlageter, praising him as a "martyr of German nationalism" and a "brave soldier of the counterrevolution who deserves to be honored by us honest men of the revolution." Radek invoked the spirit of the German generals August von Gneisenau and Gerhard von Scharnhorst in the "wars of liberation" against Napoleon, during which Prussia had been allied with Russia, asking,

> Against whom do the German ethnic nationalists want to fight: the massive capital of the Entente powers or the Russian people? With whom do they want to be allied? With Russian workers and farmers so that they can both shake off the yoke of Entente capital? Or with Entente capital so that the German and Russian peoples will be enslaved? Schlageter is dead. He can't answer this question. But his comrades in this battle swore at his graveside to continue the fight. They have to answer the questions—against whom and at whose side?

This was an open offer of an alliance between the radical Left and the extreme Right in the mutual interests of both nationalist and socialist revolutionaries. Radek continued:

> We believe that the vast majority of the nationalist masses belong in the camp of labor and not of capital. We intend to and will seek out and find the path to these masses of people. We will do

everything to ensure that men like Schlageter, who were prepared to die for a common cause, don't become wanderers into nothingness but wanderers into a better future, so that they didn't shed their passionate, selfless blood for the profits of coal and iron barons but for the welfare of the great, laboring German people, one of the family of peoples fighting for their liberation.

Radek didn't compose his attention-grabbing speech by himself. It was almost certainly approved by his comrades in Moscow. The Comintern leadership no doubt had dual aims for the "national-Bolshevik" line. On the one hand, they wanted to divide right-wing nationalists in Germany in order to gain new followers for the Communist Party. On the other, by advocating for Russian-Soviet cooperation, they were continuing in the spirit of Rapallo. The Soviets feared that the German government would soon submit in the face of French pressure and allow Germany to be maneuvered into forming a common front against the Soviet Union.[143] And there were indeed several indications that a change of German policy was in the offing.

OVER THE COURSE OF the spring of 1923, the German government faced increasingly insistent pressure to start negotiating with the occupying powers. Those who argued that Germany could under no circumstances negotiate as long as the occupation persisted were "political fools" who "in their nationalist intoxication could not think a day ahead," wrote Ludwig Quidde, the chairman of the German Peace Cartel and a member of the DDP, in early March to Hamm.[144] Passive resistance alone was not a strategy, and "active policy would have to be added," declared Hermann Müller of the SPD later that month before the Reichstag's Foreign Affairs Committee.[145] The unions in particular pressed for the government to seize the moment as long as the resistance of the working classes remained unbroken. ADGB chairman Leipart informed Hamm that the willingness of the working classes to resist had passed its zenith: "We think that the point has been reached for negotiations since it is better to negotiate before the power to resist visibly diminishes than when the adversary notices that we're on the wane."[146]

But the German government initially made no moves to start negotiations with the French, fearing that any initiative in this direction could be interpreted as a sign of weakness. In Reichstag debates on foreign policy on April 16 and 17, Foreign Minister Rosenberg repeated the familiar argument that Germany had gone as far as it could in the previous few years with its reparation proposals, combining this assertion with a polemical attack on Poincaré for stubbornly insisting on his policies of violence. As long as France didn't relent, Germans would have to "continue to grit their teeth, stand beside one another, and hold out in resistance ... trusting to our rights."[147] Skeptics like Kessler were utterly disappointed by Rosenberg's speech: "What Rosenberg lacks is stature, just as our statesmen did during the war. With his small size, small gestures, and small intellect, he's like a dwarf who's trying to stop a large wagon from rolling into an abyss by pelting it with pebbles."[148]

It was Stresemann who proved the true surprise in the debates. The DVP chairman, who had previously advocated a hard line toward France, suddenly adopted a new tone. Superficially seconding the sentiments in Rosenberg's speech but actually distancing himself from them with great rhetorical skill, he pleaded for an "active policy," which meant the possibility of using diplomacy to "clear the way for international agreements." Beyond the reparations obligations and Germany's ability to meet them, it was urgent to restore trust among Europe's great powers and find a solution that "replaced military force with international understanding." In his next breath, Stresemann suggested closer economic collaboration with France, which would perhaps "in a completely different way" open up the possibility for "healing the wounds of war."[149]

Stresemann's speech was a "special achievement," Georg Bernhard wrote in the *Vossische Zeitung*, its great strength being its courageous criticism of the time it had taken for Germany to make a proposal.

Stresemann, Bernhard wrote, had shown a way that could lead to negotiations with the Entente, and especially with France.[150] For its part, the *Weltbühne* emphasized the domestic import of the speech. Making a "bold connection," Stresemann had built a bridge from the DVP to the Social Democrats. If he turned the trick of "bringing capital and labor together for an honest reparations policy the other side could trust, it would be an achievement that would make all the past sins of the national-liberal party forgotten and forgiven."[151]

Adding to the pressure from within was increasing pressure from the outside. On April 20, the British foreign secretary, Lord George Curzon, spoke to the upper house of Parliament, demanding in moderate tones that the German government take the first step and make a new offer of negotiations. If Germany unmistakably affirmed its willingness to pay reparations and to allow the final sum to be fixed by authorities specially entrusted with the task, and if it was willing in addition to offer guarantees for the outstanding payments, Curzon was confident that progress could be made. In any case, in his view, the door for negotiations was open.[152]

Curzon's speech was taken seriously in Germany, and in the Reichstag, Stresemann expressed his conviction that it had created "a new political situation . . . that will be commensurately valued by the German government."[153] Curzon had "truly made it easy" for the Cuno government to approach the allies with an offer, Kessler remarked in his diary. He then conjectured, "If the government still hesitates, there will be no alternative but to get rid of it."[154]

THE DECISION WAS NOW before Cuno and his cabinet. More delay would be unthinkable. On April 25, the government's ministers met to decide how to respond to Curzon's speech, but they were unable to reach an agreement.[155] Three days later, Rosenberg presented a draft dispatch, but when it was discussed, major differences of opinion emerged. Whereas one group, led by Labor Minister Heinrich Brauns, wanted to make as generous an offer as possible in order to create a psychological advantage for ensuing negotiations, another faction, led by Economics Minister Johann Becker of the DVP, demanded that the government stay within the parameters of previous offers in order to deny Poincaré a justification for occupying the Ruhr Valley and to avoid squandering the trust of the people there, who might ask, with good reason, "whether more could have been offered in January and the Ruhr invasion thereby prevented."[156] The chancellor and his foreign minister vacillated between these two positions. They were concerned about eliciting the broadest possible support for their dispatch and believed they had to take into account right-wing parties' sensibilities, as they had on the issue of paramilitaries and national defense organizations. D'Abernon, well briefed on the differing opinions within the German government, doubted whether Germany would "take advantage of the opportunity." The British ambassador predicted, "They are more likely to make some rather inadequate offer with very numerous and superfluous *Voraussetzungen* [conditions]."[157]

And in fact, the final wording of the German dispatch issued on May 2 had all the hallmarks of a halfhearted compromise. While the German government emphasized in its preamble that it was determined to reach an agreement, the text also made it clear that passive resistance would continue until the areas occupied in violation of the Treaty of Versailles were evacuated and the contractually agreed-on conditions in the Rhineland restored. A concrete reparations proposal followed, but it didn't go beyond what had already been offered. The German government declared itself willing to pay, after a four-year moratorium, a total of 30 million gold marks, which would be raised by July 1931 in three installments through loans. With that, the dispatch declared that Germany "had gone to the absolute limit of what [it] could provide if it mustered all its strength." If the Allies couldn't agree to this, the German government suggested forming an "independent international commission" along the lines of what American secretary of state Hughes had suggested the previous December. Germany pledged to abide by the judgment of the commission. But the dispatch remained fuzzy on securities and guarantees. Instead, at the end of the statement, as an unalterable condition for negotiations, Germany demanded that "within the shortest possible period, the status quo ante is to be restored"—that is, the French were to leave the occupied region.[158]

The dispatch came as a great disappointment for those Germans hoping for a decisive step forward. The missive was "even much worse than I expected," SPD finance expert Rudolf Hilferding told Kessler. Above all, the demand that occupying troops be completely withdrawn from the Ruhr rendered the "whole enterprise, right from the start, hopeless" and would undoubtedly send the wrong signals abroad. Hilferding suspected that fear of the extreme Right had influenced the government: "The man who had the greatest influence on the wording of the dispatch was obviously Hitler."[159]

Other commentators objected to the nondiplomatic form of the missive. Had it been "handed over to the world in a cleverer and more gracious package," a significant amount of progress might have been made, opined Bernhard in the *Vossische Zeitung*.[160] Richard Lewinsohn of the *Weltbühne* criticized that the "bloviating preamble waved around for absolutely no good reason the weapon of passive resistance." In politics, the important thing was not what you said but how you said it, Lewinsohn wrote, complaining that the dispatch could do nothing but alienate "well-meaning people abroad ready to understand us."[161] In contrast, in an editorial in the *Berliner Tageblatt*, Theodor Wolff argued that although there was much wrong with the style and presentation of the dispatch, "the German proposal could have been a suitable basis for negotiations despite all its shortcomings" had the other side been genuinely willing to reach an understanding.[162]

The French and Belgians rejected the German proposals as "utterly unacceptable" in their response on May 6. The 30 billion gold marks on offer, the French reply pointed out, were less than a quarter of the sum laid out in the London schedule of payments from March. Moreover, no securities or guarantees had been proposed to ensure that the money would in fact be paid. Paris and Brussels also rejected the idea that a new international commission should replace the Allied Reparation Commission and redefine Germany's obligations. Lastly, the two governments made it clear that they would never return to the negotiating table so long as the policy of passive resistance continued, reaffirming their decision "only to withdraw from the occupied regions measured against and in proportion to reparations that had actually been made."[163]

Predictably, the French-Belgian response—particularly an assertion that the Ruhr had been occupied "without using any sort of violence"—outraged the right-wing press in Germany. The *Deutsche Allgemeine Zeitung* called it "an intolerably insulting document of impertinent stupidity," adding that "running through their response was the polemicizing of an impotent lawyer."[164]

The Cuno government, however, was more unsettled by the British reaction than the aggressive rejection from France and Belgium. In his response of May 13, Curzon made clear that the German proposal had called forth "great disappointment" in the United Kingdom, where both the form and content were perceived as falling far short of what London had expected. Curzon advised those in power in Berlin to review their proposals and expand them so that they could serve as a useful basis for further exploration.[165] As tactful as Curzon kept his wording, his response amounted to a diplomatic slap in the face. "Much more bitter than the agitated aggression of the French reply is the terse rebuke in the calm English dispatch, which lays out to its bewilderment how few steps the German government has proceeded down the path left open to it," commented the *Vossische Zeitung*.[166]

Germany's dispatch of May 2 was thus an utter failure. Far from driving a wedge between Britain and France, it brought them closer together. Germany was once again isolated. D'Abernon found Rosenberg the day after receiving the British response in an extremely gloomy mood about a situation he too regarded as hopeless after the German proposals had been so summarily rejected. Several days later, the foreign minister confided to the ambassador that "it would probably have been better for [him and Cuno] to have resigned."[167]

THE FOREIGN POLICY DEBACLE was a major blow to the German government, which, it was becoming increasingly apparent, was simply not capable of resolving the crisis. In late May 1923, rumors began to swirl that Stresemann, who had accrued considerable support thanks to his Reichstag speech on April 14, could be named the new chancellor of a grand coalition. Although the DVP chairman made "very caustic remarks" about the Cuno government in a private conversation with Kessler, saying that the May 2 dispatch had "cost it a huge amount of respect in parliament,"[168] he was not at this point prepared to take over the chancellorship. Doing so would be "akin to political suicide," he wrote to his wife, Käte, on May 28. Several days later, he told her, "It's not yet been determined how long Cuno will stay on, but everyone is talking about me as Germany's last great reserve, and many of them are pressing me to throw myself into the gap. You know how little I long for that."[169]

So Stresemann did nothing to try to topple Cuno. On the contrary, in negotiations with the parliamentary groups of the Center Party and DDP and in an article for the Berlin DVP party organ *Die Zeit* in late May, he came out in favor of the governing cabinet. The ongoing diplomatic initiative, he argued, had to be continued and would not allow for any major change at the moment.[170] There was also resistance within the SPD, despite its generally dim view of Cuno, to allying the party with the DVP, and Social Democrats weren't prepared to risk the government stepping down even if it meant gaining a share of power themselves.[171]

For his part, Cuno was trying to limit the damage. In an attempt to defuse the situation, the chancellor decided to take Curzon's suggestion and make certain passages in the May 2 dispatch more precise, starting with the issue of securities and guarantees. To have any chance of success, Cuno needed the support of German business. An initial attempt to get the most powerful business lobby, the Reich Association of German Industry (RDI), to help meet reparations payments foundered on the opposition of Hugo Stinnes—an indication of how powerful a position and how much influence on the government this organization had. But after extensive deliberations, the RDI did accede to the government's request in a memo of May 25 that was clearly, at least in part, Stinnes's handiwork. The industrialists agreed in principle to issue guarantees, but as they had during the "credit initiative" of the fall of 1921, they insisted on conditions that would be difficult to fulfill. The state would have to agree to lift the remaining government rules from the war on the production and distribution of necessities, to cut taxes, to ensure an "increase in general labor productivity," and to relieve industry of the burden of "unproductive wages." These demands were a transparent attempt to use the government's dilemma over reparations to return to business-friendly economic and social conditions that had prevailed before the war.[172]

It was no surprise, wrote Lewinsohn in the *Weltbühne*, that industrialists "would try to do domestic political business even in the moment of [Germany's] greatest peril." The memo was an example of their inability to get beyond "their narrowest self-interest."[173] The reaction of German unions was unsurprisingly vitriolic. "Industry is trying to negotiate with the state here as an independent power and is making demands in a situation that's about doing one's duty toward the state as a citizen," the three leading independent labor organizations wrote to Cuno on June 1.

> The authority of state would have to be intolerably weak, if the government were to give in to the RDI's conditions.... The demand that the state keep out of the private production and distribution of necessities would return us to the economic conditions we had eighty years ago. The only motor of the economy would be the desire for profits, and any considerations of common economic interest would be dead. It is impossible for us to negotiate about giving up the eight-hour workday, the revocation of all job security protections, and the other demands of that ilk made by the RDI.[174]

By this point, the "unified front" of company bosses and labor—so solemnly invoked at the beginning of the Ruhr occupation—was in tatters.

On June 7, Cuno sent the Entente governments a far shorter and more soberly worded memorandum than the May 2 dispatch. It reiterated Germany's willingness to entrust the decision about the scope and form of reparations payments to an "impartial international authority" and offered specifics, in line with Curzon's wishes, about securities and guarantees. Cuno offered to turn Germany's national rail company, the Reichsbahn, into a special company and to mortgage it for 10 billion gold marks, with an annual interest of 500 million. A further 500 million gold marks could be raised through liens on German industry, commerce, transportation, and agriculture. The memo ended succinctly and unambiguously: "Germany recognizes its obligations to make reparations. The German government repeats its request to call a conference in order to agree on how best to fulfill this obligation."[175]

The memo was positively received in Britain, where former Chancellor of the Exchequer Stanley Baldwin had taken over as prime minister from Bonar Law in late May. (Curzon remained foreign secretary.) "In drastic contrast to the case previously, the legitimacy of our offer was nowhere called into question," reported Germany's ambassador in London, Friedrich Sthamer. "The direct, on-point formulations and the omission of all controversies came in for praise."[176] D'Abernon found the new German offer an "acceptable basis for negotiation," adding that "if Paris refuses out of hand it will be clear that they do not seek an arrangement but desire a continuation of the quarrel."[177]

Indeed, all Germany got from the French capital was a gruff "no." Paris refused to even consider negotiating before Germany renounced passive resistance. On June 29, Poincaré told the French Senate, "The most recent German proposals aren't serious and don't deserve an answer. If Germany doesn't understand that, so much the worse for Germany. We will not give up such a valuable security as the Ruhr Valley before we are paid."[178]

Under these conditions, was it not time to give up passive resistance? That was the question posed by the man who ran the German embassy in Paris, Leopold von Hoesch. Germany should be under no illusions that it could extract any concessions from France, he argued. Poincaré was not going to budge from his insistence on an unconditional renunciation of passive resistance.[179] But the German government refused to accept this condition, with Rosenberg declaring that it would amount to a "complete capitulation and humiliation."[180] President Ebert, too, continued to stand behind the Cuno government on the issue. As the ministerial director in the Foreign Ministry, Carl Schubert, related, Ebert had repeatedly signaled in mid-June that both he and the government would resign should Germany simply discontinue passive resistance.[181]

For their part, the SPD directorship and the leadership of the ADGB feared that they would again be (falsely) accused of stabbing Germany in the back if they brought about an end to the policy. On May 31, at a meeting in SPD headquarters in Berlin, representatives of the regional party and the independent unions in the occupied region pledged to continue passive resistance "with the same energy as previously."[182] Nobody wanted to be the one to topple the "resistance chancellor," Lewinsohn posited in the *Weltbühne*. Many people were covertly happy that the man who had made the bed of passive resistance was now forced to lie in it. "With this in mind, Mr. Cuno can govern without disruption for the time being."[183]

NONETHELESS, THE DISASTROUS CONSEQUENCES of Cuno's policies became ever clearer in the summer of 1923. The gigantic expenditures to underwrite the occupied regions caused an extraordinary acceleration of inflation, and the currency was devalued as never before. Wages lagged more and more severely behind rising prices, especially for food. As time passed, the crisis enveloped the entire German economy. Unemployment shot up. The majority of the German populace had been seized by "great agitation and bitterness," Hamm asserted in mid-June,[184] while the SPD Reichstag deputy and former German economics minister Rudolf Wissell informed the Reich Economic Council's currency committee on June 22 of the "mixture of gall and desperation" among Germans who lived on a fixed income. The mood among the working classes had shocked him and filled him with apprehension for the future, he added. All that was missing was the proper incendiary slogan to make the still slumbering "revolutionary spirit" discharge "like an explosion," as it had in 1918.[185]

Just a few weeks earlier, the disillusionment had sparked a wildcat strike in Dortmund, in which three hundred thousand working people took part. A series of strikes was called for from June to August in nonoccupied parts of Germany as well. The strikers' demands usually centered on wage hikes to offset the rapid declines in the purchasing power of the mark. In some places, people went on hunger strikes or looted stores. Such spontaneous actions were an expression of the extreme desperation spreading across the country.[186] By the end of July, the patience of many union functionaries in the occupied regions was exhausted. In a report to Cuno, the Essen regional director of the German Metalworkers Association, Karl Wolf, warned about a "demoralization of the working classes," which would necessarily entail "the worst of consequences." Wolf pleaded, "We consider it urgent that the evil be pulled out by the roots and that once and for all an end to the Ruhr policy be serious considered."[187]

Profiting from the catastrophic economic situation were the National Socialists, who recorded a significant rise in support in Munich and Berlin. But the Communists also felt the wind in their sails, seeing impressive increases in their share of the vote in works council and regional and municipal elections. Between September 1922 and September 1923, their numbers swelled from 225,000 to almost 295,000.[188] The pure desperation of many blue-collar workers was obviously sending new followers to the KPD. Left-wing historian Arthur Rosenberg was hardly exaggerating when he asserted in his still eminently readable 1935 book *History of the Weimar Republic* that by the summer of 1923 Germany's Communist Party "undoubt-edly" had united most of the proletariat behind it.[189]

But the occasional slogans that combined nationalism and Bol-shevism slogans did nothing to hinder the KPD leadership from vigorously opposing fascism as it attacked the government. On July 12, 1923, the party's central organ, the *Rote Fahne*, ran a front-page call to arms that could hardly have been more radical. It began with the statement that the Cuno government was "bankrupt" and that the "internal and external crisis" would inevitably lead to "an abso-lute catastrophe" in the coming days. Fascist associations in southern Germany, the paper alleged, were planning an uprising, against which "proletarian defense organizations" would have to arm themselves: "The fascist uprising can only be put down if the white terror is met by red terror. If the proletarian fighters are to defeat the fascists, who are armed to the teeth, they will have to destroy all fascists without pity. If the fascists line up every tenth striker against the wall, the revolution-ary workers will have to line up every fifth member of fascist organiza-tions against the wall."[190] American historian Werner T. Angress has described this call to arms as rather implausible. There were no signs of an imminent putsch in either Bavaria or the rest of Germany in the summer of 1923.[191] And the martial language probably did more to repel than attract people who may have sympathized with the KPD.

The KPD central committee in Berlin proclaimed July 19 a "day of anti-fascism" all over Germany. It was primarily an attempt to test how easily the party's followers could be mobilized and how much influence it had on the masses. Nervous after the aggression of the most recent Communist proclamation, the German government interpreted the announcement as the beginning of an attempted coup and recommended that Germany's regional states temporarily pro-hibit open-air events. Most regional authorities followed this advice. The KPD leadership didn't want to risk an open test of its strength (or that of the government) at this juncture, so in turn it recommended to its members only to stage demonstrations where they were allowed and otherwise to congregate indoors. Karl Radek justified this retreat in the *Rote Fahne* with the idea that the time for a general battle was not yet at hand, advising his fellow Communists to fight the battles that needed to be fought but always to keep in mind that they were still the weaker side.[192]


DESPITE MOUNTING CRITICISM, neither Cuno nor his foreign minister were giving up. "We shall stay here and carry out our policy until we are cut to pieces," Rosenberg told D'Abernon in early August 1923.[193] But he was deceiving himself. The Cuno government had forfeited too much trust in the preceding months. "Politically, we're drifting swiftly toward the abyss," noted Georg Escherich, the organizer of the then defunct Bavarian Residents' Defense in late July, adding that the Cuno government "was more and more at wits' end."[194] The chancellor had failed to make any decisive progress on either the reparations or currency stabilization issues. On the contrary, the mark was in free fall, and although Curzon sent an August 11 dispatch to the French government questioning the legality of the occupation and endorsing the call for an independent expert commission to determine the total amount of reparations, that couldn't paper over Germany's still precarious foreign policy situation.[195]

On July 27, the main organ of the Center Party, *Germania*, had launched a frontal attack on the government in an editorial with the headline "In the Greatest Emergency." The Cuno cabinet, the paper wrote, was a "complete disappointment," and there was every reason to doubt whether it could still summon the energy to take substantive action.[196] The article "hit him like a bomb," Stresemann wrote to one of his fellow DVP members, saying it summed up the "general consensus" on the government's lack of activity: "An evil star rules over the government. People respect the ministers as personalities, but you have the impression that they can't achieve anything anymore."[197] The Center Party and parliamentary leadership distanced themselves from the article but around the same time, the *Kölnische Zeitung*, the Center Party's leading mouthpiece in western Germany was sounding the alarm with an editorial entitled "It's Five Minutes to Midnight!" It was a telling indication of how dissatisfied even members of the Center Party were with Cuno.[198] No one believed any longer in this "hopeless chancellor," wrote the *Tage-Buch*. The only reason he was still in office, the paper wrote, was that his successor would inherit an utterly thankless task: "No one wants to lay down on this bed of nails. But does the inheritance improve the later one accepts it?"[199]

On July 27, the day the widely read editorial in *Germania* was published, Ebert summoned the governing cabinet. He downplayed criticism of the government's shortcomings, saying, "It would perhaps have been better if one thing or another had been done earlier, but it's not yet too late." The focus now had to be on "acting swiftly to overcome our domestic difficulties." Ebert recommended addressing the public with a "timely announcement."[200] A joint appeal by the president and the government would announce a program to consolidate national finances. Incoming taxes were to be collected on a rolling basis rather than at the end of the year to reflect the devaluation of the currency, and wealth, inheritance, and consumer taxes as well as wages and salaries were to be adjusted for inflation. Furthermore, the government envisioned a solidarity levy for "Rhine and Ruhr," particularly on the wealthier classes, and a government bond that would protect people's savings from losing their value.[201] These were all measures that should have been enacted earlier. But in the summer of 1923, with the crisis coming to a head, the announcement had no effect. "All the measures the government proposed today are reminiscent of a man on foot trying to win a race against an automobile," wrote Bernhard in the *Vossische Zeitung*.[202]

On August 8, the Reichstag convened for a special session. Deputies awaited Cuno's speech with great curiosity but generally came away disappointed. For the umpteenth time, the chancellor categorically rejected France's demands for an end to passive resistance, arguing that it would take away the government's "only weapon and expose it to the whims of the adversary."[203] He then long-windedly explained the proposed new tax legislation. Observers like Thomas Wolff found Cuno no longer equal to the demands of the office, noting that he had read "his printed speech with an exhaustion" all the more apparent "when he raised his voice a little to demand strength and persistence." There had been palpable relief the next day when Stresemann spoke with "robust determination." Wolff wrote, "No one knows what Stresemann would be able to get done as a statesman, but at least as an orator he doesn't suffer from tired resignation."[204] The editor in chief of the *Berliner Tageblatt* wasn't the only one who considered a change of cabinet necessary and saw Stresemann as Germany's future chancellor.

THE END OF THE CUNO government came more quickly than expected. On August 10, German printers went on strike, including those who worked for the treasury in Berlin responsible for creating new banknotes. The immediate result was a shortage of paper marks. That evening, Ebert called together the cabinet to discuss the situation, which he described as "very serious, not to say worrisome." Everything possible had to be done to create a stable means of payment as swiftly as possible: "If the masses have no money and go hungry, there will be violence in the streets."[205] The next day, the fourth anniversary of the Weimar Constitution, a general assembly of the revolutionary works councils in Greater Berlin, which was dominated by Communists, called a general strike with the goal of toppling the Cuno government. "Cuno strikes" spread from Berlin to other places, including Hamburg, the Lusatia region, the Prussian province of Saxony, and the regional states of Saxony and Thuringia.[206]

The mood in the SPD finally turned against the government. On the afternoon of August 11, the Social Democratic parliamentary group decided to withdraw its support for the Cuno cabinet. Its announcement stated that the "grave foreign policy and domestic situation" required "a government borne and supported by the trust of the broad masses, stronger than the current one." With that, the Social Democrats declared their willingness to take on governmental responsibility in a grand coalition cabinet. But they also set a series of conditions, including financial and currency reform, inflation-indexed wages, pensions for lower-income people and assistance for the unemployed, the clear "separation of the Reichswehr from all illegal organizations," and, finally, greater "foreign policy activity to resolve the reparations question."[207]

On August 10, Hilferding pressed for a grand coalition in a meeting with Stresemann,[208] but the DVP chairman resisted turning against the government more than he already had. Because he was being discussed on so many sides as a successor to Cuno, any criticism would be seen as "not objective, but personal," he told a fellow party member.[209] Understandably, Stresemann didn't want to be accused later of having brought down the government. In the DVP parliamentary group meeting, also on August 10, he declared that should the cabinet "find the strength to decide to remain in office," he would "as a matter of course support and fight alongside it." Should Cuno not be able to summon that strength and the cabinet stand down, the formation of a grand coalition "under the leadership of the bourgeois middle" was the best solution.[210]

The *Deutsche Allgemeine Zeitung* supported Stresemann on this score. Once the SPD parliamentary group's decision was made public, the Stinnes-owned newspaper wrote, "Fundamentally we are already saying that at the moment, with the whole world waiting for a French campaign of annihilation against Germany, a grand coalition cabinet would be the strongest proclamation of Germany's willingness to stand as one and defend itself."[211]

Dissatisfaction with the Cuno government had built up among the other bourgeois, centrist parties as well, and they too saw a grand coalition as the only practical way out of the crisis. But they shied away from openly declaring their lack of confidence in the chancellor since doing so would have undermined their own members in his cabinet. Cuno's only remaining source of support was the nationalist-liberal DVP, whose spokesman, Karl Helfferich, beseeched the chancellor, even at the height of the crisis, not to step down.[212]

But Cuno wasn't a battler. In early August, he visited his defense minister Otto Gessler in his office on Bendlerstrasse with a request: "Let me sit here for a couple of hours in peace. I feel as though a house is collapsing upon me."[213] Exhausted, his nerves completely frayed, the chancellor seems to have been almost relieved when the opportunity presented itself to get rid of the position he had never loved. By the time he summoned his ministers for a conference at noon on August 12, he had already decided to resign. The decision of the SPD alone would not have made him take this step, he declared, if the leaders of the parliamentary "working community of the center" hadn't signaled that "the idea of replacing the cabinet with a grand coalition government" also resonated with their parties. With that, the basis for continuing as chancellor was gone. In a subsequent meeting with the DDP party leadership, Cuno reiterated that the moment had come to "reestablish the government on a broader basis of parties and within the parliament and in so doing to ensure domestic political unity and forceful policies abroad."[214]

That evening, Cuno tendered his resignation. Ebert immediately charged Stresemann with forming a government, a move that surprised no one. The president was unable to hold onto Cuno because the chancellor himself had given up, wrote Seeckt to his sister: "Stresemann was in the air. Things were well prepared for him, and it has to be admitted that his most recent appearances in parliament were very adroit. He is certainly a very skillful and also very stubborn politician."[215]

CUNO HAD FAILED ACROSS the board, and his departure was nearly universally welcomed. It had become increasingly apparent that his cabinet had "allowed the ship of state to drift aimlessly with a broken rudder," wrote Bernhard in the *Vossische Zeitung*.[216] The final analysis made by Carl von Ossietzky in the *Berliner Volks-Zeitung* was nothing short of annihilating. Cuno's government, he wrote, had left behind a "pile of ruins... a devastated house consumed by flames." The German people were paying for the blank check it had handed to the "cabinet of personalities" in November 1922 with "a hopelessly inept foreign policy, a completely demolished economy, and a domestic situation not far from civil war."[217] The *Weltbühne* issued the outgoing government "a report card of insufficiency and incompetence" the likes of which no previous governing cabinet had ever received.[218]

In response to such harsh judgments, Theodor Wolff recalled that Cuno had been extraordinarily popular at the start of his time in office and had been "welcomed as a hero on his travels throughout the country." His biggest mistake had been to hew, as a businessman, too closely to the "ideas of large-scale capitalist circles." Wolff concluded by quipping, "The Cuno cabinet forgot the rules of sea in the middle of the storm and put up little umbrellas to hold back the waves."[219]

The *Deutsche Allgemeine Zeitung*, on the other hand, mostly praised the ex-chancellor. Under his leadership, "the German name had reacquired some of its ring abroad." The "Ruhr war" he had initiated had completed the break with "Herr Wirth's policy of fulfillment." The paper did, however, criticize the ex-chancellor for not showing sufficient energy on domestic issues, neglecting, for instance, "to impress upon the working classes with complete insistence the necessity of additional labor and the elevation of national productivity."[220] As such statements made clear, this paper was the mouthpiece of large industrial interests. And it wasn't long before those circles would confront the new government to demand the reversal of the social-welfare and working-class achievements of 1918–19.

# CHAPTER 2

# FROM INFLATION TO HYPERINFLATION

*A long line in front of a grocery store in 1923. Such scenes became common in the period of hyperinflation in Germany.*

O N THE MORNING OF AUGUST 12, 1923, THEA STERN-
heim went shopping with her two children in Dresden. "The usual hunt there for groceries," she wrote in her diary. "No butter, no eggs, three pounds of meat cost 3 million marks."[1] Tellingly, Sternheim didn't mention that the Cuno government stepped down that day. Nor did Victor Klemperer write a single line in his journal about Cuno's resignation. The dominant topic remained the dramatic devaluation of German currency, with newspaper advertisements delivering some vivid examples: "Renner, a cheap department store offered:

mens' boots 16.5 million, men's trousers 6.5 million, caps 3.6 million, ladies' dresses 55.41 million, the cheapest one only 5.74 million, the cheapest ladies' hose 500,000, etc., etc."[2]

Nationalist circles blamed reparations payments for the out-of-control inflation, but the true causes ran deeper and stretched back to the First World War. The German Empire didn't finance the war by raising taxes but largely by issuing domestic bonds—on the assumption that Germany's defeated enemies could be made to pay them off after the kaiser's inevitable victory. Moreover, because the Reichsbank had no other way of meeting exploding costs, as of 1916 it had been extremely loose with credit. The amount of money in circulation rose from 2.9 billion to 18.6 billion marks between August 1, 1914, and December 1, 1918, and by the end of the war, Germany had racked up 156 billion marks in debt. The interest alone on this enormous sum amounted to 90 percent of the Reich's regular expenditures in the final year of the war. Practically speaking, the value of the mark had declined to almost half of what it was before the war.[3]

"The old regime conducted the war like a desperate gambler who stakes everything on a single card," wrote Felix Pinner, a business reporter at the *Berliner Tageblatt*, in late December 1918. "Insane price hikes were approved to stimulate production, and the higher prices brought higher wages and vice versa. Inflation, which to an extent was inevitable, took on forbidding dimensions."[4]

Currency reform was urgently required after 1918, but the postwar democratic governments didn't dare to take that step and prioritized keeping the social peace over reining in the national budget and stabilizing the mark. So they continued the inflationary policies of the past to finance the costs of the lost war. The government had to demobilize and reintegrate millions of soldiers into the labor force, provide for wounded veterans and the unemployed, subsidize industry to help it convert back to peacetime production, and compensate companies for lost property in the territories Germany had been forced to cede. All of this drove government debt to unprecedented levels. In addition, wages, salaries, and social benefits shot up after the war because the state, German business, and the unions saw the increases as a means of preventing revolutionary unrest and the radicalization of the working classes. Indeed, the consensus among those in power in the initial years of postwar Germany was that inflation was *desirable*.[5]

Even the reforms put forth by Finance Minister Matthias Erzberger in July 1919 didn't fundamentally change anything. Those reforms established the authority of the national government over that of the regional states and laid the groundwork for a modern tax system. Erzberger wanted to tax wealthy and propertied people more heavily using a legislative bundle that included a one-off levy of assets in December 1919. But none of these changes was able to effectively curb inflation or the national debt. Businessmen, facing higher taxes, simply raised prices. And since state expenditures were still higher than revenues, the gap could only be closed by taking on fresh obligations. In 1920, Germany's national debt was 184.9 billion marks. By 1921, it had risen to 248.8 billion.[6]

On the other hand, inflation did offer the German economy some advantages. The devalued mark created favorable conditions for exports. In contrast to the other large western industrial nations, which all slipped into major recessions after the war, Germany experienced a boom from 1920 to 1922. Unemployment remained low, reaching 1.2 percent in October 1921. That same month, the Berlin correspondent at the *Manchester Guardian* observed, "The results of the depreciation are threefold. In the first place, German industry is flourishing in an unprecedented manner. Profits are enormous, big dividends are being paid, export trade has been stimulated, production has increased, and unemployment has almost vanished. In the second place, the cost of living is going up and standard of living down. In the third place, foreign countries are being hit harder than ever by German competition."[7]

There was also a further advantage to letting inflation rise. It allowed the German government to better conceal the actual capacity of the German economy from the Entente and to argue that reparations demands could not be met. Suspicions, especially in France, that

Germany was purposely devaluing its currency to evade its obligations had some basis in fact. In January 1921, Walther Rathenau declared at a meeting in the German Foreign Ministry that he wasn't scared of inflation. To "erect a bulwark" against an economic crisis like that in Britain, he suggested "allowing the currency printers to work a bit harder." As he explained, "It simply isn't true that printing money will be our ruin."[8]

INFLATION DIDN'T RISE STEADILY. It came in spurts. But overall, between the spring of 1919 and that of 1920, the German currency dramatically lost value. Before the war, the exchange rate was 4.2 marks to the dollar. By May 1919, after the harsh conditions of the Treaty of Versailles became known, the rate was 13.5, and by the end of the year, 49. After a further severe drop, one dollar was worth more than 90 marks. After that, things stabilized until the summer of 1921. In July 1920, the mark notched an annual high of 37.95 to the dollar. Between October 1920 and July 1921, the exchange rate ranged between 62 and 75. It seemed as though German currency had finally recovered. In the belief that the mark's value would continue to rise, significant amounts of foreign capital flowed into Germany and propped up the exchange rate.[9]

But when the reparations bill in the May 1921 London ultimatum was accepted, the exchange value of the mark began to fall again, at first slowly, then beginning in October with increasing rapidity. By December, the exchange rate was 217 to one against the dollar. At the same time, German unemployment was at 1.6 percent. In his New Year's editorial, Georg Bernhard of the *Vossische Zeitung* wrote, "It's become a slogan in Germany that inflation has to be reduced." Yet no one had seriously tackled the task, for reasons that were universally known:

Inflation is a gigantic swindle that dangles pleasing images before people's eyes. All the economic activities, the rises in prices and wages may actually entail a below-value sellout, an inundation of the masses as consumers, and an underpayment of all working people as producers. But because the sums to which the old ideas cling are rising, people are slow to notice, or don't notice at all, and because everyone who wants to work finds a job and a wage, the positive employment figures increase the smoke and fog that surrounds us.

Conversely, deflationary policies would entail "a harsh awakening... as though after an opium binge." That would render not only production but government more difficult. "And that's why no one is willing to make a start," Bernhard concluded, "as long as it's easier just to print money."[10]

In his journal, Klemperer registered the continuing fall of the mark with growing unease. "Terrible price rises for the household and fuel," he wrote on September 8, 1921. "Need new trousers, doctor's bills threatening. . . . I no longer bother adding things up. I've become rather numb to money, either in terms of it being earned or dissolving away. A hundred-mark note is like a mark."[11] Two months later, he complained, "The finances are beginning to get very oppressive. Prices for everything are rising terribly. Coffee more than 30, butter above 40. And in addition constant side expenses. . . . If it continues, our savings will quickly be exhausted."[12] On December 23, after completing his final Christmas shopping in Dresden's Old Town, he recorded, "For the most trivial everyday items (sausage, hair tonic, etc., etc.) it's easier to spend one hundred than it used to be ten."[13]

Many Berliners agreed not to exchange gifts that Christmas "because the prices are slowly becoming ludicrous," theater critic Alfred Kerr wrote in one of his "Idle Chatter" columns from the German capital. "Everyone is looking ahead with a worried eye to what extremely unexpected things the future still holds in store. There's no denying that the way developments are unfolding is something like a landslide."[14]

Telephone calls were initially exempt from the price increases, inspiring "Sling," the pen name of *Vossische Zeitung* reporter Paul Schlesinger, to give his readers a tip in mid-November: "Let's sit down tonight by the telephone. A call only costs twenty pfennigs. . . . In four weeks, we'll have to pay double that. At the moment, it's the cheapest thing going in Germany. So let's take the opportunity. Raise your voices with me: talk the phone and nothing else!"[15]

By that time, the unresolved issue of reparations was playing havoc with exchange rates, as the mark moved wildly in the spring and early summer of 1922. The rate between the mark and dollar was 326 to one in early April, and the hope for a positive outcome to the Genoa Conference pushed up the German currency, but by mid-May, the rate was back to 314 to one, with the conference having proven a dud and the Treaty of Rapallo having stoked French distrust. In June, the prospect of Germany being able to take out a major international line of credit to pay some of its reparations brought a temporary respite. Yet this hope, too, was dashed, and the downward spiral began again. "We're gradually noticing that Germany lost the war," the publisher of the *Weltbühne*, Siegfried Jacobsohn—on holiday in mid-June in the village of Kampen on the North Sea island of Sylt—wrote to his most gifted and productive employee, the writer and journalist Kurt Tucholsky.[16]

Even in prison, anarchist writer and activist Erich Mühsam was affected by the enormous price hikes. "The value of the mark has been hovering for weeks around roughly the same level, 270 to 310 to the dollar," he wrote from his cell in late May 1922. "The newspaper for which I had to pay 24 marks in May has cost 40 since June 1. The Ovomaltine I take every day at breakfast to calm my nerves, which cost 3 marks in peacetime, has gone up from 35 to 45 marks over the past six weeks. Milk costs 10 marks a liter instead of 10 pfennigs as it used to. And the situation is even worse with potatoes, bread, and all important foods, including fruit."[17]

Thea Sternheim had observed much the same after strolling the center of Frankfurt am Main in late April: "Prices have doubled and tripled since January. Fantastic sums in store windows. . . . In the Frankfurter Hof restaurant, a beef dish costs 70 and the soup of the day 30 marks. If you order bread with that and something to drink, the bill for two will amount to 300 marks or more."[18]

The shock of Rathenau's assassination on June 24 destroyed what little confidence remained in Germany and abroad. "The German mark and Germany's reputation in the world have sunk lower than they ever have before," wrote Lewinsohn in the *Weltbühne*.[19] On July 1, the exchange rate was 402 marks to the dollar; by the end of that month it was 670. "Abruptly the mark plunged down, never to stop until it had reached the fantastic figures of madness, the millions, the billions and trillions," recalled writer Stefan Zweig. "Now the real witches' sabbath of inflation started."[20] Domestic prices rose by more than 50 percent a month. Germany had entered a period of hyperinflation.

The fifty-two-year-old teacher and church cantor August Heinrich von der Ohe kept records in his diary of the runaway price increases:

*August 4, 1922*: One dollar is worth roughly 800 marks. It's a crisis.

*August 18, 1922*: They're asking 2,000 marks for rye. Creamery butter costs 150 marks, regular butter 120 marks. One dollar is worth 1,040 marks. Horrific price hikes across the entire country.

*August 27, 1922*: The mark has fallen to 2,400 to one against the dollar. Catastrophe is now at our doorsteps. Over the course of a few days, prices are rising in dizzying fashion.... People are storming the stores. Everyone wants to buy now. Butter costs 200 marks, and a liter of milk 30 marks. Fifty kilos of wheat already goes for 3,000 marks.[21]

It was almost unimaginable, wrote Kerr in late August 2022, how grim the mood was when "word-of-mouth on the streets of Berlin had the dollar at 200." The only consolation the theater critic could find was that "the rapid decline of the mark must open the eyes of even the stupidest and most knee-jerk of our enemies and the rest of Europe to how bad things really are with us."[22]

But things were about to get a lot worse. On November 8, the dollar was worth 9,172 marks. "Like the fever curve of someone deathly ill, the exchange rate with the dollar illustrates the daily progression of our demise," wrote Count Harry Kessler.[23] The appointment of the business-friendly Cuno government temporarily calmed the situation. On November 22, the dollar had dropped to 6,300 marks, but by the end of that month, it was back up to 7,368.[24] Christmas 1922 took place under the baleful star of rampant inflation. Thea Sternheim, who traveled with her husband, Carl, to Dresden on December 20 to do her final Yuletide shopping, had to admit her disappointment: "The stores are empty. Who can afford to make their children clothes when simple, coarse wool costs 5,000 to 8,000 marks? Decorations for a tiny Christmas tree cost me thousands. The Saxon, with his sweet tooth, invests the last of his money in fruitcakes."[25]

HYPERINFLATION PUT A SWIFT end to the postwar economic boom in Germany. Exports began to decline in August 1922, as the competitive advantages industry had derived from the fall in the value of the mark disappeared. The Entente powers had recovered from their postwar recessions and were now producing many of the goods previously imported from Germany. Moreover, as of late 1922, transactions were increasingly taking place in gold rather than in marks. As a result, inflation no longer served business interests. The consensus acceptance of it, which had briefly ensured political and social harmony, was completely shattered.[26]

The Cuno government's strategy of passive resistance to French occupation proclaimed in January 1923 dealt the fatal blow to Germany's currency. By February 5, the exchange rate was 42,250 marks to the dollar, with the mark having lost three-quarters of its value over the previous three weeks. "The money issue is becoming increasingly dark and impenetrable," Klemperer noted in early February. "The prices are insane (margarine 4,000 marks a pound, the dollar between 40,000 and 50,000)."[27] An emergency measure by the Reichsbank to prop up the currency in mid-February succeeded in stabilizing the mark for a couple of months at around 21,000 to the dollar. But when a lack of foreign currency forced the state to end this measure, the dams collapsed. On April 18, the exchange rate dropped to 25,000 to one; by late May, to 54,300 to one; and a month later, to 114,250 to one against the dollar. Prices exploded commensurately. "We stocked up on what was still very cheap, coffee for 48,000 marks," recorded Klemperer in his diary. "Today it already costs 60,000. That's the way it is with everything."[28]

The freefall continued. By the end of July 1923, the exchange rate hit a million marks to the dollar, and the state secretary in the Reich Chancellery, Eduard Hamm, deemed all attempts to stop the fall of the currency a failure. The "last vestiges of trust" in the mark on foreign currency markets were gone, and the mark had become "almost unsellable," losing its domestic function as a "measure of value and a repository of worth."[29]

That was precisely what ordinary Germans were experiencing. "The dollar is now worth 1.2 million marks, i.e., almost nothing," wrote Ohe on August 1. "Today I saw my first 5-million-mark banknote. A pound of new potatoes costs 6,000 marks. Suit-quality material costs 3 million per meter. Stores close earlier. They're being stormed. Everyone is running away from the mark."[30] Prices were no longer rising by the day but by the hour. Klemperer recorded a telling anecdote in his journal. Returning from their vacation in East Prussia, his wife, Eva, ordered a coffee in a train station waiting area. "The price board said 6,000 marks, but that disappeared while she drank. By the time she paid, the waiter demanded 12,000. She objected, pointing out that the listed price had been 6,000. The waiter said, 'Oh, you were already here during the old price? Then you'll pay 6,000.'"[31]

When Stresemann took office on August 13, 1923, one dollar was worth 3.7 million marks.[32] Printing presses were running day and night to produce banknotes with ever greater nominal values. Hundreds of printing presses in addition to that of the central mint in Berlin worked to fill demand for paper money.[33] Amid the runaway

*Banknotes that had lost nearly all their value being weighed
during the hyperinflation in Germany in 1923.*

currency devaluation and the major imbalance between revenues and
expenditures, the *Vossische Zeitung* asked in all seriousness whether it
even made sense to collect taxes or whether the Reichsbank wouldn't
be better advised to "do away with tax offices and simply cover its
needs by printing more money."[34]

INFLATION AND HYPERINFLATION HIT disparate segments
of society with various degrees of severity.[35] It had catastrophic consequences for pensioners, especially older people, who lived from the
interest on money they had invested long term. They lost nearly everything, as their savings, life insurance policies, and capital pensions lost
their value. Also among those especially hard hit were the educated
upper middle classes, who had patriotically purchased German bonds
during the war and now watched that investment evaporate. The situation of retired people and recipients of social benefits, including the
unemployed, wounded war veterans, and the relatives of those who
had fallen, became increasingly desperate as inflation skyrocketed and

state payments were delayed and insufficiently adjusted for the dwindling value of German money.

The same was true for civil servants and white-collar employees who drew fixed monthly salaries. Inflation subsidies were paid ex post facto, by which time the mark had declined even further, so that they didn't compensate for the enormous price increases. "Extremely painful is the lowering of the standard of living for the entire so-called middle classes and among civil servants," wrote the religious philosopher Ernst Troeltsch in March 1922 in one of his famous "Letters of a Spectator." He noted, "People are spending their entire income on housing, heating, and food. Otherwise, they make do as well as they can with what they have and wear their clothing until it falls apart.... There are no more luxuries like art, science, and any sort of travel for these social circles."[36]

Many upper-middle-class families could no longer afford to pay for their children to attend universities. Their sons and daughters were forced to finance their studies themselves by working in factories, offices, and agricultural fields or as assistants in social welfare jobs. "The money parents had put aside over the years by doing without dissolved into nothing," remembered the fledgling journalist and writer Erich Kästner, who studied German literature, philosophy, and theater history in Leipzig. "I became a working student, which meant that I worked in an office, received a whole pile of money in wages at the end of the week, and had to run if I wanted to buy anything to eat with it."[37] The concept of the "working student" was something new, and the educated upper middle class saw it as a terrible loss of status.[38]

The privations civil servants faced are detailed in the diaries of Klemperer, who had been named a professor of Romance languages at Dresden Technical University in late 1919. "The financial emergency is horrific," he wrote in November 1922. "With last Friday's supplemental payment, I've gotten up to 50,000 marks this month—but it won't be enough. Food for a single day costs over 1,000 marks, and a half pound of butter 600. We're running out of coffee—how are we supposed to buy more? We lead increasingly primitive lives. A servant girl is now out of the question. Coffee is one of our few pleasures, and the cinema—where a seat now costs 80 marks."[39] A month later Klemperer wrote, "The prices have now all reached a thousandfold of what they were before the war. . . . But my professorial salary is only a million. A thousandfold would be seven million. And so we scrub our own floors and lug our own coal, etc."[40]

In the first half of 1923, civil servants' situation eased somewhat when their wages began to be paid in advance every quarter. On March 31, Ohe described the repercussions: "Our salary had already been paid. For the quarter from April to July, I received 1,086,336 marks; 99,091 marks go for taxes. I receive a monthly basic wage of 25,900 marks, with a location supplement of 2,700 marks, an inflation supplement of 269,412 marks, and a supplement for my wife of 12,000 and children of 52,100 marks. All together that adds up to 362,112 marks a month."[41] But by late April 1923, even these exorbitant increases in income couldn't compensate for the dwindling value of money.

The situation for the working classes was more complex but also ultimately more dire. Working people benefited from the initial years of inflation. Unemployment was low, and real wages remained relatively high, even if they had not returned to prewar levels. Best off were unskilled and semiskilled laborers, previously poorly paid, who significantly improved their situation relative to well-off trained workers. In this regard, inflation effectively leveled wage differences within the working classes. It wasn't until hyperinflation that this positive trend stopped. Whereas in July 1922, only 0.6 percent of union members were without a job, by January 1923, unemployment had risen to 4.2 percent and by October 1923 to 19.1 percent. Growing joblessness forced down wages. In July 1923, real weekly wages were only 48 percent of what they had been in 1913. Many working-class families faced desperate circumstances. Because price hikes for food and necessities increasingly outstripped wage boosts, many companies began paying their employees twice a week and, in the end, even day by day.[42]

Property and homeowners were better off, as was anyone paying off debts, above all the state, which used the opportunity to settle domestic obligations, including war bonds. Also benefiting were large farmers and estate owners who freed their land and buildings from debt. For instance, Helmuth Adolf von Moltke, a nephew of the famous German field marshal Helmuth von Moltke, found himself able to pay off a debt of 250,000 marks with 325 pounds the parents of his wife, Dorothy, had sent from South Africa. "Before the war, we owed [the equivalent of] 12,500 pounds, and now that's covered with 315 pounds—unbelievable!" Dorothy wrote to Pretoria in January 1922.[43] Moreover, rural producers always had enough to eat and could acquire valuables in exchange for food with hungry city dwellers who had fled to the countryside. On the other hand, hefty price increases for seed, fertilizer, livestock, and agricultural machinery partly negated the positives.[44]

The primary profiteers from inflation were large industrialists. The value of their investments remained stable, and they were able to get cheap credit that allowed them to buy up factories, property, and even whole companies at bargain prices. This dramatically accelerated the concentration of heavy industry in particular. "Ownership is being concentrated in a few, powerful hands," social scientist Franz Eulenburg wrote in 1924. "Small and medium-sized entrepreneurs may not have been completely stripped of all they own, but most of them are now part of the big concerns. As a result, the distribution of wealth has become significantly less equal."[45]

RUHR VALLEY INDUSTRIALIST Hugo Stinnes was considered the prototype of the inflation profiteer, although his external appearance hardly suggested that he was one of Germany's most powerful business magnates. Kessler, who observed him at a dinner party in May 1923, described him: "Dark, full-bearded, inelegant (while he did wear a coat and tails, he paired them with a black tie and square polished boots)—halfway between a trade union secretary and the Flying

Dutchman. In his eyes and his entire being, there's something veiled and secretive that could be a great passion, perhaps for increasing his own wealth. In addition, he has a surprisingly high, weak, almost boyish voice. If he didn't have money and weren't a famous man, I'd think he was some dubious charlatan."[46]

In 1893, at the age of only twenty-two, this entrepreneur's son from the small city of Mülheim founded his own company, which he expanded into the most important coal-trading business in Germany. Even more important was his activity as chairman of the supervisory boards for several large conglomerates, including the power utility Rheinisch-Westfälische Elektrizitätswerk, established in 1898.[47] Stinnes's business strategy was vertical integration, closely linking coal mining with the iron and steel sectors, energy providers, and transport companies. He considered it beyond question that political concerns should be subordinate to economic ones, and prior to 1914, he never took much of an interest in politics at all.

That changed with the First World War. Stinnes was a leader of the industrialist "war aims movement," which opposed a negotiated peace settlement and pushed for major annexations. He was a vigorous advocate of deploying thousands of Belgians as slave laborers in the German arms industry—a preview of the later Nazi policy of brutally exploiting "foreign workers." Even in the summer of 1918, when Germany had already effectively lost the war, he still trusted in the strategic genius of military commander Erich Ludendorff and was convinced that Germany would emerge victorious.

The November Revolution of 1918, which toppled Wilhelmine Germany after the country's defeat in the First World War and formed the Weimar Republic, was an unpleasant shock, but in what proved an extremely precarious situation for a business magnate, Stinnes demonstrated tactical flexibility, arranging the so-called Stinnes-Legien Agreement with union leaders under the direction of Carl Legien. It gave workers an eight-hour workday without wage cuts, the recognition of unions as legitimate workforce representatives, guaranteed wages, and the right to form "workers' committees"—work councils—

in businesses employing more than fifty people. Industrialists, of course, only begrudgingly agreed to form a long-term social-welfare partnership with unions, but the concessions were necessary for them to survive the revolutionary upheaval as unscathed as possible. This was all the more crucial for men like Stinnes because the movement to socialize key industries grew particularly strong in the Ruhr Valley in the spring of 1919.

In June 1920, Stinnes got himself elected to the Reichstag as a member of the DVP. In his role as parliamentary representative, together with Albert Vögler, the director general of the mining company Deutsch-Luxemburgische Bergwerks- und Hütten AG, which was part of the Stinnes conglomerate, and others from the party's conservative, industrialist wing, the magnate wasted no time in moving to secure his interests. He was unequaled in exploiting inflation, acquiring whatever there was to be bought: companies, land, ships, hotels (for instance, Berlin's Esplanade), cellulose and paper factories, and newspapers, including the *Deutsche Allgemeine Zeitung*, which had formerly been a semiofficial government organ. The result was a gigantic, untransparent conglomerate of corporations—an economic empire the likes of which Germany had never seen. Among the "kings of inflation," remarked one contemporary, Stinnes had achieved the same rank as "the kaiser once had among the regional German princes."[48] In a series of articles about Germany's economic leaders, the *Weltbühne* concluded, "There is without doubt no one else who, thanks to his property, successes, and business reputation, has united so much power as Hugo Stinnes, this small, inconspicuous, inarticulate, archetypal Westphalian whom wags in parliament have nicknamed the 'Assyrian king' because of his Oriental appearance."[49]

AMONG THE OTHER BENEFICIARIES of inflation were non-Germans with foreign currency at their disposal. For them, inflationary Germany seemed like paradise. "Heaven had opened its gates here," wrote journalist and cultural historian Hans Ostwald in 1931.

"For them, milk and honey and champagne and everything fine flowers in abundance."[50] In December 1921, Alfred Kerr met up again with an old acquaintance who had since moved to Denmark. He could hardly recognize her: "Years ago, she used to come to Berlin once in a while from her small northern city and was badly dressed. The child of civil servants. Now? Bedecked with furs, a completely different person. . . . Nothing about her social circumstances has changed, but she can come to Berlin and go shopping for clothes. Top of the world, top of the line, as we say here. Are we just imagining things, or is it really true that people like this sound a bit patronizing when they speak to us?"[51]

In August 1922, Ernest Hemingway, who was working in Paris as a foreign correspondent for the *Toronto Star*, traveled with his wife to the border town of Kehl am Rhein to report on the collapse of the mark. In the train station, he exchanged 10 francs, the equivalent of 90 Canadian cents, for 670 marks—enough for the entire day: "That 90 cents lasted Mrs. Hemingway and me for a day of heavy spending and at the end of the day we had 120 marks left!" Lunch in the best hotel in the city cost the equivalent of 15 cents Canadian. The cafés were crammed with French people who had come to "gorge on fluffy, cream-filled slices of German cake at five marks a slice." Hemingway wrote, "The proprietor and his helper were surly and didn't seem particularly happy when all the cakes were sold. The mark was falling faster than they could bake."[52]

Berlin—especially for Americans—was an El Dorado, a place where you could live as kings for a dollar a week. U.S. citizens were everywhere fun was to be had and flocked to antique shops and auctions where valuable items could be purchased for a song. Luxury hotels treated them as VIPs. Journalist and author Joseph Roth, who had moved from Vienna to Berlin in 1920, observed, "Foreigners park themselves on the expansive leather furnishings in hotel lobbies. . . . Pampered by waiters, personally greeted by hotel managers with smiles plastered on their faces, and surrounded by elevator boys in red uniforms, they listen to the music at five o'clock tea. As everyone whispers, they shout.

As everyone kneels, they stand. As everyone speculates, they wait. As everyone sleeps, they're awake. As the mark falls, they rise."[53]

In 1923, the American literary critic Malcolm Cowley visited his friend Matthew Josephson, who had moved to Berlin earlier in the decade because it was cheaper to publish his journal, *Broom*, there. Cowley was flabbergasted at what a monthly salary of a hundred dollars could buy in the German capital: "Josephson lived in a duplex apartment with two maids, riding lessons for his wife, dinners only in the most expensive restaurants, trips to the orchestra, pictures collected, charitable donations to struggling German writers."[54]

The contrast with the increasingly desperate circumstances of Germans who were paid in marks was glaringly obvious and made locals hostile to foreigners. In November 1923, an anonymous contributor to the *Weltbühne* vented his ire at the foreign diplomats in Berlin. Even the heads of medium-sized and small nations could "present themselves in the most lavish ... of styles," the author complained. "They are able to lead blissful lives with teams of servants and city and touring cars, while their wives adorn themselves with precious pearls and almost more precious furs. In short, they feel as though they're in heaven on earth." The author denied any "chauvinistic nationalism," but he also issued a demand: "As unconditionally as we support social intercourse with other countries taking place with the maximum openness and in the most engaging and polite forms, we cannot help but be repulsed when others gorge themselves on our currency misery while our intellectuals are dying of starvation and our middle classes suffer physical and moral demise."[55]


INFLATION'S MORAL EFFECTS WERE even graver than its economic and societal consequences. The almost complete devaluation of the mark was accompanied by a fundamental suspension of previous norms and values. Virtues like thrift, honesty, and communal solidarity were no longer binding, trumped by selfishness, unscrupulousness, and cynicism. In a poem entitled "Revised Folk Song"

published in the *Weltbühne*, author Hans Reimann summarized the
radical upheaval:

> *Be not devoted or constant*
> *Lest you dig your own grave*
> *And make sure to keep sufficient distance*
> *From Almighty God and his ways.*
> *Childhood lessons apply no more.*
> *You'll only croak if you live right*
> *Religion too brings no reward.*
> *So be brazen and impolite.*[56]

The trauma of losing the war was followed by another profound
blow. "We had the great war game behind us and the shock of defeat,
the disillusionment of the revolution that had followed, and now the
daily spectacle of the failure of all the rules of life and the bankruptcy
of age and experience," recalled historian Sebastian Haffner about
being a sixteen-year-old in Berlin in 1923.[57]

The loss of trust in money as a repository of value also robbed Germans of their faith in the existing political and social order. What
could people count on if money was no longer worth anything? What
did they have to cling to? As did many of his generation, Thomas
Mann's eldest son, Klaus, also sixteen at the time, asked such questions. "We grew up in a time of sweeping changes and uncertainties,"
he wrote in his biography *The Turning Point*.

> How could we be infallible when everything failed and fum-
> bled around us? Civilization boggled along, aimlessly as it were.
> Nobody had the faintest idea what would happen next. Some-
> times it looked as if Utopia were around the corner: in other
> moments we anticipated the collapse of all values and institu-
> tions of the sort we came to know in the Twenties seemed to be
> without balance, goal or affirmation of life. It was ripe for ruin,
> ready for downfall. Indeed, we became acquainted early on with

apocalyptic moods and experienced in many forms of excess and adventure. Yes, we were familiar with apocalyptic moods, versed in many temptations.[58]

Personifying the apocalyptic mood were the *Inflationsheilige* (literally, "inflation saints"): Christlike, would-be prophets who wandered Germany with long flowing hair, dressed in gunnysack frocks and sandals, preaching "salvation from chaos" and the "renewal of the world from the spirit of love" to sometimes bewildered, sometimes fascinated audiences.[59] In September 1922, the *Kölnische Volkszeitung* newspaper wrote, "People—in particular the weak-natured ones who cannot exist without support—flock to these latter-day saviors with their long hair and presumptuous fantasies. This culture of prophets is a worrisome symptom of the intellectual and emotional state of today's Germany. It should not be underestimated. It will increase even further in the crises to come."[60] Itinerants stylizing themselves as Jesus were one answer to the desperation of the time, a magnet for desires for salvation and dreams of enlightenment that spoke in particular to those who had tumbled down the social ladder or faced the imminent threat of doing so.

One well-known prophet was Friedrich Muck-Lamberty, the "Messiah of Thuringia." In 1920, he began traveling through towns and villages with a group of young dancers and actors he formed under the name the "New Flock." Wherever they stopped, they unleashed frenetic dancing, transporting thousands of people into an ecstatic intoxication in which social divisions disappeared and everyday worries could be forgotten—at least briefly.

Another would-be savior was the painter Max Schulze-Sölde. The son of a bourgeois family, he converted to religious socialism after 1918 and cofounded the rural commune "Lindehof" near the northern German city of Itzehoe. After that, he signed up to work in a mine near Hamborn in the hopes of inspiring his fellow miners to start a new revolution. When he failed, he tried out the role of a resurrected

"John the Apostle," crisscrossing Germany to promote the idea of "Christian-socialist popular community."

More influential than either of these figures was Ludwig Christian Haeusser, probably the most widely known of the "prophets" of the day. A former maker of sparkling wine, the experience of the war turned Haeusser into a radical reformer, who increasingly presented himself as a new Christ, collecting a group of male and female disciples. Many of the women became sexually fixated on him and longed for nothing more than to receive children—"new people"—from their fervently worshipped master. Haeusser used modern advertising techniques to stir up interest in his appearances. His rhetoric, which attracted mass audiences, was an idiosyncratic mélange of religious fervor, coarse obscenity, and Wilhelmine pomposity. Haeusser was the only one of the pseudo-prophets who tried to get into politics. In 1922, he founded the Christian Radical People's Party. But like the later Haeusser League, it never became anything more than a minor sect.

Haeusser and his many disciples and imitators thought of themselves as "people of truth" and seekers on a voyage to discover new forms of human community. Their voluntary existence as ascetic wanderers stood in marked contrast to the extravagant lifestyle of nouveau-riche wartime and inflation profiteers. They derived their identity not from material possessions but from the renunciation of their own egos— which not surprisingly led to pathological self-worship in some cases.

Historian Ulrich Linse has called these people "mutants of the Hitler type,"[61] and in fact there were some striking similarities, including the creation of a cult of the messianic leader, the rejection of "the wheeling and dealing of political parties," and the emphasis on an ethnic "people's community" spanning all class differences. But we should beware equating the itinerant would-be prophets with the racist Munich demagogue or seeing the former as precursors of the latter. In addition to the commonalities with National Socialism, the prophets also had affinities with Communism and anarchism and saw nothing necessarily amiss in combining the swastika and the hammer and sickle. In general, the prophets were more focused on the provocative use of symbols and in shocking and stirring up audiences than they were on carefully considered political platforms and rationally planned strategies. They never posed any real competition to the agitator Hitler. Their heyday came as hyperinflation culminated in 1923. In the years that followed, as the Weimar Republic achieved a measure of economic and political stability, their influence dwindled to the point of insignificance.

ANOTHER OF THE SELF-APPOINTED saviors during hyperinflation was the confidence man, former brush maker, and photographer Max Klante. In December 1920, he founded the "Klante concern," a "society of popular stakeholders" for the mutual protection from all "large-scale capital interests." It acquired a modern office building and soon had branches in almost all of Germany's larger cities. Klante promised his investors a return of 200 percent, and 260,000 people entrusted him with their money. His devotees greeted him with the word "Heil," and he made his entrance at public appearances to the strains of a self-composed "Max Klante March." The lyrics went,

> *There is a call in all Berlin.*
> *Forward! Let's move ahead with Klante.*
> *Though the path be steep and the path be mean*
> *We raise our voice: Hail, hail, Max Klante.*

For months, Klante was able to pay the promised dividends by betting on horses at Berlin's Hoppegarten racetrack. But in 1921, his house of cards collapsed, and he was arrested and sentenced by Berlin's main criminal court to three years in prison.[62]

Lewinsohn commented on the trial in the *Weltbühne* with ample sarcasm, writing that there was no longer a need for "little schemes" like Klante's: "The demise of the German mark is ensuring that every bit of individual wealth, in terms of numbers, grows to gigantic proportions, that today every beggar is a millionaire, and that everyone who lends loses while everyone who borrows wins. . . . At a time when the foundation of the economy, money, is flowing downstream, you don't have to push to get ahead. You just have to stand in the middle of the current, and you'll be pushed along automatically."[63]

THE TOPIC OF THE RUNAWAY monetary spiral completely dominated Germans' everyday conversations. "If it was earlier a matter of course in conversation to take interest in the other person, this is now replaced by inquiry into the price of his shoes or his umbrella," philosopher and cultural critic Walter Benjamin wrote in his essay "A Tour through German Inflation."[64] The fall of the mark after Rathenau's assassination had come as a shock, but the more rapidly the currency plummeted, the more people acclimated to it. A kind of "inflation mentality" took hold. He had "now gotten used to the lunatic numbers," Klemperer admitted on July 28, 1923, when the exchange rate was 760,000 marks to the dollar. On August 8, at which point he had to pay 75,000 marks for a fried herring and 50,000 for a cinema ticket, he no longer got upset because, as he wrote, "You become insensitive to the catastrophe, which has been declared permanent, and the lunatic figures."[65] People had "grown accustomed to the zeroes," Bernhard wrote in the *Vossische Zeitung* in late July 1923, and "most take no interest if there's a few more or a few less."[66]

The Spanish correspondent Eugeni Xammar had the impression that some Germans were positively intoxicated by all the zeroes and secretly enjoyed totting them up. He couldn't help but thinking sometimes that "the demise of the currency is deeply rooted and subconsciously desired in the [German] psyche."[67] Leopold Schwarzschild, the publisher of the *Tage-Buch*, saw things in a similar way: "Phantom numbers, tarantula figures—soon every tram conductor will be a millionaire and will rejoice (and pretend) that a million is still a million."[68]

Newspaper readers were confronted with a new variation of the numbers game. Whereas during the war the number of soldiers taken prisoner, artillery pieces captured, and the like had dominated the headlines, now all eyes were hypnotically fixed on the exchange rate with the dollar. "The fluctuation of the dollar was the barometer by which, with a mixture of anxiety and excitement, we measured the fall of the mark," Haffner recalled. "The higher the dollar went, the more extravagant became our flights into the realms of fancy."[69] Berlin journalist Hedwig Hirschbach noticed that the popular obsession with the dollar even changed the facial features of some of the German capital's residents: "The dollar face grins at you. . . . It is there in the tellingly cool, ever-calculating gaze and the prosaic mien, in which the previous evening's exchange rate was visibly recapitulated."[70]

TO PROTECT THEMSELVES AGAINST the devaluation of money, many Germans decided to buy stock, which seemed to be the only investment offering any security. A wave of speculation spread. "At the moment in Berlin, all of your friends are playing the market and never lose sight of the dollar for a single second," Xammar told his readers in February 1923.[71] There was a flurry of activity at banks as people jostled to purchase stocks. These weren't professional investors but amateurs trying their luck. "From half-starved pensioners to carriage drivers, they're all here," Lewinsohn noted in November 1922. "A mania for gambling has taken over."[72]

Stock tips were in greater demand than ever before. "People hung upon them every day in their regular bars, in the morning at the barber shop, in the bus and the suburban train," recalled Hans Ostwald in 1931. "Lovers conversed in the language of the stock exchanges, their pillow talk full of tips: I.G. Farben, Zellstoff, and Sarotti. Everyone knew what stocks he had to buy."[73]

But not everyone was willing to play the game. Haffner's father, for instance, a liberal, reformist pedagogue who would rise to become a governmental director during the Weimar Republic, refused to be infected by the fever for stocks and bonds. "A Prussian official does not speculate," he was fond of saying. His son considered this at the time and in his memoirs *Defying Hitler* extraordinarily narrow-minded. Only in retrospect was he able to understand his father's disgust at all the excitement surrounding stocks.[74]

Klemperer had a different reaction than Haffner's father. In May 1923, he allowed a relative to talk him into putting his money into a stock that, to his delight, doubled its value within a short span. "In this situation, speculating on the market now fills every mind every hour," Klemperer wrote. "Time has run all too far off the rails."[75] But his windfall was canceled out just one month later by further devaluation of the mark, leaving Klemperer to complain, "Unchecked inflation washes everything away."[76] In late June 1923, Klemperer decided to commission for the first time the Dresdner Staatsbank to buy two million shares of stocks on his behalf—an "uncharacteristically bold" move, as he himself described it in his diary. "I continue to go all in," he noted a few days later. "Playing the market is a constant thrill as well as a source of worry and diversion." After the market levels had temporarily fallen a bit, he noted, "That's the way it goes back and forth. It's a nerve-jangling sensation. Again and again, people say there's nothing behind the gigantic numbers, and again and again, they're intoxicating."[77]

GERMANS WITH ACCESS TO foreign currency enjoyed a huge advantage. Playwright Carl Sternheim, who had moved from Uttwil, Switzerland, to the Dresden area, was able to exchange 100 Swiss francs for more than 400,000 marks in late January 1923; by June, he was getting a million marks for 80 francs.[78] The liberal-centrist politician and lecturer at Berlin's new Academy of Politics, Theodor Heuss survived the hyperinflationary months fairly well by working for foreign newspapers from Stockholm to Buenos Aires as well as for the newspaper published by the ethnic German Transylvanian Saxons. He recalled, "I feel moved when I think of the Swedish crowns, Argentinian pesos, and Romanian lei—suddenly one was quite affluent."[79] Heuss, who became involved in writing the West German constitution after the Second World War, also didn't object to playing the market and in early February 1923 tried to convince his father-in-law Georg Friedrich Knapp to do the same. "I don't know if you keep track of changes on the stock market. In September, a friend of mine invested 37,000 marks; today those stocks are valued at 3.5 million. The story is similar with other stocks."[80]

Thomas Mann was also preoccupied by the vertiginous devaluation of the mark. His savings dissolved into nothing, and his Munich parents-in-law, the Pringsheims, lost much of their wealth. It was like a gift from heaven in 1923 when the American magazine the *Dial* commissioned a series of articles from him at 25 dollars per piece. The Nobel laureate would repeatedly interrupt work on *The Magic Mountain* to write his "German Letters." In early September 1923, he complained, "As soon as I catch my breath for a bit, I have to write another American article. My children are crying for food."[81]

In the *Tage-Buch*, author Siegfried von Vegesack rhymed,

> *Buy foreign currency!*
> *Especially those with desirability*
> *Dollar bills and English pounds*
> *Dutch guilders and Swedish crowns*
> *Even lira have some value*
> *And Swiss francs and yen are good, too.*
> *Buy a whole pile of them to stash*
> *Everything is up for sale*
> *If you've got the cash*
> *With a few crowns from the Czechs*
> *You can do some tidy business.*[82]

In Berlin, "dollar booths"—glass money-changing kiosks—sprang up on every corner. "They are constantly full of people, and because there's so little room, people try to press inside," observed reporter Egon Erwin Kisch. "Markets report the exchange rates without interruption . . . lei, pesetas, pounds, Polish marks, Czechs and Austrian crowns, dollars, and yen change hands. This is where the Nietzschean 'revaluation of all values' is being carried out. The [kiosks] are its temples."[83]

NO ONE PERSONIFIED THIS revaluation better than the *Schieber*, small-time mafiosi, criminals, and racketeers instantly recognizable by their appearance. "It's like something from one of my works," wrote author Carl Zuckmayer.

> The small-time criminal with their wide-cut "tango trousers" and cute little belts on the backs of their tight, broad-checked jackets in garish reds, oranges, and purples. Snappy young men and lucky winners on the market and in literature, with black horn-rimmed glasses and slicked-back hair in the "Bolshevik style," their necks cleanly shaven and heavily powdered, filled the cafés and set the tone. That tone was intentionally cynical, callous, and rakish, although it served as a jaunty mask for their permanent insecurity.[84]

*Schieber* drove fast cars, smoked expensive cigars, ate in "gourmet establishments," and surrounded themselves with cosmopolitan women. They were usually young men with no scruples about ignoring traditional rules and conventions in the predatory society of inflationary Germany. "The young and quick-witted did well," recalled Haffner.

> Overnight they became free, rich, and independent. It was a situation in which mental inertia and reliance on past experience were punished by starvation and death, but rapid appraisal of new situations and speed of reaction were rewarded with sudden, vast riches. The twenty-one-year-old bank director appeared on the scene, and also the high school senior who earned his living from the stock-market tips of his slightly older friends. He wore Oscar Wilde ties, organized champagne parties, and supported his embarrassed father.[85]

In December 1922, the *Weltbühne* published a satiric article entitled "In Defense of the *Schieber*." One section read, "We are the new
breed of men here to replace the ossified veterans and people with their
obsolete traditions. Those with two feet in real life and strong nerves.
Children of the people who are making their way up in the world.
We're the true revolutionaries. Small-time criminals. We're Germany's
future."[86]

The image of the *Schieber* was often connected with the stereotype
of the "Jewish profiteer." Because the devaluation of the mark could
not be easily explained rationally, many people blamed dark forces.
In this way, inflation intensified racist resentments that had already
been stoked by war and revolution. A report on popular sentiment in
Bavaria in the spring of 1920 concluded, "The hatred of the broadest circles is increasingly directed against the Jews, who have seized
the majority of trade and who, according to prevailing opinion, enrich
themselves most unscrupulously at the cost of their fellow human
beings. In trains and trams and on all sorts of occasions, people curse
the Jews."[87] This was ideal soil for Hitler's unbridled demagoguery.

STATE AUTHORITIES REGISTERED THE general decline
in public morals with concern. Berlin in particular became the epitome of decadence and sin. In the summer of 1923, Klaus Mann, still
shy of his seventeenth birthday, visited the German capital with his
eldest sister, Erika, and was fascinated. He recalled, "The city seemed
both pitiful and enticing: gray, shabby, demoralized, but still vibrat-
ing with nervous vitality, glistening, gleaming, phosphorescent, hecti-
cally animated, full of tensions and promise." He particularly enjoyed
observing the prostitutes parading every night up and down streets
like Tauentzienstrasse and Oranienburger Strasse. "There were girls
among them who couldn't have been older than sixteen or seventeen.
Others had wrinkled faces under their make-up." Mann also wrote,
"Pitiful creatures, all right; however, it was enjoyable to watch their
garish procession. Some of them looked like fierce Amazons strutting

in boots made of green, glossy leather. One of them brandished a sup-
ple cane and leered at me as I passed by. 'Good evening, Madame,' I
said. So she whispered in my ear: 'Want to be my slave? Costs only six
billions [*sic*] and a cigarette. A bargain. Come along, honey!' "[88]

More and more women from well-heeled families were so desperate
that they had to turn to prostitution. Russian writer Ilja Ehrenburg,
who lived in Berlin between 1921 and 1923, recalled a scene he witnessed one evening in a friend's apartment. After being given some
sparkling wine, "the two daughters appeared, naked as Eve, and began
to dance.... Their mother looked at the foreign guests expectantly.
Perhaps they would find her daughters attractive enough to spend
some money—dollars of course. 'And you call this life,' this respectable mama sighed. 'It's the end of the world.' "[89]

Male prostitutes also did brisk business. Homosexuality was illegal, but Berlin was known for turning a blind eye toward gay people.
"Along the entire Kurfürstendamm powdered and rouged young men
sauntered, and they were not all professionals," observed Stefan Zweig.
"Every high school boy wanted to earn some money, and in the dimly
lit bars one might see government officials and men of the world of
finance tenderly courting drunken sailors without any shame."[90]

What was even then known as "free love" also took on new dimensions. Young women had little incentive to remain chaste before mar-
riage with inflation disrupting the dowry system. As the mark fell,
many decided that virginity no longer paid.[91] "It became the done thing
to 'sleep with one another,' no matter whether you loved your partner or just thought you did," recalled writer Curt Reiss, who worked
as a sports reporter and later a theater and film critic for the midday
newspaper *12-Uhr-Blatt* in 1920s Berlin.[92] Haffner had similar memories: "Everywhere people were feverishly searching for love and seizing it without a second thought. Indeed, even love had assumed an
inflationary character.... Unromantic love was the fashion: carefree,
restless, light-hearted promiscuity. Typically, love affairs followed an
extremely rapid course, without detours. The young who learned to
love in those years eschewed romance and embraced cynicism."[93] An

expression of this newfound sensibility was the most popular song of the time, which began, "Why cry when a relationship is over / When there's another on the very next corner?"[94]

With such uncertainty about what tomorrow would bring, Germans lived for today, for the pleasures of the moment. "After us comes the Flood," was a common saying.[95] The desire for entertainment was boundless. Clubs, bars, and late-night haunts sprouted up everywhere. As had been the case in the first few months after the war, Germany was seized by a dance craze. "Millions of helpless, impoverished, bewildered people capered and swung in a delirium of hunger and hysteria," wrote Klaus Mann. "Dance was a mania, a religion, a racket. . . . They danced the shimmy, tango, fox trot, and St. Vitus' dance. They danced despair and schizophrenia and cosmic divinations. . . . They danced ecstasies, hangovers, orgasms, intoxications, and nervous tics. . . . Jazz was the great balm and narcotic of a disconcerted, frustrated nation."[96]

In Zweig's telling, Berlin's transvestite clubs were notable for their excesses. "Even the Rome of Suetonius had never known such orgies as the pervert balls of Berlin, where hundreds of men costumed as women and hundreds of women as men danced under the benevolent eyes of the police. In the collapse of all values a kind of madness gained hold, particularly in the bourgeois circles which until then had been unshakable in their probity."[97]

The dance craze wasn't restricted to public nightspots. One evening in March 1923, Klemperer was at a private party in the villa of a couple with whom he and his wife were friends and witnessed all the guests going into a large room after dinner to indulge in the pleasures of dancing: "They had a gramophone there, and they danced, couples by themselves and with others. . . . It was then we truly got to know them, and it was nice. American, exotic-erotic-lunatic dance songs whose melodies we knew from the cinema."[98]

The songs sung for people to dance to in the bars and cafés expressed the mood of the day. Another notable hit from the inflation years ended with the chorus, "We're drinking grandma out of her little

*A transvestite couple dances at a party in the gay club
L'Eldorado on Motzstrasse in Berlin, January 1926.*

home / We're drinking grandma out of her little home, and her first
and second mortgage." In the *Weltbühne*, the ever-cynical Tucholsky
called the song "the perfect expression of the popular soul," which succinctly illustrated "the momentary general economic situation." He
wrote, "We're consuming our substance just like pensioners who can
no longer live off the interest and are forced to draw upon the capital.
That's the situation here [in the song]. It's impressive how finely the
two generations are pitted against one another: the old generation of
the grandmother, who still owns a little house bought with dutifully
earned savings—and the second and third generations, who impu-
dently reach for the family assets and pour the sweat of their parents
down their gullets!"[99]

ALSO UNPRECEDENTED WAS THE lifting of the taboo on
many forms of public nudity. Individually and in groups, dancers displayed their barely covered bodies in variety theaters, cabarets, and
nightspots. The nude dancer Anita Berber was a sensation in Berlin.

A devotee of garish makeup and cocaine, the slim and sultry beauty embodied like no other the feverish atmosphere of inflationary Germany. In her private life as well, she was hardly a strict moralist, marrying three times and engaging in countless affairs with both men and women. When Berber died in 1928 at the age of only twenty-nine, ravaged by years of alcohol and drug abuse, the demimonde of Berlin joined the funeral procession.[100]

Unbridled nightlife wasn't the only source of amusement and diversion. Enthusiasm for sports also reached new heights during these years. Particularly popular was the six-day indoor cycling competition at Berlin's Sportpalast. Thousands of people, including numerous stars of the stage and silver screen, packed the floor and the stands of the arena. "Thirteen pairs of racing cyclists started pushing the pedals at 9:00 p.m. on Friday . . . and this lunatic carousel has been spinning day and night, day and night ever since," reported Kisch about the spectacle.[101] In 1923, the waltz "Wiener Praterleben" was played during the race for the first time, with every third beat accentuated by a shrill whistle from Reinhold "the Crutch" Habisch, who had lost one leg in an accident. The "Sportpalast Waltz," as it was renamed, became the event's unofficial anthem.

Boxing also became a major attraction, combining the desire for entertainment with the lust for raw violence. The archaic mano-a-mano duel between two men in the ring, the ups and downs of triumph and defeat, mirrored the drama of a world in which nothing was certain and many people were exposed to the whims of fortune.[102] One favorite of boxing enthusiasts was Hans Breitensträter, who turned pro in 1919, five years before Max Schmeling would start his rise to international fame. In April 1920, Breitensträter won the German heavyweight title, which he successfully defended throughout the inflation years, first losing it to Paul Samson-Körner in a third-round knockout in late February 1924. "Blond Hans," as Breitensträter was known, was not only an elegant pugilist; he also had the sculpted body of a superb athlete. Vitality and physical integrity were alluring qualities at a time when men permanently injured in the war were a common sight.[103]

THE LUXURY AND ENTERTAINMENT enjoyed by the nou-
veau riche and possessors of foreign currency contrasted with the
desperate situation of the war-wounded. "On every corner there were
victims of the lost war," remembered actress and cabaret performer
Trude Hesterberg. Dressed in rags, leaning on crutches, or squatting
on the ground because they no longer had legs, they held out their
ragged old military caps. "What was one supposed to toss them? Five
hundred, a thousand, a million? The next day it would only be worth
a pfennig!"[104] As if drawn to one another, these social opposites col-
lided in the Bahnhof Zoo train station in the middle of western Berlin's entertainment center. Ostwald presented the following tableau:

> Revelers in lace and silk, fur-lined ballroom jackets and tuxe-
> does sat between the few exhausted travelers who couldn't afford
> a hotel for the night and had to wait here for the first morning
> train. Within the former group, visitors from Dollarica and Guil-
> derland and bejeweled Russian émigrée women sat next to stars
> of stage and screen, cocky youngsters who got rich on inflation,
> banking apprentices, and black-market money dealers. Off to one
> side, heavily made-up refuse from the street, especially female
> adolescents, jostled for position. It was a cacophonous, screeching
> scene of the sort that never previously existed in Berlin. While
> some people continued to raise a ruckus under the arches of the
> city rail, others, crippled in the war, stood outside selling matches
> or shoelaces. Pitiable back-alley hookers slunk around, unable
> to earn their keep for the following day even by selling their
> bodies.[105]

The sudden collapse of the mark left many people with no other
option than to "flee into physical assets"—a phrase that established
itself as part of the common jargon of 1922 and 1923.[106] Spending
money before it lost even more of its value became a matter of sur-

*Long after 1918, men who were permanently injured in the First
World War could be seen begging on Germany's streets. They
were particularly hard hit by hyperinflation.*

vival. In the hyperinflationary phases, consumers were beset by a veritable "buyers' panic." In July 1923, the *Deutsche Allgemeine Zeitung*
reported, "Disquiet and nervousness are spreading. People descend
upon stores, buying whatever there is to buy. People horde both necessities and completely superfluous items.... The huge demand elevates
prices. Inflation grows. All the millions spent still aren't enough for
the most urgent needs of people's stomachs."[107] One month later a
journalist for the *Berliner Illustrierte Zeitung* observed,

People's nerves are jangling every day from the insane sums, the
uncertain future and what has overnight become the tenuous
matter of surviving today and tomorrow. An epidemic of fear, the
most naked of desperation. The massive lines of consumers, which
we have long gotten disaccustomed to seeing, are again standing
in front of shops ... the city, this massive city of stone, is once
again being emptied of buyable items. A pound of rice, which
yesterday was 80,000 marks, costs 160,000 marks today and will

probably cost twice that tomorrow. The day after tomorrow, the man behind the shop counter will say with a shrug, "We're out of rice." Okay, then noodles! "We're out of noodles." Okay, then barley, semolina, beans, lentils, the main thing is to buy, buy, buy! That piece of paper, the new banknote still damp from the printing, which was paid out as a weekly wage this morning, is already shrinking in value on the way to the retail store. Zeroes, ever more zeroes. "A zero is just that—nothing!" with every dollar hatred, desperation, and privation increase.[108]

Sebastian Haffner described in vivid detail what everyday life was like for a Berlin civil servant's family in these circumstances. When his father was paid at the end of each month, the first thing he would do was buy a monthly ticket for public transportation. Then he swiftly made out checks for the rent and school fees, and that afternoon, the entire family got their hair cut. Early in the day, even before dawn, Haffner's mother took a taxi with her children and servant girl to the food market. Within an hour, she spent most of the remaining family income on nonperishable groceries: "I would go through the feverish streets of inflationary Berlin with the manner and feelings of one of Mann's patricians or Wilde's dandies. These fantasies were not seriously impeded by the fact that at five in the morning I might have been packing rounds of cheese and sacks of potatoes into a handcart with the maid."[109]

But while some Germans were fleeing into material goods, others were fleeing away from them. Middle-class people who didn't have a regular income, savings, or foreign currency were forced to sell off family heirlooms and valuables at improvised auctions. "Walking through the small showroom with its tables and glass cabinets moved your heart," wrote the *Niederdeutsche Zeitung* in October 1922.

There are so many wonderful things spread out to delight the eye . . . marvelous Turkish and knit scarves, delicately carved figurines, clocks, pearls, linen embroidery, table silver—in short everything that decorates a household has been collected here.... A glance out the window—the hectic street-life of the big city goes about its business, silk stockings and expensive furs draw attention to themselves, and cars flit by with fat racketeers in them ... while here, inside, in this quiet room, impoverished Germany weeps silently, expressing its quiet, painful desperation.[110]

INFLATION DISSOLVED TRADITIONAL BOURGEOIS notions of property much as it did obsolete ideas of morality. Differences between "yours" and "mine" blurred. Small-time crime rose. Pickpockets were endemic. Bands of thieves combed through Berlin and other German cities carting off whatever wasn't nailed down— brass door handles, bronze plates on gravestones, and works of art in churches and museums. Robbers climbed up the outside of buildings and broke into apartments to steal jewelry, furs, and silverware. The petty thievery focused on items of everyday utility, and in many places, desperate city dwellers had to help themselves by plundering fruit-and-vegetable stores and bakeries.[111]

Others traveled to the countryside to stuff backpacks with butter, ham, eggs, flour, and potatoes. Farmers refused to accept paper money, bartering their produce instead for jewelry, table silver, carpets, and porcelain. In this fashion, rural Germany acquired a lot of family heirlooms from the country's urbanites. City dwellers who had nothing of value to barter often had to pilfer what they needed from farmers' fields.[112] Government calls for solidarity between town and country fell on deaf ears. In the madhouse of hyperinflation, charity began at home, and the new norm became "everyone is his own best friend." *Wolf among Wolves* was the title Hans Fallada chose for his 1937 "inflation novel," which revived memories of a time when "everybody was feverishly waiting for the dollar rate, when everybody's thoughts turned on money, money, money, figures stamped on paper, paper with more and more noughts printed on it."[113]

# CHAPTER 3

# AN ATTEMPT AT CRISIS MANAGEMENT

## *Stresemann's Grand Coalition*

*"The most difficult office in the most difficult hour"*
*—Gustav Stresemann shortly after becoming both German*
*chancellor and foreign minister on August 13, 1923.*

NOT SINCE BERNHARD VON BÜLOW'S APPOINT-
ment in 1900 had a new German chancellor been "designated
as such a matter of course," wrote the *Weltbühne* about Gustav Stresemann on August 13, 1923. For months, it had been clear that the
DVP chairman was Wilhelm Cuno's only possible successor. "It is one

of the most interesting and strangest phenomena in our by no means overabundantly interesting parliamentary life that after the death of Rathenau this tactician, who was previously considered merely a gifted juggler of interests, gained so much influence, power, and ultimately strength and skill."[1] Theodor Wolff was of much the same opinion, arguing in an editorial for the *Berliner Tageblatt* that very few politicians had learned as much as Stresemann from the experiences of the past. He deserved praise, declared Wolff, for his willingness to take on "the most difficult office in the most difficult hour" instead of "saving himself for calmer times."[2]

In fact, when he moved into the Chancellor's Palace on Wilhelmstrasse at the age of forty-five, Stresemann had already had quite a past of his own.[3] He had been born as the eighth and youngest child to petite-bourgeois parents, Ernst August and Mathilde Stresemann. His father ran a beverage store with an attached bar in the center of eastern Berlin. Stresemann's intellectual curiosity led him to attend a university-preparatory academy and get a doctorate in economics in 1901, giving him the opportunity to climb the social ladder. His dissertation, entitled "The Development of the Berlin Bottled Beer Business," revisited his family origins and was a source of amusement for his adversaries. Joseph Goebbels, for instance, who became the regional leader (Gauleiter) of the Nazi Party in Berlin in 1926, mocked him as "the doctor of bottled beer."

After his studies, Stresemann embarked on an impressive career that saw him assume key positions in business and politics within the space of a few years. In 1902, at the age of only twenty-four, he became the in-house counsel for the Association of Saxon Industrialists, one of the largest regional business associations in Germany. The job proved a springboard into politics. In 1907, before his twenty-ninth birthday, he was elected to the Reichstag as the youngest deputy of the National Liberal Party. A gifted speaker who developed into a passionate advocate of Wilhelmine naval and colonial policies, Stresemann enjoyed the patronage of party leader Ernst Bassermann. Stresemann was also adroit at making the right contacts in his private life. In 1903, he married Käte Kleefeld, the daughter of a wealthy bourgeois Jewish family, who helped smooth the rough social edges of the ambitious careerist.

During the First World War, Stresemann was among the most vocal supporters of Germany's ambitious goals in both the East and the West. His dream of a "larger Germany" and his advocacy of unlimited submarine warfare allied him with the supreme military command under Hindenburg and Ludendorff, alongside whom he helped depose the allegedly "lethargic" Chancellor Theobald von Bethmann-Hollweg. Falling for the lies of the German military, Stresemann believed up until the last that Germany would emerge victorious. Even in August 1918, with the Wilhelmine Empire obviously headed toward defeat, he wrote to Ludendorff's right-hand man, Lieutenant Colonel Max Bauer: "The German statesman who finally smacks Lloyd George in the face so hard that the man forgets his native language for four weeks will be celebrated from East Prussia to Konstanz."[4]

For Stresemann, the November Revolution brought the collapse of a cherished societal order that had allowed him to climb to the upper reaches of German life and with whose representatives he had identified completely. His desire for Germany to annex as much territory as it could in the war so discredited him in the eyes of leftists that he was one of the reasons the fusion of the nationalist and progressive liberal parties failed—a rift that continued with the founding of the rival DDP and the DVP. In December 1918, Stresemann became head of the DVP, which at least nominally opposed the Weimar Republic. Initially, he stood by his conviction that monarchy was the best form of government, and in January 1919, he sent his "reverential congratulations" to Kaiser Wilhelm II, who was in Dutch exile, on the former emperor's sixtieth birthday. Stresemann and the DVP played a decidedly ambivalent role during the counterrevolutionary Kapp-Lüttwitz Putsch, a short-lived attempt to occupy Berlin in mid-March 1920. While not involved in the plans for a coup, the future chancellor and his party fell over themselves to acknowledge "the new facts" when it looked as though the putsch might succeed—only to distance themselves just as quickly from the insurgents when the rebellion failed.

Stresemann's transformation from a monarchist to a republican was anything but abrupt. On the contrary, he had to go through a lengthy learning process. Still, gradually, the DVP chairman came to realize that a return to power of the royal family would never happen and that there was no choice but to accept democracy. The positive side effect was that his party polled 13.9 percent in the 1920 Reichstag election, leaving the DDP in its shadow. The DVP pragmatically embraced the parliamentary system and acknowledged the need to cooperate with the pro-democracy parties. It assumed power for the first time as a member of the minority coalition led by Constantin Fehrenbach and the Center Party in 1920 and 1921, and it also contributed a pair of ministers to the Cuno government. One reason for the massive approval Stresemann garnered for his Reichstag speeches on April 17 and August 9, 1923, was his unambiguous pledge of loyalty to the Weimar Constitution. This built a bridge to the political Left, a sine qua non for a grand coalition that would span every party from the DVP to the SPD.

When Stresemann was appointed chancellor on August 13, he was not the favorite candidate of President Ebert, who hadn't forgotten the role Ludendorff's party comrade had played during the war. He mistrusted the protean parliamentarian who had inspired the satiric couplet, "Everyone knows that Stresemann / Thinks differently now than when he began."[5] But Ebert was less interested in personal animosities than in finally forming a grand coalition to lead Germany. That said, in a message to Stresemann a day after his appointment, Ebert didn't fail to emphasize the German chancellor's duty to keep the German president informed at all times of the latest developments, either orally or in writing.[6]

THE NEW GOVERNMENT WAS formed unusually quickly. One day after he assumed office, Stresemann presented Ebert with his cabinet—a sign of how prepared he was for his new role.[7] The only problematic post was that of Reichswehr minister. The SPD demanded the replacement of Otto Gessler (DDP), whom they accused of being too close to the head of military command, General von Seeckt. After Ebert threatened to resign if Gessler was fired, the SPD backed down but insisted as compensation that the Reichstag deputy from Cologne and editor in chief of the *Rheinische Zeitung*, Wilhelm Sollmann, become Germany's new interior minister. The Social Democrats also got three further cabinet posts. Robert Schmidt became vice-chancellor and minister of reconstruction, and Gustav Radbruch was appointed justice minister. Both men had been part of the Wirth cabinet. The big surprise was USPD member and author of a book on finance capital Rudolf Hilferding as finance minister, since he was considered more of a theorist than a pragmatic politician. But Stresemann gave him the nod in the hope he would find unorthodox solutions to Germany's financial and currency crisis.

As a counterweight to Hilferding, the DVP deputy Hans von Raumer, a leading manager in the electricity sector and a committed supporter of the grand coalition, took over the Economics Ministry. The most powerful cabinet member after Stresemann was the food minister, the former mayor of Essen, Hans Luther, a political independent who was close to the DVP and was held over in that office from the Cuno government. Heinrich Brauns from the Center Party also retained his post as labor minister. His party comrades Anton Höfle and former supreme president of the Rhine Johannes Fuchs also became, respectively, Germany's postal minister and the head of the newly created Ministry for the Occupied Territories. The DDP, then the smallest of the coalition partners, had to content itself with the Ministries of Defense and Transportation, the latter of which was now led by Cuno's interior minister Rudolf Oeser.

In addition to the chancellorship, Stresemann also claimed the Foreign Ministry. His primary assistants were State Secretary Adolf Georg Otto "Ago" von Maltzan and Ministerial Director Carl von Schubert, the head of the ministry's England and America Division. For his Chancellery state secretary, Stresemann called on his DVP party colleague, the Reichstag deputy and former naval attaché in Rome,

Werner von Rheinbaben. Stresemann also engaged as his private secretary Henry Bernhard, with whom he had worked during the war and who would make a name for himself as the publisher of three volumes of Stresemann's personal papers after the latter's death in 1929.

The demands of being both chancellor and foreign minister would have tested even a physically robust politician, but Stresemann, despite his relative youth, was in shaky health, suffering from a hyperactive thyroid and recurring cardiac and renal conditions. A few days after his appointment, his physician cautioned him: "As overjoyed as I am that you have taken over the leadership of our people, I am still concerned that you will become more unable to shrug off the burdens of your work."[8]

But Stresemann was not the sort of person to slow down—even less so at a time of dramatic crisis that required every ounce of his strength. The chancellor's regular workday ran between sixteen and eighteen hours. Despite all the obstacles, Stresemann projected optimism. "'If you have to jump a ditch, you must fling your heart over first,'" he told the British ambassador, quoting Bismarck. "Well, I have flung my heart over, and I trust that both the horse and rider will also get to the other side safely."[9]

Within his cabinet, Stresemann's leadership style was amiable. The chancellor's "tactical adroitness" was "mixed with so much personal warmth," recalled Justice Minister Radbruch, that he was won over. At least in the first weeks of his tenure, Radbruch observed, Stresemann's relationship with his Social Democratic ministers had been "the best imaginable."[10]

ON THE AFTERNOON OF August 14, Stresemann presented his new cabinet to the Reichstag and made a short governmental declaration promising energetic action to resolve the Ruhr crisis and the larger economic crisis. Repeatedly interrupted by full-throated interjections by the Communists, he asked parliamentary deputies for their trust. Germany was facing great decisions at home and abroad, he told them—ones that demanded "the solidarity of all forces that affirmed the constitutional idea of state."[11] Bernhard described the speech as "young in tone and fresh in sound" in the *Vossische Zeitung*. "For the first time since the days of Wirth, a man who knows how to speak stood before the Reichstag from the chancellor's spot on the ministerial bench. . . . It was a pleasure to follow the skillful thrusts and parries of this clever parliamentarian."[12]

Stresemann's speech earned him enthusiastic applause from both the SPD and the bourgeois parties. The ultraconservative DNVP remained unimpressed. "They sat there with their arms crossed as though they had been turned to stone," observed Erich Dombrowski, editor in chief of domestic politics at the *Berliner Tageblatt*. "No one twitched a facial muscle or moved a hand," he added. "Silence all around. An icy cold emanated from this corner [of parliament]. Given this visible response, no one could be under any illusions how the new government went over on these benches."[13] And indeed, DNVP chairman Oskar Hergt swore that his party would vigorously oppose the government.[14]

The 239 delegates from the coalition parties proclaimed their confidence in the government, while 76 deputies—KPD, SPD, and two members of the remnants of the USPD—voted against the new leadership. Twenty-five representatives, including those of the Bavarian People's Party (BVP), abstained. Afterward, the SPD mouthpiece *Vorwärts* wrote of the "greatest parliamentary triumph" of any government of the young Weimar Republic.[15] But blighting the result was the fact that 43 SPD deputies, mostly former members of the USPD, and 23 largely conservative DVP representatives boycotted the vote. It was a sign of just how fragile the coalition forged by Stresemann actually was.[16]

Under no circumstances could the new chancellor count on absolute support from either the Social Democrats or his own party. The unease within the parts of the SPD parliamentary group had already made itself felt on August 13, when eighty-three deputies had voted for and thirty-nine against joining the government. Within the DVP,

critics objected to the SPD being given four ministerial posts, especially the major ones of finance, justice, and the interior. On becoming
chancellor, Stresemann had handed over the leadership of the center-
right DVP parliamentary group to Ernst Scholz, the former economics minister under Fehrenbach and a conservative who represented the
interests of industry and opposed cooperating with the Social Democrats. Thus, on the parliamentary level, there were cracks in the coalition from the onset. But they didn't initially restrict the government's
capacity for action since the Reichstag went into recess on August 15
and didn't reconvene until September 27.[17]

SUPPORTERS OF DEMOCRACY HAD major expectations for
the grand coalition. With it, "the broadest front for order and resistance had been established since the days of [the] November [revolu-
tion]," wrote the pro-democracy Berlin historian Friedrich Meinecke.[18]
Great hopes were attached to Stresemann personally. If he retained
as chancellor those qualities that had distinguished him as a Reichstag deputy—"a naturalness that isn't mired in forms and concepts,"
as Bernhard put it—then he would possess the most important quality needed to master Germany's challenges: "the courage to act swiftly
and unambiguously."[19] "Precisely because Stresemann's patriotism was
beyond question," the editor of the *Vossische Zeitung* added, he could
"ruthlessly do whatever reason demanded." No one could predict
whether Stresemann would succeed in maintaining the solidarity of
the coalition "through the political storms of the time to come," wrote
Dombrowski, but he deserved gratitude for having the "courage and
conviction" needed to "take hold of the rudder in a moment of general
division."[20] The new government didn't have much time, warned Stefan Grossmann in the *Tage-Buch*, to move on currency and economic
policy: "To put none too fine a point on it—Mr. Stresemann is the last
hope German parliamentarianism has to offer."[21]

The Communists saw the formation of a grand coalition as a continuation of the political status quo. A statement from KPD head-

quarters on August 14 dismissed it as "the old bankrupt policies of coalitions and working groups . . . only with open SPD participation," and further remarked that "new catastrophes are unavoidable. A fresh collapse is only a question of—very short—time."[22]

The reaction from the extreme Right was even more hostile. The fact that the new government enjoyed a broad parliamentary foundation, including the Social Democrats, was a blow to right-wing radicals' efforts to undermine democracy and prepare the ground for an authoritarian way out of the crisis. A particular target of their hatred was Hilferding on account of his Jewish background. The DNVP had nothing good to say about the new government. DNVP deputy and former Krupp boss Alfred Hugenberg, who had built a powerful right-wing media empire in the 1920s, had warned Hugo Stinnes in an August 11 letter about Stresemann being appointed chancellor. The chancellor in waiting, wrote Hugenberg, had neither "nerves" nor "firm character," possessed no "political instincts" and therefore "never does the right thing at the decisive moment." Should he in fact become chancellor, it would be "calamitous for the German bourgeoisie."[23]

Yet the obstruction of German ultranationalists from day one of the new government went too far for even Stinnes's *Allgemeine Deutsche Zeitung*, which asked "whether such a bitter opposition, which deepens our internal wounds almost beyond recovery, can possibly be in the national interests."[24] No one had expected the ultranationalist press to shower the Stresemann cabinet with advance praise, wrote the *Vossische Zeitung*, but the "aggressive tone" nonetheless came as a surprise. Even the ultranationalists, the paper added, could have no illusions that, should Stresemann fail, there was "simply no one who can replace him at the moment."[25]

The Stresemann government was also vehemently rejected by political forces in Bavaria. The overwhelming majority of the Bavarian populace considered the grand coalition not evidence of progress but "a danger to a strong national state leadership of powerful personalities that stands up for Bavarian political and economic interests," reported the DDP's Eduard Hamm, Cuno's Chancellery state secretary, on

August 16 from Munich. The new ministers of the interior, justice, and finance personified in Bavarian eyes the "abdication of political power to social democracy" since they were "not representatives of the actual relations of power within the populace." Hamm recommended that the new government engage in an "open discussion in an atmosphere of trust" with the Bavarian government.[26]

A few days later, Stresemann did indeed approach the Bavarian state premier, Eugen Ritter von Knilling, requesting his "kind support regarding the execution of the duties of the German state." Political developments, the chancellor added, had come "so frantically in recent times that the decision about the formation of a new government had to be made as quickly as possible." In any event, a grand coalition cabinet had been the "only way out" of Germany's difficulties.[27] On August 24, Stresemann went to Munich to consult with Knilling. Their talks were "initially very emotional but later very cordial," he wrote in his pocket calendar. Later he told his cabinet that "agreement had been reached on all questions."[28] But as would soon become clear, that was anything but the case.

"THE GRAND COALITION GOVERNMENT is the last one Germany will be able to form within the framework of the Weimar Constitution," reported the Austrian counsel general Richard Riedl from Berlin. "No government has ever taken office at a more difficult point in time than this one."[29] Indeed, the problems Stresemann and his cabinet confronted were overwhelming. Passive resistance in the Ruhr was on the verge of collapsing. Hyperinflation continued to spiral day after day. Germany's finances were a disaster, worse than even "the worst expectations," Hilferding told his party leadership on August 22.[30] Meanwhile extremists on the Left and Right were mobilizing against the state, and rumors of putsches were rife. As if that weren't enough, separatists were agitating on the left bank of the Rhine. On August 21, industrialist Otto Wolff told Stresemann that "anarchist conditions" had broken out in the Rhineland and that in his estimation "the movement for autonomy" in the region was making swift progress.[31]

It was clear to all with any common sense that there would be no economic recovery without currency reform. At the same time, inflation could only be reined in if the financially unsustainable state subsidies for the Ruhr campaign were discontinued. The "crux of the matter," wrote Lewinsohn in the *Weltbühne*, was whether the Stresemann cabinet would be able to "deal with the Ruhr question swiftly, in other words, if the new men in power would be able to convince the German people that victory in the conflict was impossible and the best we can achieve now is a modest, very modest, accord to avoid bankruptcy."[32]

When the cabinet met on August 23, Prussian interior minister Severing painted a gloomy picture. There could be no more talk, he said, of passive resistance. The unified front against the French was "full of holes from top to bottom." Supported by Prussian state premier Otto Braun, Severing drew the logical conclusion: "Either we'll succeed in ending the Ruhr struggle as quickly as possible, or we won't, in which case Germany will be unsalvageable."[33]

Stresemann was open to such arguments but wanted to delay the cessation of the passive resistance strategy in hopes of mobilizing international support and forcing France to make concessions. The fight "couldn't be given up entirely," he countered in the meeting. On the other hand, no one should fool themselves. "It would already be an honorable conclusion to the Ruhr struggle if Germany managed to maintain its sovereignty over the occupied regions."[34] Stresemann was interested, among other things, in saving face. While recognizing the need to change tack, he didn't want it to appear as a capitulation. It was impossible, he told the British ambassador, to unconditionally give up passive resistance "without creating grave social unrest."[35]

With the Reichstag in recess and thus unavailable as a forum for influencing public opinion, Stresemann used other means to prepare Germans for the end of passive resistance. On September 2, he addressed reporters in Stuttgart, once again offering a clear-eyed overview of Germany's position. The country was prepared to make "substantial material sacrifices," he declared, but not to abandon any "German soil to anyone." A "Germany without Ruhr and Rhine" would be incapable of survival and unable to make its reparations payments. He proposed a "Rhine pact" that would give French politicians "the greatest security of peace imaginable." But he took care to add, "Partitioning Germany, the attempt to break off German territories or the attempt to dominate German border areas economically or in terms of transportation would undercut the spirit of such an agreement in the long term."[36]

"Bravo, Chancellor!" wrote Bernhard in the *Vossische Zeitung*, asserting that with his speech Stresemann had "seized a standing equal to the leading statesmen of Europe."[37] Wolff also praised the speech in the *Berliner Tageblatt* as the "grand announcement of a statesman" that should be disseminated throughout Germany, and that it would "without doubt invigorate, enlighten and, despite its strict refusal to engage in false optimism, encourage."[38] In a conference with members of the foreign press four days later, the chancellor reiterated his policy of "concessions on material questions but relentlessness in the defense of German territory."[39]

Stresemann put little stock in British mediation. Although the British foreign secretary had conceded in an August 11 dispatch that the Ruhr was being unlawfully occupied, that admission had not yet resulted in any "concrete support," the chancellor told his cabinet on August 23.[40] At a meeting with D'Abernon on September 4, Stresemann pressed for British diplomatic action, arguing that London "had to do something soon" or the German government would be forced to "come to an arrangement with France."[41]

In fact, Stresemann had already extended feelers toward Paris. On September 3, immediately after his Stuttgart appearance, he had received French ambassador Bruno Pierre Jacquin de Margerie for confidential talks in the Chancellery. He stressed that his top priority was a resolution of the Ruhr conflict while adding that the German public wouldn't accept an end to passive resistance without at least the prospect of "an honorable conclusion." As conditions for a change in German policy, Stresemann named the restoration of German sovereignty over the Rhine and Ruhr, the return of those deported from the occupied regions, and a general amnesty for prisoners.[42]

He couldn't wait any longer for Britain, he told his cabinet on September 7. For that reason, he had begun "semiofficial negotiations" with France.[43] Eight days later, in talks with ministers and representatives of Germany's regional states, the chancellor still opposed an immediate cessation of passive resistance because he wanted to wait for the results of negotiations and because he feared that such a step would unleash "serious domestic unrest," particularly in Bavaria. The Bavarian representative in Berlin, Heinrich Karl von Papius, confirmed those fears. Suddenly discontinuing the struggle in the Ruhr would be interpreted as "a laying-down of arms" and could lead to a "dissolution" of the country, given the mood in Bavaria and especially Munich. "People are afraid of a second Versailles," Papius warned.[44]

In talks with the Belgian ambassador in Berlin, Comte della Faille de Leverghem, on September 16, Stresemann once more declared himself willing to discontinue passive resistance but insisted that any such action had to take into account German public opinion and be linked to "certain conditions." An unconditional change of strategy, Stresemann said, would render him—in the words of DNVP leader Hergt—"a dead man, at least politically."[45]

But Poincaré had no intention whatsoever of entering into serious negotiations and continued to insist on the unconditional renunciation of passive resistance. On September 17, the French ambassador told Stresemann that he had been instructed by Paris "to engage in no discussions of details as long as passive resistance wasn't discontinued."[46] The following day, Stresemann was forced to admit to his cabinet that France had dug in its heels "in most recent days," resulting in another anti-German campaign in the French press.[47]

If the chancellor had harbored any vague hopes of British support, they were dashed once and for all on September 19. After Poincaré met with Prime Minister Baldwin in Paris, they issued a joint statement making it clear that there were no differences of opinion between the two governments significant enough to endanger Anglo-French cooperation.[48] The situation was clear: Germany had no choice but to unconditionally desist from passive resistance.

The following day, in light of "the final statement of policy from Paris," Stresemann prepared his cabinet to make the crucial decision.[49] On September 24, the chancellor summoned representatives of the political parties in occupied Germany and told them that he had failed to get anything in return for the country renouncing passive resistance but that the state of German finances allowed no other option. "In the week of September 16 to 22 alone, 3,448 trillion marks in banknotes had been issued for passive resistance," he informed the group. "As a result, the bottom dropped out of the mark." All those present agreed to follow Stresemann's recommendations, except for the DNVP representative Johannes van den Kerkhoff, who was the general director of a factory and a member of the central committee of the Reich Association of German Industry. He demanded that Germany refuse to engage in any further negotiations and declare that the Treaty of Versailles was now null and void after French violations of the agreement. "The occupied region should immediately be declared an object of war," he insisted.[50] At a meeting that same day of representatives from economic associations and civil-servant organizations, the mayor of Duisburg, Karl Jarres, acknowledged the necessity of discontinuing resistance but demanded a statement from the German government that it no longer felt bound by the Treaty of Versailles. Stresemann vigorously refused because that would have meant "abandoning the population of the occupied regions to their fate and eradicating any basis for other powers to exercise their influence on Germany's behalf."[51]

On September 25, Stresemann met with Germany's regional state premiers and political party leaders and asked them to support the end of passive resistance. With the exception of Hergt, who insisted on a complete "break" with France, and Bavarian state premier Eugen von Knilling, who also advocated the abrogation of the Treaty of Versailles, everyone present acknowledged that such a step was unavoidable.[52] That very evening, at a meeting chaired by Ebert, the cabinet approved an announcement for the following day. In the statement, the German president and government once again protested about what they saw as the unlawful occupation but announced the end of the policy of passive resistance: "To preserve the life of the people and the state, we are faced today with the bitter necessity of discontinuing this struggle. We are aware that, with this step, we are making greater mental demands on the residents of the occupied region than ever before. Their struggle was heroic, their self-discipline unparalleled. . . . The president and government solemnly swear that they will not agree to any arrangement that cedes any German soil, no matter how tiny."[53]

There was no doubt that Stresemann had acted courageously in taking responsibility for a decision that was unpopular and controversial within the ranks of his own party. In terms of foreign policy, he could not even count on Poincaré honoring German acquiescence by agreeing to return to the bargaining table. On September 27, the chancellor briefed the ambassadors of the Entente. The resolution to give up passive resistance had been "very difficult," he said, since the government could foresee all too clearly that it would cause "great national agitation and passion."[54]

And indeed the reactions were extremely emotional. In the Ruhr Valley, Stresemann's announcement caused "deep despair" among working people, wrote the local correspondent of the *Berliner Tageblatt*.[55] The ultranationalist Right launched a vicious campaign lambasting the decision as a "capitulation" to the French and a "betrayal" of Germany and calling for the chancellor's assassination. "People openly say that Stresemann should be made to follow Rathenau and Erzberger as soon as possible," read a report on the mood in ultranationalist and racist circles in the Ruhr. "Nationalist instincts are stimulated to the point where passions take over." Despite knowing better, extremists claimed that the resistance had been on the cusp of victory until "[as] in 1918 the Jew government sold us out and betrayed us."[56] The *Rheinisch-Westfälische Zeitung*, a mouthpiece of German heavy industry edited by the racist nationalist Theodor von

Reismann-Grone, called for Stresemann to be brought up before Germany's Constitutional Court on charges of treason.[57] Nothing could be "more criminal and mendacious" as accusing the government of arranging a "capitulation," countered Ossietzky in the *Berliner Volks-Zeitung*. "Not at all," he wrote. "The government did the only thing left open for it to do. . . . The game is over. We should honestly admit that we've lost."[58]

THE MOST VEHEMENT PROTEST came from Bavaria. The same day Berlin announced the end of passive resistance, the Bavarian regional government declared a state of emergency and appointed its president and former Bavarian state premier, Gustav Ritter von Kahr, "general state commissar" with near-dictatorial powers. At a meeting with representatives of the national government, Bavarian state premier Knilling justified the move as necessary to offset the "very threatening situation" he had found after returning to Munich. Rightwing paramilitaries, he said, were ready to take action, and a radical step had been needed to avert a putsch. Knilling admitted that Kahr was a risky choice for the role but argued that, as the man who "most broadly enjoyed the trust of the patriotic associations," Kahr was also most likely to be able to maintain order and get people to follow his commands "without bloodshed."[59] Of course, by pursuing its own independent course, Bavaria was not just countering the Hitler movement's increasing readiness to stage a putsch but also taking a potshot at the national government in Berlin, which it blamed for the unforgivable sin of "capitulation" to the French.

Stresemann and his cabinet were quick to respond, deciding during the night of September 26–27 to have President Ebert declare a national state of emergency and authorize Reichswehr minister Gessler and his military commanders in individual German districts to use force to quell unrest.[60] From a purely constitutional standpoint, the German president and government would have been well within their rights, perhaps even bound by their offices, to demand that Bavaria rescind its regional state of emergency. Interior minister Sollmann insisted on precisely this at the cabinet meeting on September 27, arguing that Kahr's appointment represented a "direct challenge to all republican circles." In Sollmann's eyes, the Bavarian government needed to be taught that "national authority superseded regional authority." But the chancellor and his centrist allies shied away from that level of confrontation. "If we can't be certain that Bavaria will accede to our call, then we shouldn't issue that sort of call to the Bavarian government at all," declared Stresemann.[61]

The chancellor was obviously trying to avoid a public test of strength. In the cabinet meeting of September 30, he presented the draft of a letter in which he politely drew the Bavarian government's attention to the fact that with the German president's declaration of a state of emergency, the regional one had become void. He then asked Munich to "clarify" the legal position of the general state commissar and "consider" revoking the Bavarian declaration. But even such cautious requests went too far for the centrists in the cabinet. Labor minister Brauns predicted that Kahr would "simply ignore" them, putting the national government into the "most embarrassing of positions." Other cabinet members suggested that any stringent overtones from Berlin would only serve to further anger the Bavarians and that the conflict could be better resolved by compromising. But the SPD ministers insisted the letter be sent since it would show Bavarian Social Democrats, against whom Kahr's appointment was primarily directed, that the national government supported them and was working to "defuse the situation."[62] At a meeting the following day, Ebert proposed a compromise: Stresemann could announce the letter before the Reichstag but defer actually sending it.[63]

The debates surrounding a letter that was ultimately never posted revealed an underlying problem. The national government didn't believe it had any leverage to bring those in power in Munich to a reasonable position. Neither Ebert nor Stresemann thought it would do any good to take the situation before the Constitutional Court. For his part, Gessler had already ruled out sending in the military on September 30, saying, "The execution of national authority with troops in Bavaria is out of the question."[64]

There was no counting on the loyalty of the national military leadership in Bavaria—a fact made painfully apparent at the time by another controversial incident. On September 27, the Nazi newspaper, the *Völkischer Beobachter*, had run an article headlined "The Dictators Stresemann and Seeckt," excoriating the chancellor and head of military command and taking pains to mention that both of them had Jewish wives.[65] Gessler ordered a ban on the newspaper. But Kahr opposed the prohibition, and the commander of the Reichswehr's troops in Bavaria, General Otto von Lossow, defied orders and refused to overrule him. This was a clear case of insubordination, but both President Ebert and the national government reacted with curious passivity. "In Berlin, the strategy is still to handle the Bavarian question with kid gloves," Bernhard wrote, critically, in the *Vossische Zeitung*. "But it seems as though Mr. von Kahr doesn't respect such treatment. So now every attempt to strike a deal must stop. Either a unified Germany exists, or it does not."[66] It would be weeks until Ebert, in his function as supreme commander of the German armed forces, had Lossow fired—to which Kahr immediately responded by entrusting Lossow with continuing authority over Reichswehr contingents in Bavaria.[67] He could have hardly called the authority of national government into question more demonstratively.

THE SIMMERING CONFLICT with Bavaria wasn't the only thing burdening the grand coalition, which confronted other severe challenges in late September 1923. Stresemann's hope that France would return to the bargaining table with the end of passive resistance was in vain. Poincaré wasn't about to hand over his trump card, telling Germany's ambassador in Paris that negotiations couldn't begin again until reparations payments resumed. This was probably a gambit to increase chaos in Germany by, among other things, further encouraging separatist movements in Bavaria.[68]

As a result, MICUM—the Inter-Allied Mission for Control of Factories and Mines, which had been formed to oversee reparations payments—began talking directly to representatives of industry in Ruhr, above all Stinnes, about the resumption of production and reparations. Stresemann acknowledged that such negotiations had to be held as long as Poincaré refused to engage with the German government, but he insisted that no agreements would be reached that would affect "state rights, especially those concerning sovereignty."[69] The chancellor registered with alarm that without his knowledge Otto Wolff did a deal with MICUM for the Phönix-Rheinstahl Gruppe in early October. That had "badly damaged the authority of the government," Stresemann told his cabinet, determined to prevent other industrialists from following Wolff's example.[70]

Even domestically, the grand coalition faced additional pressures. German industrial magnates had decided it was time to reverse the country's new regulations concerning working hours. On September 30, Ruhr Valley mine owners meeting in Unna opted to disregard German law and instructed their employees to work eight and a half hours a day as had been standard before the First World War, instead of the seven, which had been the limit for miners since the labor reforms of the early days of the Weimar Republic.[71] As Heinrich August Winkler has shown, the offensive by big business aimed at nothing less than the "demolition of the Stresemann cabinet." With the end of passive resistance, the grand coalition had served its purpose in the eyes of German industrialists and needed to be replaced by a more conservative government. Obviously, there was no way Social Democrats were going to agree to an eight-and-a-half-hour workday, which would have voided one of their major achievements from the November Revolution, and the bosses hoped that they could thus blame the SPD for torpedoing the government.[72]

In the final week of September, Stinnes and his allies, Albert Vögler and the Essen chamber of commerce's in-house lawyer Reinhold Quaatz, had won the support of a significant part of the DVP Reichstag group under Ernst Scholz. Simultaneously, the business-friendly

German press prepared an attack on the cause of social democracy and Germany's labor unions. For example, on September 29, the *Deutsche Allgemeine Zeitung* ran a polemic against an article by ADGB chairman Leipart in *Vorwärts* rejecting demands that German workers put in extra hours: "It is nothing short of tragic to have to read here with what unrealistic arrogance labor leaders, who have succumbed to union dogma, are arguing.... We are again facing the choice of whether to work more or to die of starvation."[73]

Vögler and Scholz spread rumors that their party would "divorce itself from the Social Democrats before the week was up" and suggested overturning a major Social Democratic achievement: the eight-hour workday (seven for miners) in place since the fall of the Wilhelmine Empire. They laid out a two-part scenario: "(a) The Social Democrats would be made to quit the national government by having the DVP demand the immediate eradication of damaging Marxist legislation, especially the eight-hour workday and the aspects of the demobilization and works council law that constrained German business; (b) the German nationalists will then replace the Social Democrats in the government."[74]

But the SPD ministers proved surprisingly conciliatory in the cabinet meeting of October 1. When Labor Minister Brauns advocated extending working hours for as long as it didn't endanger workers' health or, as he put it, the introduction of a "maximum salutary working day," the Social Democrats didn't object. Vice-Chancellor Schmidt merely requested that, out of respect for the SPD, Stresemann should refrain as much as possible in his governmental declaration planned for the following day from talking about the work hours question "in order not to unleash ... a premature, overall debate in public." The idea was to "act on this issue and not talk very much about it." Without any great discussion, the cabinet approved Stresemann's suggestion of an emergency powers law that would help the government enact what it saw as the necessary financial, social, economic, and political measures.[75]

It soon became clear, however, that the SPD ministers had misjudged the mood in their party. While not fundamentally ruling out enhanced powers for the government, at a meeting between the chancellor and the Reichstag parliamentary groups on the morning of October 2, SPD parliamentary chairman Hermann Müller came out against using emergency powers to extend working hours, arguing that it would only cause agitation. The best course, he proposed, was not to even broach the topic under the present circumstances.

However, a declaration by DVP parliamentary chairman Ernst Scholz created a scandal. He demanded not only a complete revocation of workday limits but a shake-up of the government itself. No effort should be spared, he insisted, to "bring the German nationalists into the cabinet."[76] Since there was no way the SPD would ever accept this, Scholz's intent was clear. Demanding a role for the DNVP in the government, commented Ernst Feder in the *Berliner Tageblatt*, meant in practice "pushing the Social Democrats out of the cabinet." Scholz, Feder continued, had made himself into a "mouthpiece for the sort of agitation . . . fomented during the past weeks with undeniable industry by the German racists and German nationalists."[77]

The *Deutsche Allgemeine Zeitung*, which as recently as August had stood behind Stresemann, changed course and called for the nationalists to join the government, acknowledging that this would logically entail the "demise of the grand coalition and limits being placed on parliamentarianism."[78] It was an almost explicit admission that those who pulled the strings in the background wanted not just to strip the SPD of power but to replace the entire Weimar system with some form of authoritarian regime. The *Deutsche Allgemeine Zeitung* had now "cast aside its mask," wrote the *Vossische Zeitung*, not neglecting to identify for its readership who the "soul" behind the governmental intrigue was: DVP parliamentary leader Stinnes.[79] The *Tage-Buch* termed the maneuvering a "stab in the back" and asserted, "No one who has observed the crass agitation of a contemptible species of men close up can fail to feel revolted by these weavers of intrigue."[80]

As the incompatibility of the different positions within the coalition became obvious, on the morning of October 2, Stresemann canceled his government statement, saying, "I can't appear before the Reichstag with an internally fractured cabinet."[81] The crisis was coming to a head. A further conference of party leaders early that evening did nothing to defuse the situation. Scholz issued an ultimatum, demanding the resignations of Hilferding and Economics Minister Raumer, who was considered an anchor of the grand coalition in the DVP. Realizing that he no longer had support within his own party, Raumer asked to be dismissed from his post that same day. SPD leader Müller reiterated that he considered it the wrong time to "roll out" the working-hours issue and said his party would only vote for an emergency powers act if the proposed enhanced authority was limited to currency and financial issues, not social and labor politics.[82]

By the time Stresemann convened the cabinet at 9:30 p.m., it seemed inevitable that the government would stand down. But to everyone's surprise the situation deescalated. The Center Party and DDP ministers declared in unison that they had no intention of driving their Social Democratic colleagues out of the cabinet. SPD ministers for their part signaled a willingness to compromise on working hours, and a draft was agreed to that largely conformed to Brauns's concept of a "salutary maximum workday." The draft legislation stated that the "extreme desperation" in which Germany found itself left no other choice than to "increase working hours to the level that seems tolerable with respect to [workers'] health." In mining, working eight hours—including travel times down to and up from the pits—was "indispensable," and in heavy industry as well there had to be "the possibility of exceeding the eight-hour workday."[83]

But the very next day tensions rose again. The SPD faction stuck to its refusal to sanction broad emergency powers, and party deputies also rejected, by a margin of 61 to 54, a suggestion by Postal Minister Höfle that the act encompass social welfare issues but that the workday question would be settled by a separate package of legislation. In vain, Vice-Chancellor Schmidt appealed to the cabinet at an evening meeting not to scuttle the coalition. "He said it was impossible for his party to decide the working hours question by ordinance," read one account of the meeting. "It couldn't alienate the working classes. The Social Democrats wanted to take energetic financial and economic action, but they couldn't compromise any further on working hours.... The eight-hour workday was the only thing the working classes had left." Stresemann responded that in his party's view, an emergency powers act would make no sense if it didn't include the entire complex of financial, economic, social welfare, and political issues as an indivisible whole. After the factions had voted as they did, he could no longer appear before the Reichstag in good conscience and had no option but to dissolve the cabinet.[84] Shortly after midnight, the chancellor met with President Ebert and told him the government was stepping down.

"The deepest depression," Stresemann wrote in his pocket calendar on October 4, and his son Wolfgang recalled having rarely seen his father "so depressed" as on that day. Stresemann was afraid that he would go down in history merely as the chancellor who had capitulated on the Ruhr.[85]

Without question, the industrialists in the DVP, led by Stinnes, were mainly responsible for the failure of the first grand coalition. They had used the workday issue to create a conflict between their party and the SPD and break apart their alliance. But the SPD also bore its share of the blame for the crisis. "Irritated and annoyed, indeed provoked by the action of the DVP, Social Democrats couldn't bring themselves to put the higher political needs of the state before what were ultimately minor party interests," remarked Dombrowski in the *Berliner Tageblatt*.[86] Fearful of losing even more supporters to their left-wing competitors, the Communists, the majority of SPD deputies voted against a compromise agreed to by the party's ministers, albeit with heavy hearts.

LIBERAL-MINDED SEGMENTS of the public were very disappointed at what appeared to be the end of the grand coalition. "Within a few days, parliamentary intrigues destroyed months of work and the hope that a broad democratic basis would restore an orderly economy to the so sorely tested German people," Bernhard lamented in the *Vossische Zeitung*.[87] There seemed to be no chance of a parliamentary solution to the crisis. Enemies of the Weimar Republic inside and outside the German parliament felt they had achieved their goal of bringing down Stresemann and had taken a huge step toward instituting a right-wing government that would largely ignore the Reichstag.

But they were mistaken. To the surprise of many, the grand coalition arose from the dead only two days later. Ebert played a decisive role in the unlikely resuscitation. The German president had charged Stresemann at their meeting on the night of October 4 with forming a new government. Yet it soon proved impossible to form a minority government that included the bourgeois parties and leaders of industry. The DNVP staunchly refused to join a cabinet under Stresemann, and the majority of the DVP was unwilling to sacrifice its chairman. The situation called for a revival of the grand coalition, an option vocally preferred by the Center Party and the DDP.[88]

The night of October 5–6 brought a breakthrough on the issue of the workday. After hours of negotiations, the various parties agreed to retain the principle of the eight-hour workday but to permit exceptions in labor agreements and legislation. That allowed the Social Democrats to claim at least partial victory. Now nothing stood in the way of a new version of the grand coalition.[89]

Stresemann presented his new cabinet on October 6. The Social Democrats retained only three ministers: Schmidt, Radbruch, and Sollmann. Hilferding, who had attracted the ire of the Right, was replaced as finance minister by Hans Luther, the former food minister who had no party affiliation. Another independent, Joseph Koeth, who had headed the Reich Office for Economic Demobilization in 1918 and 1919, took over from Raumer, who had stepped down as economic minister. The post of food minister remained vacant for several days but was then filled by Count Gerhard von Kanitz, who gave up his membership in the DNVP to take the job. As the owner of a large agricultural estate, Kanitz was closely connected to agrarian circles, and his appointment was the clearest indication that the new cabinet had moved to the political right. Stresemann also dismissed the director of the Reich Chancellery, Werner von Rheinbaben, tapping Reichstag deputy and chairman of the DVP's operative committee, Adolf Kempkes, who was a loyal ally.[90]

Every seat in the Reichstag was occupied on the afternoon of October 6 as Stresemann led his new cabinet onto the floor of parliament. "The crowd was pressed shoulder to shoulder on the governmental dais, the deputies' benches, and the spectators' rostrum," reported the *Berliner Tageblatt*. "After all the tense moments and ups and downs of the last few days and nights, things now relaxed to a degree. The chancellor looked pale and tired, and his ministers no less so."[91] But Stresemann showed no signs of fatigue during his speech, defending his decision to discontinue passive resistance with great conviction: "I was aware in the moment I did what I did, as leader of my party, which was positioned in a completely different direction, that I was risking not just my position in the party but indeed also my life. But what do we, the German people, lack? We lack the courage to take responsibility." That was precisely what was lacking among those who flirted with the "ideas of dictatorship," Stresemann emphasized. The chancellor was equally adamant in his defense of the decision to declare a state of emergency, which, he said, was intended to prevent Germany from drifting into "a war of citizen against citizen." Stresemann concluded by telling his listeners that there had scarcely been a cabinet in "a more difficult time and a more difficult emergency." But he promised that "we will not perish as long as we do not doubt in ourselves."[92]

Two days later, DNVP spokesman Count Kuno von Westarp sharply attacked the new government in a Reichstag debate, making clear the ultranationalists' real aims for Germany: "We demand and are working toward the detachment of the government from social democracy. That is our dominant perspective." Only when the call to "rid ourselves of Marxism is finally taken seriously can the DNVP take part in a government."[93] Stresemann rejected as pure demagoguery the notion that the government was "dominated by Social

Democratic ideology or the ideas of Marxism." Working together in a coalition, he added, required readiness to compromise, particularly from the two parties on either end of the political spectrum. Anyone who attacked that as weakness didn't understand that "coalition politics are the only realistic politics" that could be pursued in Germany as long as the government was based on constitutional grounds. "A storm of ovations lasting minutes sounded through the building, and the German nationalists were forced to listen," reported Bernhard. "The applause, augmented against the rules by the spectators, will have shown the chancellor that he's on the right path . . . and that he enjoys the unqualified support of the country as long as he remains true to himself."[94]

ON OCTOBER 7, STRESEMANN noted in his calendar, "Immense mental calm after the past weeks' storm."[95] His respite would be brief. Well-informed observers like the American ambassador in Berlin, Alanson B. Houghton, predicted that the second grand coalition cabinet wouldn't last long either.[96] The first test was to convince the Reichstag to approve emergency governmental powers—by no means a sure thing. According to the Weimar Constitution, two-thirds of deputies had to be present to pass such a measure, and two-thirds of those present had to vote for the legislation. It was a "clear duty" for the parties in government to ensure that their votes were cast, without exception, for the law, warned the *Berliner Tageblatt*. Should the legislation fail, taking with it the possibility to do "what was absolutely necessary in accordance with the Constitution," the result would be "upheavals whose scope cannot be foreseen."[97] But before the third and final reading of the draft legislation, scheduled for October 11, it turned out that not enough deputies would be present for the vote to be valid. The coalition avoided defeat only by delaying the vote for two days and by Stresemann getting authority from Ebert to dissolve the Reichstag if it didn't approve the emergency powers act.[98]

Stresemann's threat to call new elections brought his nominal polit-

ical allies into line. With 348 votes present, he easily exceeded the necessary quorum, and 316 deputies from the parties in power voted for
the legislation, with only 24 "nays" and 7 abstentions. "Bravo, Reichstag!" cheered the *Vossische Zeitung*.[99] Yet the result was less impressive
than it initially seemed. Although the SPD had ordered strict parliamentary discipline, 13 of its deputies had failed to appear for the vote,
and 31 issued a declaration that they had only given their assent under
duress and in the interests of party unity. Meanwhile 6 right-wing
DVP deputies, including Stinnes, Vögler, and Quaatz, had abstained.
Thus the vote also showed the power of those forces trying to rupture
the grand coalition from within.[100]

The emergency powers act gave the government extraordinary, sweeping authority on economic, financial, and social matters, although the issue of the length of the workday was officially
exempted. The act was temporary. It was only valid until the government or the governing coalition changed and would expire under any
circumstances on March 31, 1924.[101]

THE EMERGENCY POWERS ACT gave the Stresemann government an instrument to take the decisive action needed to resolve
Germany's crises, particularly the second major issue the coalition had
tackled: reforming state finances and stabilizing the currency. What
the government did in response to those related crises, the mainstream
newspapers of record all agreed, would be a "test of its ability to correctly use the powers now entrusted to it by the Reichstag."[102]

Since Stresemann had taken office on August 13, hyperinflation
had radically accelerated. On that day, a dollar had been worth 3.7
million marks. On September 1, it was worth 10.5 million; two
weeks later, 109 million; and by the end of September, 160 million.[103]
Prices climbed commensurately. By the end of August, Victor Klemperer had to pay 300,000 marks for the movie ticket that had cost
him 10,000 a couple of weeks earlier. "Senseless heights on the stock
market, in the exchange rate with the dollar and in prices," he noted

on September 6. "The feeling of imminent catastrophe. . . . Everyone senses something threatening approaching. No one knows what will happen."[104] Twenty-four days later, he complained, "Yesterday a bread roll cost a million and a tram ride ten million. The lunatic inflation and torturous state of our finances is devouring all our qualities of spirit and soul."[105]

No longer able to afford public transportation, many people in Berlin switched to bicycles. "Berlin is now the city of the cycle," reported the *Berliner Tageblatt* in early September. "If you stand in the morning and the late afternoon beside the access roads from the suburbs, rows and rows of bicycling Berlin, with no end in sight, glide past you. The bike is now the most affordable mode of transportation for white-collar employees, businesspeople, and day trippers."[106]

In late September, trade unions reported receiving "cries for help" from broad segments of the working population, which were no longer able to afford the potatoes and coal they needed. People were looking toward the coming winter "with the greatest of trepidation."[107]

By early October, as though driven by an unstoppable flywheel, the value of the dollar was rising in increments not of tens but of hundreds of millions every day. "The dollar is at 200 million, 300 million, 400 million," Klemperer recorded on October 4.[108] Because the amount of money printed was often insufficient to cover daily needs, many communities and businesses began issuing emergency currency. With unsurpassed black humor, one businessman brought out a 500,000 note with the words, "Should a briquette of coal be more expensive, go ahead and use me to fire your oven."[109]

On October 9, the dollar cracked the billion-mark threshold for the first time. That day Betty Scholem, the wife of a Jewish printing-press owner in Berlin, wrote to her son Gershom, a writer who had left for Palestine to escape the antisemitism rife in Germany: "I can imagine that over there the strangest ideas about Germany prevail, but the reality is much weirder. When you departed, the sausage I gave you, for instance, cost 12 million a pound. Now it's 240 million. The price of everything has risen at that speed and even faster.

The electric train costs 10 million, and you can only go shopping with billion-mark notes. The economy has completely collapsed." Arthur Scholem's business actually profited from the crisis since he printed money on behalf of the government. "In the entire company, great joy and industry is the rule since the threat of being fired had hovered over everyone's heads."[110]

Only six days later, Betty Scholem reported to her son that conditions had gotten "catastrophically worse." The weekly wages of the family's employees totaled 8 billion, but negotiations were under way because the workers wanted double that. "Bread ration cards have been revoked. A loaf costs 540 million today, and without doubt twice as much tomorrow. The electric train 20 million (tomorrow 50 million). My God, you probably can't conceive any more about this witches' sabbath."[111]

THE DAY BETTY SCHOLEM wrote those lines—October 15, 1923—the Stresemann government announced an important measure it hoped would help master hyperinflation: the formation of the Rentenbank (annuity bank). This attempt to financially liberate Germany in one fell swoop was preceded by tense negotiations during which a wide variety of proposals had been considered. Stresemann, who had little financial or currency expertise, had given his former finance minister Hilferding a free hand to prepare the reforms. Hilferding was at pains to form as broad a consensus as possible. On August 18, he invited the DNVP Reichstag deputy Karl Helfferich to address the cabinet. A former banker and state secretary in the Reich Treasury Office, Helfferich had developed an idea for reforming the currency in the final days of the Cuno government that he now presented to Stresemann's ministers. The idea was to create a transitional currency bank run by representatives of private industry and independent of both the Reichsbank and the national government. Helfferich justified the idea by arguing that the economic "professions"—industry, agriculture, manufacturing, and trade—"at least had credit at their disposal, unlike the Reich." The private bank would issue a new currency guaranteed by Germany's stockpiles of rye. In return for ensuring the value of the "rye mark," private industry was to be freed of the special taxes that had been levied as recently as August 11.[112]

Hilferding couldn't accept the notion of a currency bank managed by private commercial "professions," and he suspected that the suggestion was an attempt by the old large-scale industrial and agricultural elites to wrest control of financial and economic policy from the government. The "primacy of the state," Hilferding insisted, had to be "unconditionally preserved."[113] He also considered rye insufficient as a guarantee. A solid currency, in his mind, could only be backed by gold. But Hilferding initially didn't present a detailed plan of his own, believing that the Ruhr conflict had to be resolved before the currency could be reformed. Only "a foreign-policy operation" could help, he told the cabinet on August 30.[114]

Under pressure from Stresemann and his fellow ministers, by the start of September, Hilferding was ready to prepare basic guidelines for his own concept, which he presented for discussion within the cabinet on September 7 and 10. He proposed establishing a "gold banknote bank" that Germany would finance by using its remaining gold reserves to buy more gold on credit. To prevent the devaluation of the new "gold mark," it would be decoupled from the old "paper marks," which would, however, remain in circulation for a time. The only suggestion by Helfferich that Hilferding adopted was to involve private industry through a mortgage on its assets to create credit lines for the state and make it easier for banknotes to be cashed in. On September 10, the cabinet broadly approved Hilferding's plan and pressed for it to be put into practice swiftly.[115]

The Stresemann cabinet was "energetically in the process of introducing some order into the economy, which has been shattered and shaken up by frivolous financial charlatans," Theodor Wolff told readers of the *Berliner Tageblatt*. "If it should succeed . . . in cleansing the moral atmosphere by shoring up state finances and in constraining the filth that has sprouted from the swamp, the rampant corrupters of the health of the people, and the tarted-up, bon-vivant, gambling brats, our gratitude would know no bounds."[116]

But one day after the cabinet resolution, the Reichsbank refused to establish a separate bank based on gold. The time wasn't right for such a new currency, it argued, and for that reason Helfferich's project should be seen as an interim solution. Additionally, the Reichsbank articulated the wish "to be completely separated from the conducting of state finances for the immediate future" and declared that it intended to discontinue treasury bonds.[117] The head of the Reich Association of German Industry also expressed skepticism, and even within the cabinet itself, Economics Minister Raumer and Food Minister Luther came out in favor of a transitional solution.

When the cabinet met again on September 13, ministers agreed to a compromise between Hilferding's and Helfferich's proposals. On the one hand, a gold-note bank was to be established as quickly as possible, but a means of payment capable of holding its value and "mobilizing the harvest" would be introduced for a transitional period. A currency based on rye would "greatly appeal to the psychology of agriculture," Stresemann declared. In any case, agricultural producers had to be prevented from falling behind on deliveries. A commission led by Hilferding was formed to complete the currency reform package.[118]

Pressure was growing on the government to act, and Prussian finance minister Ernst von Richter of the DVP warned that time was of the essence. The endless negotiations were partly responsible for the mark every day losing more and more of its value as a means of payment. Germany, Richter argued, had arrived at the point where financial misery was fueling economic and political disintegration and threatening the unity of the nation itself.[119]

On September 26, the same day passive resistance was abandoned, the cabinet approved draft legislation to be introduced a few days later to the two chambers of the German parliament. Helfferich's influence was noticeable in several major points. For a transitional period, a currency bank supervised by one of the "professions"—in other words, industry and agriculture—was to be created. But in a departure from

Helfferich's idea, the national government would appoint that institution's president. The new currency was also to be called the "soil mark" and not the "rye mark," and it would be based on concrete assets. The reference value, as Hilferding had demanded, wasn't grain but gold.[120] The *Vossische Zeitung* welcomed the news that "at least the toxic idea of the rye mark had been removed," while criticizing the government for succumbing "to no small influence from business circles." Editor Richard Lewinsohn, the future head of the paper's business section, went so far as to call for preventing "the botched Helfferich-Hilferding proposal from being carried out."[121]

The proposal was never put to a vote because of the crisis within the coalition and the dissolution of the first Stresemann cabinet. Hilferding was forced out because, as his successor Luther recalled, he "gradually got on the nerves of the entire cabinet" with his "inveterately theoretical manner."[122] With Luther at the helm, the original proposal was revised even further, and on October 15, the second Stresemann cabinet approved the creation of the Rentenbank, as the new financial institution was now called. Correspondingly, the new currency was known as the Rentenmark and not the rye mark or soil mark. The bank was to be provided with 3.2 billion Rentenmarks in capital, which would come from agriculture, industry, trade, and manufacturing in equal measure: 1.2 billion would be placed at the disposal of the national government, with 500 million in the form of an interest-free loan. Parallel to the introduction of the new currency, which was planned for early November, the Reichsbank would discontinue treasury bonds, thus sealing off one of the main causes of inflation. Rentenmark banknotes could be exchanged at any time for annuity bonds that paid 5 percent interest. The paper mark would remain an instrument of payment alongside the new currency. To bridge the short time until the latter was issued, one-, two-, and five-dollar increments of the gold the government had borrowed were to be provided as temporary means of payment. The underlying idea of the currency reform was to find an interim solution until the situation was stabilized and a return to the gold standard was possible.[123]

There was an entire month between the creation of the Rentenbank on October 15 and the issuance of the Rentenmark on November 15. Whether people inside and outside of Germany would trust the new money, prophesied the *Vossische Zeitung*, would depend on the state taking immediate action to reform its finances: "If in the coming weeks we hear about progress on tax reform, an increase in government revenues, and an equally energetic reduction in expenditures, the Rentenmark will retain its value, despite all the theoretical arguments to the contrary."[124]

THERE WAS ALSO LIGHT shining on the foreign-policy horizon. On October 15, as the creation of the Rentenbank was announced, the cabinet decided to follow a proposal made by former finance minister Hilferding eleven days earlier. The government would write to the Reparations Commission, declaring itself temporarily unable to resume payments because of the "complete collapse of the currency" and inviting that authority to audit Germany's finances.[125] A dispatch to that effect was sent nine days later. Stresemann and his colleagues were convinced that Britain had no interest in driving Germany into total economic ruin and that their initiative would be positively received in London at least. On October 12, the British government had called on the United States to participate in the sort of experts conference Secretary of State Hughes had proposed back in late December 1922. The reaction in Washington to the new suggestion was encouraging for Germany. On October 25, Poincaré agreed to the initiative, albeit on the condition that the Reparation Commission's expert committee be convened. The main reason for the French prime minister's surprising willingness to engage with Germany's proposal was the assurance via Hughes that in return for French participation, the United States would link the audit of the reparations issue to the question of debts owed by the Allies to one another, potentially reducing France's American debts. "The Americans have agreed to come into the inquiry as to Germany's capacity

*After the currency reform: Crowds of people congregate before
the new Rentenbank building in Berlin, November 1923.*

to pay," D'Abernon noted with satisfaction, "and Poincaré has reluc-
tantly agreed to the proposal."[126]

With that, a way out of the foreign-policy dead end seemed at
hand. Nonetheless, the German government couldn't rest even for a
moment. Indeed, the second edition of the grand coalition would face
stiff new challenges on the domestic front in the latter half of October.

# CHAPTER 4

# THE GERMAN
# OCTOBER

*Street barricades in the working-class Hamburg district*
*of Barmbek on October 23, 1923. As part of the uprising, left-wing*
*insurgents attacked police stations in the city.*

IN MID-SEPTEMBER 1923, THE JOURNALIST AND SPD Reichstag deputy Ludwig Quessel wrote in an article for the *Welt-bühne* about a "Ninth of November mood" growing in Germany: "A wild, all-consuming anxiety is bringing bitterness into every relation-ship in human lives. Panic and obsession are taking over our souls. We have seven weeks of revolutionary fermentation behind us without a single sign of improvement on the horizon. On the contrary, every day, things get worse."[1] One month later, the chaos persisted. "Every day you say that a catastrophe must arrive, without knowing which one, but believing something will happen: the disintegration of the nation, civil war, some sort of storm, something unprecedented or something else," noted Victor Klemperer on October 14. "And always the same pestilent silence remains. There is absurdity upon absurdity, humiliation upon humiliation, ten-billion-mark notes upon one-billion-mark notes, and in the immutable silence, desperation and misery grow."[2]

It was the quiet before the storm. The tensions had intensified over the late summer and early fall to the point that a violent eruption seemed inevitable. It wasn't just the Far Right that saw an opportunity and began to make plans for a coup. In Moscow, too, Communists considered the situation ripe for an armed uprising, a "German October," that would bring the proletarian revolution to central and western Europe and release the Soviet Union from its isolation.

At the conference of the Executive Committee of the Communist International in June 1923, at which Karl Radek had made his incendiary speech praising German paramilitary activity, there had been no talk of preparing an uprising. The German Communists of the KPD, for all their revolutionary rhetoric, weren't eager for a test of strength either. From his vacation home in the Caucasus in late July, Comintern chairman Grigory Zinoviev pressured the German KPD leadership under Heinrich Brandler and August Thalheimer to go on the offensive. But Stalin himself—the secretary general of the Russian Communist Party and the center of power in the Soviet leadership since Lenin had fallen seriously ill—urged caution: "If today the powers-that-be in Germany fall and the Communists revolt, they will go down to a crushing defeat—in the best-case scenario. At the worst, they will be hacked to bits and set back enormously. . . . In my opinion we have to restrain, not encourage, the Germans."[3]

Nonetheless, starting in mid-August, as the crisis in Germany came to a head and the Cuno government resigned amid the threat of mass strikes, opinions changed in Moscow. In a set of guidelines entitled "The Situation in Germany and Our Tasks," Zinoviev declared that a "second, truly proletarian revolution" was brewing, and no step should be omitted to support it.[4] On August 21, the Politburo endorsed this view. After the hoped-for upheaval in Germany, still the most powerful industrial nation on the European continent, there was reason for the Soviet Union to believe that it could master the difficulties of building up socialism domestically. For Stalin, this was an existential issue: "Either the revolution in Germany will fail and kill us, or the revolution will succeed there, everything will be fine, and our position will be secured. There is no other alternative."[5]

The next day, the Politburo issued a declaration. On the assumption that "the German proletariat is ready for the decisive struggles for power," the Comintern's activity should be directed at preparing for the armed uprising in Germany. The Central Committee of the KPD was allocated a special fund of 400,000 dollars to procure weapons. Leon Trotsky's deputy in the Revolutionary Military Council, Josef Unschlicht, illegally entered Germany to help with the establishment of a covert military apparatus.[6]

The proclamation was greatly influenced by reports from KPD circles that spoke of "massive agitation" among the German working classes.[7] To leading Bolsheviks, the situation in Germany in the late summer of 1923 seemed comparable to that in Russia between April and October 1917. But they overlooked the facts that Germany as a society was very different from Russia and that the KPD Central Committee had neither a Lenin nor a Trotsky.[8]

At a series of conferences beginning on September 20 in Moscow, the KPD delegation was sworn to the common cause. "We see the situation of events ripening to the point that they can be decided in short order," declared Zinoviev. "We . . . have every chance of success if we deploy our entire force." Trotsky came out and demanded, "The aim now is to seize power in Germany. That's our task. Everything else will follow from that." KPD chairman Brandler, who had warned against drawing premature conclusions as recently as August, pivoted to present the most optimistic outlook for Communist prospects. A quarter of a million proletarians, he claimed, were ready to fight. Within six to eight weeks, they could be formed into fifteen divisions. There was enough weaponry available. The remaining problem was distributing it.[9]

In the final days of September and the first days of October, a concrete plan of action was decided. To start, the KPD was to join the government in Saxony and use this strategic position to continue to arm the working classes. November 9—the fifth anniversary of the German Revolution of 1918—was provisionally set as a date for the uprising. A "quartet" of ranking Communist functionaries, led by the Germany expert Radek, was sent to Berlin to help the comrades in the German capital make preparations.[10]

IT WAS NO ACCIDENT that Saxony was selected as the springboard for the "German October."[11] The SPD had governed the regional state since 1919, initially alone, then in a coalition with the DDP and as of 1920 as part of a minority government with the USPD. In late January 1923, a vote of no confidence engineered by the centrist parties and the Communists had forced the Saxon government under State Premier Wilhelm Buck to step down. In early March, a regional SPD conference, strongly influenced by the left wing of the party, disregarded the advice coming from Social Democratic headquarters to seek a coalition with the DDP and instead sought to reach a consensus with the KPD. On March 18, the two parties agreed to a platform for a purely SPD government that would be tolerated by the Communists. The main points were the formation of "proletarian defense organizations" against fascism and the establishment of price-control offices and committees to combat usury.[12] On March 21, the Saxon regional parliament in Dresden elected former justice minister Erich Zeigner the new state premier by a margin of 49 to 46.

The thirty-seven-year-old lawyer and representative of the party's left wing was a "November socialist" who had first joined the SPD after the revolution of 1918. As the Buck cabinet's justice minister, he had advocated modernizing the penal system, democratizing the judicial administration, and more vigorously pursuing Far Right groups.[13] He continued his drive for decisive reforms as state premier. While he stirred the hopes of leftist supporters of Weimar democracy, the national SPD leadership considered his cooperation with the KPD a dangerous experiment detrimental to the party as a whole. And Zeigner was a thumb in the eye of the military, never tiring of excoriating the illegal cooperation between the Reichswehr and right-wing extremist militias. From the start, in his government declaration of April 10, he took the military to task, proclaiming, "The army that is supposed to protect and serve the Republic and that is conceived as an instrument of power of the Republic has increasingly developed into a threat to the Republic." For that reason, he added, the working classes were well within their rights if they took "defensive actions against putschist elements" to protect themselves.[14]

That was beyond what the commander of the Reichswehr in Saxony, General Alfred Müller, was willing to tolerate. Zeigner's statements, he reported to Berlin, showed that the Saxon government had "almost without exception bound itself to the wishes of the Communist Party." Müller also called upon the Reichswehr minister to deliver a sharp rebuke to the "value judgment" about the German military.[15] In late May, Gessler went to Dresden to meet with Zeigner. The two men agreed to put their previous bickering behind them and to direct future disagreements to the responsible authorities rather than making them public.[16] But the conflict wasn't settled. In particular, the establishment of working-class defense organizations, known as "proletarian battalions" (*proletarische Hundertschaften*), created new friction. Whereas Prussian interior minister Carl Severing banned them that May, in Saxony they were benevolently tolerated and in some cases even directly encouraged by the government. The associations drew their members from communists, socialists, and union activists, and most were led by the KPD. As a rule, the battalions didn't carry firearms but rubber truncheons.[17]

In mid-June, the representatives of the Association of Saxon Industrialists complained in Berlin about conditions in their state, especially pointing to the proletarian battalions, whom they claimed were organizing demonstrations, making impossible demands, and bringing "street terror" to negotiations between business and labor. The result, they asserted, was that no more business contracts were being awarded to Saxony. Such complaints were exaggerated, but they made the intended impression on the national government and the armed forces. Interior Minister Rudolf Oeser was deaf to appeals to deploy the military to Saxony but conceded that one "would of course have to crack down" if the situation deteriorated. Deputy Reichswehr Minister Major Kurt von Schleicher was able to reassure the Saxon industrialists that the proletarian battalions didn't possess any serious weapons. But he also left no doubt that armed forces would be ready to "restore order any time at short notice."[18]

Zeigner did little to defuse the situation. On June 16, he gave a speech at an SPD parliamentary conference in Planitz that raised bourgeois hackles. In it, he reemphasized the accusations he had leveled against the Reichswehr, denounced large industrialists for alleged corruption during the Ruhr conflict, and took aim at the Cuno government, which, he said, was "bankrupt" across the board. The Social Democrats and Communists had to block a vote of no confidence launched after the speech by the bourgeois parties in the Saxon regional parliament. Cuno summoned Zeigner to Berlin and threatened him with legal consequences should he continue his agitation "without any consideration for the interests of the nation." Although the Saxon state premier attempted to partially disavow his statements, blaming the media for misrepresenting a speech not intended for the public at large, the mood remained sour.[19]

Zeigner poured more oil on the fire during an August 7 speech in Leipzig, when he again questioned the Reichswehr's commitment to defending democracy, criticizing the national government's murky stance toward covert right-wing organizations and calling upon the SPD to distance itself unambiguously from the Cuno government.

At that point, Ebert, too, ran out of patience, admonishing the Saxon state premier that it was time to use "serious and considered language."[20] Gessler used Zeigner's speech as a pretext to prohibit the Reichswehr from participating in the constitutional celebrations in Dresden on August 11. He also instructed officers in regional and district Reichswehr units to avoid any further contact with the Saxon government.[21]

As part of the celebrations, Zeigner's government booked Heinrich Mann to speak in Dresden's main concert hall, the Semperoper. The political Right had particularly loathed Mann since the publication of his 1918 novel *Man of Straw* (Der Untertan), which had depicted Wilhelmine Germany as a society of craven underlings. Klemperer was in attendance in a third-level loge, noting, "Beethoven before and after the address Heinrich Mann delivered onstage. Green trees, violet velvet walls, a red ribbon on the podium. I didn't recognize the man with his dark, little moustache and otherwise clean-shaven face. He read his speech in a soft but very clear voice, only speaking freely for a few sentences at a time, also in a quiet voice. But his muted tone carried a terrible embitterment and bitterness."[22] Mann made clear that he was appalled by events since 1918. The broad liberty promised by the Weimar Constitution, he complained, was increasingly coming under threat from enemies of democracy in the military and heavy industry. Responding to the German government's threats to use force against the Saxon government, Mann asked, "Should the national executive be making preparations against those [regional] governments that see the state as a free body of the people?"[23]

WITH THE FORMATION OF the first grand coalition, relations between Saxony and Berlin initially relaxed. On August 17, a few days after taking office, Stresemann met Zeigner for talks. In the subsequently published message to the press, Zeigner stressed "the staunch determination of the Saxon government to preserve peace and order." To calm the situation, the state premier wanted to avoid "politically escalating" differences with the Reichswehr Ministry in the future. The communiqué ended with the words, "Overall, the chancellor has determined that the Saxon state premier completely supported protecting the current state system, alongside the national government, with all means at his disposal."[24]

At a second meeting between the two men on August 22, Stresemann promised to use his influence to get the Association of Saxon Industrialists, with whom he had become well acquainted as a corporate lawyer, to "distance themselves from continuing the fight against Zeigner's government." For his part, the state premier signaled his desire to work toward a "similar political constellation" as in the Reich and Prussia, that is, to form a grand coalition—something of which Stresemann heartily approved.[25] But political observers in Saxony doubted Zeigner's honesty. Saxon DVP secretary general Johannes Dieckmann, for instance, felt he had to warn Stresemann that he was being deceived. In private conversations, Dieckmann commented, Zeigner may have consistently portrayed himself "as a man who himself suffered greatly under Communist pressure and strove to alter the present situation toward cooperation with the bourgeois parties." But in reality, Dieckmann warned, Zeigner had no such intention since he existed in "a kind of pathologically subservient state" to the Communists.[26]

Gessler also had little interest in conciliation. The day after Stresemann's second consultation with Zeigner, he presented the chancellor with a memo that recapitulated the conflicts between his ministry and the Saxon state premier, threatening to make everything in it public. The point had now been reached, he insisted, that mutual relations could "only be normalized by the Saxon government completely altering its behavior and taking back the accusations leveled against the Reichswehr." Under the present circumstances, Gessler added, he had no choice but to ban any contact between the Zeigner government with either himself or his subordinates. He also asked Stresemann to consider whether Zeigner's August 7 speech in Leipzig should be investigated as an instance of "treason."[27]

Nonetheless, as he told the Reich Council on Foreign Affairs on September 7, Stresemann continued to believe that the "unedifying quarrel" could soon be resolved. And Zeigner, who was present at that meeting, again presented himself as willing to compromise. But he had hardly returned to Dresden before he once more vehemently attacked Gessler. As if that weren't enough, he publicly revealed statements made in confidence by Stresemann concerning the end of the Ruhr standoff. That was too much for the chancellor. At a cabinet meeting on September 10, he condemned Zeigner's behavior in no uncertain terms, saying the Saxon leader had made it "impossible to direct national policy in a responsible manner."[28]

RELATIONS BETWEEN THE NATIONAL government and Saxony had reached a new low, and Thuringian state premier August Frölich, who had led a Social Democratic minority regional government since the fall of 1921, intervened. As was the case with its neighbor Saxony, the SPD in Thuringia had begun negotiations in the spring of 1923 with the KPD about forming a coalition, but talks were discontinued after Social Democrats deemed the Communists' demands unacceptable. On September 10, Ebert asked Frölich to mediate in the quarrel between Zeigner and the national government. Frölich suggested that the state premiers of the regional states "that had thus far shown particular commitment to the German Republic"—all of them Social Democrats—be invited to a conference to clear the air in Berlin. But the very next day, the Frölich cabinet received a request for a vote of confidence from the bourgeois parties, with the support of the Communists, in the regional parliament in Weimar. As a result, when Frölich's proposal reached Ebert on September 12, he responded that Thuringia would first need to form a new government. That turned out to be unnecessary since the Communists refused to support the bourgeois motion to dissolve the parliament and call new elections. Frölich was able, for the time being, to continue his minority government.[29]

Nonetheless, the conference of state premiers never materialized. Instead, Stresemann summoned Gessler and Zeigner to a meeting that included several national ministers, SPD co-chairmen Otto Wels and Arthur Crispien, and Severing. As far as is clear from the minutes, which contained only bullet points, this attempt at mediation was also fruitless. The two sides merely traded accusations, and in the end the only agreement was that Gessler would publicly declare that the Reichswehr didn't maintain any contact with organizations hostile to the Constitution.[30] In a subsequent statement on September 14, Gessler played down the extent to which the Reichswehr had cooperated with extreme right-wing paramilitary groups. Any such connections, he claimed, had "long been prohibited by clear orders," and where they had "truly existed in the past as individual cases," they had long been dissolved. "I am convinced," Gessler said, "that in the difficult times to come the honor of the German soldier will remain unbesmirched."[31]

Stresemann was coming under increased pressure from his own party. In a DVP parliamentary group meeting on September 12, Deputy Siegfried von Kardorff characterized Zeigner's behavior as "thoroughly embarrassing," arguing that the government had to "put its foot down and potentially institute a state of siege" in Saxony. Franz Brüninghaus, the deputy from the Saxon electoral district of Chemnitz-Zwickau, declared that the citizens of his regional state no longer enjoyed the protection of the law: "If the government doesn't intervene energetically, we will have Communism in Saxony and Thuringia in no time." And Hugo Stinnes tersely demanded, "Assume control over Saxony and Thuringia. There's not a day to lose. Otherwise, the street will depose the Stresemann cabinet." But Stresemann was still able to resist the pressure. The option of the national state taking over a regional state, he asserted, was the very last resort. If it proved necessary, however, he would "ruthlessly deploy the entire power of the state."[32]

The chancellor faced a difficult balancing act. On the one hand, he didn't want to alienate Social Democrats over Saxony and risk the end of the grand coalition. On the other, he had no desire to be accused within his own party of failing to act, and under no circumstance did he want conflict with Gessler and the Reichswehr, on whose loyalty he depended.

WITH THE DECLARATION OF a national state of emergency on September 27, the Reichswehr minister was given executive authority. In Saxony, Gessler immediately passed on this power to General Müller, the commander of Reichswehr District IV, and in Thuringia to former Prussian minister of war General Walther Reinhardt, the commander of Reichswehr District V. That brought the conflicts between the regional government and the military to a head in Thuriniga as well. In his first official measure on September 28, Reinhardt prohibited all large gatherings and marches, threatening to rigorously suppress "every attempt to disturb public peace and order" in Thuringia. Müller additionally granted soldiers in Saxony police authority and ordered that all flyers and new newspapers be subject to military approval.[33]

Gessler exploited his newly gained position to insist on a more hardline approach in Saxony. At the first meeting of Stresemann's second cabinet at noon on October 6, he argued that the imminent convening of the Saxon parliament should be prevented because the Communists had petitioned for an investigation into the Reichswehr and were planning to demand the resignation of the German Reichswehr minister. The three Social Democratic ministers, however, rejected the idea of Berlin intervening against a regional parliament, arguing that such an act would have no legal basis. It was politically "most questionable," they added, to show severity toward Saxony at a time when rebellious Bavarians were effectively being coddled. Gessler threatened to resign, even warning, ominously, that in that scenario he could "not be held responsible for what the Reichswehr would do."[34]

When the cabinet reconvened that evening, Gessler went a step further, demanding that the Saxon government be deposed and an autocratic Reich commissar appointed in its stead. "The nation must exercise its authority over Saxony," he thundered. Stresemann disagreed that the point for such a drastic step had been reached. They would await the Saxon government's next move, he said, while remaining prepared "to utilize the most severe measures." Justice Minister Radbruch supported that view, saying there was no cause to "play the preemptor," and Interior Minister Sollmann argued that Zeigner's position had already been "shaken" and that the cabinet could achieve its goals without sending in federal troops. In the end, Gessler gave in and agreed not to do anything before the Saxon regional parliament was convened. After that, however, "the final consequences" would have to be drawn.[35]

As the 1920 Kapp-Lüttwitz Putsch had also clearly revealed, the tense back-and-forth pointed to a fundamental structural problem of the Weimar Republic, that is, its inability to rely on the Reichswehr. As soon as it wanted to take action against right-wing governments like the one in Bavaria, the political leadership couldn't count on assistance from the military. Yet when it came to left-wing governments like the one in Saxony, the Reichswehr didn't have to be asked twice. In fact, its desire to intervene with force could hardly be restrained.

DEVELOPMENTS IN SAXONY PLAYED into Gessler's hands. On October 5, the KPD, acting on the directive from Zinoviev, declared its willingness to help form a government in Saxony. Five days later, the Social Democratic–Communist coalition was sealed. The KPD received two key ministries—finance under Paul Böttcher and economics under Fritz Heckert—while KPD chairman Brandler was named the director of the Saxon State Chancellery. The coalition agreement foresaw the expansion and arming of the proletarian battalions and the "formation of a central German defensive bloc in Saxony-Thuringia to counter the Bavarian fascist attack."[36] In his governmental address on October 12, Zeigner characterized the re-formed cabinet as a "government of republican and proletarian defense," whose primary task was to "fend off the danger of a military dictatorship of big capitalism."[37]

The SPD and KPD also agreed on a common platform in Thuringia. On October 16, the Communists joined the Frölich government, with Albin Tenner named economics minister and Karl Korsch justice minister. Several days later, Frölich issued a governmental declaration in which he underscored the special situation in Thuringia, which bordered on Bavaria, the regional state in which "the enemies of the Republic" were de facto in charge of the government and were readying a "march on Berlin." That, Frölich warned, would unleash "open bloodshed and civil war" and cause the "disintegration of the German nation." By contrast, Frölich assured his listeners of Thuringia's "unbreakable fidelity" to the unity of Reich and Republic.[38]

With the formation of left-wing unity governments in Saxony and Thuringia, the conflict entered its decisive phase. Those regional governments were the result of democratic means, and in contrast to General State Secretary Kahr in Bavaria, neither Zeigner nor Frölich failed to declare their loyalty to the national government. But the powers-that-be in Berlin were convinced that both men had revolutionary designs. There was no precise information as to what Moscow decided in August and September 1923 concerning the "German October." Nonetheless, Reich Commissar for the Supervision of Public Order Hermann Emil Kuenzer was certain that the Communists entering the regional Saxon and Thuringian governments were plotting a violent national revolution. The entire Communist Party, he fretted, was "at the moment in a state of high alert." In Kuenzer's eyes, the primary threat came from the proletarian battalions: "Their organization is thoroughly military. They want to arm themselves to the greatest extent possible, and military intelligence and courier service have been prepared. They are primarily designed to carry out armed, open rebellion."[39]

General Müller was quick to act. On October 13, he ordered the proletarian battalions and "other similar organizations" disbanded since they exercised the "terror" of a "violent minority" against the vast majority of the population.[40] Three days later, he put the entire Saxon police force under the direct command of the military—a major step toward completely disempowering the Saxon government. But that wasn't enough for the general, who continued to provoke his political adversaries. On October 15, he admonished Zeigner for failing to secure the permission of military command to put up posters of his governmental declaration.[41] Two days later, Müller issued an ultimatum to the state premier, requiring him to distance himself from a speech by his Communist finance minister Paul Böttcher about arming the working classes and the coming "proletarian struggle for liberation."[42]

In a protest to the national government that same day, Zeigner lodged "the most vigorous objection" to Müller's behavior, arguing that his interpretation of the state of emergency would "worsen antipathies and lead to politic unrest." The ban on the proletarian battalions in particular, the state premier fumed, was the "sharpest sort of declaration of war on the governments of the republican-minded regional states." Likewise, the Saxon government had no choice but to resist "the last vestige of sovereignty being taken from [its] hands" when the police were put under military command. All of this, Zeigner wrote, had given the pro-republican segments of the population the impression that the Reichswehr was "primarily taking action against Saxony and the other states with socialist governments . . . while great restraint is being shown toward Bavaria." For that reason, he demanded that the national government end "these intolerable conditions" and suspend the state of emergency and martial law.[43]

On October 18, Zeigner again excoriated the Reichswehr's alleged cooperation with right-wing paramilitary organizations in a speech to the Saxon parliament, this time going so far as to call on French general Charles Nollet from the Military Inter-Allied Commission to end such practices, which violated the Treaty of Versailles. In the eyes of the German military, this was an act of high treason, and it would only be a matter of time until the Reichswehr was sent into Saxony. On the Saxon borders, troops from various district Reichswehr units were readied for a "concentric invasion."[44]

The Communists' entry into the Saxon and Thuringian governments also led Stresemann to abandon his conciliatory position and
take the military's side. During a cabinet meeting of October 17, when
Sollmann described the situation in Saxony and complained in particular about General Müller's behavior, characterizing it as "a provocation for the entire social democratic movement," the chancellor
responded coolly that he considered Zeigner "not a completely men-
tally competent person." The military commander had intervened
with the absolute support of the German president, Stresemann added,
characterizing the moves thus far as "quite moderate." Stern action
had to be taken, he argued, to ward off the danger that segments of the
Saxon bourgeoisie, who felt threatened, would ask Bavaria for help.
"He didn't need to spell out that this would mean civil war and the
disintegration of the nation," read the meeting minutes.[45]

Two days later, Stresemann informed his cabinet that to preserve
law and order in Saxony and Thuringia, Reichswehr troops would be
"assembled at certain points." The minutes recorded him saying, "This
is expected to throw a scare into radical elements, who are readying
for action, and to restore public order and security."[46] In making this
announcement, Stresemann was risking the resignation of the SPD
members of his cabinet. It was obvious that if the Reichswehr intervened against the governments of Saxony and Thuringia, the Social
Democrats would be at their limit.


THAT WAS THE STATE of play when a Communist conference
convened on October 21 in the Saxon city of Chemnitz. Originally,
the KPD had wanted to invite works councils from all over Germany,
but there wasn't enough time to do so after the first reports circulated
on October 20 that the Reichswehr was about to march on Saxony.
The hastily thrown-together event in Chemnitz, in which several
SPD representatives participated along with delegates from the KPD,
some revolutionary works councils, unions, and supervisory committees, was intended to test the attitude among the working classes

toward Communist ideas and, if the result was positive, to proclaim a general strike, which would in turn send a signal for rebellion. The main speakers were Zeigner's SPD labor minister, Georg Graupe, and the Communist ministers Paul Böttcher and Fritz Heckert. All three criticized the tenuous food supply, Germany's catastrophic finances, and the misery of the unemployed. The subsequent discussion focused on the crisis in Saxony and the imminent threat of "military dictatorship."

At that point, KPD chairman Brandler took the floor to call for a vote on a general strike. Yet he was greeted not with applause but with frosty silence. Graupe declared that he and his fellow SPD members would immediately quit the conference if the Communists pushed ahead with the vote. Several years later, August Thalheimer, one of the leading minds of the KPD along with Brandler, recalled, "At a truly revolutionary conference, committed to battle, a storm of outrage would have swept away the spiritless weaklings, but the opposite happened. The conference decided not to hold an immediate vote but instead to name a small commission to make a recommendation. It was a third-class burial."[47]

It was obvious that both the Comintern and the German Communists had misjudged the mood of the German working classes. They couldn't inspire party members to take the plunge into mass revolutionary action even in Saxony. The KPD chose the only option available under the circumstances: without waiting for the arrival of Radek, the party decided to set aside plans for an armed insurrection. Couriers set off from Chemnitz that evening to communicate the decision to the KPD district leadership.[48]

Radek, who arrived from Berlin on October 22, gave the decision his unqualified approval. The idea of "first seizing power in Saxony," then extending it to Germany as a whole, had turned out to be a "total illusion," he reported to Moscow. The same man who only weeks before had thought, despite considerable doubts, that Germany was ready for a proletarian revolution, now dismissed any talk of a general strike unleashing an armed uprising as "empty sloganeering."[49]

ALMOST ALL COMMUNISTS IN Germany strictly abided by the KPD's decision to call off the "German October." The lone exception was an armed uprising in Hamburg on October 23. It has never been conclusively determined how the unrest began. One theory is that it happened accidentally. Due to a series of unfortunate events, the theory goes, word of the KPD leadership's decision didn't reach the northern German city in time. Another hypothesis holds that Hamburg's KPD leadership willfully ignored the news from Chemnitz, believing that by taking to the streets they would make a statement that would launch rebellion across all of Germany.[50]

Whatever the case, the leadership of the Northwest German KPD under Ernst Thälmann, the party's chairman in Hamburg, met on the evening of October 22 and resolved to act the following morning. Since party commandos were inadequately armed, with a mere nineteen rifles and twenty-seven pistols, their first move would be to attack suburban police stations to procure the necessary weaponry. The insurgents would then march on the city center and occupy strategically important locations.[51]

On October 23, at exactly 5:00 a.m., individual commandos began their raids, taking seventeen of the twenty-six police stations they assaulted. Officers were stripped of their guns and ammunition but otherwise, if they didn't resist, were left to their own devices.[52]

Although Hamburg police leaders had received advance warning that something was afoot, the beginning of the rebellion took them by surprise. But they quickly collected themselves and by the afternoon had begun to take countermeasures. The fiercest fighting took place in the traditionally left-wing district of Barmbek, where many people sympathized with the insurgents. Rebels and sympathizers quickly erected barricades, fifty-eight in the southern part of the district alone, with women and children pitching in. "The barricades went up as though growing from soil, multiplying with unbelievable speed," wrote Russian revolutionary Larissa Reissner, Radek's lover, in an article about events in Hamburg.[53] By nighttime, city authorities still hadn't managed to put down the insurrection, and Police Colonel Lothar Danner ordered the fighting to be suspended overnight.

The insurgency in Schiffbek, a working-class neighborhood in eastern Hamburg, was special in that Communists didn't just cut off police stations. They also prepared to declare a republic of councils. A provisional executive committee issued a public declaration threatening looters with the death penalty and calling upon all able-bodied workers to volunteer for the "proletarian self-defense." "Working brothers!" the proclamation read. "Victory is ours! The time is now at hand to defend and expand what we've achieved."[54] The insurrectionists in Schiffbek held out for two days. It wasn't until the fighting in Barmbek ended on the afternoon of October 24 that a large police contingent moved into Schiffbek as well.

Over the course of that day, the KPD leadership in Hamburg decided to quit fighting and make an orderly retreat. It had become evident that, despite their courage, insurrectionists were no match for the police. To make matters worse, the uprising remained an isolated event. Although dock and harbor workers had been on strike since October 20, the rebellion didn't succeed in enlisting them to the cause. To his disappointment, the military director of KPD headquarters, Valdemar Rose, who arrived in Hamburg on October 24, had to admit that they had carried out "a putsch, not a mass action" and that "on the whole, Hamburg workers had not reacted to the insurrection with a general strike."[55] Ultimately, Hamburg, too, showed that the notion of Germany being ripe for a proletarian uprising was completely erroneous.

Twenty-four Communists and seventeen police officers were killed in the fighting, while many others were wounded. There were even more casualties among those who constructed the barricades and on whom police had opened fire. At least sixty-one, many of them women, were killed.[56]

The Hamburg rebellion was the final chapter of the "German October." Moscow began searching for a scapegoat for the disaster and soon found one. In a November 15 missive, the Executive Committee of the Communist International accused the KPD leadership of misrepresenting the situation in Germany: "It is fully clear to us that your reports to Moscow about the level of organizational and technical preparation, particularly in terms of weaponry, were egregiously exaggerated."[57] The Comintern neglected to mention that it had itself grotesquely overestimated Germany's revolutionary potential and had pushed its German comrades toward their fateful adventure. The troika at the head of the Soviet Communist Party (Stalin, Zinoviev, and Lev Kamenev) exploited the criticism of the Brandler group, which was painted as "opportunistic" and "right wing," to go after Trotsky and his supporters.

The debate about the origins of the "October defeat" was thus linked with the battle for power within the Soviet leadership, from which Stalin would emerge triumphant. He and his followers in the Comintern would see to it that the old KPD leadership was replaced with a new one in which party radicals (Ruth Fischer, Arkadi Maslow, Ernst Thälmann) set the tone. The events of October 1923 didn't damage Thälmann's reputation. In fact, the relatively pathetic Hamburg insurrection gave birth to the legend that Thälmann had stood amid the rebels as a glorious hero and an "excellent leader of the Hamburg proletariat."[58]

ON OCTOBER 22, the day after the Chemnitz conference, trains full of Reichswehr soldiers rolled across the Saxon border from all parts of Germany. Before long, sixty thousand federal troops armed for battle were in the regional state. "Saxony is flooded with the Reichswehr," noted Thea Sternheim in Dresden. "Countless groups of six to eight men, heavily armed and imported from Württemberg and Mecklenburg, patrol the streets."[59] Soldiers clashed with civilians in Meissen, Pirna, Freital, Chemnitz, and other locations. In the most serious incident, on October 27 in Freiberg in the foothills of the Erzgebirge range, troops opened fire on demonstrators, killing twenty-three and wounding twenty-one. People were arbitrarily arrested, and prisoners were mistreated.[60] "Anyone who experienced the dull, desperate, impotent rage on the faces and in the words of the workers, together with the grave, sometimes bloody incursion of the Reichswehr, the horrible and ridiculous reports of the regional Reichswehr unit in Dresden, the bloodbath in Freiberg, and the sardonic joy of order-loving citizens, will be forever cured of any illusions about the present-day German Republic," wrote a correspondent in the *Weltbühne*.[61]

On October 25, the Saxon government had its envoy in Berlin, Georg Gradnauer, officially complain about the deployment of the Reichswehr, but it was two days before the cabinet again discussed the issue. At that cabinet meeting, Gessler used the clashes between the military and demonstrators to set in motion an action he had been mulling for some time: he demanded the installation of a Reich commissar in Saxony to exercise state authority until a new government could be formed without the Communists. If no such appointment were made, Gessler insisted, the position of the Reichswehr would become "intolerable." Radbruch objected on legal grounds, arguing that Article 48 of the Weimar Constitution didn't allow for a regional government to simply be dismissed. Moreover, he added, the Reichswehr's aggressive behavior was itself to blame for the troops' situation. Sollmann expressed doubts that the grand coalition could continue if Gessler got his way. Most working people would never understand—and Social Democratic deputies would never approve—a "one-sided action against Saxony."

But Stresemann sided with Gessler, saying that he "couldn't recognize as constitutional" a government with Communist ministers. Yet his true motives become clear when, in the same breath, he asserted that a "restitution of constitutional conditions in Saxony" would "significantly strengthen" the position of the national government with respect to Bavaria. In other words, he hoped by treating the left-wing government in Saxony with severity, he would arrive at a modus vivendi with the Kahr regime in Munich.

Stresemann was supported not only by the cabinet members from the bourgeois parties, who voiced their approval for "energetic action against the intolerable terror from the Left," but also Otto Meissner, the ministerial director in the presidential chancellery, whom Gessler had installed in the cabinet as a hedge against possible objections to his proposal on constitutional grounds. A confidant of Ebert, Meissner summarily declared all the proposed measures constitutional insofar as the Reich president or the wielder of executive authority deemed them necessary for restoring calm and order. At this point, the SPD ministers asked for a recess from the meeting so that they could review the situation and consult with fellow party members.

Once the meeting resumed, Vice-Chancellor and Reconstruction Minister Robert Schmidt announced the results of those consultations. The Social Democrats refused to depose a regional government based on a parliamentary majority that had come to pass in accordance with the Constitution. Instead, an attempt should be made to get Zeigner to step down voluntarily. Should he refuse, the cabinet would be given a "free hand" to take all necessary measures. Following similar lines was an attempt at a compromise solution proposed by Meissner at the behest of Ebert. Stresemann should write to Zeigner, calling on him to resign and setting as short a deadline as possible. At the same time, the Reichswehr minister as the executing authority should make all preparations needed to replace the Saxon government with a Reich commissar should the answer from Dresden prove unsatisfactory. Gessler was none too pleased but assented to the proposal because he didn't want to "ignore the advice of the Reich president." The general outline of the letter to Zeigner was agreed to, and the SPD ministers made no demands to review the final communication beforehand. Radbruch merely requested that the accompanying press release be worded as tactfully as possible to avoid putting the Social Democrats in an even more difficult position.[62]

In fact, the letter Stresemann sent to Zeigner on October 27 dropped all diplomatic niceties. In extremely brusque terms, the chancellor demanded that the Saxon state premier submit his resignation by the end of the following day. Should the government not be re-formed without the Communists, a Reich commissar would be installed to administer Saxony until "constitutional conditions were restored." To justify his demands, Stresemann cited KPD propaganda, particularly Brandler's October 21 speech in Chemnitz calling for the violent overthrow of the Weimar Republic.[63]

In a last-ditch attempt to head off a confrontation, an SPD delegation, including Ministers Schmidt and Radbruch, former finance minister Hilferding, party board member Wilhelm Dittmann, and Saxon envoy in Berlin Gradnauer, went to Dresden to persuade Zeigner to leave office. In the meantime, because of both external pressure and the actions of his Communist ministers, the state premier had himself arrived at the conclusion that the experiment with a left-wing unity government had failed. In consultations with the Berlin delegation on October 28, he agreed not only to stop cooperating with the Communists but to announce he would step down at the October 30 session of the Saxon parliament. But the outrage of the regional labor committee and the majority of the regional SPD parliamentary deputies over Stresemann's ultimatum was so great that they refused to follow the recommendations of their own state premier. That left Zeigner with no option other than to reply that the national government's demands were unconstitutional: "Only the Saxon regional parliament can legitimately depose the Saxon government. As long as that doesn't happen, the members of the Saxon government will remain in their posts."[64]

Before Zeigner's answer arrived in Berlin, Stresemann learned from a semiofficial press release from Dresden that his ultimatum had been rejected. He immediately announced that the national government had resolved to install a Reich commissar in Saxony. Late that evening, he informed Radbruch, Hilferding, and Gradnauer of his decision. Apparently, the SPD leadership had started to wonder whether they might have yielded too much ground the day before, and the three Social Democrats requested that the commissar not take any action unless discussed first in the cabinet. But the chancellor made it clear he wasn't interested in showing regard for his Social Democratic coalition partners. Everything further on the matter of Saxony, he snapped, was contained in his letter to Zeigner, and the cabinet had already extensively covered the consequences of refusing his ulti-matum. After this discussion, Stresemann tried to reach Ebert to ask for permission to seize power in Saxony. But Ebert was asleep, so the chancellor would have to wait several hours.[65]

AROUND 11:00 A.M. ON October 29, a decree from Ebert arrived at the Reich Chancellery authorizing Stresemann under the pow-ers granted in Article 48 of the Weimar Constitution to "relieve . . . members of the Saxon regional government of their duties and entrust other individuals with carrying out those official responsibilities."[66] But even before he had Ebert's authorization in his hands, Stresemann had named Rudolf Heinze as Reich commissar. Heinze, a former min-ister in the Kingdom of Saxony during the Wilhelmine Empire, was hardly an independent, and his appointment was effectively a nod and a favor to Stresemann's old party and industrial friends in the regional state. Heinze made immediate use of his new powers, sending a mil-itary captain at around 12:30 p.m. to tell the Saxon government that it was removed from office and had until 3:00 p.m. to vacate public premises. Ebert was not pleased about Stresemann's display of inde-pendence because he had issued his edict in the expectation that the chancellor would reach an agreement with the party leaders in his cab-inet before taking any concrete steps.[67]

Stresemann had in fact convened those party leaders at 11:00 a.m., but by that point Heinze's appointment was a fait accompli. That drew bitter recriminations from the chairman of the SPD parliamen-tary group, Hermann Müller. Nothing was being done in Bavaria, he complained, while the harshest measures were employed against Sax-ony. Supporters of the Weimar Republic felt betrayed, he added, and if Stresemann continued to apply double standards, it would be impossi-ble to convince a majority in his parliamentary group to remain in the coalition. Stresemann defended his actions, arguing that conditions in Bavaria would not return to normal until the Saxon issue had been "cleaned up."[68]

*The national government sends troops into Saxony: a company
of Reichswehr soldiers on their way to the Saxon regional
parliament building in Dresden to dissolve that body.*

Stresemann continued to defend his policies against Social Democratic criticism in the subsequent cabinet meeting. Sollmann complained that Stresemann had neglected to procure a cabinet resolution before appointing Heinze. "He said he considered the path chosen wrong and in particular the appointment of a DVP member misguided," the minutes of the meeting read. Schmidt argued that no further major measures should be taken until an attempt had been made to form a new government without Zeigner. The SPD protest seemed to have some effect. In the end, Stresemann promised to tell the commissar "not to take any steps before he had received further instructions."[69]

But in Dresden, Heinze had already created a new predicament. Shortly after 3:00 p.m., while the cabinet was still convening, he sent a Reichswehr company, with weapons drawn and heralded by marching music, to the Saxon Ministry of State to remove those ministers who refused to leave. A short time later, another Reichswehr company occupied the Saxon regional parliament building, refusing entry to elected deputies. "The city and its inhabitants are extraordinarily tense," reported a special correspondent from the *Vossische Zeitung*. "After dark, Reichswehr soldiers on bicycles and in motor vehicles crisscrossed the streets, where a massive crowd of people ebbed and flowed. Only the next few days will show where things are headed."[70]

The Reichswehr's ruthless behavior in deposing the Saxon government was the subject of intense arguments in the national cabinet meeting on the evening of October 29. Stresemann admitted that "much has happened in Dresden that could have been done differently" but disputed that the military and Heinze had intend to provoke anyone. Sollmann countered that he and his fellow Social Democratic ministers weren't prepared to take responsibility for developments in Saxony and saw no other option than to quit the cabinet. The final decision, however, would be left up to the SPD parliamentary group. Stresemann and the cabinet members from the bourgeois parties appealed to the Social Democrats not to act rashly. Stresemann also held out the prospect of the first hopeful signs of French conciliation on reparations. It would be "almost like a blow of fate" if such a promising development were scuttled by an internal government crisis.[71] But Stresemann's remarks betrayed not the slightest acknowledgment that it was his own brusque ultimatum to Zeigner and overly hasty appointment of Heinze that had gotten him into the dilemma he now bemoaned.

Stresemann made several attempts on October 29 to rein in his all-too-independent and industrious Reich commissar. Without any explicit authorization, Heinze had already begun forming an extreme right-wing "cabinet of civil servants" to bypass the regional parliament entirely.[72] Stresemann put a stop to that, ordering Heinze to end the military occupation of the parliament building in Dresden and allow parliamentary groups to meet. The idea was that they would of their own accord form a government, albeit one with no Communists. Stresemann also emphasized that as soon as orderly conditions had been restored in Saxony, the mandate of the Reich commissar would expire.[73]

The military withdrew from the parliament building the next morning. After lengthy debate, the SPD parliamentary group, supported by the SPD bigwigs Otto Wels and Wilhelm Dittmann, who had hastily arrived from Berlin, agreed to put forth former economics minister Alfred Fellisch to head a purely Social Democratic minority government. On October 31, SPD and DDP deputies elected Fellisch to succeed Zeigner. The new state premier immediately sent Stresemann a telegram announcing the formation of an "impeccably" constitutional government and demanded the swift withdrawal of the Reich commissar. The following day, Ebert, at Stresemann's request, revoked his edict of October 29, putting an end to Heinze's short-lived regime.[74]

Even after being deposed, Erich Zeigner remained in the crosshairs of his political adversaries. In November 1923, he was arrested and convicted by the regional court in Leipzig on charges of passive corruption during his time as Saxon minister of justice and sentenced to three years imprisonment. When he was released, he would face disciplinary proceedings that resulted in punitive cuts to his state pension.[75]

THE MILITARY HAD NO interest whatsoever in a speedy resolution to the crisis in Saxony. It was already disappointed that Ebert had given Stresemann and not the Reichswehr minister, Gessler, the mandate to enforce the authority of the national government over the regional state. Even worse, the Social Democrats continued to head the Saxon government, and Heinze was forced out after only two days: the military had hoped the office of the Reich commissar would be a means of seizing decisive power in the region. The "overly hasty formation of a new government" in response to pressure from Stresemann and its recognition by Berlin, combined with the dismissal of Heinze, had had a "positively paralyzing effect," General Müller reported from Dresden. "The wheel we thought had finally and hopefully begun to roll forward ... has suddenly been halted. Indeed, it's begun rolling backward. ... The deployment of the Reichswehr will have been for naught if the Fellisch government remains at the helm."[76]

On November 6, the new Saxon state premier filed a complaint with Germany's highest court, the Staatsgerichtshof, against the federal intervention in the regional state. It argued that the Reich president's October 29 edict, which was based on Article 48, had exceeded his authority and violated the German Constitution.[77] Ebert accepted responsibility for the edict but pointed out that the chancellor had been the one to enact it—a further indication that he had by no means approved of all the measures taken by Stresemann. After a lengthy back-and-forth, Saxony withdrew its complaint in 1926.[78]

Contemporary commentators already saw the imposition of national rule on Saxony as a dangerous precedent. Bernhard, for instance, wrote in the *Vossische Zeitung*, "What has happened to Saxony today can be visited tomorrow on any regional state. Imagine what the consequences would be if an ultranationalist German government decided to dissolve the Prussian government. . . . We have to admit that we have a sinking feeling when we see how the constitution is being applied right now."[79] That scenario would indeed come to pass in July 1932, when Chancellor Franz von Papen's presidential regime simply removed the Prussian government under state premier Otto Braun by fiat.

In a letter to the chancellor on October 30, the Thuringian regional government, too, had lodged the "most vigorous protest" against the "unconstitutional" intervention in Saxony, saying that it feared the same instrument would be employed against Thuringia.[80] As it happened, that regional state was spared. Nonetheless, on November 6, Gessler strengthened troops under General Reinhardt, ostensibly to protect Thuringia against attacks from right-wing gangs from Bavaria but actually to increase pressure on the regional government to dismiss its two Communist ministers. On November 12, those ministers, Karl Korsch and Albin Tenner, resigned, and Frölich remained state premier in a minority Social Democratic government.[81] By that point, the SPD had already quit the grand coalition in Berlin.

AS WAS ONLY TO be expected, the brutal coup against the Zeigner government unleashed howls of protest from SPD supporters. "Great uproar in Social Democratic circles," noted Stresemann in his calendar on October 30.[82] People were particularly outraged at the government treating Bavaria and Saxony so differently. No one in the SPD faithful could understand targeting the latter with such draconian severity while ignoring the constant provocations from the former.[83] Even when, on October 20, Kahr not only openly refused to dismiss District Reichswehr Commander General von Lossow but promoted him to Bavarian regional commander and put the Seventh Reichswehr Division under the command of the Bavarian regional government, there was no meaningful reaction from Berlin.

As we have seen, on the evening of October 29, Sollmann had already announced the resignation of the Social Democratic ministers from the Stresemann cabinet, albeit leaving the final decision in the hands of the Social Democratic parliamentary group. Two days later, that group convened for acrimonious debates between supporters and opponents of the grand coalition. The president of the Reichstag, Paul Löbe, no longer considered it sensible to remain in the government to prevent things from getting worse. Instead, he declared, "Back to class struggle in its pure form!" Severing, no doubt also concerned about preserving the grand coalition in his own regional state, countered: "Think of the consequences!" In the end, a large majority followed Hermann Müller's recommendation and issued new conditions for the SPD to remain in the government. Social Democrats demanded 1) the lifting of the military state of emergency; 2) an unambiguous declaration by the national government that it considered the actions of those in power in Bavaria as a "violation of the Constitution" and would take "immediate, appropriate steps" against it; and 3) the limitation of Reichswehr activities in Saxony to assisting civilian authorities and the discharge of members of extreme right-wing movements from the force.[84]

"Even if nothing certain can be said about the outcome of negotiations between the government and the Social Democrats," prophesied the *Vossische Zeitung*, "you would be well-advised not to be too optimistic about the prospects for a continuation of the grand coalition."[85] Indeed, at the cabinet meeting on November 1, which had been postponed from the morning to the evening after Stresemann came down with a cold, all signs pointed to a breakup. Sollmann laid out the SPD's demands, telling the bourgeois party members in the cabinet they had to decide "whether they want to govern through the winter with or without the Social Democrats." Stresemann said he regretted that the SPD parliamentary group's decision had immediately become public. It was imperative "at all costs" to avoid the impression that the coalition stood "under Marxist pressure." In any case, it was "impossible for a coalition government to accept ultimatums from any one parliamentary group." And for practical reasons, the military state of emergency could not be revoked given the tense domestic situation.

Gessler was blunter. With regard to Bavaria, there were two paths: a strictly constitutional one that would inevitably lead to secession or a negotiated one that, however, couldn't be taken while the SPD was still part of the national government. "The Social Democrats must consider whether they want to depart the government in this situation," Gessler said. "If that happened, Mr. von Lossow would immediately disappear."[86] There was no ambiguity anymore. No one contradicted the minister responsible for the exercise of state force as he blamed Social Democrats for the Bavarian crisis and practically pushed them out the door. Gessler's statement was, in the words of historian Heinrich August Winkler, "nothing less than a partial capitulation to Bavarian general state commissar von Kahr and the forces that supported him."[87]

In a separate meeting with Stresemann on the morning of November 2, cabinet members from the bourgeois parties unanimously rejected the SPD's demands. Even Transportation Minister Oeser from the DDP, previously one of the most enthusiastic supporters of the grand coalition, believed that nothing more could be achieved "by long-term cooperation with the Social Democrats." He added, "We now have to stop forever going around in circles." Stresemann cautioned that the bourgeois remnants of the cabinet might not command a majority at the next session of the Reichstag. Thus he could only continue to govern if he secured orders from the German president to dissolve parliament and call for new elections.[88]

In the subsequent cabinet meeting on November 2, Stresemann made the position of the bourgeois parties known. "With that," Sollmann attested, "the breakup has become inevitable." However, Schmidt declared that it was "not absolutely impossible" for the SPD to remain in the cabinet, saying, "The parliamentary group will have to decide about that."[89] There was no doubt, however, what decision SPD delegates would reach. That afternoon, they opted—with only nineteen dissensions—to withdraw the party's ministers from the cabinet. At 6:00 p.m., the three Social Democratic ministers tendered their resignations to the chancellor.[90]

THE FIRST GRAND COALITION under Stresemann, which had taken office with such high hopes, had come apart after only two and a half months. Its demise also put an end to the emergency powers act that was nominally valid until March 31, 1924, but that automatically became null and void when the constellation of political parties in the government changed. For seventy-two-year-old Hermann Molkenbuhr, the longest-serving member of the SPD party board, the parliamentary group's decision was an act of "stupidity." He argued, "We're maneuvering ourselves out of government and creating a situation the reactionaries in Bavaria and the landed aristocracy would have been unable to bring about on their own."[91] But Molkenbuhr was arguably demanding too much compromise. How could the SPD remain in a cabinet whose bourgeois majority refused to take energetic action against the rebellious Kahr regime but had no scruples about using an iron fist against the left-wing governments in Saxony and Thuringia? And the leading Social Democratic functionaries couldn't predict that after leaving the Stresemann government they would spend almost five years outside national power.

The leftist segment of the pro-democracy press expressed deep regrets about the breakup of the grand coalition, albeit with considerable understanding for the bind in which the SPD found itself. The three conditions Social Democrats had named for remaining in the cabinet could have provided a basis for collective understanding had the coalition members from the bourgeois parties not feared losing face and rejected them out of hand, wrote Erich Dombrowski in the *Berliner Tageblatt*. But the Social Democrats' tactical clumsiness, he asserted, had "given all the light-brown [quasi-fascist] elements on the Right and quasi-Right the opportunity they had long desired to force the 'Marxists' from the coalition and the national government."[92] Bernhard, for his part, reminded readers of the *Vossische Zeitung* that from the start, the reshuffled Stresemann cabinet had experienced "significant birth pains under the influence of large-scale industrialist intrigues." With the breakup of the grand coalition, the "efforts to undermine social democracy" had achieved another incremental victory. Ultimately, Bernhard argued, the right-wing attacks had targeted the Social Democratic Reich president Ebert and Stresemann himself, whom the extreme Right saw as the main obstacles to establishing an authoritarian regime.[93]

The *Deutsche Allgemeine Zeitung* couldn't conceal its glee at the SPD's withdrawal from the government, endorsing wholesale the positions Gessler had represented in the cabinet meetings. A break had become "unavoidable," the paper wrote, since as long as Social Democrats controlled national policy, "no determined stance . . . externally, as well as no satisfactory agreements with the powerful right-wing segments of society internally and no compromise in Bavaria, would ever be possible." In a further dig, the paper concluded that the fruitless attempts to reach any deals with this "obsolete and disintegrating party" had been bound to fail sooner or later.[94]

How could things continue? The remnants of Stresemann's cabinet had found themselves in a situation that was anything but enviable. The cabinet no longer had a parliamentary majority, and it was unclear whether the SPD would tolerate a minority regime. If the Social Democrats left the cabinet, Sollmann had warned on November 1, it would be impossible to maintain a "benevolent neutrality."[95] Nonetheless,

Stresemann decided to pursue a minority cabinet, while telling his
ministers on November 5, the day before the formation of his second
grand coalition, that he was "prepared at any time . . . to cede his position to men who enjoyed the trust of the nation at a higher level." But
he continued to say that it was "impossible to resign his office in such
a labile and unsettled situation as the one at present." On the contrary,
he had a responsibility to carry out the task with which the Reich president had entrusted him and "take hold of the rudder."[96]

Although there were three vacant ministerial posts, Stresemann
named only one successor, appointing as the head of the Interior Ministry former Duisburg mayor Karl Jarres, who had been deported from
the occupied Ruhr and who, much to the dismay of the DDP, had
close ties to the right wing of the DVP.[97] Apparently, the chancellor
intended this decision to mollify his own party, which was pressur-
ing him to move to the right, in the best-case scenario by cutting a
deal with the DNVP. But Stresemann had assured his ministers from
bourgeois parties on November 2 that he had no plans to form "a cabinet with an ultranationalist character" since he knew only too well
that neither the DDP not the Center Party would go along with that.[98]
Thus, the chancellor was still on shaky ground, all the more so because
various plots to establish a right-wing dictatorship were about to cul-
minate in an attempted coup.

# CHAPTER 5

# THE CALL FOR
# A DICTATORSHIP

*The Shock Troop Hitler Munich, a group of Hitler bodyguards
who took part in what is often known as the Beer Hall Putsch.*

I N MID-SEPTEMBER 1923, ONLY A FEW DAYS BEFORE passive resistance came to an end in the Ruhr Valley, Hugo Stinnes invited American ambassador Alanson Houghton to a meeting in Berlin. What the industrial magnate told Houghton in confidence so alarmed him that several days later he drew up a lengthy report for Secretary of State Hughes. "The end is nigh," Stinnes had said at the start of the meeting. "The Ruhr and the Rhineland have no choice but to capitulate." To prevent the German economy from collapsing completely, production would have to be increased significantly, something only possible with the reintroduction of a "normal ten-hour workday." Since the working classes resisted this demand, they would have to be forced. "For that reason . . . a dictator must be found, equipped with all the power to do anything remotely necessary. Such a man has to speak the language of the people and himself be bourgeois, and such a man stood at the ready." Stinnes didn't reveal whom he had in mind, and as Houghton asked him what France would think about the installation of a dictator in Germany, Stinnes responded that no one would be asked for permission.

The ambassador made no attempt to conceal his skepticism but wanted to know more. Stinnes presented the following scenario. By mid-October, three to four million Germans would be unemployed, and the Communists would try to launch an armed insurrection. Because the Stresemann government would prove unable to resolve the situation, Reich president Ebert would equip either a lone individual or possibly a three-man directorship with full dictatorial powers and put this person or these people in charge of the military. "From then on the parliamentary government will be over," Stinnes said. "The Communists would be ruthlessly smashed, and if they called for a general strike, this, too, would be put down by force." If everything went according to plan, Stinnes told Houghton, the whole thing would be finished within three weeks, with socialism "swept away forever as a form of politics in Germany." Stinnes's only worry was that the Right would strike first rather than waiting for the Communists to act. The provocation had to originate from the Left, in Stinnes's eyes, or else the "outside world" would turn against a right-wing Germany.

Houghton wasn't certain how seriously Stinnes embraced these views. But the ambassador's report to his superior left no doubt that if the magnates of industry did in fact support right-wing plans for a coup, a decisive crisis would follow.[1]

CALLS FOR A STRONGMAN, a savior to lift Germany out of misery and desperation, had been constant since the collapse of the Wilhelmine German Empire in 1918. Indeed, they grew louder on the political Right in the initial, chaotic postwar years.[2] It was expected that a charismatic leader could liberate Germany from the trauma of defeat and lead the country to new national glory. Domestically, the leader was to make short work of the "economy of political parties" and create order by ruthlessly sweeping out the filth. The March 1920 monthly report of the Bavarian regional recruitment center of Reichswehr Group Commando 4 read, "Again and again, loud calls go up for a dictator who will tackle with the utmost severity the corruption that reaches all the way up to the highest circles."[3]

That month, on March 13, right-wing enemies of the Weimar Republic tried for the first time to seize power. But the Kapp-Lüttwitz Putsch, backed by military leaders and Prussian aristocrats, failed after meeting stiff resistance from the working classes. The largest general strike in German history to that point forced the conspirators to give up after a few days.[4] Still, would-be insurgents continued to plot to bring down German democracy, despite significant differences of opinion on the anti-democratic Right. While monarchists dreamed of a return to Wilhelmine authoritarianism, racists wanted to create an ethnically homogenous "popular community" under strict dictatorial leadership.

The desire to bring down democracy enjoyed the powerful support of the Pan-Germanic League (Alldeutscher Verband), which had already been at the vanguard of extreme German nationalism in Wilhelmine Germany. Led by chairman Heinrich Class, the league's desire to destroy parliamentary democracy and create a "national dictatorship" became the central political platform of the Far Right in the early 1920s.[5] Both monarchists and racist nationalists considered Social Democratic president Friedrich Ebert a major obstacle to realizing their goals. In October 1922, when the Reichstag agreed to extend Ebert's term in office until June 1925, thereby postponing the popular election mandated by the Weimar Constitution, Georg Escherich, the leader of one of the most prominent German anti-democratic militias, fumed in a letter to Stinnes that the move had prevented "a shift in the relations of power toward the nationalist side." The "president, tied down to the Social Democrats and to the demagoguery of the masses," he contended, needed to be replaced with a "representative of the Reich ... capable of awakening all nationalist energies through the strength of his personality." As Escherich made abundantly clear, he was envisioning a leader, a *Führer,* who would liberate himself from all the "impotent parliamentarianism."[6]

AS GERMANY'S SITUATION DETERIORATED in the spring of 1923, hopes for a national messiah grew and grew. The ultraconservative nationalist professor Karl Alexander von Müller, whose Munich lectures were regularly attended by Rudolf Hess and Hermann Göring, would later recall that even among academic circles at the time, there was lots of talk of the necessity of a dictatorship as the only way out. It was part of the legacy of the Bismarck era "that a great many—indeed what felt like most—Germans sought salvation in a lone, great individual."[7]

The example of Italy, where Benito Mussolini had seized power in a coup in late October 1922, fired the imaginations of those Germans who despised the Weimar Republic. For example, the son of a prominent publisher and an early fellow traveler with Hitler, Ernst Hanfstaengl, observed "a certain aggressive admiration for what had taken place south of the Alps, for the elan of the fascist movement, for Mussolini and New Italy" among the bourgeois patrons who frequented Munich's Hofgarten park. He recorded typical statements, such as "yes, indeed, we need someone like that in charge—a Renaissance man and Machiavellian, someone without scruples."[8]

In late July 1923, an article for the Center Party's newspaper *Germania,* which rang in the end of the Cuno government, wrote of hearing "from almost all social circles, even those on the left, calls for a dictatorship or the installment of a public welfare committee that would have to be given the authority to take dictatorial measures."[9] By mid-August, the left-leaning *Tage-Buch* published a diagnosis by the liberal Italian historian Guglielmo Ferrero that had originally run under the title "In Search of a Dictator" in Milan's *Il Secolo,* before that newspaper was taken over by the fascists. It argued, "Under today's conditions, the striving for a dictatorship, so widespread among the educated and uneducated alike, is nothing but a romantic form of cowardice. Many people are looking for a dictator because they hope he will know what they all do not and that he will find what all of them search for in vain: a cure to end the various ills afflicting the world." *Tage-Buch* editors prefaced the article with the remark that it was important to become acquainted with the opinion of this "greatest of all living historical researchers" because "the idea of 'dictatorship' is being considered everywhere in our society right now."[10]

The philosopher, battalion leader, and highly decorated First World War officer Ernst Jünger was one of the intellectuals who joined in the chorus of those calling for dictatorship. In his first political article after being discharged from the Reichswehr, he wrote in the culture section of the Nazi newspaper *Völkischer Beobachter* on September 23, 1923, "The true revolution has yet to take place. It is marching unstoppably forward. It is not a reaction. It is a real revolution with all its characteristics and statements. Its basic idea is the racist one, honed to previously unknown incisiveness, its banner the swastika, its form of expression the concentration of will onto a single point—dictatorship!"[11]

In his book *The Third Reich*, published in the fall of 1923, right-wing intellectual and "conservative revolutionary" Arthur Moeller van den Bruck attacked the liberal parliamentary democracy of the Weimar Republic as a system imposed by the West and alien to German political tradition. As an alternative, he sketched out the contours of a new order, which would free itself from what he considered the paralytic rule of political parties and combine the age-old dream of a German empire with the racist principle of a strongman Führer: "We need . . . racial leaders whom we . . . have no need of asking which party they belong to because their party, right from the start, is Germany."[12] The idea of the "Third Reich" would of course be adopted by the Nazis to great propagandistic effect.

Even high representatives of the Weimar Republic made statements in August and September 1923 that no longer ruled out a dictatorial solution as a last resort to resolve the crisis. The Social Democrat Wilhelm Sollmann, for instance, declared in a cabinet meeting on September 23 that if the Stresemann government should fail, a "certain amount of dictatorship" would perhaps be unavoidable "under the circumstances." In late September, when the grand coalition faced that scenario for the first time, Sollmann came out in favor of a temporary suspension of the rules of parliamentary democracy given the perils of the moment: "The signs of storms brewing on the Right and Left are constantly multiplying. . . . It is generally felt that dictatorial measures are needed. But a form will have to be found that doesn't cause major new turmoil."[13] The interior minister apparently meant an emergency government, supported by the president and operating on the basis of Article 48, that would temporarily divorce itself from the Reichstag—but without fully emasculating the parliament or setting up a permanent authoritarian regime, as enemies of the Weimar Republic envisioned.

THE HOPES OF BOURGEOIS right-wingers, the business community, and the military focused on one man in particular: the head of army command, Hans von Seeckt, who seemed to them to be best able to master the extraordinary situation. As of mid-September 1923, immediately before passive resistance was discontinued in the Ruhr, people on many sides beseeched the commander to forgo neutrality and become politically active. On September 19 and 20, leading representatives of the Reich Rural League (Reichslandbund), a lobby of powerful large agriculturalists east of the Elbe River, met with Seeckt and implored him to deploy all the resources of the Reichswehr to eradicate "every Social Democratic influence on the government." In return, they declared themselves prepared to provide the general with "large quantities of food in the case of a dictatorship."[14]

Three days later, representatives from the DNVP, Oskar Hergt and Count Kuno von Westarp, also paid their respects, telling Seeckt they would love to see him in the role of a "military chancellor" since they had no faith in Stresemann. The general was wary of such advances. Confidants in the Reichswehr Ministry, especially Major General Otto Hasse, the head of the "troop office," a cover for officially prohibited German General Staff, had strongly advised him, as a potential future dictator, not to make himself "dependent on the wishes of any one party." The German nationalists only wanted to use him in order to "get to the trough themselves."[15]

Seeckt was also courted by the nationalist associations, and on September 24, Heinrich Class paid him a visit. The chairman of the Pan-Germanic League had already tried to enlist the general to the cause of a military dictatorship at two meetings in February and March and had come away with the impression Seeckt wasn't disinclined. But Class was disappointed by their talks this time. Seeckt left no doubts that he would oppose any attempt at a putsch, whether from the Right or Left, with all means at his disposal. From that point on, Pan-Germanic League circles considered Seeckt an "Ebert devotee," whose insistence on legality prevented the steps necessary to set up a "national dictatorship."[16]

Another person Seeckt disappointed was Oswald Spengler. The Munich writer, whose 1918 tome *The Decline of the West* had made him popular among ultranationalists and racists, was aligned with the industrial magnate Paul Reusch, also an enemy of parliamentary democracy and a supporter of an authoritarian resolution to the crisis. Spengler gained access to Seeckt on Reusch's recommendation, but their discussions went nowhere. Subsequently, Spengler dismissed the head of the Reichswehr as a "complete opportunist," and Seeckt wrote his wife that he wished Spengler "had declined along with the West— he's a political fool."[17]

On September 25, Seeckt received Friedrich Minoux, the director general of the Berlin division of the Stinnes conglomerate and a confidant of its conservative owner. Minoux was no stranger to the head of army command. In February, Seeckt had gone to Minoux's villa in the upscale district of Wannsee to meet General Erich Ludendorff, Germany's de facto dictator in the final two years of the First World War.

*One of the main figures
in the story of right-wing
unrest in the fall of 1923
was the head of the army
command, Reichswehr
General Hans von Seeckt,
shown here with Reichswehr
Minister Otto Gessler.
Seeckt sympathized with
the enemies of the Weimar
Republic but refused
to violate the Weimar
Constitution.*

In August, Minoux had put forward a plan of his own for reforming the currency. Now he wanted to introduce a whole political program that was "massive in all areas" and would "change the entire internal structure" of Germany. Major General Hasse noted that "Seeckt was bowled over by the gigantic impression made by this personality."[18]

Minoux's ideas influenced two documents Seeckt drew up in September to prepare himself should he be suddenly called upon to form a new government. One was entitled "Government Policy," the other "Government Declaration," and they were basically identical. In the draft of his governmental declaration, Seeckt wrote, "In a serious and difficult hour, a soldier has been summoned to head the government, and as a soldier serving the government, I have heeded that summons." In the document's introduction, the cabinet to be named under his authority was described as "a government of an emergency and transitional state," whose main task was to "preserve and shore up the unity of the nation externally and internally."

When it came to foreign policy, Seeckt favored fulfilling the terms of the Treaty of Versailles until "a new foreign policy constellation allows a revision." While recognizing "the duty of reparations," he strictly opposed "any new obligations beyond the lines of the Treaty of Versailles." To bolster the secret cooperation between the Reichswehr and the Red Army, Seeckt supported enhanced efforts to deepen Germany's economic, political, and military relations with the Soviet Union.

Seeckt's domestic policy was to be governed by the principle that "all hostility acts directed against the continued existence of the Reich and the order of state was to be put down by employing national force." As he had in his meetings with Class and Spengler, Seeckt pledged to oppose "all efforts to bring about a coup d'état." The general wasn't categorically against changing the foundations of the Weimar Constitution, but he felt that any such alteration should be postponed "until a calmer hour."

Most of his economic program was music to the ears of German industry. "Decisive refutation of Marxist theory and practice, especially the abandonment of all efforts at socializing [private property]," Seeckt wrote. Unions were to be replaced by professional chambers, which would be far more favorable to the interests of employers, but the right to strike would be preserved. On the controversial issue of the workday, Seeckt stopped short of Stinnes's demands: "Revocation of the absolute eight-hour template, which will remain the basis for labor performance but which is to be increased or decreased depending on the type of work."[19]

Seeckt seems to have envisioned a three-man directorship of the sort Stinnes had raised in his talks with the American ambassador. Seeckt himself would serve as spiritus rector, while the most promising candidates for the remaining spots in the troika were Minoux and Germany's ambassador to the United States, Otto Wiedfeldt. In late September and early October, Seeckt had several talks with them about the crisis within the Stresemann cabinet and a possible new direction for the government.[20] Because Ebert charged Stresemann with forming a new government on October 3, even after the resignation of his first cabinet, and Stresemann was able to continue leading the grand coalition, Seeckt's plans would never come to fruition. But the general remained a figure of hope for many Germans. "Internal situation very confused," noted Hasse. "The idea that only a strongman, a soldier, can help is gaining ground in the Reichstag as well. Seeckt is often named."[21]

This tense situation was further exacerbated by the news of a right-wing putsch. On October 1, retired Major Ernst Buchrucker and a five-hundred-man battalion attempted to take control of an old Prussian fortress in Küstrin an der Oder (today, Kostrzyn nad Odrą, Poland). The intention was to spark a national right-wing rebellion, but the Reichswehr quickly put down the insurrection, which came at a bad time in the eyes of Far Right strategists, who wanted the Communists to move first and thus provide justification for their own agitation. "In any case, this unprecedented incident illustrated the domestic perils and the gravity of the situation and should end, once and for all, the hypocritical efforts of German racists and ultranationalists, whose threat as sources of right-wing putsches has always been dismissed as the product of overactive imaginations," wrote the *Berliner Tageblatt.*[22] Meanwhile Carl von Ossietzky warned in the *Berliner Volks-Zeitung* on October 5 that "support is diligently being whipped up for a 'directorship' on the narrowest of bases, that of bayonets." The time of a "great decision" had arrived: "On the one side is parliamentarianism, democracy, and a state based on the authority and will of the people—and on the other dictatorship, fascism, a copy of Mussolini, and caprice."[23]

THE PLANS FOR ESTABLISHING a "national dictatorship" had progressed further in Bavaria. There, it was primarily the National Socialists who benefited politically from Germany's catastrophic economy. "Whereas political gatherings are otherwise only moderately attended due to the enormous prices for admission and beer, National Socialist rallies constantly sell out their locations," the Munich police directorate reported in early September 1923.[24] Great numbers of people were drawn to the Nazis over the course of the year. Between January and November, the party registered 47,000 new members, taking its total to 55,000.

The main attraction was the party chairman, Adolf Hitler, who had elbowed his way past all party competitors in July 1921. With his hateful tirades against the "November criminals," the "shameful peace of Versailles," and international "Jewish lending and stock exchange capital," he filled Munich's biggest venues week after week. Like no other, Hitler understood how to stir his listeners' emotions, playing on their fears and resentments like a skilled pianist. "The fact that none of the large event venues in Munich, not even the Zirkus [Krone] can accommodate the crowds, so that thousands of people are turned away, is today already considered standard," reported the *Kölnische Volkszeitung* in early November 1922.[25]

Stefan Grossmann, the publisher of the *Tage-Buch*, was one of the few journalists who gave early warning not to underestimate the danger Hitler represented. All the repugnance for the Munich demagogue notwithstanding, he pointed out, it was "foolish" to deny his "indisputable talents," above all his abilities as a speaker: "In the Zirkus, his preferred speaking venue of late, he commands the gigantic space. He possesses a national pathos that comes from deep within, he carries people along, and he knows exactly when Munich audiences are tired of being serious, when he needs to switch to Bavarian-Austrian dialect, and even when, as a last resort, he has to pull out some humorous Jewish-isms."[26]

A Munich woman who attended one of these overcrowded rallies wrote to Hitler in a letter that he had "spoken with such warmth and such passion for the cause" that his speech "could hardly have passed anyone by without leaving an impression." The hours had been "a miraculous elevation" that had reminded her of the days "when our troops marched out of Berlin on August 14 [1914]." Her daughter added both a "German greeting" and the words, "Germany's youth still recalls the traditions of its fathers and will prove this in the hour of action."[27]

The greater the response Hitler was able to draw, the more self-confident he grew and the more convinced he became that he had been chosen for a special historic mission. Whereas in the initial years of his career he had seen himself as a "drum major," whose task was to prepare the ground for a future dictator, he increasingly saw himself in the role of the Führer and savior, called to liberate Germany from its "shame and misery" and put it back on the "world stage." When he declared in early December 1922, "We need a strongman, and the National Socialists will produce one," he was thinking of himself.[28]

CONTRIBUTING TO the change in Hitler's self-understanding was the worship he received from his entourage. Impressed by Mussolini's "March on Rome," some of his closest followers began to promote an idea of a German *Führer* based on the Italian *duce*. "What a horde of courageous men in Italy were able to do, we can in Bavaria as well," Nazi journalist Hermann Esser proclaimed in early November 1922 in the Löwenbräukeller beer hall. "We have our own Mussolini. His name is Adolf Hitler."[29]

In the fall of 1922, Munich University announced a prize for the best essay on the topic "How will the man be created who will lead Germany back to its former heights?" The winner was a student named Rudolf Hess, one of Hitler's earliest party comrades. Hess submitted a portrait of a dictator equipped with "the power of motivating speech" and awaited by millions of Germans as the coming messiah. In a letter to Karl Alexander von Müller, Hess confessed that he had Hitler in mind. In "many respects," Hess wrote, he had envisioned Hitler in this exalted role as he had gotten to know him "after two and a half years of sometimes daily contact." He reiterated that to set in motion the "spiritual renewal" and "moral recovery" of the German people, a man was needed at the top "who had the power and will to carry out the commensurate measures."[30]

The cult of the Führer reached an initial high point on April 20, 1923, Hitler's thirty-fourth birthday. The *Völkischer Beobachter* ran a

banner headline reading "Germany's Führer" atop a poem by the journalist and former Hitler mentor Dietrich Eckart:

> *Five years of misery, such as no people has known*
> *Five years of filth, and mountains of vulgarity*
> *Destroyed all the proud fire and purity*
> *And all the greatness Bismarck once made our own!"*

But the savior, in Eckart's verses, was already waiting in the wings.
"Raise your hearts! He who wants to see, will see! / The strength is
there, before which the darkness will flee!"[31] In the same edition of
the newspaper, Alfred Rosenberg, who had replaced Eckart the month
before as its editor in chief, also praised Hitler's positive effect on Germany. Masses of desperate people longing for a "Führer of the German
people," he wrote, were looking "with increasing hope at the man in
Munich." Rosenberg added, "We can already say today that the name
Hitler has taken on a mystical ring—and not only for us. One day,
under the name, the German people will be separated into the wheat
and the chaff."[32]

The unique mutual reinforcement between Hitler's self-image as a
national savior and the hopes and expectations for a messiah his followers projected onto him was reflected in the countless congratulations he received on his birthday. A letter from a postal secretary in
Breslau read, "For us you are the breaking of dawn and the only ray of
hope in the lamentations of the present day. The eyes of all suffering
Germans are today directed toward you as a figure of leadership."[33]

Among the congratulants was one of Hitler's former comrades
in the List Regiment during the First World War. He sent the Nazi
chairman several photos from their days in battle and concluded with
the words, "My dear Hitler, those who have had the opportunity to
follow you from the start of the movement until today cannot help
but honor you. . . . You have achieved what no other German man has
been able to, and we front-line comrades stand at your disposal to do
with as you see fit."[34]

DESPITE MANY PROVOCATIONS, THE Bavarian regional government was remarkably tolerant of Nazi agitation. "Fascism, which in Munich goes under the name of the 'National Socialist Workers Party' [*sic*] is blossoming, growing, and flourishing under the protection of the authorities," criticized the *Weltbühne*.[35] Apparently the Bavarian leadership feared losing popular support if it decisively went after Hitler, who was becoming increasingly well regarded in conservative circles.[36] The result was that his supporters could more or less occupy public spaces in Munich whenever they wanted and act with ever greater impunity. Their activities were more and more directed not just against the political Left but against Jews. Jewish people were berated on public streets and also physically attacked, while Jewish businesspeople were threatened.[37]

But young Sturmabteilung (SA) brownshirts occasionally visited violence even on Munich residents who sympathized with the Hitler movement. In May 1923, one of them forced a bookstore owner on Brienner Strasse to remove a book he found objectionable from the shop window. The proprietor sent an outraged letter to Hitler, complaining about the "dictatorship of punks." As a man of "venerable Germanic family heritage," who had volunteered to fight in the First World War at the age of forty-two, he claimed the right to inform the party leader that the behavior of a segment of his young supporters was "reversing the sympathies felt for you."[38]

After one Hitler rally in Zirkus Krone in late April 1923, an older woman who had been taking notes during the party leader's speech was surrounded by several young security guards, taken into a separate room, and searched. Her companion, a practicing doctor, expressed her outrage over the incident in a letter addressed to "my very honorable Mr. Hitler." She wrote, "What we encountered there is naked terror, worse than what went on in Eisner's day. If this spirit comes from your spirit, then you are not destined to bring Germany ultimate salvation but rather a fatal blow."[39]

Amid the general climate of antisemitic agitation and violence, more than a few Munich residents felt called to develop ideas and initiatives of their own to fulfill what they assumed was the Führer's will. For example, a salesman approached Hitler in May 1923 with the suggestion of "inconspicuously but practically taking action against Jewry by getting the patriotic populace to neither buy from nor sell to Jewish firms." Since it was impossible to distinguish reliably between Jewish and "racially German" companies, the Hitler admirer proposed publishing an "Aryan address book."[40]

Moreover, people in the Bavarian capital regularly informed on their fellow city residents. An anonymous person claiming to be a "true supporter" of the National Socialists demanded that a campaign be launched against a pair of brothers named Goldschmidt and a leather shop owner named Rosenzweig for "agitating in the most unheard-of manner" against Hitler's cause. "Because I cannot be sure this message will end up directly in your hands, I'm omitting my name and social station at the bottom," wrote the would-be denouncer to Hitler. "But you can rest assured that I have provided the above information to the best of my knowledge and with a clear conscience, with the intention of keeping people from undermining your great work for the fatherland in even the smallest way."[41]

RUMORS SWIRLED ABOUT IMPENDING putsches in Munich throughout the spring and summer of 1923, with Hitler's public appearances stoking such desires. "What can save Germany is the dictatorship of national will and national determination," he proclaimed in early May in Zirkus Krone. "Our task is to provide the dictator, when he comes, with a people ripe for him! German people, wake up! The day is coming!"[42] One month later, in the same venue, he thundered, "Our misfortune grows day by day. The people don't want any more ministers. They want leaders. They long not for parliamentarians but men prepared to take the lead in our liberation."[43] Hitler left no doubt as to his willingness to play this role. "As the leader of the National Socialist party, I see my task as being the assumption of responsibility," he told a crowd in Augsburg's Sängerhalle concert venue in early June.[44] On August 21, a few days after the end of the Cuno government and the formation of Stresemann's first grand coalition, he attracted massive applause in Zirkus Krone for proclaiming, "We want dictatorship! ... We are drawing ever closer to the hour of decision!"[45] Afterward, one enthusiastic audience member wrote Hitler, "The thing now is to keep the masses in motion since we won't have to wait long for a decision in one form or another."[46]

Later in August, accompanied by one of his early patrons, chemist Emil Gansser, who worked for Siemens in Berlin, Hitler traveled to Switzerland. The purpose of the trip was to secure money from Germanophiles in the Alpine nation for the Nazi Party, which despite its increasing membership was facing acute financial challenges. The excursion was a significant success. Hitler reportedly took in some 30,000 Swiss francs—a huge sum in a time of hyperinflation. In the Zürich villa of Swiss general Ulrich Wille, whose entire family were Nazi sympathizers, Hitler gave a talk before a small circle of chosen guests, in which he discussed with unusual frankness how he imagined the coming coup would work. "The situation in Germany is heading unavoidably toward chaos," he emphasized. Stresemann would be unable to last in office even for as long as Cuno: he would be undone by the "food issue" since farmers would no longer be willing to sell their products for worthless pieces of paper. Starving people in the cities would riot, and the government would find itself powerless against them. The Communists would exploit the situation to try to launch a national revolution, and their success in northern Germany was as "good as certain." That, however, would prompt a counterreaction from Bavaria, where a considerable force of twenty thousand men stood ready to march on Berlin to eradicate the "Bolshevik peril" and establish a "dictatorship of the Right." Like Stinnes, Hitler still thought that a Communist uprising would have to precede his own bid for power. And like the industrialists and his own supporters, Hitler was also convinced that Germany couldn't "convalesce" through parliamentary means. "Such an upheaval can never be carried out by a parliamentary government, only a dictatorship backed by a determined, if small, minority."⁴⁷ A member of the Wille family who attended the talk noted in her diary, "Hittler [*sic*] extremely likable. His whole body quivers when he speaks. And he speaks wonderfully."⁴⁸

IN SEPTEMBER 1923, THE sense of crisis in the south of Germany spread. "The pressure of economic misery is increasing every day," opined the head of the governmental administration of Upper Bavaria. "That has an effect on the mood of the masses who are growing ever more agitated and ready to wage a dog-eat-dog battle."⁴⁹ On September 1 and 2, the Bavarian political Right assembled for a "Germany Day" in Nuremberg. The event was a demonstration of strength, featuring a two-hour parade of patriotic clubs, veterans' associations, and officers' leagues. "The street marches were swathed in an ocean of black, white, and red and blue and white [the Bavarian regional colors], [and] blusterous cries of 'Heil' resounded from the guests of honor and the parade from all sides," a local police station reported. "It was an outcry from hundreds of thousands of despondent, intimidated, buffeted, and desperate people to whom a ray of hope appeared for liberation from servitude and misery. Many men and women stood crying, overcome by emotion."⁵⁰

The Nuremberg event included a demonstration of solidarity between Hitler and Ludendorff. Ludendorff had pulled the strings behind the scenes during the Kapp Putsch, and after it failed, the general had moved to Bavaria, where his villa in the south of Munich became a meeting place for anti-democratic agitators. Hitler valued the connection to the former First World War commander, who still possessed considerable clout in military and ultranationalist circles, since Hitler hoped that an alliance would ensure Reichswehr support for his own plans for a coup d'état.⁵¹ "What a marvelous acknowledgment that the magnificent Ludendorff has joined you and the movement you have unleashed!" wrote the geriatric Houston Stewart Chamberlain—

Richard Wagner's son-in-law and the author of the best-selling antisemitic tome *The Foundations of the Nineteenth Century*—to Hitler after
a visit by the latter to Bayreuth in late September 1923.[52]

Another important event in Nuremberg was the founding of a
"German Fighting League," which brought together the SA, the Bund
Oberland militia, and the Reichsflagge—the politically activist segment of the Reichswehr. Its leadership was entrusted to the Ludendorff intimate and former chief of staff of the volunteer militia, retired
First Lieutenant Hermann Kriebel, and the Baltic German Max
Erwin von Scheubner-Richter was given responsibility for managing
daily affairs. On September 25, Hitler assumed its "political leadership." A secret "action program," agreed to the day before, defined the
alliance's actual purpose as the "overpowering of Marxism," stating
that the "proclamation of the national revolution" could "only then be
pursued successfully . . . when the fighting units were in possession of
the instruments of state power in Bavaria." Moreover, attempts should
be made "to get hold of state police authority in a way that appeared,
at least to the outside, legal."[53]


THE NAZI PARTY HEADQUARTERS on Corneliusstrasse and
the editorial offices of the *Völkischer Beobachter* on Schellingstrasse
received letters from all parts of Germany in September and October
imploring Hitler to act. "You must strike while the iron is hot," one
former army captain wrote, adding a reference to the fourth Roman
emperor. "Don't let it cool off. . . . Don't become Claudius Cuncta-
tor."[54] Hitler could do Germany "an enormous service" by taking "truly
energetic, indeed extraordinary action," asserted another admiring letter writer. The entire hopes of the nation were pinned to the "savior
from Bavaria," who would "clean up the Augean stable with an iron
broom."[55] There were signals of support from northern Germany as
well. The head of a company in Hamburg promised, "When this entire
corrupt episode finally unravels and the great 'cleaning up' is at hand,
you will find many friends and effective help in the North."[56]

In his speeches in the Zirkus Krone, Hitler encouraged expectations that he would strike soon. Things "couldn't continue this way for much longer," he announced on September 5. There were "only two possibilities: either Berlin will march on Munich or Munich will march on Berlin."[57] Seven days later, he promised, "In a few months, perhaps even in some weeks, the dice will be rolled again in Germany. . , . We accept the challenge to do battle and are convinced: victory will be ours, as it must be!"[58] But privately Hitler was far less confident and still hesitated to put everything on the line. In mid-September, Hess found him "as solemn . . . as seldom before." The "tribune," as Hess often referred to Hitler, was having trouble resolving to "put the flame to the powder keg."[59] The Nazi Party chairman was planning to call for fourteen mass events in Munich alone on September 27, yet it is unlikely, as some observers later claimed, that this series of rallies was intended to spark a putsch. More likely, Hitler just wanted to encourage his followers' readiness for a fight at some point.[60]

KAHR'S APPOINTMENT AS GENERAL state commissar on September 26 threw a wrench into the Nazis' plans. An official party statement criticized the move as "a massive blow" that would have a "confusing and paralyzing effect on the ethnic-patriotic movement."[61] One of Kahr's first acts was to prohibit the fourteen Nazi events planned for the following day. Hitler immediately lodged "the most vigorous of protests," but Kahr was unmoved.[62] The Munich correspondent of the *Vossische Zeitung* believed that Hitler's reputation might take a hit: "Maybe this will finally open the eyes of people in Munich to their hero—this man who has known for the past four years how to use the petty tools of the rabble-rouser, his gift for populist speech, and a temerity born of utter irresponsibility to stir up trouble in Bavaria and Munich and swindle the uncritical segment of the public into thinking supernatural forces have sent him to rescue an enslaved region."[63]

Kahr, however, also used the extremely broad powers he had been given to curry favor among Bavarian racists. On his orders, some thirty Jewish families were forcibly removed from Munich. The act was justified with the argument that the people concerned had "immigrated in impoverishment" but had become affluent and had thus enriched themselves from the "misery of the people."[64] Kahr also took a hard line toward the Bavarian Left, particularly the KPD, ordering the dissolution of its paramilitary organizations, banning Communist publications and events, and taking activists into "protective custody."[65]

Still, the relationship between Kahr and the Nazi Party chairman remained tense. On the one hand, Hitler didn't want to vehemently attack Kahr and rule out any possibility of a future alliance, but on the other, he took pains to publicly maintain his distance from the state commissar. Kahr was only an "obedient civil servant," Hitler complained at "German Day" in Bamberg on October 7, not a man "to lead the decisive battle."[66] One week later, he explained why the Nazi Party didn't support Kahr: "A true statesman, a true dictator, doesn't lean on any man. Instead he supports the nation. He puts it back on its feet. And leads it down the path he has recognized as the correct one." The implication was that Hitler, not Kahr, was the right man to be a "trailblazer for the great German liberation movement."[67]

Munich simmered during October, with one observer noting that Kahr and Hitler were like "two predators in a single cage … slinking around and eyeing each other up."[68] Overtures were followed by veiled threats and vice versa. Amid all the ill-tempered political jockeying, it was hard for the national government's representative in Munich, Edgar Haniel von Haimhausen, to keep a handle on events. In fact, Ebert occasionally joked, "Something important happened in Munich. Has anyone told Haniel?"[69]

The opaque situation was additionally complicated by the conflict between the Bavarian and the national German government. Over the course of the standoff, power in the southern German regional state in essence devolved to a triumvirate: Kahr; the regional state commandant of the Bavarian Reichswehr troops, Otto von Lossow; and the head of Bavarian regional police, Colonel Hans Ritter von Seisser.

GENERAL ANIMOSITY TOWARD THE national government in Berlin temporarily papered over the rift between the trio and the putsch-ready forces around Hitler and the German Fighting League, but behind the scenes the contest continued. There was full agreement on the goals of "liberating Germany from Marxism" and creating a "national dictatorship," as Lossow assured representatives of patriotic associations including the league at a meeting on October 24.[70] Yet there was no consensus about the proper point in time or the methods to be used to achieve those ends. The triumvirate felt the spark should come from Berlin. The three Bavarian leaders were aware that plans were being drawn up in the German capital for a directorate under Seeckt—an idea they backed. The point, as Kahr testified at Hitler's trial for insurrection in March 1924, was to "bundle national forces and . . . create a strong Bavaria that would be capable of standing at the side of the move toward such a directorate and supporting it."[71] The Fighting League was welcome to become part of this movement, but as Kahr made clear on October 1, it would have to subordinate itself to the cause of bringing together all nationalist forces and integrate itself into "the greater whole." As Kahr put it, "Special wishes won't be tolerated."[72]

Hitler and the league, on the other hand, thought that the "national dictatorship" should first be proclaimed in Munich, followed by a "march on Berlin." In a conference with SA leaders on October 23, Hitler described the first stage of his planned enterprise: "[We must] pose the German nation question at the last minute in Bavaria [and] call for a German liberation army under a German nationalist government in Munich."[73] He expanded on these ideas at the Zirkus Krone on October 30: "Today, Bavaria faces a great mission. . . . We have to carry out the battle that will stab at the heart. . . . For me, the German question will only be resolved when the black, white, and red swastika flag waves above the Berlin Palace."[74] It was clear who was to do what. Ludendorff would assume leadership of the military, since his aura seemed to guarantee that the Bavarian Reichswehr troops under Lossow would fall in line with the coup. Political leadership would be Hitler's. "When someone believes he is called to do something, then he has a duty to do what he feels he is called to," Hitler testified at his 1924 trial in Munich.[75]

By conjuring up visions of an imminent "act of liberation," Hitler fed the expectations of his followers to the point that he couldn't back down without losing their faith. "You are our final and hopefully our most potent and successful reserve,"[76] a Catholic priest wrote to the Nazi leader on October 14, adding that every day he feared that Kahr wasn't up to the job. On October 26, the director of the Bayreuth Festival, Winifred Wagner, confided to a friend, "Everyone is feverishly awaiting that everything will be different and better."[77] Never had one of Hitler's speeches "so captivated and moved" her, wrote a Munich woman from the wealthy neighborhood of Bogenhausen after Hitler's appearance at the Zirkus Krone on October 30. "That's the only way the man who will bring about the great work of liberation can be. . . . And now let the Almighty make your arm as strong as your word already is so that, finally, the day of liberation will come."[78]

In reality, though, the prospects for a successful putsch had significantly worsened by late October and early November. The Reichswehr's intervention against the leftist governments in Saxony and Thuringia removed any pretext for Bavarian paramilitaries to march toward the border with those two regional states. Meanwhile, the failure of "German October" eliminated any prospect of a Communist insurrection that could be exploited for launching a right-wing rebellion. The national government's introduction of the Rentenbank in mid-October, moreover, was a major step toward domestic reform and stabilization.

The Bavarian conspirators were running out of time. At a meeting with Seisser on November 1, Hitler repeated his earlier promise to take no action without the Reichswehr and regional state police. "Don't think I'm that stupid: I'm not going to start a putsch," he declared. But he simultaneously insisted that the time for joint action was at hand.

"Economic desperation is driving our people, so that either we act or our circles of supporters will defect to the Communists."[79]

On November 3, Seisser traveled as a representative of the trium-virate to Berlin, where he met with Minoux, Seeckt, and spokesmen for the Agricultural League. On behalf of Stinnes, Minoux warned Seisser against striking prematurely in Bavaria, saying that the time for concrete action had yet to arrive. "Hunger and cold" had to be "allowed to do their job," so that the resulting unrest could be exploited to effect fundamental change. Meeting with Seeckt, Seisser pointed out the "heavy pressure . . . all patriotic forces in Bavaria" were put-ting on Kahr to "intervene against Berlin" with the goal of "creating a national dictatorship." Seeckt countered that this was his goal as well, but, whatever happened, the "legal path" had to be maintained. The Agricultural League, by contrast, welcomed Seisser with open arms, despite their doubts that the general would ever decide to break with Ebert and Stresemann. A "violent solution," however, would only be possible if the Reichswehr participated, so it was imperative to keep up the pressure on the head of army command to "make that leap."[80]

THE SKEPTICISM CONCERNING SEECKT was only partially justified. On November 2, immediately after the Social Democrats quit the grand coalition, he had made another attempt to realize his plans for establishing a dictatorship. In the draft of a letter to Kahr, he wrote that he didn't consider the Stresemann coalition, even after being re-formed, "capable of survival." Without a "dramatic shift in the national governments," he foresaw civil war, and the Reichswehr couldn't afford to be put in a position of "being deployed against its political allies on behalf of a government it found alien." On the other hand, there was no tolerating "change through violence." As he had in conversation with Seisser the day before, Seeckt insisted on sticking to "constitutional forms and paths," arguing that abandoning them entailed "great dangers" and could only be considered "in an extreme emergency." He articulated a principle that he would drop from the finished version of the letter, sent on November 5—apparently because it revealed his own political outlook all too clearly: "The Weimar Constitution isn't a *noli me tangere* [touch me not] in my eyes. I played no role in it, and its fundamental principles contradict my own political beliefs."[81]

On November 3, the Bavarian consul in Berlin, Konrad Ritter von Preger, announced that Bavaria would send the Seventh Reichswehr Division north if a "nationalist government" wasn't formed within forty-eight hours. The announcement—which soon proved baseless since no Bavarian troops were sent anywhere—created fury in Berlin. Ebert demanded that Seeckt "march immediately on Bavaria," to which the head of the army command demurred, saying that neither the numbers nor the morale of his troops would allow such an operation.[82] As Gessler remembered it, Ebert melodramatically threatened to step down: "If you are of the opinion that the Reichswehr is incapable of protecting constitutional conditions in the nation—because they either can't or won't—you have to declare that now. Then I will depart from this house." Gessler recalled that afterward Seeckt relented, while also making clear that the chancellor no longer enjoyed the trust of his troops.[83]

Ebert apparently was reminded of the days of the Kapp Putsch in March 1920, when Seeckt, then in charge of the Troop Office, had acted disloyally and refused to use the Reichswehr against the putschists, declaring, "Soldiers don't fire on their fellow soldiers."[84] But any resentment caused by Seeckt's renewed reticence to use his forces seems to have been short-lived. One day later, Ebert charged Seeckt with asking Germany's ambassador to the United States, Otto Wiedfeldt, if he would be willing to take on the office of chancellor.[85]

Wiedfeldt's name had already been mentioned in early October amid discussions of forming a ruling directorate. Ebert thought highly of the former Krupp director, who combined economic expertise with diplomatic experience. On November 4, Seeckt wrote to him "not only with the knowledge but at the express wish of the Reich president," sketching out the following scenario: "The Str[esemann] cabinet will hardly be able to survive. . . . An effective government with the parliament is out of the question after the departure of the S[ocial] D[emocrats]. The only alternative is a small cabinet with the character of a directorate and full emergency powers." Wiedfeldt should be ready for that eventuality, which could be "accelerated or perhaps also disrupted by unforeseen events."[86]

Seeckt didn't specify the role he himself was to play in the directorate. Ebert did not want to make him chancellor since he both feared the reaction of the Entente powers and was unwilling to do without him as the "leader of the military." But the fact that the president had warmed to the idea of a directorate and seemingly come around to Seeckt's perspective can only have reflected a profound disappointment with his own party, the SPD, which in his view had frivolously risked the destruction of the grand coalition. Ebert reckoned that the rump Stresemann cabinet would not command a parliamentary majority and believed that he needed to be open to alternatives to prevent a power vacuum. A cabinet independent of parliament, propped up by the military and equipped with extraordinary powers, was a problematic but temporarily tenable option. Ebert told Gessler that while he "was trying to find legal ways to encourage Germany's recovery," he wouldn't hesitate to "act otherwise to save Germany, if the Constitution or the future [of the country] were at stake."[87] Nonetheless, it remains bewildering that the Social Democratic German president would go behind his own chancellor's back and ask the head of army command to make such a controversial inquiry in Washington.

Stresemann seems to have learned of the intrigue. On the evening of November 4, he sent his personal secretary, Heinrich Ehlers, to the Reichswehr Ministry to check into the situation. Seeckt was blunt, speaking against Stresemann remaining chancellor because he considered him incapable of pulling "the errant government wagon out of the mud."[88] When Ehlers reported back after midnight, Stresemann was "deeply shocked," sighing, "So we've reached the point where the Reich chancellor is dismissed by the Reichswehr." That very night, he called Ebert and told him that Seeckt had demanded his immediate

resignation. Ebert, apparently surprised that the head of the Reichswehr had acted so rashly, tried to calm Stresemann down and prevent
him from quitting in response to the attack on his authority.[89]

The following morning, Stresemann and Seeckt met to clear the
air, with Gessler present as well. In the Reichswehr minister's recollections, Seeckt declared, "Mr. Chancellor, there is no way to go to battle with you at the helm. You no longer have the trust of the troops."
Stresemann tried to lure the head of army command out into the open
by asking, "So you are refusing me the obedience of the Reichswehr?"
Seeckt said nothing. Instead, Gessler answered, "Mr. Chancellor, only
I can do that." The Reichswehr minister's recollections concluded,
"Thus, understandably, we parted ways in rancor."[90] Seeckt was forced
to accept that he had gone too far. Ebert stuck by the chancellor, and
for the time being, the general avoided another confrontation, stepping back from the idea of seizing governmental authority and installing a directorate against the will of the German president.

For his part, Stresemann had to stand up not only to Seeckt but to
opposition within his own party. In a meeting of the DVP parliamentary group on November 5, Ernst Scholz, DVP's parliamentary chairman, called for an "energetic shift to the right," which would see the
chancellor officially ask DNVP ultranationalists if they were willing
to join the cabinet. Stresemann refused, calling the suggestion "impudent" and asserting that there was no way to form a parliamentary
majority with the DNVP since the Center Party and the DDP would
surely refuse to play along. In the middle of the constant crossfire from
his own party, Stresemann uttered a line that would become famous
in Germany: "I'm tired of this dog's life." In response to the rumors
that Bavarian fighting units were readying a "march on Berlin," he
declared, "If those gangs encroach on Berlin . . . they should shoot me
dead on the spot where I have every right to be sitting."[91]

The DVP chairman's impassioned pleas temporarily silenced the
critics, but the very next day they renewed their attacks. Deputy Oskar
Maretzky told the parliamentary group that Seeckt had literally said to
Stresemann's face, "You are no longer a possibility as chancellor. Please

step down. Make that sacrifice for the fatherland." This information caused a considerable stir among deputies, but the chancellor hastened to smooth things over by offering a less damning version of the pressure Seeckt had applied. The head of the Reichswehr had merely expressed his personal opinion that it would be easier with a different government to "coopt" the radical Right, Stresemann claimed. That had nothing to do with the actual position of the Reichswehr itself, as Gessler had confirmed.[92] Stresemann had made possible a brief respite in his party's internal struggles. But in the days that followed, events in Bavaria would completely command his attention.

IN THE AFTERNOON OF November 6, Kahr convened a crucial meeting of the leaders of all patriotic associations, including Hermann Kriebel from the German Fighting League and Friedrich Weber from the Oberland League. He warned them explicitly against launching a putsch on their own. He, too, aimed to "form a nationalist government" free of "parliamentary hindrances." But this "great national goal," he said, could only be achieved if everyone maintained discipline and submitted to his authority. Kahr himself and no one else would give the signal to act when the time was right. "Flights of fancy" would not be tolerated.[93]

When Kahr was finished, Lossow spoke up, telling the group he would use the Reichswehr to put down any and all independent coup attempts. He, too, declared himself willing to support the establishment of a right-wing dictatorship but only if the undertaking had a chance of success. Likely with the thought of the Kapp fiasco in mind, he declared, "If we're just being hounded into a putsch that will come to a pathetic end in five or six days, I'm no longer in."[94]

The triumvirate was clearly playing for time, waiting to see how things developed in Berlin and only ready to side with the directorate if rebellion broke out there. After his bold declarations of the preceding weeks, however, Hitler couldn't afford any delays without alienating the powerful parts of his movement that were prepared to act.

"We couldn't always keep people prepared for the cause and then call them off," he said at his trial, describing the pressure he had put himself under. "We couldn't inflame them constantly. We had to reach a clear decision."[95]

On the evening of November 6, Hitler made that decision. The next day, he briefed the leaders of the Fighting League—Kriebel, Weber, Scheubner-Richter—and Göring as the head of the SA. Originally the uprising was planned for November 11, the fifth anniversary of the armistice that ended the First World War, but it was moved ahead three days when it became known that Kahr intended to hold a speech in the Bürgerbräukeller, another leading Munich beer hall and event venue, on November 8. Every powerful person in the city would be in attendance. Occupying the beer hall would offer a unique chance to take the entire political elite of the Bavarian capital hostage and launch the putsch. Kahr, Lossow, and Seisser were to be presented with a fait accompli and forced to participate. The idea, Hitler said at his trial, was to give the "three laggards" a "little push," so that they would "finally take the leap into waters that are apparently too cold for them."[96]

The military leaders of the Fighting League issued their orders throughout Bavaria on the evening of November 7 and the morning of November 8. In the town of Landshut, for instance, the SA congregated in front of party headquarters after the orders arrived, and their commander, the apothecary Gregor Strasser, later the Nazi Party's organizational director, announced that he needed a hundred men for a "serious mission," declining to explain precisely what it was. "He insisted that all of those who had to take family into consideration or were worried on account of age or health stay behind," one eyewitness recalled years later.[97]

As few people as possible were told of the plans to avoid jeopardizing the surprise. There could be no doubt, the Munich police directorship determined in retrospect, that knowledge of Hitler's impending action "didn't go beyond the innermost circles until directly before the putsch."[98] Even several of Hitler's closest intimates weren't taken into confidence. Dietrich Eckart, for example, whiled away the evening of November 8 in a Munich bar with some drinking buddies, first hearing unspecified rumors around 11:00 p.m. that a putsch had taken place.[99]

Early in the morning of November 8, Hitler went to see Ernst Pöhner, the former Munich police president and a friend and patron of the Nazi Party, and offered him the office of Bavarian state premier in the post-putsch regime. With Kahr, Lossow, and Seisser still wary, Hitler told him, the event in the Bürgerbräukeller would be used to make it easier for them to "take the plunge." Hitler's announcement had taken him by complete surprise, Pöhner testified at the trial of the putchists, but he had felt an "internal satisfaction" at the thought of "someone finally finding the courage to act." Pöhner added, "So when Hitler asked me, I answered without hesitation, 'Yes, I'm on board!'"[100]

At 9:00 a.m., Hitler summoned his most ardent supporter, Hess, by telephone. The latter was back in Munich after spending several weeks at his mother's home in the Fichtelgebirge hills, devoting himself to his university studies. In early October, he had written to his mentor, Professor Karl Haushofer, that although he had no concrete plans to return to the Bavarian capital, "I'm waiting for the call." Hess immediately knew that Hitler was about to bypass Kahr and completely and utterly agreed with the idea: "The rehabilitation of the whole should and must proceed from Bavaria."[101] Hess's task was to arrest the members of the Bavarian government in the Bürgerbräukeller, first and foremost State Premier Eugen Ritter von Knilling. He would later be given the address of a house where the "elevated gentlemen" were to be kept under guard. "I shook his hand and promised not to say a word, and we parted until that evening," Hess recalled of his meeting with Hitler.[102]

Around noon, Hitler, his face pale and agitated, riding crop in hand, stormed into the editorial offices of the *Völkischer Beobachter* and declared to the astonished editor in chief Alfred Rosenberg and to Ernst Hanfstaengl that he had decided to launch a coup. "You must swear not to speak a word of this to any living soul!" he demanded.

"The hour for action is at hand. You, party comrade Rosenberg, and you, Mr. Hanfstaengl...will be among those who accompany me directly at my side." Both men were to appear that evening in the Bürgerbräukeller. "Bring your pistols," Hitler ordered.[103] In such fashion, the principals were gradually informed of the putsch and given specific orders.

Because it had been moved to an earlier date, the entire endeavor was poorly planned, significantly reducing its chances for success, if it had any to begin with. Perhaps it would have been better, Hess admitted several months later, "to postpone the operation rather than being overly hasty—but it's, of course, easy in retrospect to say that there was still time!"[104] Neither Hess nor any of the other co-conspirators tried to prevent Hitler from taking such a risky step. Even those who were given no advance warning about the putsch followed Hitler's call to action without hesitation.

THE BÜRGERBRÄUKELLER WAS PACKED to the rafters on November 8, with hundreds of people who had been refused admission crowded around the entrance. Shortly after 8:00 p.m., Kahr arrived with Lossow and Seisser. Kahr's address was feverishly anticipated. Would he finally come out and say what he envisioned Bavaria's role to be in the "national uprising" he had so often invoked? But the audience was disappointed. "Kahr didn't hold...a speech for a mass rally but rather an academic presentation, indeed a lecture, about Marxism," the historian Karl Alexander von Müller remembered. "A couple of good sentences at the beginning, then completely bland, wordy, and boring."[105]

Once Kahr began speaking, Hitler was driven up in his Mercedes-Benz, accompanied by Rosenberg, his bodyguard Ulrich Graf, and Max Amann, the head of the Nazi-affiliated Eher publishing house. Because of the unexpectedly large crowd in front of the beer hall, Hitler was afraid that the SA men who would arrive shortly would be unable to get to the entrance. On the spur of the moment, he ordered the police officers on duty to clear the street, which they did. "At Hitler's command, the police opened up the path for Hitler's putsch," wrote his earliest biographer Konrad Heiden.[106]

Soon, the first trucks full of SA men pulled up, and the "Hitler Commando," a precursor to the Schutzstaffel (SS), surrounded the Bürgerbräukeller, sealing it off from all sides. Hitler, dressed that evening in a dark suit, went into the foyer and started to pace, sipping a glass of beer Hanfstaengl had given him.[107] Finally, at around 8:45 p.m., he threw the glass to the ground, pulled out his pistol, and stormed with three armed associates into the auditorium while Göring had SA troops set up a Gatling gun at the entrance. "It was obvious you couldn't go in waving a palm frond," Hitler would later testify. It took considerable effort to push through the crowds and get to the stage. At one point, Hitler pointed his pistol at the forehead of an officer who approached him with his hand in his pocket, with Hitler hissing, "Take your hand out!"[108] A few steps away from Kahr, he climbed on a chair and fired a shot into the ceiling to silence the din in the auditorium. Then he jumped down to the floor, ascended the stage, and cried out in a quavering voice, "The national revolution has broken out. This hall is occupied by six hundred heavily armed men. No one is allowed to leave. If there is not immediate silence, I will have a Gatling gun set up in the gallery. The Bavarian government is hereby dismissed. The national government is dismissed. A provisional national government will be formed."[109]

Thereupon Hitler brusquely ordered Kahr, Lossow, and Seisser to follow him into an adjacent room, where he guaranteed their safety. At the subsequent trial, Lossow testified that he had whispered to the others, "Play along with this comedy," and the three men had agreed by exchanging glances that they would pretend to submit to Hitler.[110] It's unlikely, however, that the triumvirate spontaneously reached any such agreement to playact obedience in order to regain their liberty. In the discussions that took place in the adjoining room, they initially rejected all of Hitler's proposals, even as he employed all his powers of persuasion, excusing his actions with the pretense of having no other choice. In clipped words, he elucidated how he envisioned the new Bavarian state: "Pöhner will become state premier with full dictatorial authorities. You . . ."—addressing Kahr—"will become regent, national government Hitler, national army Ludendorff, Seisser police minister." He knew how difficult it was for the men to take this step, Hitler told them, but he wanted to help them "find a way out." Then he immediately followed these overtures with a threat: "I have four bullets in my pistol. Three for my associates, if you leave me. This final bullet is mine." He gestured with the gun toward his head as he said this. Kahr remained unmoved. "You can detain me and shoot me dead," he told Hitler. "Dying or not dying makes no difference."[111] This went on for around ten minutes, with Hitler making no progress.

Meanwhile the auditorium was in tumult. Many in the audience were shocked at the Nazis' violent disruption and voiced their outrage by crying out "theater," "South America," and "Mexico!"—suggesting that Germany was becoming a tinpot dictatorship.[112] To calm things down, Göring got onstage and boldly declared that the action was not aimed at Kahr. On the contrary, it was hoped that he would join the rebellion. But Göring couldn't help adding, sarcastically, that the crowd had nothing to complain about since everyone was supplied with beer.[113] This frivolous remark naturally did little to soothe emotions in the hall.

Hitler then returned to the stage, and to the astonishment of many eyewitnesses, the man who had behaved like a hysterical semilunatic only minutes before now seemed very much in control and equal to the situation. With a short speech, a masterpiece of crowd control, he completely turned the mood in the hall. In his memoirs, Karl Alexander von Müller wrote that never in his life had he "experienced such a reversal of a mass atmosphere within minutes, almost seconds." When Hitler was sure he had the crowd on his side, he asked a leading question. "In the room next door are Kahr, Lossow, and Seisser. They are having trouble reaching a decision. Can I tell them that you will stand behind them? 'Yes,' swelled the answer from all sides like a storm." That, at least, was Müller's depiction.[114] With a triumphant gesture,

Hitler ended his theatrical performance by proclaiming, "Tomorrow will either find a German nationalist government in Germany, or it will find us dead."[115]

After Hitler returned to the room where he was holding the triumvirate, commands and cries of "Heil" could be heard from the entrance to the auditorium, as retired general Erich Ludendorff arrived. He had been called at 8:00 p.m. and told that his presence in the Bürgerbräukeller was urgently required and that he should ready himself. Scheubner-Richter picked him up in a car. At the insurgents' trial, Ludendorff testified that it was only then that he was told what was going on.[116] This is hardly believable. That very afternoon, he had called on Kahr unannounced and asserted, in the presence of Lossow and Seisser, that the situation was crying out for a decision. When Kahr once again rejected the notion of a right-wing dictatorship originating in Bavaria, Ludendorff took his leave with the barely veiled threat that the Fighting League could "now strike." In his unpublished memoirs, a sarcastic Kahr wrote, "When Ludendorff had left the room, the three of us asked what he had intended to achieve."[117]

But that evening in the beer hall, Ludendorff acted as though he, too, had been presented with a fait accompli. "Gentlemen, I'm as surprised as you are," he said by way of a greeting when he joined the triumvirate waiting in the room next to the auditorium. "But this step has been taken. The fatherland is at stake, as well as the great cause of our nation and our kind, and I can only advise you to close ranks with us and do as we do!"[118]

With Ludendorff present, the atmosphere immediately changed. The pistols disappeared, and cordial arguments were made in the attempt to convince the triumvirate to cooperate. Lossow, whom Ludendorff addressed as a former comrade in arms, was the first to give in, then Seisser folded. Only Kahr still resisted, although he, too, relented in the end, declaring, "I am prepared to assume responsibility for Bavaria's fate as a placeholder for the monarchy."[119] Hitler, who had no intention whatsoever of restoring the monarchy, said that "nothing at all stood in the way" of that end. He himself would immediately

inform "His Royal Majesty," Crown Prince Rupprecht, that the coup
in the Bürgerbräukeller wasn't directed against him but was solely
intended to "pay back the November criminals" and thereby redress
the "injustice" that had been done to the House of Wittelsbach. Once
again, Hitler displayed his talents as a dissembler, feigning subservi-
ence to Kahr: "Your Excellency, I assure you that from this moment I
will follow you as loyally as a dog."[120]

Hitler insisted that he and Kahr return to the main hall to officially
seal their agreement. But Kahr again refused, saying he couldn't go
back out onto the same stage from which he had just been so igno-
miniously removed. Hitler was having none of this, promising that the
crowd would "receive him with great celebration" and indeed would
"kneel down" before him.[121]

In the end, they all returned to the stage. Kahr, his face frozen in
a mask, reiterated to thunderous applause his willingness to serve as a
"placeholder for the monarchy," while saying it was only with a heavy
heart that he had agreed to participate in the rebellion "for the welfare of our beloved Bavarian homeland and our great German fatherland."[122] Hitler grasped his hand and held it for quite some time, with
an "expression of beaming, almost childlike, completely open delight,"
as Karl Alexander von Müller observed. The scene, he added, allud-
ing to Schiller's *Wilhelm Tell*, was like a "kind of Rütli oath in front
of the German people."[123] Once the tension had dissolved, Hitler felt
euphoric, speaking to the hall with pseudoreligious fervor. "Now, in
the weeks and months to come, I intend to carry out what I swore I
would do five years ago, when I lay as a blind cripple in a military hos-
pital: never to relax or rest until the criminals of November 1918 are
brought down! Resurrected atop the ruins of today's pitiful Germany
will be a Germany of strength and greatness, freedom and splendor.
Amen!"[124]

Ludendorff was next to speak. Standing up straight, barely able to
conceal his excitement, he declared that he was "at the ready thanks
to the innate right of the German national government." He proclaimed, "The hour represents a turning point in our history. Let us

enter into it with profound moral gravity, in the knowledge of the immense difficulty of our task, aware of and suffused by our grave responsibility."[125] Summoned to the rostrum one after another by Hitler, Lossow, Seisser, and Pöhner also declared their support for a coup. Several eyewitnesses, however, noticed that in contrast to Ludendorff, Lossow adopted a relaxed posture and wore a mocking smile on his fox-like face, as if to suggest that the issue was anything but settled.[126] Hitler shook hands with all of them, relishing his role as the director of the action on the stage and enjoying the fact that he seemed to have bent the others to his will. Nearly everyone present was carried away by the spectacle. It never occurred to Hitler, wrote Müller, that the whole spectacle might only be a charade performed by the triumvirate for ulterior motives. On the contrary, many people seemed to share his sense of having witnessed a "historical hour."[127] At the end of the event, when the audience broke out into a rendition of the German national anthem, some people were too choked up to sing along.

Before everyone went their separate ways, an SA commando under the direction of Rudolf Hess and following a prepared list arrested all the Bavarian government ministers in attendance as well as the Munich police president and the head of the Bavarian crown prince's cabinet, Count Josef von Soden. They were taken to the villa owned by the publisher Julius F. Lehmann, a member of the Pan-Germanic League, and were released the following day.[128]

AFTER SUCCESSFULLY CLEARING HIS first hurdle, Hitler made a serious error. Having received word that his allies had occupied the Pionierkaserne military academy, he decided to hasten there with Friedrich Weber from the Oberland League, leaving Kahr, Lossow, and Seisser under Ludendorff's supervision. When Hitler and Weber returned, they discovered that the general had released the triumvirate on their own recognizance, after being assured they felt bound to the promises they had made onstage. Ludendorff brushed aside criticism of this move, saying that Lossow had given him his word of honor and a German officer would never break that word.[129]

But hardly had Kahr, Lossow, and Seisser left the Bürgerbräukeller than they turned their backs on Hitler and Ludendorff. The entire enterprise depended on the triumvirate cooperating. There were few contingency plans in case they didn't. "It was surprising," wrote Kahr in his final report on the putsch in December 1923, "that Hitler made hardly any serious attempts that night to gain control over important public buildings like the telegraph and telephone centers, government offices or the main train station." Given the Nazi leader's grandiose proclamations, one would have expected him to proceed in a maximalist fashion.[130]

The consequences of the premature launching of the putsch now became apparent. The attempt to occupy the Pionierkaserne and the barracks of the First Battalion of Infantry Regiment 19 ultimately failed. The only significant victory was achieved by SA Captain Ernst Röhm, who secured control of Lossow's headquarters at the district Reichswehr command. It was there that Hitler and his fellow conspirators set up their base for the night of November 8 before returning to the Bürgerbräukeller early the next morning.[131]

In the meantime, however, the triumvirate had taken countermeasures. With his office occupied, Lossow drove to the city command center, where his subordinates greeted him with the question, "Your Excellency, was that all just a bluff?" If the head of the Reichswehr in Bavaria had previously hedged his bets, he now assured his underlings that he had only promised what he did in the Bürgerbräukeller "as a pretense and under duress."[132] Together Lossow and his staff went to the infantry barracks, where Kahr and Seisser also arrived at 1:00 a.m. There, they crafted the wording of a radio telegram that was sent to all German military transmission stations at 2:50 a.m.: "General State Commissar Kahr, Colonel von Seisser, and General von Lossow repudiate the Hitler Putsch. The statements extorted under the threat of weapons in the Bürgerbräukeller are null and void. Caution is advised since those names are being misused." Another radio telegram followed at 5:30. "Barracks and the most important public buildings are under the secure control of the Reichswehr and the Bavarian police. Reinforcements are on their way. The city is calm."[133]

The conspirators remained unaware of this turn of events for some time. A messenger sent by Hitler and Kriebel to the infantry barracks in the early hours of November 9 to check on the position of the triumvirate was immediately arrested. "There are no negotiations with rebels," Lossow told him.[134]

In his 1930 roman à clef *Success*, in which Hitler appeared in the guise of the fictional character Rupert Kutzner, novelist Lion Feuchtwanger described the events in the Bürgerbräukeller as a folkloristic farce.[135] But as cavalierly as the putsch had been launched and as melodramatically as it might have proceeded, the events of the night of November 8–9 in Munich were eminently serious. For several hours, storm troopers believed they had seized power and immediately set about terrorizing political leftists and Jews. Members of the "Shock Troop Hitler" marched on the editorial offices of the SPD newspaper *Münchner Post* and ransacked them. Shortly after midnight, they broke into the apartment of well-known SPD politician and the paper's editor in chief, Erhard Auer, to arrest him. When they found only his wife and son-in-law on the premises, the two were taken in Auer's place and confined to a room at the Bürgerbräukeller. Already imprisoned in the room was the chairman of the Central Association of German Citizens of the Jewish Faith in Munich, Ludwig Wassermann, who had been identified and taken into custody as he tried to leave the main hall. SA troops moved throughout the city to round up Jews as hostages. Several prominent Jewish families had already left the Bavarian capital or had gone into hiding. In the morning, storm troopers went to the Rathaus and arrested the Social Democratic city mayor, Eduard Schmid, and city councilors from the parties of the Left. They, too, were held as hostages in the Bürgerbräukeller.[136] The putsch's rapid collapse prevented more harm. But the events nonetheless offered a preview of what was to come ten years later when Hitler became chancellor of Germany.

Before night was done, the conspirators posted a "Proclamation to the German People" around the city, announcing that the "government of the November criminals" had been overthrown and that a "provisional national German government" had been formed.[137] On the morning of November 9, the headline in the *Völkischer Beobachter* read "Proclamation of a German National Government in Munich." An editorial entitled "The Triumph of the Swastika" read, "The ethnic revolution is triumphantly marching forward! Germany is awakening from its terrible feverish nightmare, and a great new age is breaking through the clouds with its gleaming light, night is lifting, dawn is upon us, and the symbol of German power and greatness—the eagle—is proudly rising up again!" The Nazi Party central organ celebrated Hitler for making the racist movement great enough that it "was finally able to deal the debilitating blow to the internal enemies of our fatherland," concluding with an appeal, "And now off to the march upon Berlin."[138]

By the time such proclamations of victory were published, it had become clear to the conspirators that they couldn't count on the triumvirate, and every new report that arrived confirmed that the Reichswehr and the Bavarian police would oppose the putsch. In the Bürgerbräukeller, the intoxication of the previous evening had given way to disillusionment and helplessness. Debates went on for hours about what to do next. Kriebel proposed making an orderly retreat to the Nazi stronghold of Rosenheim, halfway between Munich and Austria. But Ludendorff objected, saying he didn't want the entire movement to end in "street filth" and suggesting a protest march into Munich's city center. When Hitler, who had suddenly become very meek, wondered whether that might lead to them being "shot down," Ludendorff barked officiously, "We're marching!"[139] But there was little more than a vague hope that a march might win over public opinion and turn the tide.

The demonstration came together around noon, with Hitler, Ludendorff, and the other leaders of the Fighting League at its head, backed by some two thousand men equipped for a military field march. A Bavarian police division initially blocked their way at the

*At noon on November 9, Hitler supporters began marching
from the Bürgerbräukeller on Rosenheimer Strasse
toward Munich's city center.*

Ludwigsbrücke, a bridge over the Isar River, but after a few minor
skirmishes, they eventually allowed the columns of would-be putschists to pass. The demonstration pressed on to Isartor gate and then
toward Munich's central Marienplatz square. Thousands of onlookers
lined the streets and cheered on the marchers. "The enthusiasm was
unprecedented," Hitler later testified, "and I would have to say that
during this march the people were behind us."[140] Yet the demonstrators surely must have noticed that many of the posters proclaiming the
new nationalist German government had already been torn down or
covered over with a counterproclamation by Kahr.[141]

The demonstration proceeded from the Marienplatz down Wein-
strasse, turned right onto Perusastrasse, then left onto Residenzstrasse.
Just before it reached the Odeonsplatz in front of the monumental
Feldherrnhalle loggia, it ran into a second police blockade. Pushing
and shoving broke out, and a shot sounded: it remains unclear where
it came from. The two sides exchanged fire for thirty seconds, leaving
fourteen putschists and four police officers dead.[142]

One of the first casualties was Scheubner-Richter, who had locked arms with Hitler and whose weight pulled the Nazi leader to the ground, dislocating his shoulder. "Had the bullet which killed Scheubner-Richter been a foot to the right, history would have taken a different course," historian Ian Kershaw has remarked, correctly.[143] Göring was shot and seriously injured, as was Hitler's bodyguard Ulrich Graf in an attempt to protect his boss. As the demonstration disintegrated in panic, Ludendorff marched straight through the rows of police and allowed himself to be arrested, without resistance, on Odeonsplatz.

In the general confusion, Hitler got back to his feet and dragged himself to Max-Josefs-Platz, where Dr. Walter Schultze, the head of the SA medical division, had a car waiting.[144] They sped to Hanfstaengl's vacation home in Uffing on Staffelsee lake. Hitler would be arrested there two days later, on November 11, and immediately taken to prison in Landsberg am Lech. "A dark lock of hair fell onto his pale face, drawn from all the uproar and sleepless nights, from which a pair of steely eyes stared into emptiness," recalled a prison employee.[145]

The badly wounded Göring was treated in a private Munich clinic and then managed to flee to Austria. He was followed by a number of other putschists, including Hermann Esser, Hanfstaengl, and Hess. Pöhner and his accomplice in the Munich police directorate, Wilhelm Frick, had already been arrested during the night of November 8–9. Röhm was apprehended after the district Reichswehr command surrendered on November 9. Ludendorff was released after giving his word of honor to refrain from any further political activity.[146]

In the hours after the putsch was suppressed, Munich was in an uproar. Large segments of the population sided with the insurgents. "Anger at the 'treacherous Kahr' is widespread," observed Hedwig Pringsheim. "The Reichswehr, which is trying to maintain order, is greeted with catcalls, hissing, and cries of 'pfui.' The soldiers are insulted as 'mercenaries for Jews, oath-breaking facilitators of the Kahr Jew government.' People spit and generally behave intractably.

On Odeonsplatz and Briennerstrasse, there have been wild scenes with crowds that include Hitler supporters, who have been disarmed, and the Reichswehr. The Jew-baiting is terrible."[147]

In the days that followed, angry citizens staged demonstrations in Munich and other Bavarian cities against the "clique of traitors" Kahr, Lossow, and Seisser.[148] Support for Hitler and his co-conspirators was particularly significant among students. At an event at Munich University on November 12, the speakers were constantly interrupted by cries of "Up with Hitler! Down with Kahr!" In the end, when the university rector called on the students to sing the German national anthem, they sang instead "The Battle Song of the Ehrhardt Brigade," which honored the Kapp putschist Hermann Ehrhardt.[149] It would take quite some time for the mood in Munich to calm down.

In the early days of his confinement in Landsberg, Hitler was utterly depressed and contemplated suicide, telling a prison psychologist, "I've had enough. I'm done. If I had a revolver, I'd use it."[150] Instead, he went on a hunger strike for ten days, ending it after being implored by prison management and his lawyer Lorenz Roder. By mid-December, his half sister Angela Raubal found him once again "intellectually and emotionally back on top."[151] At that point, the well-known prisoner had begun preparing for his trial, which was to commence in February 1924 in front of Munich's Volksgericht I court.

Kahr banned the Nazi Party and the various organizations of the Fighting League on November 9. The *Völkischer Beobachter* had to cease publication, and the party's offices were shut down and its property confiscated.[152] After four years of what seemed to be an unstoppable rise, Hitler faced the prospect of losing all his power. The *New York Times* prophesied that the putsch would mean his certain end,[153] and the *Frankfurter Zeitung* published an obituary for the Hitler movement on November 10: "In its first step from populist gatherings with their cheap triumphs into reality and action, National Socialism has failed, and that will kill it off for all time."[154] By contrast, several days before Christmas 1923, Hess wrote from hiding in Austria to his parents, "Hitler and Ludendorff's role in German history has not yet been played out."[155] Where Hitler was concerned, Hess would be proved right.


ALTHOUGH THE NATIONAL GOVERNMENT in Berlin had repeatedly received alarming reports about the situation in Bavaria, the news of the Hitler Putsch still caught it somewhat off guard. In the evening of November 8, Ago von Maltzan, state secretary in the Foreign Ministry, had told a worried D'Abernon that the situation there had begun to ease.[156] Stresemann was dining with the future president of the Reichsbank, Hjalmar Schacht, when the first reports of the Munich uprising arrived just after midnight. He immediately called a cabinet meeting in the Chancellery, to which Ebert, Seeckt, Prussian state premier Otto Braun, and Prussian interior minister Carl Severing were also invited.[157] The participants all believed that Kahr, Lossow, and Seisser had joined the uprising. In his diary, Seeckt's adjutant, Hans-Harald von Selchow, noted that Ebert had seemed "the calmest," while Stresemann had been "completely beside himself."[158] The all-important question was how the Reichswehr would react if its Bavarian division should join with the Fighting League and march on Berlin. No minutes survive from the meeting, so it cannot be reconstructed in detail. Seeckt seems to have initially been noncommittal, responding ambiguously when Ebert asked which side the military would choose if things came to a head, merely saying that the Reichswehr would be loyal to him.[159] Only when news arrived that Lossow, his longtime rival, had been selected as Reichswehr minister in the new "national government," did Seeckt stand up and declare, "Mr. Reich President, gentlemen, the time has now come to act."[160]

After a brief discussion, Ebert invoked Article 48 of the Weimar Constitution and transferred to Seeckt command of the Wehrmacht and the executive powers that had been held by the Reichswehr minister since September 26 with the instruction to "take all measures necessary for the security of the Reich."[161] This was Gessler's idea, but apparently not all the ministers were in agreement. Finance Minister

Luther, who only joined the meeting after the resolution had been decided on, asked ironically, "And who is now finance minister?" The question, as Luther recalled in his memoirs, injected "a certain levity into a very depressed mood."[162]

In light of the dubious behavior of the head of army command in the preceding weeks, handing Seeckt executive power was a risky move. "So now he has acquired power by legal means," crowed his adjutant Selchow.[163] The others could not be certain that he would not abuse the immense power that had fallen in his lap to establish a covert military dictatorship in the form of a directorate. On the other hand, Ebert, by having Seeckt report directly to him, had bound the military commander to his own person and obliged him to defend the existing constitutional order. In that sense, it was a clever way of flouting the hopes that enemies of the Weimar Republic had placed in the general. For that reason, Gessler recalled, Seeckt had been in a "sour mood" afterward and hadn't felt "like the winner in the slightest." Instead of gaining a free hand for carrying out his plans for a directorate, he had become "Stresemann's constitutional defender." That, wrote Gessler, was "neither what he had intended nor wished."[164]

The cabinet also agreed on a joint statement by the president and the rest of the government declaring the Munich proclamations "null and void" and promising to take the necessary measures for putting down the putsch with "ruthless energy."[165] In a telegram, Stresemann asked the governments of the regional states to support the national government with all the means at their disposal.[166] When Stresemann returned to his private rooms in the Chancellery at 4:30 a.m., he said, "We don't know what tomorrow will bring, but I won't back down."[167]

THE HOURS THAT FOLLOWED quickly brought clarity to the situation. At 9:30 a.m., State Secretary Maltzan went to the British ambassador and told him the government had received reassuring news from Nuremberg and Bamberg that Kahr and Lossow had "dissociated themselves altogether from Hitler and Ludendorff and had only given their assent last night under menace and compulsion."[168] Count Harry Kessler, who was in the Hague, heard from the German envoy in the city, Baron Hellmuth Lucius von Stoedten, that Berlin hoped to deal with the Bavarian rebels that very day. Kessler wrote, "Kahr and Lossow, he said, had both declared that they wanted nothing to do with the lunatic Hitler."[169]

In the cabinet meeting at noon, Seeckt read out the latest reports from Munich, which confirmed that Hitler had failed to win over the triumvirate. The Reichswehr was holding firm behind Lossow, and one could be certain that the "uprising in Munich would soon be put down." In response, Seeckt proposed that the ban on rail travel and postal deliveries in Bavaria be lifted.[170] A report from the national government's official representative in Munich that afternoon removed any remaining doubts. It described the confrontation between "the main Hitler force" and the police and Reichswehr in front of the Feldherrnhalle, which had ended with "the National Socialists being driven apart and disarmed, Ludendorff taken prisoner, and Hitler forced to flee." Although, admittedly, "mass pro-Hitler demonstrations" were taking place, Kahr and Lossow nonetheless had "a firm grip on power."[171]

Stresemann informed his cabinet of a conversation he had just had with the French ambassador to Germany, Pierre de Margerie, who had communicated on behalf of Poincaré his country's concerns about the events in Munich. The French feared that in the event of a right-wing dictatorship, Germany would abrogate the Treaty of Versailles and begin preparations for a war of revenge against France. Peace would best be served, Margerie said, "if the democratic form of government could be consolidated in Germany." Stresemann replied that the rise of the extreme Right in Germany was in part due to the desperate situation the country had been put in by the occupation of the Ruhr Valley. He added, however, that the end of the Munich Putsch also showed that the national government "possessed enough strength and authority to bring this movement to heel."[172]

THE TRANSFERRAL OF EXECUTIVE power to Seeckt encouraged the segment of the DVP parliamentary group that opposed Stresemann to resume their attacks on the chancellor. Another motion instructing the government to negotiate with the ultranationalists over the formation of a "bourgeois bloc" was put forward on November 9 and passed by a vote of 31 to 15. An additional motion stipulating that Stresemann should lead the negotiations failed 22 to 20 with 2 abstentions. Feeling that he had finally achieved his goal, one of Stresemann's staunchest enemies, Alfred Gildemeister, made it known to the news agencies that the parliamentary group had withdrawn its confidence in the chancellor. Such crass disloyalty was too much even for parliamentary group chairman Ernst Scholz. That evening, in an announcement passed on via the Wolff's Telegraphisches Bureau news agency, he made it clear that while parliamentarians wished to see negotiations with the DNVP, they still stood behind the chancellor. The upshot was that since the ultranationalists insisted that Stresemann be removed, the motion that had been accepted was moot. The next day, a large majority of DVP deputies came out in support of this position.[173]

Stresemann now counterattacked. On November 11, at a large public event in Halle following a regional party conference of the Saxon DVP, he lambasted those who constantly talked about a "national dictatorship" but did nothing to solve Germany's urgent problems: "One cannot get help to the German people by declaring in a beer hall that Mr. Adolf Hitler is now in charge of steering Germany's political destiny!" Stresemann rejected the accusation that he hadn't acted "nationally" as "shameless slander" and once again called for the "courage to be unpopular even within one's own political party."[174] That earned the chancellor standing ovations—something, as he noted in his calendar, that "gave him the greatest psychological boost."[175]

But Stresemann's party rivals weren't the only ones working busily behind his back. Seeckt, too, continued his efforts to topple the chancellor. Having received no answer to his letter of November 4, Seeckt wrote again to Wiedfeldt, again with Ebert's permission and this time by telegram, asking if he would be prepared to take over the office of chancellor and serve as the head of the foreign ministry.[176] But the German ambassador in Washington still dallied with his response. It wasn't until November 24 that he definitively declined. He didn't have the necessary support among the parties and the important segments of society, he told Seeckt, and after two years away from Germany, he didn't feel familiar enough with the domestic political situation.[177] That left the leaders of the Reichswehr searching for a suitable replacement. Seeckt saw "no other way to liberation than a dictatorship of some sort," he confided to his sister around this time, and he would welcome "if a man for this role could be found." He himself, he added, desired "only the ultimate goal, not [dictatorial] rule itself."[178]

With their prematurely launched and amateurish putsch, Hitler and Ludendorff discredited radical right-wing plans for a dictatorship. "The slogan of national dictatorship has been revealed as empty," wrote Ernst Feder in the *Berliner Tageblatt*.[179] Stinnes's *Deutsche Allgemeine Zeitung*, whose morning edition on November 9 had proclaimed the "victory of the national Reich dictatorship in Bavaria," hastily distanced itself from Ludendorff that evening, writing that he had displayed a conspicuous "lack of political vision."[180] That inspired the *Vossische Zeitung* to comment, "What ingratitude!" and to pillory the rival newspaper's about-face: "The circles behind the Stinnes paper did not just find out yesterday morning what Hitler and Ludendorff wanted. They have always pursued the same goal, and they have done everything to create the conditions for their endeavor."[181] Editor in chief Georg Bernhard rejoiced that Ludendorff's true nature had now been revealed. The conspirator who had always managed to hide in the background, wrote Bernhard, had come out openly in favor of high treason together with the "charlatan Hitler . . . revealing for all the world to see the general dangerousness of his activity going back to the Kapp Putsch."[182] Carl von Ossietzky concurred: "The idol has fallen.

This November 9 has delivered the belated but fair judgment about the worst and most unfortunate leader in German history."[183]

The rapidity with which the Munich Putsch was quashed removed the danger of a right-wing coup d'état, at least for the moment. There was also no more justification for the pseudo-legal variant of a directorate. Hitler and Ludendorff had unintentionally helped defuse the conflict between Bavaria and the Reich, shoring up the Republic they so despised. "It's a great benefit that Hitler's putsch was such a comprehensive failure," reported Dorothy von Moltke in mid-November 1923. "If we develop a stable currency, we can get through this. If not, there will be chaos."[184]

# CHAPTER 6

# "FREEDOM FROM BERLIN"

## *Separatist Movements in Rhineland-Pfalz*

*Street battles between separatist demonstrators and the police on
so-called Bloody Sunday in Düsseldorf, September 30, 1923.*

"AS COULD BE ANTICIPATED, THE RHENISH SEPA-
ratists have . . . gleefully received the signal given in Munich,"
commented Theodor Wolff in a *Berliner Tageblatt* editorial about
unrest in Aachen on October 21, 1923. "They have stormed the
Rathaus in Aachen, proclaimed a 'Rhenish Republic' and are preparing similar heroic deeds in other cities."[1] The "signal" in question
was the rebellion against General Lossow's dismissal from office,
which marked the tensest point in the conflict between Bavaria and

the Reich. But separatist movements in the Rhineland were not a reaction to the crises in the fall of 1923. They had started in the immediate aftermath of the fall of the House of Hohenzollern in November 1918.

Separatism was the product of many factors converging at once. The Rhine provinces had been part of Republican, then Napoleonic, France for twenty years, before being awarded to the Prussian crown at the Congress of Vienna in 1815, and as a result they had developed a strong sense of regional identity independent from the German national one. This was reinforced by the confessional difference between Protestant Prussia and the largely Catholic Rhineland. Memories of Bismarck's anti-Catholic "Cultural Battle" (*Kulturkampf*) in the 1880s remained very much alive, and the conflict flared up again in late November 1918, when the culture minister of the provisional Prussian government, Adolf Hoffmann of the USPD, announced plans to radically secularize Rhenish schools. Even at the beginning of the 1918 revolution, there were vocal calls for the Rhineland to become "free from Berlin," and they dovetailed with ideas about how the Reich could be reconfigured to end Prussia's hegemony. With the downfall of the Hohenzollern monarchy, the Prussian system lost its historical justification, noted historian Friedrich Meinecke in late 1918, adding that Germany could "not flourish as long as Greater Prussia remained."[2]

Traditional Rhenish resistance to Prussian domination was accompanied by worries that France might annex all territories west of the Rhine. When the armistice ended the First World War on November 11, 1918, it had yet to be decided what would become of the Rhineland, but by occupying the Lower German Limes and the cities of Mainz, Koblenz, and Cologne, each with a bridgehead across the Rhine, France went into the peace talks in Versailles in a very strong position. France's political and military leaders—first and foremost, Poincaré, Clemenceau, and Marshal Ferdinand Foch—made clear they would not be content only with the return of Alsace-Lorraine but would press long-standing French demands for the Rhine as a buffer region that would protect France against future German attacks.[3] By separating from Prussia, supporters of a Rhenish Republic hoped the region could both avoid being annexed by France and reduce the expected burden of reparations.

The separatists' chief organ was the *Kölnische Volkszeitung*, the leading newspaper of the Catholic Center Party. On the evening of November 9, 1918, editor in chief Karl Hoeber, political editor Josef Froberger, and a number of party politicians sought out Cologne mayor Konrad Adenauer and sought to win him over for the idea of separating from Prussia and creating a "West German Republic." Adenauer was noncommittal but promised to keep the issue in mind and to discuss it with politicians from other parties.[4] On December 4, 1918, two days before occupying British troops entered Cologne, the Center Party staged a large event hosted by the city's main citizens' association. It resulted in a resolution calling on all political parties in the Rhineland to "pave the way for an autonomous Rhenish-Westphalian Republic as part of the German Reich."[5]

Adenauer didn't take part in that event and later said that he had been "completely surprised" by it.[6] But on February 1, 1919, he took a public stand. Addressing the Rhenish deputies elected to the German national and Prussian regional assemblies as well as mayors of occupied cities, he came out in favor of a partition of Prussia and the forming of a "West German Republic in the confederation of the German Reich." Adenauer argued that such a move would assuage French concerns and "rule out the subjugation of Germany by a Prussia dominated by the spirit of the east and militarism." The Cologne mayor summarized his logic in a simple formula: "Either we will become a direct part of or a buffer state for France, or a West German Republic—there's no third alternative." The state Adenauer envisioned was by no means restricted to territory west of the Rhine; it also included areas to the east of the river. Its size and economic significance alone would ensure that this "West German Republic" would play a leading role in a new Germany and be able to "influence the nation's foreign policy in the spirit of peace and friendship." Still,

Adenauer warned against acting prematurely. All measures taken would have to follow "legal paths," abiding by the still-to-be-written national constitution.[7]

The resolution unanimously passed by the conference reflected Adenauer's views and recommendations. It began by solemnly objecting to all efforts to separate the Rhineland from the Reich. But it went on to say, "Because the partition of Prussia is being seriously considered, we authorize our elected committee to continue to work out the establishment of a West German Republic within the confederation of the German Reich and based on the Reich Constitution to be written by the German National Assembly."[8]

This was not enough for hard-line Rhenish separatists, who had hoped a Rhenish Republic would already have been proclaimed by that point. One of those most disappointed was the man who would emerge as a leader of the movement in the months and years that followed: Hans Adam Dorten. Born in 1880 to a merchant family in the village of Endenich near Bonn, Dorten studied law, worked for the Düsseldorf Magistrates Court, and was appointed city prosecutor in 1914. He turned to politics after being discharged from the military in late 1918. Dorten rejected the November Revolution, and his fear that the socialists would reshape Germany was a major reason he joined the separatist movement. In early 1919, he began acquiring official powers in various communities east of the Rhine that supported joining a West German Republic.[9]

Introduced by Hoeber, Dorten contacted Adenauer, on whom he made "a positive but rather erratic impression."[10] Adenauer's and Dorten's respective views on how best to proceed indeed diverged dramatically. Whereas the Cologne mayor favored the creation of a West German Republic by constitutional means, in cooperation with the national German and Prussian governments and the National Assembly charged with writing a new German constitution, Dorten wanted to force the issue. The decision about the destiny of the Rhineland, he wrote to Adenauer on February 5, 1919, "was solely a matter for the groups within the people directly concerned, not the Prussian government or the National Assembly." Dorten and his supporters were calling for "the immediate creation of the West German Republic as the most urgent task of the hour."[11] A few weeks later, on February 28, he issued Adenauer an ultimatum. Either the Cologne mayor would do something, or Dorten himself would "take action."[12]

Dorten was supported by circles within the *Kölnische Volkszeitung* and the Center Party. Together they drew up a public appeal, approved at an assembly on March 10 in Cologne, for an immediate popular referendum in the Rhineland. The "West German Republic" that would subsequently be declared, the document specified, would offer "a guarantee for peace in Europe" as well as a "bulwark against being overwhelmed by Bolsheviks." The committee founded under Adenauer on February 1 was declared "void because of its complete inactivity."[13]

On February 10, 1919, however, the National Assembly in Weimar had decided as part of the "Law on Provisional Reich Authority" that "the territory of the sovereign regional states can only be altered with those states' consent." And on March 13, the assembly endorsed a declaration by National State Premier (the preconstitutional precursor to the chancellor) Philipp Scheidemann, a Social Democrat, that the resolution to the Rhineland issue could only proceed "after a peace treaty and by constitutional means." Any "constitutional reconstruction" before such a point in time, he warned, would "threaten the unity of our fatherland."[14]

This did nothing to deter separatists, who tried to advance their cause in negotiations with French occupation authorities. Yet it emerged that while the French were sympathetic to the idea of founding a Rhenish state, they had little affinity for the idea of it remaining part of the confederation of the German Reich and preferred that it become a buffer state with close ties to France.[15] Moreover, when the harsh terms of peace imposed on Germany became known in May, Rhenish enthusiasm for a split with Prussia cooled. Several of Dorten's supporters from the Center Party only considered it sensible to continue their plans if they promised to yield milder conditions from France.[16]

Despite the challenges in front of him, Dorten decided to act. On June 1, 1919, in his home city of Wiesbaden in the French occupation sector, he proclaimed the "Rhenish Republic." That night, posters containing an appeal "To the Rhenish people!" were put up in parts of the region, informing its surprised populace that "an autonomous Rhenish Republic within the confederation of the German Reich will be established that will include Rhineland, Old Nassau, Rhine-Hessen, and Rhine-Pfalz." As soon as possible, elections would be held for a "Rhenish regional assembly." Until such time as that body could convene in Koblenz, the "provisional government" would reside in Wiesbaden.[17] The following afternoon, Dorten appeared in the company of a French officer and commandeered the Landeshaus, the building where the municipal parliament met.

Dorten and his supporters had misjudged the mood of the populace. On June 2, working people called a general strike, public transport was suspended, and shops closed. The commander of French troops in the Rhineland, General Charles Mangin, summarily forbade all strikes and protest actions, threatening organizers with deportation from the region. The visible protection French troops offered Dorten cast a poor light on his cause. His farcical provisional government lasted only four days, and with its demise the idea of a Rhenish Republic within the confederation of the Reich was, for the moment, completely discredited. A Reich court in Leipzig issued a warrant for Dorten's arrest on suspicion of high treason, but it could never be carried out because Dorten remained in French-occupied territory.[18]

THE TREATY OF VERSAILLES was signed on June 28, 1919. The opposition of President Woodrow Wilson and Prime Minister David Lloyd George prevented the French from splitting the territory to the west of the Rhine off from Germany. The Prussian Rhineland remained part of the Reich. In a concession to French security concerns, a fifty-kilometer-wide demilitarized zone was established to the east of the river. The occupation to the west of the Rhine was to be ended in three stages after fifteen years.[19] The Inter-Allied Rhineland High Commission in Koblenz was created as the highest agency of the occupation government, and French civil servant Paul Tirard was named its chairman.

In late July 1919, the German National Assembly ratified the Weimar Constitution. Article 18 left open the possibility of reordering the territory of the regional states within the Reich, but in a departure from the original draft of the document, which had been authored by DDP politician and constitutional law expert Hugo Preuss, political representatives and municipalities no longer had the right to call referenda to that end. Furthermore, Article 167 stipulated that Article 18 would not take effect for two years. That blocked any plans for partitioning Prussia.[20] With the Treaty of Versailles in place and the Weimar Constitution ratified, Adenauer and his circles in the Center Party abandoned the "West German Republic" plans for the time being.[21]

FROM 1920 TO 1922, the Rhineland separatist movement led a shadow existence. In January 1920, the undeterred Dorten founded the Rhenish Popular Association in the town of Boppard, but it was little more than a cult. The same was true of the Rhenish Republican People's Party founded by Cologne Social Democrat Josef Smeets, who in contrast to Dorten advocated for an independent state outside the Reich confederation. A third group, the Rhenish Independence League, coalesced around the journalist Josef Friedrich Matthes, who was thought to be on the French payroll. He primarily recruited his followers from the Düsseldorf area in northern Rhineland.[22]

It wasn't until the crises of 1923 that the movement for a Rhenish Republic regained momentum. The failed policy of passive resistance against the French occupation of the Ruhr Valley and the devastating economic and societal effects of hyperinflation drove people not only to extremist parties on the Right and Left but also to separatism. At a conference in Koblenz on August 15, 1923, the various separatist organizations joined to form the United Rhenish Movement. For the first time ever in public, Dorten came out at the conference in favor of the Rhineland splitting from Prussia and forming a "Rhenish Republic" as a French protectorate. The movement's declaration read, "We are free Rhinelanders. We won't allow ourselves to be paid off. We want to decide our own destiny." The new state's independence from Berlin was to be underscored by a currency of its own.[23]

The United Rhenish Movement was quick to take action. It held increasingly well-attended events in cities including Trier, Bonn, Duisburg, Mainz, Mönchengladbach, and Wiesbaden. The high point of the campaign was a mass rally in Düsseldorf on September 30, a Sunday. The French railway administration, the Régie, provided demonstrators from all over the region with free special trains so they could attend. Unions and civil servant organizations distributed flyers addressed to "the entire population of Düsseldorf," calling on residents to vacate the streets at 1:00 p.m. to "leave the Rhine League people alone with their activities."[24] Nervous tension crackled in the air amid rumors that the separatists were about to proclaim a Rhenish Republic. The head of the Düsseldorf municipal administration, Walther Grützner, who had been banished from the city for obstructionism and had set up an office in exile in the town of Barmen, instructed Düsseldorf mayor Emil Köttgen and the police forces under him to "ruthlessly" put down any such "treasonous action" with all means at their disposal.[25] Thus, on the morning of September 30, police officers were put on high alert.

The special trains of the Régie began arriving at Düsseldorf's main train station around noon. Eight thousand to ten thousand people, including several hundred members of the armed militia calling itself Rhineland Defense, formed a column and began marching in closed ranks toward the city center. That triggered a series of events. There was a chaotic exchange of gunfire, then pitched street battles, between separatists and police. It is not known who fired the first shots, but both sides acted with brutality. The results were ten dead, mostly separatists, and well over one hundred wounded. Only when the worst was over did French occupation troops intervene—unmistakably on the side of the separatists. Police officers were disarmed, and more than a few were called to answer for themselves in front of courts-martial. Grützner was sentenced in absentia to twenty years in prison and banned from entering Düsseldorf for twenty years.[26]

"French troops protected defenseless people against police who were misusing their weapons," wrote the Parisian newspaper *Le Temps* about what was becoming known as the Düsseldorf "Bloody Sunday." "An occupying army would have done the same thing in any country."[27] The one-sided depiction of events by the French highlighted how the occupation authorities would behave in the conflicts to come. The separatists could only feel emboldened to force through a Rhenish Republic.

BY THE NIGHT OF October 20–21, the time to do so seemed to be at hand. Belgian-occupied Aachen provided the spark, as some two thousand armed separatists seized the most important public buildings, including the Rathaus, the main postal directorship, the district office, and the local branch of the Reichsbank, and raised the separatist movement's green, white, and red flag over them. On posters plastered all over town, the rebellion's spokesmen—factory owner Leo Deckers and Emil Karl Guthardt, a corporate lawyer who was the commander of the Rhineland Defense—proclaimed the formation of the "Rhenish Republic." The "hour of freedom" had come, they asserted. Berlin had "declared bankruptcy," and the Rhineland would have to save itself.[28]

Although the coup had gone as well as its plotters could have hoped, a response followed the very next day. A conference of civil servants from all city offices, union representatives, and political parties decided to ignore all orders from the putschists: "Negotiations with those who presume to be the government are out of the question." Conversely, Rhenish republicans disregarded demands from a representative of the mayor's office to vacate city buildings so "that a condition of constitutionalism can be restored and peace and order preserved." On the evening of October 21, a large crowd gathered before city hall, but police were able to prevent them from storming the building. The demonstrators proceeded to the separatists' administration office and demolished it.[29]

By October 23, the leaders of the rebellion that initially had ruled the streets barely appeared in public. The previous evening, they had evacuated most of the buildings they had occupied, taking down the movement's flags, while some remained holed up in Aachen's venerable Rathaus and the city administration building. At around 11:00 a.m., a group of them sallied forth in a car through the city, with shots apparently being fired along the way. A special correspondent for the *Vossische Zeitung* described the events that followed: "A great agitation seized the crowd, which stormed a furniture store belonging to one of the leaders of the movement, where some twenty separatists were in hiding. They were dragged out and lynched. Several were literally beaten to death; others wounded so badly they had to be driven away by car. Others who had managed to flee from the rear of the building also fell into the hands of the enraged mob and were beaten bloody. One of them was killed."[30] On October 24, only a small number of separatists remained. Belgian occupiers declared a state of emergency, which allowed these people to escape.

Yet the failed Aachen putsch inspired attempts by separatists to seize power in cities throughout the French and Belgian occupation zone. All over the region, rebels took over government buildings and raised the green, white, and red flag, but as in Aachen, their reign was usually over after a few days.[31] In the town of Rheydt, a twenty-five-year-old unemployed scholar with a doctorate in literature named Joseph Goebbels described one such attempted putsch on October 23:

In the streets around the railway station are the Rhenish republicans, four guards at the entrance, guys between the age of eighteen and twenty, revolvers in their hands, the obligatory cigarettes in the corners of their mouths. Wild rumors swirl around the city and are eagerly passed on and even more eagerly believed. The *jeu-*

*Posters in Aachen proclaiming the "Rhenish Republic,"*
*October 1923.*

*nesse dorée* of Rheydt sits around the Rathaus, armed with rubber
truncheons, together with the police, and are ready to receive the
attack units of the separatists.... Many of those who are talking
the loudest are known for not exactly earning their *pour merité*
during the war. Rabble here, there, and everywhere.[32]

Occupation authorities were clearly on the side of the separatists,
despite their official stance of strict neutrality. In reality, they tolerated and sometimes even aided separatist efforts, causing the German national government to repeatedly lodge protests with Paris.
The French government rejected all accusations of meddling. French
troops, Paris claimed, had in all cases "restricted themselves to maintaining order and preventing slaughter among the peaceful population," but that flew in the face of the facts.[33]

DORTEN APPEARS TO HAVE been surprised by his fellow
movement members' initiative. The proclamation of the Rhenish

Republic seems to have originally been planned for a week later. General Mangin, who had been recalled from his post in October 1919 but had remained on cordial terms with Dorten, wrote to his protégé on October 22 from Paris that he would have wished for a less hasty action. If Dorten wanted to remain the "master of events," Mangin counseled, he was now forced to "go over to a general attack... as quickly as possible."[34]

Dorten didn't need much encouragement. On October 23, he and his ally Matthes in Koblenz formed a "preliminary government of the Rhenish Republic." That afternoon, separatists occupied Koblenz Palace, the seat of the Prussian provincial government. As they were raising the green, white, and red flag, the rope got tangled, and the flag remained at half-mast. It was a bad omen, and after a couple of hours, police drove off the rebels. That night, the French occupiers declared a state of siege and assumed command over the German police. The mayor of Koblenz and forty city employees were dragged from their beds and deported into nonoccupied territories.

This allowed the separatists to retake possession of the palace and to seize the Rathaus, the post center, and the telegraph office on October 25. The following day, Chairman Tirard received Dorten and Matthes and recognized them as the "de facto possessors of power." Their first ordinance, signed by Matthes as the head of the executive branch, suspended freedom of the press. Newspapers and other printed material were only allowed to be published if the authors agreed "to heed most exactly the directions of the executive of the provisional government."[35]

As in Aachen, the provisional government in Koblenz was more or less operating in a vacuum. Following instructions from the Prussian Interior Ministry, most civil servants refused to follow the would-be government's orders, with the result that public administration broke down. How little support the separatists had among the public at large became apparent in a report in early November by the deputy of Koblenz's mayor, who had been banned from the city: "The scenes on the streets have again calmed down thanks to the French measures, the state of siege at the 7:00 p.m. curfew. But things are still fermenting within the populace. If the separatists weren't backed by French weapons, these desolate-looking fellows clad in torn green uniforms slinking through the streets, including State Premier Matthes with his dubious appearance and Alpine French cap, would have been physically driven from the city in no time."[36]

The separatists' enemies stereotyped them as "alien, armed rabble" aiming to "trample the feelings of the Rhenish populace and drive a wedge between these people and the Reich and the [other] regional states."[37] But that was unfair. There were no doubt dubious elements in the separatist ranks, but the Rhineland Defense, the armed wing of the movement, recruited most of its members from the working class, who were native to the Rhineland or had lived there for quite some time. Most were relatively young, between twenty and thirty, and many of them had lost their jobs amid the concatenation of crises. These people had been uprooted and now sought salvation in the separatist self-defense movement, as other people their age did in right-wing and left-wing paramilitary organizations.[38]

From the start, the provisional government in Koblenz faced financial troubles. The French and Belgian occupiers throttled the flow of money into the government because they recognized that the separatist movement had so little public support. In early November, Matthes had to cut the wages of the members of the Rhineland Defense and reduce the size of the force by a quarter.[39] As a result, some of the armed members of the movement began requisitioning anything they felt they needed, creating bitterness and growing enmity within the populace. In many places, citizens formed militias to resist the separatists. In mid-November, a pitched battle broke out between the "Home Defense" and a troop of Rhineland Defense forces in the Aegidienberg district. Fourteen separatists were killed and later buried in the local cemetery.[40]

Internal power struggles further weakened the puppet government in Koblenz, with no clear lines of authority existing among the leadership. Even after it was agreed that Dorten would administer the southern and central Rhineland and Matthes the north as "general plenipotentiaries," rivalries persisted. The cabinet split into two factions, each issuing its own decisions. On November 27, worn down by endless quarrels, Matthes declared in a letter to Tirard that the "provisional government of the Rhenish Republic" was dissolved.[41]

Dorten had already relocated in the middle of the month to Bad Ems, where he tried—in vain—to establish a new center of power. The French occupation authorities lost interest in, although never fully abandoned, the separatists, who had by this point been completely discredited in the minds of many Rhinelanders.[42] By the end of November, the *Vossische Zeitung* was convinced that "the Rhenish separatism so vocally promoted for three years but without any ideas at all" was finally over and done with. The paper concluded acidly, "French nationalists are one hope poorer."[43]

ALONG WITH THE RHINELAND, the Pfalz (Palatinate) to the west of the Rhine also emerged as a center of separatism after 1918. This process, too, was related to the area's history. In the Rhine-Pfalz, as it was also known, memories of the republican traditions begun during its period under French rule from 1797 to 1814 remained. In 1816, as part of a land swap in the post-Napoleonic reordering of Europe, the region passed from Austrian control to Bavarian, although it wasn't contiguous with the latter. Nonetheless, the Pfalz maintained its liberal orientation. In 1832, it was the location of the national-democratic Hambach Festival, a political event disguised as a country fair, and in 1849 republicans from the region joined with like-minded activists from Baden to the south to wage a final battle for the Frankfurt Constitution to form a constitutionally unified German nation-state. But that came to nothing. With the end of the Bavarian Wittelsbach dynasty and the proclamation of the "free state" of Bavaria in November 1918, separatist movements also arose in the French-occupied Pfalz, where Bavarians had never enjoyed great sympathy. In the town of Landau, the chemist Eberhard Haas founded the Free Pfalz League, but as they had in the Rhineland, all attempts to form an autonomous republic failed. In early June 1919, a "Pfalz Republic" proclaimed by the league in Speyer fell apart before it even really began, after Social Democrats and the unions in particular opposed the enterprise. Haas and his allies retreated from the town empty-handed.[44]

Nonetheless, the dream of an autonomous Pfalz state wasn't dead and would be revived in the early 1920s as Bavaria developed into a reactionary "cell of order" and home for ultranationalists and the racist Right. "The Pfälzerist is above all a Pfälzer and a German," explained the regional writer Wilhelm Michel in the *Weltbühne*. "His Bavarian identity barely runs skin deep. The intellectual atmosphere that predominates in today's Bavaria couldn't be more alien to the Pfälzer. He is naturally revolted by the sinister, pigheaded, and obdurate nature of Hitlerism, the tyrannical inability to acknowledge difference, the crude inhumanity and primitive simplemindedness of all this nationalistic foolishness."[45]

The Social Democratic Reichstag deputy Johannes Hoffmann from Kaiserslautern became a leader of the efforts to split the Pfalz from Bavaria. After the assassination of revolutionary leader Kurt Eisner in Munich by the right-wing terrorist Count Anton von Arco in February 1919, Hoffmann had become Bavarian state premier, but he had been forced to step down in March 1920 after the Kapp Putsch and had then withdrawn from politics. Hoffmann was deeply concerned with the increasing radicalization of Bavaria under General State Commissar Kahr starting in September 1923. But Hoffmann didn't reenter the political arena until after the Lossow affair, when Bavaria began openly opposing the national government and showed it would have no scruples about violating the national constitution.[46]

At a hastily convened meeting of the SPD regional committee on the evening of October 22, Social Democrats vented their outrage over Bavaria's unconstitutional actions and the tolerant attitude of the national government. Following a motion brought by Hoffmann, the delegates decided to form an autonomous Pfalz state "within the Reich confederation" while explicitly rejecting any state formed "outside the Reich." The decision was not only in reaction to Kahr and his hostility toward the Weimar Republic but also to the Rhineland separatists. A few hours before the meeting, Hoffmann had received word of the attempted putsch in Aachen, and he feared that the rebellion could spread to the Pfalz, resulting in a split from the rest of Germany.[47]

At the insistence of his fellow party members, Hoffmann was forced to agree to inform French occupation authorities about the new state. On the morning of October 23, together with two members of the committee, Paul Kleefoot and Friedrich Wilhelm Wagner, he went to see General Adalbert François Alexandre de Metz in Speyer and presented him with a declaration of an autonomous Pfalz "within the confederation of the Reich." As a representative of the Inter-Allied Rhineland High Commission, the general was asked "to register with benevolence" the existence of the new state.[48] He made it understood that the commission was open to the enterprise and held out the prospect that elections for a Pfalz parliament could be held within weeks. But at a second meeting that afternoon, after speaking to his superior, Tirard in Koblenz, Metz insisted as a condition for his support that the words "within the confederation of the Reich" be struck from the document. "I refused on the spot and in no uncertain terms, and he relented," Hoffmann would remember.[49] By that point, the Pfalz SPD must have realized that French interests went considerably beyond merely divorcing the region from Bavaria.

The following morning, Hoffman sent a telegram to the chairman of the SPD parliamentary group in the Reichstag, informing him of the situation: "Our patience with Munich at an end. Great danger of separatism. Formation today of Pfalz Republic within Reich confederation. Chancellor to be informed." The national party leaders were likely somewhat surprised by this announcement, but they didn't reject it out of hand, although they did advise the Pfalz SPD not to act unilaterally: "I urge you to reach agreement with coalition partners on the Pfalz issue. All measures that support French Rhine League plans, even indirectly, to be avoided," wrote Müller in his telegraphed answer.[50]

But the bourgeois centrist parties in the Pfalz had already rebuffed

Hoffmann's attempt to reach an agreement the day before, and on the afternoon of October 24, he received another major disappointment. At a meeting of the Pfalz District Council, from which Hoffmann himself was absent, a representative of Metz, a Major Louis, read out a proclamation that made no mention of the Pfalz retaining its connection to the Reich: "In view of the fact that the present situation cannot go on with endangering the most crucial moral and material interests of the populace, and in view additionally of the most worrisome and dangerous situation in Bavaria, from today forth, an autonomous Pfalz state has been formed with a provisional government until further developments take place."[51] The words "within the confederation of the Reich" had been purposely left out, leaving the delegates with the impression that Hoffmann's project was in line with French separatist policy concerning the Rhineland. As a result, the proclamation was rejected by all the parties in attendance, including the SPD. The chairman of the council, Michael Bayersdörfer of the Center Party, said he had received word by telephone that the national and Bavarian governments were "most urgently examining" the issue and considered the "formation of a new state in whatever form an act of treason."[52]

The liberal press in the German capital, led by the *Berliner Tageblatt*, also condemned Hoffmann's project and not just because it clearly contradicted Article 18 of the Weimar Constitution:

> Even if all reports thus far state that the Social Democrats involved in the preliminary discussions are only interested in a split from Bavaria within the confederation of the Reich, it is still absolutely contemptible that such discussions have taken place with the French general behind the backs of the official German authorities. For our part, we consider it out of the question, especially after the welcome decisive action taken by Social Democrats and the unions against the Rhenish separatists, for the Social Democratic Party to participate in an enterprise like this one in our hour of need.[53]

On October 25, Hoffmann sought out Tirard in Koblenz and finally determined that his vision of an autonomous Pfalz within the Reich was incompatible with the French plans for a Greater Rhine state that would unify the Pfalz and the Rhineland and be closely tied to France. Without permission from Poincaré, Tirard told his visitor that he could offer no assurances about the future status of the Pfalz. Hoffmann countered by repeating that he could never vote for splitting the Pfalz from the Reich, if he "didn't want to stand accused of high treason."[54]

After returning from Koblenz, Hoffmann called the district committee of his party together and proposed that their project be immediately discontinued. A subsequent press release read, "After the intentions of the Social Democratic Party were met with significant resistance from various circles in the Pfalz, and after the national government refused to acknowledge the secession of the Pfalz from Bavaria while remaining within the Reich, and given that for the Social Democratic Party secession from Bavaria outside the Reich is out of the question, we are abandoning the pursuit of those intentions."[55]

Despite the statement, the national and Bavarian SPD distanced themselves from Hoffmann. Referring to Hoffmann's profession, Ebert remarked that the affair further confirmed the old adage that "as a rule schoolmasters make unhappy politicians."[56] The Bavarian representative in Berlin, Konrad Ritter von Preger, noted that the SPD deputy from Kaiserslautern was "so fanatically pigheaded" that he had been willing to consider an autonomous Pfalz state outside the Reich—a complete untruth.[57] In early November, the German superior prosecutor applied for an immediate investigation of Hoffmann on suspicions of high treason. In a lengthy memo to the Reichstag committee that would decide on whether to suspend his parliamentary immunity, Hoffmann claimed that he and his allies in the Pfalz were exercising a "right to self-defense" against a Bavarian government that had "systematically, unnecessarily, and without justification frivolously violated the Reich Constitution."[58] Before the month was out, Bavarian culture minister Franz Matt expelled Hoffmann from the civil service and canceled his pension. Ultimately, Hoffmann was able to hold onto his seat in the Reichstag, but he was permanently tarred by the stigma of his alleged "treason."[59]

THE ABANDONMENT OF HOFFMANN'S project brought about what he had hoped to prevent: the Rhineland separatist movement spread to the Pfalz. The man behind the initiative was Franz Josef Heinz, nicknamed Heinz-Orbis, a reference to his hometown. Born in 1884, Heinz was the chairman of the Free Farmer's Association, the largest agrarian group in the Pfalz. In 1920, he was elected as a DVP deputy to the Pfalz District Council, but he quit the party on October 24, 1923, to protest its rejection of Hoffmann's project. On November 5, three days before the Hitler Putsch in Munich, Heinz took action, occupying the Kaiserslautern city administration building with several hundred supporters. One week later, on November 12, Pfalz separatists in Speyer proclaimed the "Pfalz Republic in Confederation with the Rhenish Republic," whose government declared martial law and called upon "all law and order–loving citizens regardless of party affiliation" to support the new dispensation.[60]

The leading separatists were a motley crew. Alongside Heinz-Orbis, who represented conservative farmers, the most important leader was his deputy, printer Adolf Bley from Kirchheimbolanden, a leftist who had been politicized by the war and the revolution. He had sheltered Eisner's widow in his house after her husband's murder and had represented the USPD on the town council. Bley was a committed pacifist who wanted to prevent hostilities from ever breaking out on Pfalz soil and conceived of an autonomous Pfalz state as a "republic of peace." Even further to the left was the career revolutionary Georg Viktor Kunz, who had been active as an agitator for the Communist Workers' Party of Germany (KAPD), a group that had splintered from the KPD because the latter was insufficiently radical. He moved to the Pfalz in late 1922, where he made a name for himself as an organizer of the unemployed in the city of Ludwigshafen.[61] In the Speyer government, he served as head of the labor department. In a proclamation, he promised a "complete shake-up" of conditions, declaring "the poorest of the poor must and will be helped." Pensions for war invalids, widows, and orphans would be guaranteed; retirement payments for civil servants continued; old age and sickness support expanded; social amenities improved; unemployment assistance maintained; and workers put back to work and paid so that they could "escape as soon as possible the serious situation in which Berlin politics has placed them."[62]

The government of the "Autonomous Pfalz" in Speyer faced the same hurdles as the "Rhenish Republic" in Koblenz. Public employees refused to cooperate, and the separatists faced an overall lack of trained personnel. Moreover, the financial resources were insufficient to keep all the grand promises. The sums the French occupiers covertly gave to the separatists weren't even close to enough. Thus, in Speyer, too, the leaders turned to requisitioning, leading people to joke that the state was named the "Autonomous Pfalz" because when it came calling, your auto was no longer yours but ours.

On top of those difficulties, the introduction of the Rentenmark in November 1923 was gradually stabilizing the domestic political situation, and in foreign policy, there were signs of a thaw in relations with France. Increasingly, the government of "Autonomous Pfalz" was fighting a losing battle. The cause had already been lost by January 9, 1924, when Heinz was assassinated while dining at the Wittelsbacher Hof hotel in Speyer. The killing was carried out by right-wing militants with the knowledge and approval of the Bavarian government. The final sad chapter of "Autonomous Pfalz" took place in the city of Pirmasens on February 12, 1924, when an angry mob attacked a district office to which separatists had retreated and set it on fire. Seven of the attackers and fifteen separatists died in the violence.[63]


THE SEPARATISTS IN THE Rhineland and the Pfalz weren't the only ones who revived plans from 1919 during the crises of the fall of 1923. Cologne's mayor, Adenauer, revisited his plans for a "West

German Republic." His primary motivation was concern that the simmering conflict between Germany and France would end with the permanent or temporary separation of the territories west of the Rhine from the Reich.[64] But Adenauer never seriously considered a Rhine state existing outside the Reich confederation, as envisioned by Dorten and his followers. On the contrary, like Hoffmann's "Autonomous Pfalz," the "West German Republic" was supposed to counter the efforts of separatists backed by France and reinforce the internal stability of the Reich. For that reason, Adenauer rejected any suggestion of cutting off the occupied German territories by no longer pumping money into the area. Among the proponents of that idea was Duisburg mayor Karl Jarres, whom Stresemann would appoint Reich interior minister in early November 1923. He proposed making the occupying powers responsible for the fate of the occupied territories while at the same time abrogating the Treaty of Versailles, which would have dramatically increased tensions with France and possibly led to renewed war.[65]

On October 25, alarmed by the most recent separatist forays, Stresemann traveled to the unoccupied city of Hagen to get a feel for the situation from representatives from the occupied territories, including Adenauer. Leading off the discussion, Jarres summarized the outcome of a preliminary meeting held the day before in Barmen. All districts reported that the vast majority of the populace from all walks of life "thoroughly rejected" separatism. Nonetheless, the danger posed by the movement could not be underestimated in light of the "uncertainty and insecurity" concerning the Rhine regions.[66] Stresemann started his remarks by making clear that as chancellor he had no choice but to "refuse as a matter of course any discussion splitting off parts of the German Reich." He added, "We haven't given up the Rhineland, and as a result we cannot regard the Rhineland as a part of the German Reich that can decide for itself to break away from the Reich." The stenographer recorded a loud "Bravo!" at this point in the minutes. Countering Jarres, Stresemann declared that he would resist "us bringing about a break with France with the same premature haste as we brought about a declaration of war in 1914." The minutes recorded calls of "Entirely right!" Abrogating the Treaty of Versailles might be a popular move in the moment, but it would also be "eminently undiplomatic. . . . It would put us on the side of injustice, whereas we likely have the most just cause of any abused people ever in the world."

Stresemann was equally critical of Adenauer's project. It was "utopian" to believe that the "Rhine issue" could be solved and the "harassments and sanctions" from France ended by forming a Rhine state: "They would just try to keep cutting us down to the bone to scrape out what we would not yield voluntarily." Stresemann did leave it up to the Rhinelanders themselves to decide if they wanted to negotiate directly with France and Belgium over possible alleviations of foreign dictates in the occupied areas, "so as not to abandon such matters to separatist elements such as those of Dorten, Smeets, Matthes, etc."[67]

Adenauer responded that secession from the Reich was the last thing on his mind. The picture he painted of the occupied regions, old and new, was gloomy. The attempted separatist putsches in a number of locations may have been beaten back, Adenauer said, but in view of rising unemployment, currency shortages, and concerns about the food supply, the separatists might well be more successful in subsequent attempts to seize control of large parts of the Rhine regions. Because the Reich and the other regional states couldn't help even though they wanted to, the question became, "Should we let the misfortune we see coming simply wash over us, should we let the French or their henchmen lord over the Rhineland and the Ruhr, or should we at least try to defend ourselves?" No one was under any illusions, Adenauer said, in a nod to Stresemann, that the formation of a Rhenish confederated state would solve all problems. On the contrary, everyone was aware such a state would have to "bear a significant share of the reparations." But it would help enormously to inject some movement into the gridlocked relations between Germany and France. Speaking with great urgency, the Cologne major assured the others that he was guided not by "selfish perspectives" but "only by the purest love for our homeland and our nation."[68]

The results of the meeting in Hagen were modest. A fifteen-member committee of representatives from the occupied regions was formed to try to initiate a dialogue with the Inter-Allied Rhineland High Commission. But the national government provided no clear instructions about the goal of such talks. Adenauer was the most important figure on the committee. In late October, he gave an interview to the Belgian socialist newspaper *Le Peuple*, in which he clearly distanced himself from the separatism of Dorten and his supporters. The creation of a neutral Rhenish buffer state, he insisted, wouldn't guarantee the security of either France or Belgium. The best thing for the cause of peace in Europe would be to create a "community of interest" between the three countries.[69]

Tirard initially refused to meet Adenauer. The mayor of a city in the British occupation zone was persona non grata in the eyes of the French.[70] On October 28, the archbishop of Cologne, Cardinal Karl Joseph Schulte, went to the high commissioner to ask him to receive committee representatives. Tirard explained that it was impossible for him to defy French public opinion, which believed that the proclaimed "Rhenish Republic" was already a reality. Even if it was headed by "impossible people," the French would never agree to go after a separatist movement that had "arisen spontaneously" and had been "successful almost everywhere." Tirard assured Schulte that France didn't aim to annex the Rhine territories but merely wished for the sort of "security" that could only be achieved with "an independent state of a neutral character."[71]

The next day, after speaking with other leading Rhenish personalities, Tirard traveled to Paris to receive new instructions. He had started to question whether it was really in France's best interest to bet everything on the separatists. It had become clear that while short-term successes could be achieved with the support of occupation troops, separatist movements were unable to maintain effective administrations or mobilize the broad support of the populace. For that reason, he believed it wasn't advisable to refuse to engage with the fifteen-member committee. Poincaré ordered Tirard to continue to use the separatist movements to aid his diplomatic goals but also allowed him to talk to the committee.[72]

When he returned to Koblenz on November 3, Tirard received the president of the Cologne Chamber of Industry and Commerce, the banker Louis Hagen, and informed him that his government had agreed to talks with the committee about "the future form of state of the occupied regions." Hagen declared his support for such negotiations but insisted the separatists be completely excluded and the Rhenish state that would be created remain "under all circumstances in the confederation of the German Reich." Hagen also insisted that Adenauer be included as part of the negotiating commission, a condition to which Tirard ultimately agreed.

The second half of the meeting was dominated by one of the Cologne banker's pet projects: the establishment of a Rhenish gold-standard bank. Because it was uncertain whether the Inter-Allied Rhineland High Commission would permit the Rentenbank Law to be enforced in the occupied regions—and it had yet to be decided whether the Reich government even wanted to introduce the Rentenmark in the Rhineland—Hagen saw the creation of a securely valued means of payment in the Rhineland as the only way of reviving its economy. Tirard was open to the idea, and the two discussed the details, including the amount of capital required and the question of whether foreign entities would be involved.[73]

At its meeting on November 9, the Stresemann cabinet extensively debated the situation in the occupied regions. What most darkened the general mood there, reported the minister for the occupied regions, Johannes Fuchs, was "separatist terror." Only a minuscule part of the populace, he added, was in favor of splitting from Prussia, and "no respectable element" supported leaving the German Reich. Nonetheless, the danger existed that individual cities like Koblenz and Trier could "form tiny republics if the economic concerns of the occupied territories weren't taken into account." Prussian state premier Otto Braun was particularly critical of Adenauer's and Hagen's plans. France's goal remained to pry the Rhineland from the Reich, he argued, and it would never be satisfied with the Rhineland as a new regional state within the German confederation. "If the Rhineland is now divorced in any form from Prussia, it will be bound for all time to come, sealing its fate. It would be a commitment for the ages if Berlin were now to agree to the formation of a Rhineland gold-standard bank." Stresemann agreed with Braun, albeit with the qualification that nothing from his perspective spoke against "privately extending feelers to the occupation powers even in the political arena."[74] But before the discussion could be continued, the remnants of the Stresemann cabinet became embroiled in a crisis that would topple the chancellor.

# CHAPTER 7

# STABILIZATION

## *From Stresemann to Marx*

*A Hebrew bookstore with signs in both
Hebrew and German. The year 1923 saw bursts
of violence against "Jewish businesses" and other
prominent Jewish sites throughout Germany.*

GERMANY SAW UNUSUALLY PLEASANT AND MILD
weather in the fall of 1923. "It's almost as though nature were
trying to calm the passions that have been unleashed with unprecedented tricks of the light and atmospheric fineries," gushed Thea Sternheim in late October in her diary. "A benevolent, gently warming sun

hangs in the turquoise sky."[1] It was a strange counterpoint to the economic and political chaos in Germany, as hyperinflation approached its zenith. "How desolate it is to walk though the streets of the city today," remarked Goebbels in Rheydt. "On every corner, groups of the unemployed stand around arguing and speculating about the future. It's a time for both laughing and crying." The first journal Goebbels used to record his experiences, starting on October 17, 1923, cost one billion marks. "For that sum you would have been previously able to buy half the world."[2] As Victor Klemperer recorded, "Every day things get worse and more oppressive. It's impossible to catch your breath. Above all, money and more money. The dollar rises by billions day after day... and prices follow suit. Bread now costs 1.5 billion."[3] The unprecedented plunge of the mark on the New York currency exchange rocked Germany, and its purchasing power decreased by unimaginable proportions. The official exchange rate of the mark to the dollar was 72 billion to one on October 31, 130 billion to one on November 1, 320 billion to one on November 2, and 420 billion to one on November 3. The rate remained constant for three days before vaulting to 630 billion to one on November 7 and 840 billion to one on November 13.[4]

Such numbers had "freed themselves of their material existence" and were "leading lives of their own like fascinatingly frightful ghosts," wrote a journalist in the business newspaper *Berliner Börsen-Courier* on November 6. The writer added that the "obvious comparison with an asylum" didn't apply because "no common lunatic... even in his most insane flights of fancy would have imagined sums of the sort now denoted by paper marks—for the simple reason that they were unknown to him."[5]

Count Harry Kessler, traveling from Paris to London in the second half of October, witnessed peddlers on the streets of the British capital offering million- and billion-mark notes for sale as curiosities for a couple of pence.[6] When he returned to Germany on November 10, he was astonished to pay 500 billion marks for a half bottle of water for his sleeping car. He was even more flabbergasted when, after arriving back in Berlin, he went to a restaurant with a friend. He noted in his diary, "The two of us ate very badly last evening for three billion: soup, a meat dish, a bottle of mediocre wine and coffee. In London, a meal like that would have cost perhaps ten to twelve shillings."[7] After his long absence from Germany, Kessler needed some time to get used to the absurd prices in the country.

The overwhelming majority of Berliners couldn't afford to patronize restaurants. Many had to seek out soup kitchens for cheap, warm meals. It was a miserable experience, as one *Berliner Tageblatt* journalist described: "People of all ages sit pressed together on wooden benches at long tables. A young mother carries a pale infant in a shawl who cried and screeched with hunger. The mother extracts a tip of a spoon full of rice from a tin bowl, makes sure it's not too hot and dribbles the food into the hairless infant's tiny mouth. How greedily it swallows the boiled mush. Its face, cramped from crying, smooths out in contentment. Next to the mother sits an ancient fellow with a long white beard. You can tell he's been catapulted from a life of personal worth and security into this public soup kitchen. Everywhere are malnourished children, all of them with those wide, prematurely knowing, dark-ringed eyes and translucent skin. A middle-aged laborer leaves the rows of people and approaches me, not to beg but to get a few things off his chest. 'Who would have ever thought things would again be this bad?' he says. The man has been without work for six months and has four children who suffer dizzy spells because of extreme privation."[8]

"Our collapse is complete," Betty Scholem wrote to her son Gershom, who had just found a job as the director of the Hebrew department at the Jerusalem National Library. "There's some looting here and there, but not much. The desperate women are too worn out. They accept their fate. There has been no noticeable unrest, although we've been expecting it for weeks. You scratch your head as to why it hasn't happened yet."[9]

ON MONDAY, NOVEMBER 5, the expected unrest arrived, as pogrom-like violence broke out in Berlin's Scheunenviertel neighborhood near Alexanderplatz square with its large population of Eastern European Jewish immigrants. The attacks were sparked by a sudden, extreme rise in the price of bread over the weekend from 25 billion to 140 billion marks for a single loaf. Antisemitic agitators fomented violence by spreading the rumor that the "Galicians" had bought up all the state-issued, value-guaranteed emergency money so that none was left over for thousands of jobless people. The hate-mongering landed on fertile soil. Around noon on November 5, people began looting Jewish-owned shops and dwellings. "Before terrified neighborhood residents could shut their businesses, gangs of young men forced their way into shops and apartments, beating the occupants and stripping them of their clothes before fleeing," wrote the reporter for the *Vossische Zeitung*. "The marauders proceeded systematically from building to building for an hour, until the police were notified. Every pedestrian who looked Jewish was surrounded on the street by a bellowing mob, knocked to the ground, and had his clothes stolen." The violence continued until late in the night. Only the following day did a massive police presence, assisted by Reichswehr units, succeed in dispersing the mobs.[10]

"Berlin now has had its anti-Jewish pogrom," wrote *Vorwärts*. "Berlin has been defiled. Shame upon a people that considers itself among the world's civilized."[11] The *Vossische Zeitung* was equally appalled: "Something that would have been considered utterly impossible in Germany before the war but that has been slowly prepared by regular, hateful tirades since 1918 and has broken out here and there in smaller places, including even some outside Hitler's sphere of influence, became a reality yesterday in the national capital."[12] The violence in Berlin was a sign of darker days to come. Unlike with the Hitler Putsch and the accompanying anti-Jewish unrest, those who had mistreated Jews and looted their businesses in Berlin bore no signs of being part of the extreme right-wing, racist segment of society. Most were simply unemployed and desperate. It was clear that even a relatively minor event was capable of pushing ordinary people in antisemitic directions. "Pogroms in Berlin," noted Thea Sternheim.

"Popular rage in search of victims descended upon the Jews."[13] Betty Scholem registered with alarm how widespread pathological hatred of Jews had become during the worst of hyperinflation: "Antisemitism has so infused itself within and infected the people that everywhere you hear Jews being berated, in public, with a brazenness that never existed previously."[14]

IN MID-NOVEMBER, HYPERINFLATION REACHED its bizarre high point—and simultaneously an end. "Inflation took the final frenetic lap of its rampage," recalled the theater director Bernhard Reich. "It was a time when a single hard dollar was the equivalent of trillions in worthless German paper money. The popular comic Karl Valentin, a typical Munich native if there ever was one, used to joke, 'One dollar costs three trillion marks? What's the problem? That's exactly what it's worth.'"[15] On November 14, the exchange rate for one US dollar topped a trillion; the following day the value of a dollar was 2.52 trillion marks.[16] That was the day the Rentenmark, agreed on by the grand coalition in mid-October, was issued. The governing cabinet had finally set a date for the new mark at a meeting on November 7, although Finance Minister Luther had warned that it would be "a total blunder, if it didn't succeed in bringing the monstrously inflated expenditures of the Reich back down to acceptable levels." Therefore, Luther argued, financial support to the occupied territories—unemployment support made up the largest portion—had to be discontinued. The government ministers drew up a corresponding resolution two days later. In a none-too-subtle dig at the French, it read, "The entire responsibility for the immense economic misery that has arisen in the occupied region must rest with the powerful people who created these conditions."[17]

But in response to objections by the new interior minister, Karl Jarres, the decision was revised on November 12. Financial support would now continue after November 15 for a period of around ten days. Luther could barely be prevented from immediately resigning.

When the decision was approved by the cabinet, according to his memoirs, he broke out in tears for the first and only time in his life.[18]

During the same cabinet meeting, Hjalmar Schacht, a founder of the DDP and the director of the Danat (Darmstadt and National) Bank, was appointed Reich currency commissar. He was assigned to work for the finance minister and to serve as an advisory vote at all future cabinet meetings. But after Reichsbank president Rudolf Havenstein unexpectedly died on November 20, Schacht succeeded him in that post.[19] The banker would go on to play a fateful role as one of Hitler's most important supporters in the business world in the early 1930s.

Together, Luther and Schacht succeeded in establishing the new currency. On the same day it was first issued, the Reichsbank discontinued Reich treasury bills. Paper marks remained Germany's official currency, but printing them was no longer allowed. It wasn't until November 20 that a fixed exchange rate was announced. The rate of the paper mark to the dollar was stabilized at 4.2 trillion to one, while the exchange rate of Rentenmarks to the old paper marks was set at one trillion to one—a de facto return to the prewar exchange rate of 4.2 marks to the dollar.[20]

Because of an extended strike by Berlin printers in mid-November, at first it was only possible to print a limited number of the new banknotes. It would take another couple of days before Germans could pick up Rentenmarks from bank counters. "Notes are being handed out in dominations of 1, 5, 10, 50, 100, 500, and 1,000 marks," reported the *Vossische Zeitung*. "The bills are printed on both sides in various shades of iris and are relatively small and in panel form."[21] The key to the success of the new money was popular faith in its stability. Having lived in the unreal world of astronomical numbers for years, Germans now had to readjust to normal figures.

They did this fairly quickly, as Sebastian Haffner recalled in his memoirs:

> Then something really unexpected did happen. The incredible fairy story began to circulate that there would soon be stable

money again, and a little later, it materialized. Small, ugly, gray-green notes with "One Rentenmark" written on them. When you offered them in payment for the first time, you waited in suspense to see what would happen. Nothing did. They were actually accepted, and you were handed your goods—goods worth a billion marks. The same thing happened the next day and the day after. Incredible. The dollar stopped climbing, so did shares. And when one converted them into Rentenmarks, they were reduced to nothing, like everything else. So no one was left with anything. But wages and salaries were paid out in Rentenmarks, and some time later, wonder upon wonder, small change also appeared, solid bright coins. You could jingle them in your pockets, and they even kept their value. On Thursday, you could still buy something for the money received on the previous Friday. The world was, after all, full of surprises.[22]

On November 22, Klemperer was paid for the first time in Rentenmarks. For him, as for many others, this brought significant relief to everyday life. He wrote, "The fear of sudden monetary devaluation and the rush to go shopping is over for the time being."[23]

Nonetheless, the "miracle of the Rentenmark"—a description people began using at the time—didn't happen overnight. The new currency was "no magic potion that took effect immediately," Finance Minister Luther pointed out. "There will be long dry periods to get through before we reach lands of green and somewhat solid ground."[24] But even as early as December 1923, small signs of improvement were already detectable. "You see salesgirls in grocery stores looking pleased again," observed Kessler in Berlin. "An initial ray of hope cutting through the darkness."[25] In mid-December, the correspondent for the *Manchester Guardian* reported that the mood had turned around "profoundly" in the past fourteen days: "Despondency has given way to confidence, not very exuberant perhaps, but unmistakable.... The predominating cause is the stabilising of the mark. The nightmare of astronomic figures and of brain-wearying

calculation in millions, milliards, and billions over every petty trans-
action has vanished."[26]

Farmers, too, had faith in the new currency and resumed supplying
cities. By Christmas, Lord D'Abernon noted that food was plentiful
again: "Food has become abundant in the great towns; potatoes and
cereals are brought to market in large quantities, while butter, which
was obtainable only in the better quarters, is now offered at stable, if
high, prices. Animals crowd the abattoirs, and queues have disappeared
from in front of the shops of butchers and provision merchants."[27]

A WELCOME COMPLEMENT TO the currency reform was the
signing of an agreement between the six-member commission of the
Mining Association, headed by Hugo Stinnes and Albert Vögler, and
MICUM. The negotiations began in October but were continually
on the verge of failure; they were, however, brought to a successful
conclusion on November 23. It was agreed that German coal mines
would deliver 18 percent of their yield to France, with their full value
being booked against Germany's reparations obligations. A fee of ten
francs was also to be paid per additional ton of coal delivered. The
coal tax collected by the Reich since the occupation of the Ruhr Valley had to be transferred retroactively to the occupation authorities
and was paid, along with other fees, into a "repossession account." The
agreement was initially scheduled to run until April 15, 1924, and was
obligatory for all mines that had not reached separate arrangements
with MICUM. As harsh as these conditions were, the accord created
a reliable framework, allowing production to resume. "The heart of
the Ruhr economy has begun to beat again," Luther remarked.[28] The
burden on mine owners was tolerable since they could pass on most of
their additional costs either to the Reich or to consumers.

BY MID-NOVEMBER, THE DAYS of Stresemann's rump cabinet
were looking numbered. The scheming of the Reichswehr leadership,

the constant battles with rivals in his own party, the Hitler-led putsch in Munich, and the machinations of the separatists had all affected the chancellor, whose health was not perfect to begin with. After a meeting with Stresemann on November 15, US ambassador Houghton described him as looking exhausted, even half-dead.[29] Nonetheless, Stresemann had no intention of giving up. D'Abernon, who had an intense meeting with Stresemann over dinner in the Chancellery on November 17, came away with the impression of a tired but still entirely confident person.[30]

Stresemann had called a meeting of the DVP central board for November 18. It consisted of representatives from electoral districts and Reichstag and regional parliamentary groups, from whom the chancellor hoped he could elicit a clear decision about the future direction of the party. "The atmosphere must finally be cleansed, and we have to deal with those among us who do nothing but pursue German ultranationalist policies," he had confided to a party colleague on November 8.[31] From the very beginning of the meeting, Stresemann was on the offensive: "Either the party is dissatisfied with the chancellor, in which case he must face the consequences. Or the party stands behind the chancellor, in which case others will have to face the consequences of their behavior." After a whirlwind summary of the domestic and foreign policy landscape, he directly posed the question of whether those "others" wanted him to continue his cabinet: "You have the right . . . to judge whether the path we have taken was correct or not. But you can't demand from the leader of your party that he make sacrifices to continue along this path if he doesn't have his party behind him." The minutes of this moment in the meeting read, "Storms of applause. Those present stood up and gave the chancellor a furious ovation."[32]

In the debate that immediately followed, many of the delegates vented their outrage at the disruptions caused by the chancellor's party rivals. Parliamentary group leader Ernst Scholz found himself forced to declare that none of the party's Reichstag deputies intended to sacrifice the party chairman in order to form a "bourgeois bloc" with the ultranationalists—a lie, as everyone present knew. In the end, the party gave Stresemann a 206-to-11 vote of confidence and called upon the parliamentary group to support the chancellor "without exception in his policies."[33] It was a personal triumph for Stresemann. "He now has the party and the parliamentary group behind him," wrote Bernhard in the *Vossische Zeitung*. Even if it was worrisome that Stresemann's fiercest enemies were still members of the parliamentary group, they had no choice but to hold their tongues for a while. "In parliamentary terms," Bernhard added, "it would certainly have been a relief if the right wing of his parliamentary group finally defected to the ultranationalists."[34]

NONETHELESS, THE DVP ALONE couldn't decide the destiny of Stresemann's minority government. On November 20, at the request of the SPD, the Reichstag was set to reconvene, after going into recess for an indeterminate period following the passions of the Emergency Powers Act on October 13. The ultranationalists and the Communists had made clear their opposition to Stresemann's government, and after intense internal conflicts, the SPD had also decided to call for a vote of no confidence. It justified that move by noting the national government had gone after Saxony and Thuringia in the "harshest form" while "taking no substantial action against the unconstitutional circumstances in Bavaria." That may have been an accurate description of the situation, but there was no indication of what the SPD thought it could achieve by bringing down Stresemann. "The Social Democrats accuse him, undoubtedly not without reason, of having responded weakly to the conflict with Bavaria," wrote the *Berliner Tageblatt*. "But are they sure that a successor would be stronger, more inclined toward their own ideas and more able to satisfy their wishes?"[35] There was no prospect of a new grand coalition. On the contrary, the danger existed that the remnants of the cabinet would be replaced by a government further to the right or perhaps even be deposed by a directorship supported by the Reichswehr. The

Social Democrats had nothing to win and a lot to lose. Calling for a vote of no confidence may have pacified the left wing of the party, yet it was not only short-sighted but stupid.[36]

On November 19, Stresemann discussed the political situation with his cabinet, telling them that Ebert intended to use his influence to prevent an SPD motion for a vote of no confidence. But regardless of whether the German president was successful, it was scarcely imaginable that any of the no-confidence motions by the DNVP, KAP, or SPD would attract a majority in the Reichstag. Stresemann rejected the idea of staging a vote of confidence himself and dismissed the suggestion by several of his ministers to try to dissolve the Reichstag, saying fresh elections would bring "no relief in terms of the political balance of power."[37]

It appears that Ebert had refused to give the chancellor the permission to dissolve parliament, a source of leverage he could have used—as he had before the vote on the Emergency Powers Act in October—to get his way. D'Abernon surmised that the president had no interest in preserving a minority cabinet at all costs and would have welcomed a chancellor who was easier to handle.[38] Ebert's relationship to Stresemann had never been straightforward and had been further complicated by the former's flirtation with Seeckt's plans for a directorship, so D'Abernon's theory hardly seemed off the mark. But constitutional concerns outweighed personal animosities in the mind of the German head of state. Granting a government susceptible to a vote of no confidence full power to dissolve parliament did not square with Ebert's understanding of his office—at least not as long as there was hope of forming a new government with parliamentary support.[39]

"THE STRESEMANN CABINET IS under grave threat from the attacks of the Social Democrats and the ultranationalists, who, though acting independently from each other, are striking simultaneously," commented the *Vossische Zeitung* when the Reichstag reconvened on the afternoon of November 20.[40] The session took an unexpected turn. After Otto Wels had spoken for the Social Democrats and Oskar Hergt for the DNVP, Stresemann prepared to approach the podium, only for Wilhelm Koenen of the KPD to speak up on a point of procedure. When Reichstag president Paul Löbe refused to recognize him, saying that the chancellor had the floor, the Communists created a commotion the likes of which had rarely been seen in the German parliament. The Communists were upset that Löbe had allowed police into the Reichstag to protect members of the government and parliament who had received threatening letters and feared for their lives. "Are we in a parliament or a prison?" shouted KPD deputy Hermann Remmele three times, his voice breaking, whereupon Löbe excluded him from further proceedings.

The Right wasn't about to let this provocation pass without a response. "Waves of outrage made their way to the president's seat," wrote Erich Dombrowski in the *Berliner Tageblatt*. "All the deputies took to their feet in agitation. Groups formed everywhere and engaged in heated discussions. Here, there, and everywhere was a terrible racket." Löbe suspended the session for an hour, but even after it reconvened, Stresemann was unable to give his speech because Remmele refused to obey the parliamentary president's instructions and leave the room. In the end, Löbe postponed the session until November 22.[41]

That morning, Stresemann surprised his cabinet by announcing that he had changed his mind and would have his coalition introduce a vote of confidence in the Reichstag should the Social Democrats put forward a corresponding no-confidence motion. (Any similar motions from the ultranationalists and Communists would simply be ignored.)[42] Historians can only speculate about the rationale behind Stresemann's reversal. Did he hope that in the end the three opposition parties wouldn't vote together against him? Did he want to force the SPD to choose a side and accept the blame for bringing down the government? Or was he simply tired of ensuring the survival of his government by "rejecting votes of confidence on the back stairs?"[43] Whatever his thinking, Stresemann knew he was taking a big risk.

EARLY IN THE AFTERNOON of November 22, Löbe opened
the session of parliament. Beforehand, the Reichstag building had
been witness to extraordinary scenes. Only two of its gates were
open, and police and parliamentary officials carried out strict checks
at both entrances to prevent interlopers. Around noon, Remmele,
who was excluded for the remaining twenty sessions of the legislative
term, tried to sneak into the building surrounded by a group of party
colleagues, but he was recognized and turned away.[44] The mood on
the floor was extremely tense. The diplomatic box was full of VIPs,
including D'Abernon and Russian ambassador Nikolai Krestinski.
Everyone there knew that the moment of truth was at hand for the
Stresemann government.[45]

The chancellor spoke for almost two and a half hours, an unusually
long time. Stresemann's son Wolfgang considered it the best speech
his father had ever made, and Wolfgang wasn't alone in that opinion.[46]
Full of passion and fight, wittily parrying interjections from the Left
and the Right, the chancellor comprehensively recapitulated his three
months in charge. "Rarely has something so difficult to defend been
defended so well," concluded Bernhard. With "unusual dialectic skill,"
Stresemann was able to "bridge the gaps between then and now and
to answer attacks that were not without justification, winning over listeners with his words."[47] The attacks to which the editor in chief of the
*Vossische Zeitung* referred were perfectly reasonable SPD criticisms of
the different treatment accorded to Saxony and Bavaria, which Stresemann hastily brushed over.

Once again, the chancellor laid bare his articles of faith: "Not restoration and counterrevolution, but evolution and togetherness must
be the basis of the major strains of our politics. . . . There is hardly a
land anywhere that is so split along political, economic, and social
lines." If for no other reason than to counteract this polarization, the
decision had been made to form a grand coalition. The coalition had
not been an "end unto itself," Stresemann conceded, but it was "also

more than just some tactical maneuver." He stressed his regret that that alliance had fallen apart earlier in the month and didn't rule out on principle renewed cooperation in some form with the Social Democrats. He had the impression, he declared at the end of his speech, that the current situation was "more of a parliamentary than a cabinet crisis," since no constellations of parties capable of forming a majority had emerged as an alternative to his government. Nonetheless, he added, he had asked the president of the Reichstag not to delay but to accelerate the parliament's decision.[48]

Political observers disagreed about what to make of Stresemann's speech. Was it the swan song of a politician who knew his time was over? Or a last attempt to close ranks and mobilize support for his cabinet? Whatever the case, the situation was clear within a matter of hours. Late that evening, the SPD parliamentary group did in fact decide to ask for a vote of no confidence. The fate of the second Stresemann government was sealed.

On the morning of November 23, the Reichstag convened for the decisive session. The DNVP, KPD, and SPD issued their motions for a vote of no confidence. Stresemann spoke up, saying that he wanted a "clear, unambiguous decision" and thus asked the parties in the government to move for a vote of confidence themselves.[49] The parliamentary groups of all the parties consulted internally until the late afternoon. Tensions, already running high, increased when it was announced that Seeckt had banned the KPD, Nazi Party, and German Ethnic Freedom Party (DVFP). The news unleashed howls of protest from both the extreme Left and the extreme Right.[50]

It wasn't until 7:30 p.m. that Löbe was able to call for a final vote. The motion put forward by the governing parties for a vote of confidence in the government was rejected by 231 to 156, with 7 abstentions and one invalid ballot. Six DVP deputies had boycotted the vote. Even more conspicuous were the breaks in the ranks of the Social Democrats, 20 of whom decided not to vote against the motion. Silence greeted the announcement of the result. "There was no applause or signs of unhappiness, and the parliamentary president ... continued on with the day's agenda," reported the *Vossische Zeitung*.[51]

Directly after the vote, Stresemann summoned his ministers and informed them that he was going to Ebert to ask him to dismiss the cabinet.[52] A Social Democrat would tell him that the Reich president wrote in the party logbook about his SPD colleagues, "Whatever cause you have to topple the chancellor will be forgotten in six weeks, but you will feel the consequences of your stupidity for the next ten years."[53] According to Wolfgang Stresemann, his father was "not at all depressed" when he returned to the Chancellery. He had wanted a decision in parliament and had provoked one with great aplomb. Not without pride, Stresemann told foreign press representatives a short time later that this was the first time in the Weimar Republic's history "that a government has fallen in open battle."[54]

STRESEMANN'S TENURE AS CHANCELLOR lasted only 103 days. Obituaries differed dramatically within the various political camps. The *Deutsche Allgemeine Zeitung* proposed that the chancellor who had been "so adroit in parliamentary debates and nearly uniquely skilled in the art of give-and-take and compromise" had ultimately lacked the "iron first and hardened will" absolutely necessary in times of crisis. Above all, the Stinnes newspaper faulted him for not soliciting the cooperation of the ultranationalists and for instead sticking "almost fanatically to the politics of centrism."[55] The *Berliner Tageblatt* declared that the time given the chancellor had been insufficient to solve Germany's multitude of problems: "As soon as one wound on Germany's sickly body seemed to have healed, another opened up. Thus, it was impossible for him to focus his ideas and will on a single problem. He was continually distracted by new issues suddenly appearing on the political horizon."[56]

The *Vossische Zeitung* attributed Stresemann's failure to the fact that he had "not stayed true" to his policies but had become too deeply "ensnared in the net of tactics." In the face of his right-wing adversaries, who had made common cause with the opposition within his own party, Stresemann had "retreated step by step, always with the same negative result—his enemies only got bolder, and his parliamentary basis narrower."[57] The *Weltbühne* was particularly uncharitable, accusing Stresemann of using his chancellorship to "subjugate the people to the military." His anxiety over the radical Left, the paper added, had caused him to throw himself "upon the breast of the Imperial General" Seeckt: "Cuno cost us the Ruhr Valley. Stresemann cost us civic freedom."[58] The *Tage-Buch* also drew a damning overall conclusion, writing that Stresemann "had squandered more political capital in the space of three months than any chancellor since Bethmann."[59]

Most historians today credit Stresemann with important foreign and domestic policy achievements during his short tenure in office. By discontinuing passive resistance, he created the conditions for easing international tensions, clearing the way for a solution to the reparation issues. The establishment of the Rentenbank and the Rentenmark curtailed hyperinflation and laid the groundwork for the currency to be stabilized and the economy to recover. Finally, during the Weimar Republic's gravest existential crisis thus far, in which powerful forces within the Reichswehr, the business community, and the political scene had favored dictatorial solutions, Stresemann proved a committed defender of the constitutional system. That fact, in particular, made it clear how much he had changed since the revolution of 1918–19.[60]

NONETHELESS, PART OF THE legacy of Stresemann's chancellorship was an episode that left even many of his supporters confused: his leading role in allowing Crown Prince Wilhelm of Prussia back into Germany in the fall of 1923. The eldest son of Kaiser Wilhelm II had, like his father, gone into Dutch exile in November 1918, finding sanctuary in a former parsonage on the small island of Wieringen. The prince's name was at the top of the list of those considered war criminals by the Entente, which called for his extradition in the Treaty of Versailles—without, however, insisting on it. Stresemann visited the prince in exile for the first time in September 1920 and came away impressed. Wilhelm was "a very likable and broad-minded person of the best of qualities," he wrote, who in contrast to his father lived in the "real world."[61] Stresemann seems never to have abandoned his feelings of loyalty to the German monarchy, and without doubt he was flattered by the attention the crown prince showed him, an ambitious man from a modest background.[62] The two men remained in contact in the years that followed. In July 1923, when Wilhelm was trying to engineer a return to his homeland and ran into resistance from the Cuno government, which feared the potentially serious domestic ramifications of his return, Stresemann assured the crown prince in a long letter that he would do everything in his power "to open the path for His Eternal Imperial Majesty to enter back into Germany."[63]

Once Stresemann was chancellor, Wilhelm redoubled his efforts to force his way back to Germany. After the end of passive resistance, he even went so far as to issue an ultimatum to the German government that it would have to decide his case by October 5 or he would enter Germany on his own.[64] Stresemann asked for patience, citing the extremely fluid situation, but on October 23, he broached the issue with his ministers. Under the condition that the crown prince would mainly reside in his Silesian estate, Oels Castle, not Potsdam, and would renounce all political activity, the cabinet sanctioned Wilhelm's return.[65] Stresemann promptly communicated this decision to the prince, writing that things were still "extraordinarily tense" but that his wish could no longer be refused: "Your Eternal Imperial Majesty will find your German homeland, which you knew in earlier times as a member of the ruling house in all its glory and greatness, in a condition of grave confusion, impoverishment, and desperation. But it is still the German nation and the German homeland."[66] On November 10, the crown prince crossed into Germany without informing Entente authorities, and a few days later he arrived in Oels (today Oleśnica, Poland).

The former kaiser Wilhelm was none too pleased about the step his son had taken. In his Dutch home in exile, Doorn, he was brought to tears when he read Wilhelm's letter of farewell and declared that the whole enterprise had been carried out behind his back. It was incomprehensible to Wilhelm II that the crown prince had behaved in this matter: "How is it possible that he went begging for permission to the government of Stresemann, Hilferding, Braun, and consorts? The government that expelled his father and himself? It's simply unworthy."[67]

The return of the crown prince created a major stir internationally. British foreign secretary George Curzon was beside himself, telling Germany's ambassador to the United Kingdom, Friedrich Sthamer, that it was an act of foolishness that played into Poincaré's hands. Yet at a conference of Entente ambassadors in Paris in mid-November, Curzon resisted French demands for fresh sanctions against Germany because of the prince's return, and the Belgian and Italian ambassadors followed the British lead. The French government saw that it had been isolated and agreed to forgo punitive measures.[68]

Kessler had foreseen the hostile reaction to Wilhelm's return and expressed his concern to the German foreign ministry. State Secretary Maltzan and Ministerial Director Schubert admitted that the timing was "unfortunate," but there was no option of leaving Wilhelm in Wieringen "because it was too sad for him there." Moreover, Wilhelm could alternatively have returned to Germany illegally. Secret organizations in Bavaria had offered to smuggle him across the border, something the German national government would have been powerless to prevent.[69]

Stresemann himself justified the decision to D'Abernon by arguing that his SPD ministers had also voted to allow Wilhelm to come home. It was better, he said, for the crown prince to return "with republican permission" than against the will of the Weimar Republic, which would have provided the Right with "a great weapon of attack."[70] But those probably were excuses. Stresemann's sense of loyalty made him feel duty-bound to the Hohenzollern monarchy, and he may have believed, at the same time, that he could earn the heir to the throne's support if he helped him return to his homeland.

The crown prince would prove less than grateful for the generosity he was shown. Although he did in fact abstain from politics in his first years back in Germany, in 1930 he began to push his way into the political arena and sought out contact with the anti-democratic Right. In the critical spring of 1932, he was mooted as a potential successor to Hindenburg as Reich president, and when that came to naught, he threw his weight behind Hitler in the second round of voting.[71]

"WHAT NOW?" ASKED THE *Kölnische Volkszeitung* after the fall of Stresemann.[72] And indeed many Germans had no idea what would come next. Was Seeckt's hour now at hand? Kessler thought it could be: "It's entirely unclear what will follow. To tell the truth, probably a dictatorship under Seeckt, who is increasingly acting as the sole wielder of power in northern Germany and yesterday ordered the Communist, National Socialist, and German Ethnic parties dissolved and banned."[73] D'Abernon also doubted whether a new government could be formed on a parliamentary basis, writing, "The tendency that has prevailed in Italy and in Spain, and that has established something like a military dictatorship in those countries, will probably be followed here."[74]

But those predictions would turn out to be wrong. The head of army command may have tested how far he could go as the temporary possessor of executive authority, confiding in a private letter that he had "interpreted the power that had fallen to him in a somewhat broader sense than it had been intended."[75] One example was his November 23 ban of the KPD, Nazi Party, and DVFP, as described by Kessler. He also repeatedly meddled in the affairs of the ministries, leading to considerable friction with the ministers. But Seeckt remained unwilling to violate the law and establish a military dictatorship against Ebert's will.[76]

Conversely, once the immediate danger to the Weimar Republic was gone, Ebert set about showing the general his limits. He considered revoking the state of emergency in Germany's regional states, most significantly Prussia, leaving it in effect only in Saxony and Thuringia. Moreover, he wanted to restore executive authority over the military to Gessler as a parliamentary-approved minister. That caused bitter arguments with Seeckt.[77] Ultimately, the latter was able to get around both of these moves. But there was no more talk about installing a directorate, which both Seeckt and Ebert had considered an option as late as early November. "I've gotten too powerful for his taste, that much is certain," Seeckt complained. "He wanted to restrain me, not get rid of me, but he still intended to take me down a peg."[78]

IMMEDIATELY AFTER STRESEMANN STEPPED down, Ebert summoned the parliamentary leaders of all the democratic parties to explore the possibilities for forming a new national government. His preferred candidate for the chancellorship was the chairman and parliamentary leader of the Center Party, Wilhelm Marx. But Marx demurred, saying that his party had provided the head of government often enough and had been rewarded only with ingratitude. Former chancellor Constantin Fehrenbach informed Ebert around noon on November 24 of the parliamentary group's decision. Instead, the Center Party and the DDP suggested DVP deputy Siegfried von Kardorff as someone who could attempt to create "a cabinet of the center." Cooperation with the ultranationalist DNVP was no longer ruled out on principle.[79]

The DVP parliamentary group agreed to support Kardorff's candidacy, if he contacted Stresemann and asked him to serve as foreign minister. But the ex-chancellor, irritated at the notion that he could be succeeded by someone from his own party, waved them off. Negotiations with the DNVP, which was offered two ministerial posts, also proved fruitless, as the ultranationalists flatly refused to serve under a chancellor Kardorff. Their reasoning stemmed in part from the fact that Kardorff had previously been a member of the German National

Party (DNVP) but had gone over to the German People's Party (DVP) to protest the Kapp Putsch. That very evening, Kardorff told Ebert he was no longer willing to lead negotiations.[80]

Interior Minister Karl Jarres, who was more popular with the Right than Kardorff, was also briefly considered as a candidate. But Ebert was by then convinced that he couldn't expect any rapid agreement among the parties, and on November 25, he charged the former treasury minister and reconstruction minister under Cuno, Heinrich Albert, with the formation of a nonpartisan "caretaker cabinet." Ebert had been keeping tabs on Albert even before Stresemann's fall. Now he wrote him a letter, summarily released to the press, saying that his only option was "to form a government of proven men" who didn't answer to any political parties.[81] Albert's nomination was fiercely criticized by all the centrist parties. On the afternoon of November 26, the parliamentary leaders of the DVP, Center Party, and DDP went to Ebert to discuss Albert's candidacy. It was already clear that Ebert's protégé had no chance of attracting a parliamentary majority. After Seeckt also refused to transfer executive powers, Albert stepped aside. It was a painful defeat for Ebert, who had clearly underestimated the resistance he would encounter.[82]

"Unfortunately, it must be admitted that the current cabinet crisis offers a less than welcome spectacle," commented Dombrowski in the *Berliner Tageblatt*. Stresemann, who was battling a bad case of the flu, noted, "Great confusion in the formation of the government."[83] The carousel of candidates continued to spin. The next one up was the Center Party politician and Christian union leader Adam Stegerwald, who was rumored to have good connections to the DNVP. On November 28, Ebert gave him a mandate to form a coalition government across the five bourgeois parties, including the ultranationalists. But negotiations foundered on a DNVP demand for a similar "bourgeois bloc" in Prussia, which would have meant the end of the governing grand coalition there. The Center Party, DDP, and DVP in the Prussian regional parliament immediately refused. Stegerwald, too, had failed in his appointed task.[84]

"We're not getting anywhere like this," wrote the *Deutsche Allge-meine Zeitung* on November 29. "The people are losing patience. Let the president appoint a chancellor who has the parties of the people and ultranationalists behind him.... He can dissolve the Reichstag and will find that a majority of the people enthusiastically follows his policies. Without such a decision, it is no longer possible to solve the cabinet crisis by constitutional means."[85] But Ebert had no inter-est in such a solution. Appointing a DNVP politician to head the government was out of the question for him because of the possible foreign-policy ramifications it would have. Thus, the only remaining alternative was to continue to try to engineer a centrist bourgeois coa-lition that wouldn't command a parliamentary majority but might be tolerated by the SPD. The key was to find a person who would be able to hold such a minority government together and was trusted by Social Democrats. On the afternoon of November 29, Ebert returned to Marx, and this time the Center Party politician didn't refuse the German president's request. The very next day, Marx presented a cab-inet based on the previous coalition of the DDP, Center, and DVP, supplemented by the Bavarian People's Party.[86] Helping expedite the formation of the new government was a letter from Luther to Ebert tendering his resignation, in which he argued that the urgent decisions required in the area of finance could not be made by a mere acting finance minister.[87]

THE NEW CHANCELLOR, A Cologne Rhinelander, was sixty years old. After studying law, he had embarked on a successful career as a judge. From 1910 to 1920, he served in the Prussian regional parliament, and since 1910 he had also been a member of the Reich-stag. In September 1921, he was elected parliamentary group leader of the Center Party, and the following January he assumed the party chairmanship. Unlike Stresemann, Marx wasn't a gifted pub-lic speaker. His greatest talent was said to be his ability to engineer compromises, for which he had earned the respect of political adversaries. That made him the ideal consensus candidate who could be trusted to cobble together sufficient parliamentary support on a case-by-case basis.[88]

Marx's cabinet was nearly identical to Stresemann's final one. At the express wish of the Center Party, Stresemann had been asked to stay on as German foreign minister, and he agreed, ensuring continuity in that all-important arena.[89] Jarres remained interior minister and became vice-chancellor. Also keeping their posts were Gessler as Reichswehr minister, Heinrich Brauns as labor minister, the East Prussian estate owner Count Gerhard von Kanitz as food minister, Rudolf Oeser as transportation minister, and Anton Höfle as postal minister. Höfle was also appointed as the deputy head of the Ministry for the Occupied Regions. The only new members of the cabinet were Eduard Hamm, Cuno's former state secretary in the Chancellery, who succeeded Koeth as economics minister, and the BVP deputy Erich Emminger, who was appointed justice minister.[90] "No one looking at the list of ministers in the new cabinet will understand why the whole infernal fuss was necessary to create a team that could have easily been put together without any black magic," Bernhard wrote critically in the *Vossische Zeitung*.[91]

THE NEW GOVERNMENT HAD to swiftly decide on a series of comprehensive financial, economic, and social policy measures. Draft legislation had already been drawn up in the various ministries but had stalled during the seven-day governmental crisis. Because the reform program could not be expected to pass via the normal parliamentary means, the Marx cabinet agreed in its first meeting on December 1 to ask the Reichstag for emergency powers of the sort Stresemann's cabinet had been given in October. Should that request fail to achieve the necessary two-thirds majority, Marx planned to ask Ebert to dissolve parliament and call fresh elections. In a cabinet meeting the following day, Gessler even went so far as to suggest suspending the rule that new elections had to be held within sixty days if parliament was dissolved. That would have entailed a clear break with the Weimar Constitution.[92]

Ebert wanted to delay dissolving the Reichstag for as long as possible because he believed the complexity of events in the occupied regions made it an unfortunate time for new elections. On December 2, the head of his office, State Secretary Otto Meissner, told the cabinet that Ebert would be prepared to issue emergency edicts on the basis of the Constitution's Article 48 but only if the parliament refused to pass an emergency powers act. This was a maneuver Ebert had also used during the Cuno government.[93]

The crucial question was what the Social Democrats, whose 170 seats made them the strongest group in parliament, would do. Initially the SPD party leadership had been unwilling to unconditionally support a government of which it was no longer part, stringently rejecting a new edition of the emergency powers act. But Ebert's announcement that he would once again make generous use of Article 48 was an effective means of applying pressure. Although the Reichstag retained the right to rescind emergency decrees, that prerogative was of little use if the SPD was unable to get a simple majority of deputies on its side. Thus, a temporary emergency powers act seemed like the lesser of two evils, and on December 4, the parliamentary group voted for it 73 to 53. A concession from the government eased the Social Democrats' decision: committees from the Reichsrat and the Reichstag would be invited for "confidential consultations" before any decrees were issued.[94]

On the afternoon of December 4, Marx presented his new cabinet to the Reichstag. "There were the usual scenes in parliament on a big day," wrote the *Berliner Tageblatt*. "People were crowded shoulder to shoulder wherever you looked. In essence, all that has happened is a reshuffle. . . . Stresemann, who until recently occupied the historic corner seat, has been moved two seats further back. In front of him are throned the chancellor and the vice-chancellor."[95] When Marx approached the rostrum, an expectant hush fell over the crowd. Even the Communists desisted from interruptions—perhaps a reaction to the disciplinary exclusion of Deputy Remmele.

Marx delivered a short address, his tone calm, measured, but resolute on the main issue at hand. A new emergency powers act was indispensable, he argued: "The government is of the opinion that, in view of the great urgency of the time, lengthy negotiations in the Reichstag, which would require consultations on incisive economic and financial legislation, are not only undesirable but nearly unsupportable." He appealed to deputies to vote for the act: "This is a matter not of weeks or months but of days, which will show whether we will be able to save ourselves at the last second from total demise."[96]

A vote on the measure scheduled for December 6 had to be postponed as it became clear that too many deputies would be absent to reach the necessary qualified majority. The SPD leadership ordered its deputies to vote as one, and on December 8, the emergency powers act passed 313 to 18 with one abstention. Contrary to expectations, the ultranationalists, presumably wanting to avoid blame should the resolution fail, hadn't boycotted the vote. But 39 representatives of the left wing of the SPD had in fact protested by failing to appear.[97]

THE EMERGENCY POWERS ACT, which was valid until February 15, 1924, enabled the government "to initiate measures deemed necessary and urgent with respect to the desperation of the people and the nation."[98] Marx's cabinet thus possessed the leverage needed to continue the stabilizing policies of his predecessor. The most immediate concern was to get the state budget under control by rigorously cutting back expenditures while increasing revenues just as drastically. Without exception, Marx carried out the personnel reductions in the civil service that had been decided on by Stresemann's grand coalition on October 17. By the end of March 1924, the number of people employed in public administration, including the post office and national rail, was to be cut by 25 percent. Some four hundred thousand civil servants and white- and blue-collar employees were made redundant.[99] Moreover, the government froze civil servants' wages at significantly below their prewar levels. Those at higher echelons received less than half of what they had been paid in 1913.[100] "Our finances weigh us down quite a bit," Klemperer noted on December 10. "According to the latest regulations, we won't even earn 4,000 marks a year. That's 50 percent of our peacetime wage, even though prices across the board are 150 percent higher even after being lowered. A joke is making the rounds now that the correct answer to the question, 'How's it going?' is 'Terrible—multiplied by the Reich index.' "[101] (The Reich index was a measure of the cost of living, excluding clothing.)

Three emergency tax hikes aimed to alleviate the government's financial crisis. The first, prepared in advance on December 7, moved up the due dates for taxes to generate urgently needed revenues. The second, issued on December 19, raised the value-added tax and increased income, corporate, and wealth taxes. And the third, on February 14, 1924, instituted special taxes, the *Hauszinssteuer* on property and the *Obligationssteuer* on bonds. National support to the regional states to counteract inflation was discontinued, and compensation for those badly hurt by rising prices was restricted to a very modest level. In total, the effects of reducing expenditures and raising taxes proved far more beneficial than many skeptics had predicted. By the spring of 1924, Germany had already come through the crucial first phase of stabilization.[102]

The emergency powers act of December 8 also helped the Marx government push through several reforms on social issues, first and foremost the hotly debated one of working hours. On December 14, the cabinet increased the working week for civil servants from forty-eight to fifty-four hours. A week later, it issued a general decree on working hours that maintained the eight-hour working day "until such a time as there is a permanent agreement." But the decree also admitted the possibility of extending the workday by two hours based on union wage compacts and emergency public regulations. With that, the eight-hour workday—one of the greatest social achievements of the November Revolution—was de facto superseded. It was a major defeat for labor unions, which were already hard hit by high unemployment and declines in membership.[103] In mid-January 1924, the central committee of the ADGB announced it was ending the "central working community" with employers' associations that had been called into existence in November 1918. But that was nothing more than a "declamatory gesture" since by that point the arrangement no longer served any purpose.[104]

ADVOCATES OF A NEW regional state in western Germany also suffered a significant defeat. In mid-November 1923, the committee of fifteen began negotiations with Tirard. In response to their demands that France remove its "protecting hand" from the separatists, the high commissar was evasive, but he did offer reassurances that his country was not aiming to annex the Rhine regions and held out the prospect of reductions in the number of occupying troops.[105] On November 28, Tirard presented Adenauer with a memo outlining his ideas concerning the future composition of a Rhine state: a confederation of several small states with a joint parliament in the capital Koblenz. This new state was to have unrestricted legislative powers in all areas, a currency of its own, and diplomatic missions abroad. In essence, it would be a buffer that was nominally part of the Reich but effectively under French control.[106] On December 12, Adenauer responded with a "counterproposal," in which he repeated what he had argued in his interview with *Le Peuple* in late October. The creation of a buffer state would do nothing for French security. The best guarantee of lasting peace between Germany and France would be a "western German state within the Reich confederation," whose connection with the German nation as a whole would not be restricted in any form.[107]

Two days later, Adenauer briefed Marx about the state of the negotiations and secured the chancellor's approval for continuing them. Foreign Minister Stresemann, however, was now purposely left out of the loop.[108] Since their confrontation in Hagen on October 25, Adenauer and Stresemann's relationship had permanently soured, with each man deeply distrustful of the other.

Despite the lack of encouragement from Paris, Adenauer was not deterred. After a further meeting in late December with Tirard, who for the first time sounded conciliatory, he thought he might be nearing a solution in line with his vision. On January 9, 1924, he had the chance to secure support at a meeting of the Reich cabinet. The reality, Adenauer argued, was that Germany would have to "choose between two evils": the loss of the occupied regions or the creation of a West German state within the Reich. "The members of the cabinet in attendance took note of these remarks," the minutes drily stated.[109] But Stresemann, who had left in the middle of the meeting, refused to sign the minutes. In a memo to Marx on January 16, he summarized his concerns about Adenauer's plans. With the Cologne mayor's pessimistic prediction that Germany might break apart, Stresemann contended, Adenauer was acting contrary to Germany's interests. Domestic conditions had "largely calmed down," and on the foreign policy front, Stresemann believed that the chances of reaching agreement with Paris and Brussels had substantially improved. He now considered the separate negotiations of the committee of fifteen with the Inter-Allied Rhineland High Commission, which he had approved early in the preceding November, a burden on his own foreign policy. It would be "extraordinarily dangerous," he told Marx, for the national government to give the impression that it was "supporting negotiations whose outcome was so difficult to envision."[110]

This was the end of Adenauer's plans for an autonomous state in the Rhine regions. On January 23, he informed Marx that he and his supporters would refrain "from all further activities" toward that end.[111] Around the same time, Louis Hagen and the Rhenish bankers followed suit, drawing the logical conclusion that the weakness of France's own currency would not allow it to participate in the formation of a Rhenish, gold-standard central bank.[112]

"ADIEU, 1923—YOU WEREN'T very nice," Hedwig Pringsheim wrote in her diary.[113] It was a euphemistic choice of words for what she and her family had been through. "A very sad old year" was coming to an end, Kessler noted on New Year's Eve. The worst thing in his estimation was the desperation of broad swaths of the German population: "There's hardly anyone who doesn't beg from you. Today's Berlin is like the church square in a small city in Spain or southern Italy. You're besieged by pushy beggars without any human dignity or shame."[114]

By contrast, the sixteen-year-old high school student Sebastian Haffner felt upbeat as 1923 drew to a close, later recalling, "There was a feeling of 'the morning after' in the air, but also of relief." The worst seemed to be over, and there were lots of things available to buy at Berlin's Christmas markets: "Everything cost ten pfennigs, and everyone bought rattles, marzipan animals, and other such things just to show that one could really buy something for ten pfennigs again, and perhaps also to forget the past year, indeed the past ten years, and feel like a child once more. All the shops had notices: 'Peacetime prices.' For the first time since the war, it really felt like peace."[115] In an article entitled "Berlin Christmas," novelist Alfred Döblin described a "veritable tumult of buying." He wrote, "Suddenly everything is there, even pineapples. That was a rarity in years past: you only ever saw them through storefront windows. Overnight, books are cheap, affordable. You can sit in a café and even enjoy a piece of cake without devouring the basis of your existence. You can take the tram without any second thoughts. The war has been overcome, and the enemy—foreign currency—is outside the country."[116]

The journalists and publisher of the *Tage-Buch* presented their readers with an optimistic take on 1924: "If the hope we all share is fulfilled, it will be a year in which the most horrible of all calamities, the currency calamity, no longer forces us to struggle every day for our most basic needs."[117] D'Abernon also saw light at the end of the tunnel. In his end-of-the-year review, he recalled how close Germany had come to the abyss. The French occupation of the Ruhr Valley, an unprecedented currency crisis, the Communist challenge in Saxony and Thuringia, Hitler's attempted putsch in Munich, the separatist movement in the Rhineland—each endangered the very existence of the Weimar Republic. The British ambassador credited German politicians with avoiding a massive collapse: "Political leaders in Germany are not accustomed to receiving much public praise; those who have seen the country through these perils deserve more credit than is likely to be their portion."[118]

The mood among military officers was exemplified by a letter sent on New Year's Day 1924 by Lieutenant Colonel Waldemar Erfurth, the chief of staff of Reichswehr District Commando I in Königsberg (today Kaliningrad, Russia). The predominant feeling was disappointment, he wrote, that the Reichswehr had failed to establish itself as a force for order and to then establish a dictatorship. The "military offensive that had begun with such promise in September" had "come to a standstill," while "silence had again descended" on the "national revival in Germany" and "parliamentarianism and political corruption" continued "unbroken." The nationalist Right, Erfurth predicted, would now turn its back on the Reichswehr because it had proven unequal to "the task it had been given." He concluded, "Thus, 1923 ends as the saddest and worst year we have ever experienced."[119]

# CHAPTER 8

# CULTURE IN A TIME OF CRISIS

*More than any other film, Robert Wiene's* The Cabinet of Dr. Caligari *epitomized the cinematic creativity and dark visions of the Weimar Republic.*

THE GENERAL GERMAN TRADE UNION FEDERA-tion (ADGB), in a retrospective published on New Year's Day 1924, proclaimed, "1923 will necessarily be described in German history books as one of the blackest years ever."[1] That may have been true of the year's economic, social, and political crises, but culturally it was a different situation. The instability in the wake of the First World War was accompanied by a remarkable efflorescence of German culture. Inflation and hyperinflation didn't constrain artists and writers as much as might have been expected. Indeed, the crisis seemed to stimulate their creativity, with the need to improvise in response to the collapse of the currency fueling experimentation. "Weimar culture" flourished well before conditions in Germany were stabilized in 1924. Right from the start, the Weimar Republic proved a laboratory for modernism, in which a multitude of new forms of cultural expression were experimented with.[2]

Democracy created a framework for the free development of the powers of the imagination. Literature, theater, art, and music—no longer dominated by the educated upper and upper middle classes—opened up to a broader audience. New media like film and radio sped the transition to mass culture.[3] Spurring this trend was the desire of many Germans to distract themselves from the misery of everyday life. "Now amid the great turmoil . . . people welcome every bit of variety, entertainment, and diversion from everyday worries—to the point of craving them," wrote theater critic Alfred Kerr in December 1921.[4]

Naturally, the avant-garde didn't completely dominate Weimar culture. New cultural currents met fierce resistance from conservative circles, which clung to traditional conceptions of art and denounced alternatives as "cultural Bolshevism." The gap between the avant-garde and traditionalists was wide. Weimar culture was nothing if not divided.[5]

THE BEGINNINGS OF CINEMA stretch back to before the start of the First World War, but it wasn't until after the war that it experienced a boom and became a leading cultural medium. There was no better way to reach the masses than through the movies, wrote the young Social Democrat and later leader of the resistance against Hitler, Carlo Mierendorff, in a 1920 pamphlet: "Whoever has film will pry the world from its moorings."[6] The center of the growing German film industry was the Universum-Film AG, or Ufa, a company founded in 1917. It operated a host of cinemas, including the iconic Ufa-Palast am Zoo in Berlin, which opened in September 1919 and which, with its 2,165 seats, was one of the largest of its time. "Everything in red and gold," was how the *Tage-Buch* described the interior. "Heavy, luxuriant purple on the floors and walls. Despite its gigantic size, it feels cozier than many smaller movie theaters. With its sensational seventy-five-piece orchestra and impressive folding golden curtains, it is illuminated by dozens of spotlights that constantly bathe the performers in fantastic colors."[7]

In the 1920s, Ufa established Europe's largest film studio complex in Neubabelsberg, southwest of Berlin. In July 1923, the magazine *Kinematograph* reported about shoots in its immense spaces: "Hundreds of lights shine from above and can be raised and lowered, together or separately, with the pull of a lever. Spotlights beam from a distance of forty meters, almost as high as the heavens, and shimmer on the sides. Truly a sea of light. The massive gates open slowly as if pushed by divine hands. Natural light floods and mingles with the thousand electric candles. The shoot can begin."[8]

Before the First World War, cinema had primarily been a lower-class pastime. Educated circles were skeptical of the new medium. "'Learned people' considered it unseemly," recalled the film critic for the *Weltbühne*, Hans Siemsen. "One 'went along occasionally,' but only under the cover of darkness, and one didn't talk about it."[9] After 1918, however, film began to be accepted in bourgeois salons. At the same time, movies were becoming artistically far more sophisticated. In October 1919, after seeing a film adaptation of Gerhart Hauptmann's play *Rose Bernd*, Kerr began trumpeting the virtues of the cinema: "The pictures are a form of art like any other. The form just needs to be practiced. In all genres of art, kitsch will remain kitsch. Dross in painting, opera, and live theater is just as much dross as it is in cinema. . . . But that doesn't mean at all that cinema can only produce dross. If we reject shallow pictures, then we should reject shallow pictures but not the genre as a whole."[10]

The movies were one of Victor and Eva Klemperer's favorite forms of entertainment in Dresden in the early 1920s. "We must have been at the cinema thirty-one times," he noted in October 1922. "I've seen almost the entire lineup. It was rare for an evening to be a complete waste. At least we've had our fun. For me, cinema is an amusement and an inspiration, a substitute for theater, opera, concerts, and travel.

Sometimes I feel sheepish when I see all the young and uneducated people in the movie theaters, but this sort of shame is nonsense."[11] On New Year's Eve 1923, Klemperer ended his yearly journal by looking back and confessing, "I have a true mania for the cinema. Everything about it entertains and stimulates me. We divide people into those who partake of film and those who reject it. Those who reject it are the narrow-minded and prejudiced ones."[12]

ONE OF THE MOST important, artistically ambitious German pictures of the postwar period was *The Cabinet of Dr. Caligari*, which premiered in the Marmorhaus Cinema on Berlin's ritzy Kurfürstendamm boulevard in February 1920. Erich Pommer, one of the most influential film producers of the time, hired Robert Wiene to direct it. The story revolved around the mysterious hypnotist Dr. Caligari, played by movie star Werner Krauss, who puts the sleepwalker Cesare, played by the equally popular Conrad Veidt, into a trance and sends him out at night to commit murders. With its occult and fantastical subject matter, gloomy atmosphere, and bizarre sets, the film was a masterpiece of expressionism. He hadn't "sat so attentively in the cinema" in years, wrote Kurt Tucholsky. The reaction of the audience had vacillated between "amusement and incomprehension." Tucholsky added, "But it's that great rarity—a good film. More of them!"[13]

In his book *From Caligari to Hitler*, written in American exile, film critic Siegfried Kracauer saw the film as giving an intimation of what would later become reality under National Socialism. Just as Caligari used hypnosis to bend his subjects to his will, the mass hypnotist Hitler overpowered the collective German soul in order to achieve his criminal goals.[14]

In April 1922, the Ufa-Palast am Zoo hosted the premier of a movie that would create a similar furor. *Dr. Mabuse, the Gambler* was the wildly successful film adaptation of a novel by Norbert Jacques. It was directed by Fritz Lang, one of the Weimar Republic's greatest directors. It, too, centered on a nightmarish figure. Mabuse, a man of a thousand faces, played by Rudolf Klein-Rogge, mesmerizes people in order to steal their wealth and ruin their lives. Lang later called the picture "a portrait of its time," and indeed it reflected the anxieties of the age more vividly than practically any other work of culture. One could find in it everything the past few years had brought "in terms of overstimulation, sensation, and speculation," wrote Kurt Pinthus, the editor of the expressionist poetry anthology *Twilight of Humanity* (Menschheitsdämmerung) and the film critic for the *Tage-Buch*. "Scientifically plotted crimes, stock market tumult with corrupt, rapidly alternating bear and bull markets, eccentric casinos, hypnosis, the power of suggestion, cocaine, gin mills ... morbidly psychologically and sexually dependent human beings, and all those rootless human existences, for whom immorality has become a matter of course because all they have to lose is this one life, which would be even more lost without such unscrupulousness."[15]

Director Friedrich Wilhelm Murnau also played upon the fears of the age in *Nosferatu: A Symphony of Horror*, which was based on Bram Stoker's *Dracula*. Premiering in March 1922, it tells the story of Count Orlok, a vampire from the Carpathian Mountains, who brings death and decay to the small port city of Wisborg. "This is film," wrote the *Vossische Zeitung* after the picture's debut. "Spectral carriages rush through forest ravines, terrifying ghosts hunt people, a plague breaks out, ships arrive unmanned in harbors, coffins are full of soil, and mice flit out of cellars onto wagons and ships and into the holes in derelict buildings."[16] In the blood-sucking aristocrat with his bat's ears, claws, and long incisors, wonderfully played by Max Schreck, Murnau created one of the creepiest figures that had ever been seen on the silver screen to that point.

THE MOST FAMOUS DIVA of the silent films of the early 1920s was Danish actress Asta Nielsen. Her 1910 picture *The Abyss* had made the twenty-nine-year-old unknown a star in Germany overnight, and after 1918, she picked up where she had left off at the onset of war.

In 1919, she made *Intoxication* (Rausch) with director Ernst Lubitsch. "This woman makes the movie," enthused a critic for the magazine *Film-Kurier*. "She is not merely one of our greatest film actresses. She stands completely apart from all others. . . . She leaps off the screen. Her face smolders, twitches, contorts in pain, yells, and laughs. When she cries, her whole being cries too."[17] The secret to Nielsen's success was her range, which allowed her to take on a variety of roles and consciously flout convention. In 1921's *Hamlet: A Drama of Revenge*, she even played Shakespeare's famous prince. The film was a huge hit. "Half of Tauentzienstrasse stood in front of the sold-out box office," reported the *Berliner Tageblatt*. "Asta Nielsen is mesmerizing. The audience was beside itself with delight."[18]

Nielsen also performed brilliantly in pictures whose scripts were of lesser quality, such as *Navarro the Dancer* of 1922. "Incoherent back staircase kitsch," sniffed Klemperer. "But the lead is Asta Nielsen. She is always wonderful, and she's wonderful in every act of this drama, too, as a dancer, lover, lady, mother, and a woman condemned to death."[19]

One of the high points of the diva's storied career was the film *Downfall* (Der Absturz), which had its German premiere in May 1923. In it, Nielsen played a singer who rejects a younger lover. In his desperation, he commits a murder and is sentenced to ten years in prison. When he's released, he doesn't recognize his former lover, who is waiting, old and ugly, for him outside the prison gates. Instead, he passes right by her. The reviews were rhapsodic. "There is nothing in European film drama to compare with this spine-tingling performance," gushed the *Tage-Buch*. "How alone she stands there, disfigured by life. No film has ever given audiences such powerful tragic and ethical shivers. We kneel down before you, Asta. You're one of a kind."[20] Klemperer was also very taken by Nielsen's performance: "I have never witnessed such ruthless self-destruction as Asta Nielsen engages in in this film's final act. Yet even in complete squalor, the suffering that breaks her is something endlessly spiritual."[21] By the mid-1920s, Nielsen was turning more and more to the stage, and with the advent of sound movies at the end of 1920s, this silent movie star's film career was over.

The antipode to Nielsen was the nine-year-younger Henny Porten, who also conquered audiences' hearts before 1924. Whereas Nielsen was a tall, exotic brunette, "blonde Henny" was considered a "paradigm of German womanhood," and while the Dane embodied the modern, self-confident, emancipated woman, Porten stayed within the confines of traditional femininity.[22] Critics particularly lauded her comedic talents. In 1920, she costarred with Emil Jannings in the Lubitsch-directed farce *Kohlhiesel's Daughters*. But not everyone considered her a great actress. Siemsen in the *Weltbühne* sarcastically panned the 1922 comedy *She and the Three*, which had Porten in the lead role: "There isn't a single even halfway funny scene in the entire picture. . . . I rarely left the cinema sadder than after this really, really great German monumental comedy. I would have rather had ten dentist appointments."[23]

In 1923, these two very different actresses appeared together in Wiene's blockbuster film about the life of Jesus, *I.N.R.I.* Nielsen played Mary Magdalene, and Porten played the Virgin Mary. There was no sign of rivalry between the two divas on the set. In the role of Jesus was Nielsen's real-life lover, Russian actor Gregori Chmara, with Alexander Granach as Judas and Krauss as Pontius Pilate. The critic for the *Tage-Buch* praised the film for "proving once and for all that the greatest story ever told can indeed be filmed, as long as the approach is the right one."[24]

Emil Jannings was among the most famous male Ufa stars of the early Weimar Republic. Joe May's four-part *Tragedy of Love*, which premiered between 1922 and 1923, was a sensationalist crime story about a murdered count, and Jannings played the boxer Ombrade. You could reject this genre of cinema, wrote Tucholsky in the *Weltbühne*, but if you didn't, you had to recognize that "the best German, naturalist detective film has been created here." Tucholsky singled out Jannings for particular praise. "Now that's a real character: the goodhearted, powerful Ludewig, as strong as a bear but also as clumsy."[25]

The unknown young actress Marlene Dietrich played one of the minor roles. Seven years later, she would achieve global fame as Lola at Jannings's side in Josef von Sternberg's talking picture *The Blue Angel*.

In the spring of 1923, as hyperinflation was starting, Jannings starred in *Everything for Money*, playing an uncouth inflation profiteer and social climber. It was a role tailored for him. "How to become a money grubber, but a money grubber of the sort the world has never seen," Pinthus wrote, summarizing the message of the film. Jannings was simultaneously "brutal, deceptive, boastful, childish, lustful, paternal, tragic, hectic, love-besotted, vulnerable, petty bourgeois, megalomaniacal but with a portion of good in him—in sort he's the very essence of the money grubber."[26]

That said, very few movies addressed contemporary issues. Historical dramas were more common and successful. "Film began as a cheap novel and is well on its way to becoming a history seminar," joked Ossietzky in the *Berliner Volks-Zeitung* in March 1923. "The entire history of the world is being plowed through. All the Friedrichs, Catherines, pompadours, military commanders, kings, villains, heroines, paramours, and all the coups, beheadings, deflowerings, torture, in short, the entire spectrum of unpleasantness we rather grandiosely call world history is today nothing more than a collection of subjects for German cinema."[27] The most active director in the costume-film genre was Lubitsch. In 1919, he made *Madame DuBarry* with the young Pola Negri; in 1920 he followed it with *Anna Boleyn* with Porten and Jannings (as Henry VIII); and in 1922 came *The Loves of Pharaoh* with Jannings and Albert Bassermann.

Movies that played to nostalgia for lost national glory were especially popular. "Every day, films about the German past roll through projectors from one end of the Reich to the other—to packed houses," wrote the *Weltbühne* in 1923. "What we can conclude is that people in Germany enjoy being lied to."[28]

One of the biggest hits of 1922 and 1923 was Ufa's four-part *Fridericus Rex* starring Otto Gebühr. The first two installments, *Storm and Stress* and *Father and Son*, premiered in the Ufa-Palast in January 1922, and in March 1923 the third and fourth parts, *Sanssouci* and *Twist of Fate*, were released. To mark the first two premieres, Tucholsky wrote a poem:

> *Fridericus Rex, our king and master*
> *Called us once more to the movie theater.*
> *Of celluloid, this nonsense takes up six thousand feet*
> *And the tickets all cost twelve marks apiece.*[29]

*Weltbühne* journalist Curt Rosenfeld observed in July 1923 that whenever Frederick the Great's battalions marched with flags unfurled, storms of applause broke out in cinemas, and he reflected on the source of such films' appeal. "Three things attract the audience: past military glory, connections with the present day, and the figure of the great king, the paradigm of the vigorous man so many people long for right now." In this sense, Rosenfeld concluded, film was proving an effective means of propaganda for ultranationalist ideas of Germany's glorious military past.[30]

*Vorwärts* called upon its readers to boycott the picture, and there were Social Democratic and Communist protests in many cities. But the right wing also mobilized their supporters to march in support of *Fridericus Rex*.[31] In the busy months leading up to the Munich putsch, film enthusiast Adolf Hitler found time to see all four parts of the epic. He was particularly taken with the scene from the second installment, in which the young Frederick is forced to witness the execution of his friend Katte. "Off with the head of anyone who blasphemes against the cause of the nation, even if it's your own son," Ernst Hanfstaengl recalled him saying. That was how Prussia had become great, and this spirit had to be revived if the fight against the French occupation of the Ruhr was to be successful.[32]

After viewing the first two parts of the epic in March 1922, Klemperer found himself in "great emotional confusion." The "past German greatness that had been destroyed" had also filled him, a patriotic Jewish German, with "a lot of pain," and at a couple of points in the film, he had hardly been able to "choke back tears." On the other hand, he had to admit that it was the "repulsive swastika lovers, the most immature elements and the worst self-styled Teutons," who had applauded the picture most loudly.[33] In May 1923, he saw the final two parts, which he found even more moving, notably Otto Gebühr's performance.

> Gebühr appeared much older, with a striking facial resemblance to Goethe and Hauptmann, and the posture of an old man fighting to keep himself standing up straight. The great emergency. Bad news in the farmhouse near Leuthen. . . . Then in a broad landscape, the long battlefront of the grenadiers near Lethen. The battle. Fantastic performance by Gebühr. "Retreat is not an option." Laboriously moving forward with his cane, he leads his troop into the maelstrom. . . . Finally exhausted grief in his armchair during the victory celebration. . . . A great pleasure of a film.[34]

Offering a contrast to the glorification of war in the *Fridericus Rex* series were the films of Charlie Chaplin, which enjoyed growing popularity among pro-democracy circles in 1920s Germany. "He only needs to appear with his little hat, cane, and mustache, waddling around on those impossible legs, and suddenly everything around us is wrong, and he's right, and the entire world is ridiculous," Tucholsky wrote of the "most famous man in the world" in 1922.[35] Siemsen saw Chaplin's works as a "continued undermining of everything that claims respectability, high office, and dignity today." Siemsen asked, "Who can take the military seriously after seeing Chaplin as a firefighter, police officer, or trench soldier? When Chaplin salutes as a firefighter, when he performs his first, leg-bending complicated little twirl on his heels as a policeman, everyone laughs, and the whole pathetic brainlessness of the military and its drills are revealed to devastating effect."[36] In the fall of 1922, the film critic for the *Weltbühne* introduced his readers in a five-part series to the great actor, comedic scriptwriter, and director, singing his praises: "This funny little clown is the best thing a man can be: an improver of the world. God bless him!"[37]

In 1923, one of Chaplin's most famous films, *The Kid*, arrived in German movie theaters. It was the first time Chaplin had directed and starred in a feature-length film. The film was about a tramp who finds an abandoned baby and raises the boy, played by child star Jackie Coogan, in ever more threatening circumstances. It was precisely the combination of comedy and social drama that made the picture such an unusual success. Pinthus in the *Tage-Buch* praised the film as a "benefaction." *The Kid* was not just a piece of entertainment, because Chaplin appeared "not only as a comedic acrobat but as the personification of the dictum 'Love Thy Neighbor.'" Pinthus added, "Serious and grotesque elements are mixed here into a potion of both emotion and amusement."[38]

Klemperer, by contrast, came away disappointed. The film was "nothing new," he wrote, merely wedding "American emotional primitivism with the American love of clowning."[39] The Dresdener's reaction was an expression of the traditional arrogance of the German educated classes toward American popular culture. The opinion of the Bonn professor of constitutional law, Carl Schmitt, on the other hand, was an expression of deep-seated antisemitism. After seeing the film in January 1924, he simply noted, "Garbage, Jewish sentimentality."[40]

THEATER HAD AN EVEN greater influence than film on the cultural life of the early Weimar years. Major theatrical events were the talk of the town, with people debating performances of expressionist works just as passionately as modern stagings of the classics. The arts sections of newspapers published extensive reviews, and the leading critics were constantly crossing swords. "The social significance of the theater, especially major literary premieres, was reflected in the attention the media devoted to it," recalled the philosopher and writer Ludwig Marcuse. "We flip through all the papers! How little space they have for a weighty book and how much for the second understudy of the third Amazon in [Heinrich von] Kleist's *Penthesilea*."[41]

Berlin surpassed Paris and London as the theatrical capital of

*Hans Poelzig's Grosses Schauspielhaus (later the Theater
des Volkes and the Friedrichstadt-Palast) could accommodate
five thousand spectators in an imposing atmosphere.*

Europe. The city had forty-nine theaters, twenty-three of which could
seat more than a thousand spectators apiece. Nowhere was the desire
greater to experiment and shock people, and nowhere were the arguments thereby engendered so intense. Even hyperinflation couldn't
deter theatergoers. On the contrary, houses were more packed than
ever. "He who had nothing but money sought to spend it as soon as
possible," director Bernhard Reich remembered. "Those who had the
evening free bought tickets for the theater or a concert, even if they
weren't all that interested in the fine arts. The despair of that time was
a blessing."[42]

Three figures stood out among the major theatrical directors in Berlin: Max Reinhardt, Leopold Jessner, and Erwin Piscator. Before 1914,
Reinhardt had established his reputation with performances of the
classics and his gift for technical innovations, such as revolving stages
and sophisticated light effects. After 1918, his monumental approach
and opulent sets remained unrivaled. Although indebted to Wilhelmine tradition on the one hand, on the other, Reinhardt sought to

reflect the new circumstances of Weimar democracy and open the theater to a broader audience. To this end, he bought the Schumann circus building and had it redesigned by architect Hans Poelzig into the Grosses Schauspielhaus (Great Playhouse)—a modern theater arena with a capacity of around five thousand.[43]

The new venue opened in late November 1919 with Aeschylus's *Orestes*. The premiere prompted the *Berliner Tageblatt* to note, "It was the first great event to see and to be seen at of postimperial Berlin. There were scores of ministers and parliamentarian deputies, poets, musicians, directors from other stages, actors, foreign diplomats, and international press representatives. . . . Astonishment at the building, particularly the dome that towered like a grotto made of ice, was written across all their faces."[44]

But the great expectations Reinhardt attached to his "people's theater" were to be disappointed, and in late 1920 he withdrew to his home stage, the Leopoldskron Palace in Salzburg. He handed over the directorial reins to his dramaturgist of many years, Felix Hollaender, who passed them on to Karl Rosen in 1923. The Grosses Schauspielhaus eventually became a venue mainly for operettas and theatrical shows.[45]

Reinhardt's great rival was Leopold Jessner. In the summer of 1919, the committed Social Democrat was named director general of the Staatliches Schauspielhaus (State, or Royal, Playhouse) on Gendarmenmarkt square. His very first production, a version of Schiller's *Wilhelm Tell* that premiered on December 12, 1919, caused a veritable scandal. Jessner broke radically with the tradition of court theater, stripping the stage of all decorative elements and nonessential props. Instead, it was dominated by a massive, freestanding, green staircase. Albert Bassermann played Tell, while the young Fritz Kortner took on the role of the bailiff Hermann Gessler, who was decked out in a glittery uniform covered with German imperial army medals—the very caricature of a Prussian general. Moreover, Jessner omitted the lines "To the fatherland, so precious, attach yourself," muting the pronounced patriotism of Schiller's play.

A small but vocal part of the audience believed that Jessner was defacing a classic and mocking nationalist values, and expressed its displeasure with a series of interjections that grew louder with every act. When Bassermann began delivering Tell's famous monologue, "Here through this deep defile he needs must pass," a member of the audience yelled, "Where the hell is it?" and chants arose of "Jewish swindle, Jewish swindle!" For actor Fritz Kortner, who described the tumultuous evening in his autobiography, the vicious reaction was a harbinger of evil to come: "It was the brown beast appearing in sheep's clothing of outraged, art-loving theatergoers."[46] Jessner continued to forgo the stylistic devices of realistic theater in his next production, a version of Frank Wedekind's *Marquis of Keith*, which premiered on March 12, 1920, the day before the start of the Kapp Putsch. "What this Jessner has made of the Schauspielhaus in the shortest of time is a miracle, believe me," gushed Kerr in the *Berliner Tageblatt*.[47]

The third member of Berlin's trio of experimental directors, Erwin Piscator, was from the very start decidedly political. In the fall of 1920, this doctrinaire Communist started his first "Proletarian Theater," staging plays in working-class social clubs and meeting places. Performances featured professional actors as well as amateurs. "We radically excluded the word 'art' from our repertoire," Piscator would write, retroactively describing his intentions. "Our 'works' were calls to action with which we wanted to intervene in current events and have a political effect."[48] In keeping with this aim, he was drawn to dramas of a social and revolutionary bent. "That's what is fundamentally new about this theater, that fiction and reality overlap in a thoroughly idiosyncratic manner," wrote the *Rote Fahne* about the world premiere of Franz Jung's play *Die Kanaker* in April 1921. "Often you don't know if you're in the theater or at a rally."[49]

But the Berlin police president shut down the theater that same month. After an attempt in 1922 and 1923 to call to life a "Proletarian People's Stage" (Proletarische Volksbühne) in Berlin's Central-Theater, Piscator took over the Berliner Volksbühne on Bülowplatz (today Rosa-Luxemburg-Platz) in 1924. It was there he earned a reputation as one of the most successful theater directors of the 1920s. In 1927, he departed the Volksbühne due to political differences and opened a theater of his own on Nollendorfplatz, which also enriched the Berlin theatrical scene with a repertoire of both modernist and classical plays.[50]

THEATER CRITICISM WAS THE heart and soul of every major paper's arts section and was considered just as important as directorial inspiration itself. Critics were respected and feared—and none more so than the veteran Alfred Kerr, who was born in 1867, and Herbert Ihering, who was twenty-one years his junior. Kerr had started his illustrious career at the newspaper *Der Tag* in 1901, and in September 1919, he became the main theater critic for the *Berliner Tageblatt*. In 1918, Ihering took over as the editor of the *Berliner Börsen-Courier*, a periodical respected particularly for its high-quality arts reporting. The two men approached the theater from opposite directions. "Alfred Kerr was an imaginative man of enjoyment, who rendered judgments subjectively, from case to case, an impressionist for whom criticism was a concentrated continuation of an evening in the theater," wrote author and critic Hans Sahl. "Ihering on the other hand was systematic, doctrinaire, and focused on a single point of which he never lost sight. . . . His reviews were manifestos, tracts, and declarations of war."[51]

Critics could make or break actors' careers. For example, Kerr's review of the world premiere of Hans Müller-Einigen's *The Flame* in Berlin's Lessing Theater in October 1920 helped make thirty-year-old Käthe Dorsch an overnight star. "The name of the evening was Dorsch," Kerr wrote. "Germany's stage has another member. Another force. Another power. Another blossoming talent. Another big thing. Another soul. . . . We cannot be impoverished if something like this is growing back [after the war]."[52]

Another great discovery of the early 1920s was the young actress Elisabeth Bergner, who arrived in Berlin via Vienna and Munich in

1922. Her star began to ascend when she played the title figure in August Strindberg's *Kristina*, which premiered in the Lessing Theater in December 1922. Again, it was Kerr who raised her to prominence: "What a flattering voice, what a gently analytic voice, what an unwilling voice, what a commanding voice, what an idiosyncratic voice, what a fearful voice. . . . She doesn't send clamorous signals like a bell. Everything comes from—absorption."[53]

Bergner had massive success in the year of hyperinflation, quickly becoming Germany's favorite stage actress. Her name was on everyone's lips. Even the notoriously skeptical Tucholsky was carried away by her: "So there is still a point to going to the theater," he wrote. "The Lessing Theater echoes with calls of 'Bergner! Bergner!' And with complete justification."[54]

ONE OF THE MOST-PERFORMED playwrights of the later war years and early postwar years was Georg Kaiser. His first great successes were his episodic drama *From Morning to Midnight* (which premiered in Munich's Kammerspielen in April 1917) and his rite-of-passage play *The Burghers of Calais* inspired by Rodin's sculpture of the same name (which was first performed in Frankfurt's New Theater in January 1917). In both works, Kaiser addressed a fundamental theme of expressionist drama: the coming of the "new man." He proclaimed, "The poet gives many forms to one thing—the vision of a beginning. What sort of vision is this? There is only one—the vision of the rejuvenation of man."[55] In keeping with this attitude, Kaiser had the father of Eustache de Saint-Pierre, who sacrifices himself, declare at the end of *Burghers of Calais*, "I have seen the new man—he has been born tonight!"[56] In his *Gas* trilogy (1917's *The Coral*, 1918's *Gas I*, and 1920's *Gas II*), Kaiser revisited this topic, but instead of leaving audiences with the hope of a renewal of humanity, he offered a bleak, apocalyptic account of a "day of judgment." Technology, in these works, has become an end unto itself and is driving humanity to ruin. "In the foggy gray distance, rounds of artillery fire hurtle toward one another and collide—in a clear act of self-destruction," reads the stage direction that concludes *Gas II*.[57]

Although Kaiser had established himself as a successful dramatist, his royalties apparently weren't sufficient to support himself and his family. In October 1920, he was arrested after he pawned valuables from a furnished villa he had rented in Tutzing near Munich. In February 1921, a court in the Bavarian capital sentenced him to a year in prison.[58] His case attracted considerable attention and inspired mocking commentary, particularly in the right-wing press. In the Prague magazine *Tribuna*, Milena Jesenská, a friend of Franz Kafka, took up Kaiser's cause and excoriated the "stupidity" of journalists "who spilled idle words of such astonishing obtuseness and ignorance, such unfamiliarity with the simplest human mysteries, without the most primitive human goodness, so that it repulses even an uninvolved stranger."[59]

After his release from prison, Kaiser settled in the town of Grünheide near Berlin and began increasingly to tackle contemporary problems in his work. In 1923, he published his play *Side by Side* (Nebeneinander), which he subtitled "People's Play in Five Acts 1923." The premiere in early November 1923 in Berlin's Lustspielhaus was directed by Berthold Viertel, who had assembled his own theatrical company, called "The Troupe," the previous September. The play features three parallel plot lines. In the breast pocket of a misplaced tuxedo, a pawnbroker finds the farewell letter of a man named Otto Neumann to his former lover, Luise, who had threatened to commit suicide. Wishing to save the life of this unknown woman, the pawnbroker sets off in search of her and her lover: his journey develops into a passion play that ends with the suicides of the pawnbroker himself and his hunchbacked daughter. The second plotline features the young woman, Luise, who is not contemplating suicide but rather has retreated to the countryside and is consoling herself through a relationship with a reliably staid engineer. The third plotline revolves around Otto Neumann himself, an unscrupulous social climber with extraordinarily sharp elbows who fights his way to a position as director general of a movie studio. "This is the type of person who gets his way," Kaiser writes at the end of the drama. "While we all perish in filth and squalor, he whistles *The Watch on the Rhine* with puffed cheeks."[60]

The play's premiere was a sensation, and Berlin recognized itself in Kaiser's drama. "The murky air of the hour swirls around in it, and our time is reflected in crass, bitterly distorted images," wrote the critic for the *Berliner Lokal-Anzeiger*. "This is how people live in a German city. This is how a lost people hungers and squanders. This is how we are crammed in 'side by side.' This is what our German hell looks like."[61] Siegfried Jacobsohn, the editor and theater critic of the *Weltbühne*, praised Kaiser's departure from the "oh, humanity" pathos of his expressionist works as a "huge step forward," writing that "Georg Kaiser has climbed out of the cloud that previously surrounded him and now has both feet on the ground." The "cold and good-humored mastery he has finally achieved" was "thoroughly appropriate for the turbulent insanity of our day."[62]

Ernst Toller was the period's other leading serious playwright. Born in 1893 to a Jewish grain merchant from Samotschin (today Szamocin, Poland) in the Prussian province of Posen (Poznań), Toller had, like many Jewish Germans, volunteered to fight in the First World War in August 1914. But the horrors of the trenches turned him into a radical pacifist. He achieved fame as a dramatist with his antiwar play *Transformation* (Die Wandlung), the episodic expressionist drama par excellence, in which he depicted his own changing views as a process of enlightenment. At the end, he has his protagonist Friedrich proclaim, "Now go to the possessors of power and announce to them with the voice of a thunderous organ that their power is an illusion. Go to the soldiers and say that they should beat their swords into plowshares. Go to the wealthy and show them your heart, which has become a pile of rubble. . . . Brother extend your martyred hand, calming and joyful in inflection. Stride throughout our liberated land, crying 'Revolution! Revolution!'"[63]

The play debuted on September 20, 1919, in the newly founded experimental theater Die Tribüne in Berlin. Twenty-seven-year-old

Fritz Kortner played the part of Friedrich and immediately became one of the most coveted actors in Germany. The critics were rapturous. "I can only offer my overwhelming thanks to one person for the purest theatrical evening Berlin Theater has bestowed in quite some time," wrote Ihering of Toller. Kerr was no less flattering: "He is one of those among us, of whom you feel not only that he has a passionate heart, but often that he's a poet. . . . [Toller] takes the bull by the horns. He summons up all the horrors of the war . . . not in a long lament but with a massive force no one previously has brought to the stage."[64]

When the play premiered, Toller was behind bars, having been sentenced to five years in prison for his leading role in the Munich uprising and formation of the brief Bavarian Soviet Republic in April 1919. It was the most artistically productive time of his life, as he churned out four plays, one after another. In *Masses and Man: A Fragment of the Social Revolution of the Twentieth Century*, which attracted international recognition thanks to Jürgen Fehling's production in the Berliner Volksbühne in September 1932, Toller addressed the fundamental conflict in every revolution, between adherents of nonviolence, embodied by the female character Sonja Irene L., and apostles of force, represented by the figure of a "nameless" man.[65]

In *The Machine Wreckers: A Drama from the Time of the Luddite Movement in England*, Toller used historical subject matter, the rebellion against mechanical looms in early British capitalism. The world premiere, directed by Kerl-Heinz Martin, took place at the Grosses Schauspielhaus in Berlin on June 30, 1922, six days after the murder of German foreign minister Walther Rathenau. It quickly turned into a political demonstration. In the final scene, when the character of Jimmy Cobbett, an advocate of human kindness, is killed by the machine wreckers, the audience cried out "Rathenau!" and "Down with the murderers!"[66]

In *Hinkemann* (literally "Limping Man"), written in 1921 and 1922, Toller depicted the suffering of a veteran whose injuries have rendered him impotent and who prepares after a series of humiliations to hang himself. "I no longer have the strength," the protagonist says.

"The strength to fight on, the strength to live on ... I don't want to go on."[67] The jingoistic Right saw it as an insult to wounded veterans and mobilized to protest the play. Although the audience at the premiere in Leipzig's Altes Theater in September 1923 had applauded the play, a performance in Dresden's Schauspielhaus in January 1924 was subjected to major disruptions. The *Frankfurter Zeitung* reported, "Before the curtains had even parted for the first scene, there was a wild symphony of coughing. That was, so to speak, the marching order for a company of swastika disciples to infiltrate the audience, which began to 'take offense' extremely vocally at the production."[68] Further performances were canceled after the director and the actors received death threats.[69]

With his comedy *Wotan Unchained*, written in 1923, Toller sought to satirize racist demagoguery and virulent antisemitism. The play depicts the rise and fall of a megalomaniacal barber, Wilhelm Dietrich Wotan, who launches a scheme to swindle innocents but gets caught and then announces he will write his memoirs in prison. Toller wrote the play before Hitler's putsch on November 8–9, but there were astonishing parallels between the fictional character and the leader of the Bavarian extreme Right, anticipating the dramatist's later warnings about the perils of National Socialism.[70]

In 1923, Toller published a cycle of poems entitled *The Swallows' Book*, one of his most beautiful works, which was inspired by the sight of two swallows nesting in his cell. The prisoner suffered greatly under the hardships of his confinement in Niederschönenfeld Prison, which bore no resemblance to the cushy treatment Hitler enjoyed in Landsberg. Unlike Hitler, who was released after only nine months, Toller served the entirety of his five-year sentence. He was released in July 1924. "Greetings!" Tucholsky welcomed him. "You have come to the light!"[71]


WITH ITS MANY CINEMATIC palaces, theaters, cabarets, variety halls, and newspapers, Berlin became an irresistible magnet for artists, writers, and journalists. "Berlin punched above its weight," dramatist Carl Zuckmayer recalled about the early 1920s. "The city devoured talents and human energy with an unparalleled ravenous appetite, quickly grinding them up, digesting them, and spitting them out again. Like a tornado, it drew in everything aspiring to make it to the top in Germany, the true artists and the pretenders, the zeroes and the bull's-eyes, only to show them, initially, the cold shoulder."[72]

One of those who set out to conquer the German capital was Bertolt Brecht of the Bavarian city of Augsburg. On February 21, 1920, only days removed from his twenty-second birthday, the unknown dramatist traveled for the first time to Berlin. The commotion in the metropolis made both an intoxicating and a sobering impression on him. "Berlin is a great place," he wrote to his friend Caspar Neher the day after he arrived. "It's overfull with examples of lack of taste, but in what dimensions, my boy!" In another letter a few days later, Brecht added, "The swindle perpetrated by Berlin differs from that of all other big cities in its shameless proportions. The theaters are wonderful. With charming verve, they pump out little bladder stones. I love Berlin, but I wouldn't swear by it."[73] On March 14, 1920, one day after the beginning of the Kapp Putsch, Brecht left Berlin again, having failed to achieve any of his goals.[74]

By the time Brecht returned for a long stay in the German capital from November 1921 to late April 1922, he was no longer an unknown, having published the short story "Bargan Leaves Well Enough Alone" (Bargan läßt es sein) in the journal *Die neue Merkur* and thereby attracting the interest of literary circles. Now he set about establishing the contacts necessary for making a name for himself in the capital. Brecht negotiated simultaneously with several publishers, including Kiepenheuer, run by Hermann Kasack, and he eventually secured a lucrative contract that guaranteed him a fixed monthly income.[75]

In December 1922, the actress Trude Hesterberg engaged Brecht for six evenings in her cabaret the Wild Stage in the basement of the Theater des Westens. It was one of the many artistically ambitious cabarets that sprang up in the early postwar years between Schiffbauerdamm and Kurfürstendamm, and well-known names like Walter Mehring, Tucholsky, Joachim Ringelnatz, and Klabund composed chansons, couplets, and poems for these venues.[76] In mid-January 1922, Brecht appeared at the Wild Stage, singing in his raspy voice and accompanied by guitar, the "Legend of the Dead Soldier"—a macabre antiwar poem in which the German kaiser unearths a half-decomposed soldier from his grave and has him die a second "heroic death." No sooner had Brecht begun his performance than tumult broke out. "I had to drop the curtain to end the riot," Hesterberg recalled in her memoirs. Mehring then stepped onstage and spoke words that would often be quoted later: "Ladies and gentlemen, that was a huge embarrassment, not for the poet, but for you! One day you will boast that you were here!"[77] In November 1923, a fire broke out in the basement of the Theater des Westens, and amid hyperinflation, Hesterberg lacked the funds to rebuild the Wild Stage.[78]

During his longer stint in Berlin, Brecht met the dramaturg Arnolt Bronnen, who immediately gravitated toward him. "The heart of our time beats within this inconspicuous little fellow," Bronnen would recall decades later.[79] The two became friends and were soon inseparable, with Brecht even changing the spelling of his first name (originally Berthold) to parallel that of his chum. Bronnen, who was three years older, had created a stir in 1920 with his drama *Patricide*—one of a series of expressionist works, also including Walter Hasenclever's *The Son*, that examined generational conflicts.[80] In February 1922, *Patricide* was chosen for production by Moritz Seeler's theater Junge Bühne (Young Stage), which wanted to give up-and-coming authors a forum. Although he had no practical experience, Brecht was offered a chance to direct, and during rehearsals he feuded bitterly with the actors, above all Heinrich George and Agnes Straub, who refused to heed Brecht's instructions to play their roles unemotionally. The conflict ended the production, but, Bronnen told Brecht, that was just as well: "I congratulate you. Everything would have come to nothing with these people."[81] Austrian author and theater director Berthold

Viertel adopted the project and got *Patricide* to the stage at the Junge Bühne in May 1922. The play became a surprise hit. "A memorably alarming Sunday performance with the right stuff to make history," wrote critic Emil Faktor in the *Berliner Börsen-Courier.*[82]

Brecht had to wait several months to celebrate a premiere of his own. His play *Drums in the Night*, directed by Otto Falckenberg, was performed for the first time at the Munich Kammerspiele on September 28, 1922. The play was set against the historical background of the so-called Spartacus uprising in Berlin in January 1919. Brecht has the returning soldier Kragler find that another man has taken his place at home, with his bride-to-be Anna Balicke carrying the child of a wartime profiteer. Shocked, he decides to join the revolution but is dissuaded when a regretful Anna comes back to him, saying, "I'm a swine, and the swine is going home. . . . Now comes the bed, our big white bed, come with me!"[83] The stage directions for the premiere read, "It is recommended that signs be hung amid the audience saying things like 'Don't stare so romantically.'"[84] The audience was not to abandon itself to any theatrical illusion of reality or have its emotions stirred by the events onstage but rather was to maintain its critical distance. Here, Brecht was anticipating the alienating effect that would become a hallmark of his "epic theater."

Ihering had traveled to Munich for the premiere and was completely overwhelmed. "Twenty-four-year-old Bert Brecht has changed the literary face of Germany overnight," he wrote on October 5 in the *Berliner Börsen-Courier.* "With Bert Brecht, there is a new tone, a new melody, a new vision in our time."[85] Ihering used his influence to ensure that Brecht was awarded the Kleist Prize, the most prestigious literary award in the Weimar Republic, in November. Ihering also defended Brecht against attacks from all quarters, including from Kerr, who panned the second performance of *Drums in the Night*, which took place on December 20 in the Deutsches Theater in Berlin. It was "the age-old prerogative of every dramatic poet to run out of inspiration in the fifth act," wrote Kerr, but not, as in Brecht's play, "already in the third to last" one. Kerr conceded that Brecht had talent

*According to Herbert Ihering, "With Brecht, there is a new tone, a new melody, and a new vision in this period." Shown here is a scene from the 1922 world premiere of* Drums in the Night *in Munich's Kammerspiele, which made Brecht an overnight star in German theater.*

but not at all in the same dimensions as Toller.[86] Ihering's and Kerr's opposing reactions to Brecht's work ignited a feud between the two critics that was also fueled by personal animosity.

After the Kleist Prize, Brecht suddenly found himself in great demand. On May 9, 1923, Munich's Residenztheater premiered his play *In the Jungle of Cities*, which was set in Chicago and centered on the battle between the wood merchant Shlink and the librarian Garga. Erich Engel, who had left the Hamburg Kammerspiele for Munich in 1922, directed, and Caspar Neher, a boyhood friend of Brecht's from Augsburg, designed the sets. During the second performance of the play, Nazis threw stink bombs into the audience, forcing the evacuation of the theater. In the Nazi newspaper *Völkischer Beobachter*, Josef Stolzing admitted that he had "no clue at all ... what actually took place onstage" but scoffed that "*In the Jungle* shows most potently" Brecht's "impotence as a writer." The play was "not only unspeakably foolish but also terribly boring," so that "only the sons and daughters of Zion" had "obsessively" clapped once the curtain had fallen.[87] The play was canceled after only its sixth performance because of the protests. Munich's racist conservatism did not tolerate any Bolshevik art, opined Thomas Mann in one of his letters from Germany published in the American magazine the *Dial*.[88]

In the summer of 1923, Nazis dominated Munich's public spaces with their marches and rallies. "Swastikas, uniforms, provocative posters, and incendiary bellowing" was the first impression Bronnen had of the Bavarian capital. In early June, he and Brecht went to one of Hitler's large rallies at Zirkus Krone. Brecht was less interested in what Hitler said than in the evening's clever choreography and bombastic theatrical effects. Bronnen would remember his friend saying, half in jest, that Hitler had "the advantage of a man who has only ever watched theater from the fourth balcony."[89]

On December 8, 1923, the first play Brecht ever wrote, *Baal*, premiered at the Altes Theater in Leipzig. Brecht had written it in 1918 and had made a number of revisions since. As might have been expected, the cynical story of Baal, an epicurean driven by his lust for pleasure, unleashed heated reactions. After the curtain fell, Hans Natonek reported in the *Vossische Zeitung*, "Amid the din of whistles, cries of 'pfui,' and applause, a shy, pale, thin young man, the playwright Bertolt Brecht, appeared only to immediately seek refuge by fleeing into the background before timorously emerging once again holding hands with the protective director."[90]

In September 1924, Brecht finally moved for good to Berlin, finding a steady job as a dramaturg at the Deutsches Theater together with Carl Zuckmayer, who would have a huge hit in 1925 with his comedy *The Cheerful Weinberg*. With that play, Zuckmayer turned his back once and for all on the bathetic, visionary style of expressionism in an attempt to better serve the popular tastes of the day.[91]

ANOTHER WRITER WHO MOVED to Berlin was Joseph Roth. Born to a Jewish family in the district of Brody in Galicia in 1894,

Roth started as a journalist at the left-wing, pro-democracy Viennese newspaper the *Neue Tag*, which first appeared in 1919. He was a born columnist, gifted with the "sharply pointed quill of a mocker and a light-handed polemicist."[92] But the *Neue Tag* was forced to shutter after only thirteen months. Facing poor employment prospects in Vienna, Roth left for Berlin, Germany's newspaper capital. He arrived in June 1920, and the Prussian metropolis proved to be a springboard for a successful career. Emil Faktor, the editor in chief of the *Berliner Börsen-Courier*, immediately recognized the twenty-six-year-old's extraordinary talent and hired him as a full-time columnist. Roth wrote commentaries about everyday life in Berlin; reviewed books, films, and exhibitions; and reported on everything from court trials to entertainment events. His writings often began with seemingly insignificant details, from which he wrung out "the poetry and import of a particular moment in time."[93]

Roth was a bohemian and continued to live like one in Berlin. Along with fellow writers like Brecht and Egon Erwin Kisch, he was a regular at the Romanisches Café, which supplanted the older Café des Westens as the most important artistic meeting place in Berlin in the early 1920s. Located across from the Kaiser Wilhelm Memorial Church, the Romanisches Café was a large, mostly open, not particularly cozy space, but the clientele made it irresistible. "The people read, write poetry, draw, compose, clap, flirt, debate, do business, drink one more coffee, and smoke one more cigarette," one contemporary wrote of the unique atmosphere. "Everyone knows, respects, and hates everyone else and probably hates the eternally agitated monotony of the place's commotion as well. But the next day they'll be back."[94] Roth was fond of sitting in one of the back rooms, writing his articles. The hustle and bustle didn't distract him in the least. Indeed, he seemed to draw inspiration from it.

In September 1922, feeling insufficiently appreciated, Roth quit the *Berliner Börsen-Courier*. From that point on, he wrote most often for *Vorwärts* and the *Neue Berliner Zeitung—12-Uhr-Blatt*. His reports on the trial of the conspirators in the murder of Rathenau at the State Court for the Protection of the Constitution in Leipzig in October 1922 attracted particular attention. In them, he revealed the homicidal impulses camouflaged within the new ultranationalist phraseology: "These people proclaim their love for everything 'national,' but what they mean are firearms. They say they're serving the 'national cause,' but in actuality they're preparing for murder."[95]

In June 1923, Roth decided to go back to Vienna because his earnings couldn't keep pace with galloping inflation. When he returned to Berlin at the end of the year, his first novella had been published. *The Spider's Nest* (Das Spinnennetz) had appeared in serialized form in Vienna's *Arbeiter-Zeitung* starting in early October 1922. The paper had announced the publication of Roth's work with the words, "The novel . . . describes the swamp of reaction and the moral and intellectual brutalization from which swastika fetishism sprouts."[96]

The main character was Lieutenant Theodor Lohse, who returns from the First World War but is unable to reintegrate into civilian life: "There was no superior whose mood one could divine or whose wishes one could foresee."[97] Lohse joins a secret organization based in Munich, where it weaves its webs like a spider, and driven by a wanton desire to rise in society, he literally walks over corpses to get what he craves: "He wanted to be a leader, a member of the Bundestag, a minister, a dictator. He was still unknown outside his own circles. The name Theodor Lohse did not make headlines in the paper."[98] In the end he succeeds. He, a murderer, becomes the "Head of Security" and marries an aristocrat, Elsa von Schlieffen. Nothing stands in his way anymore. The final installment of the narrative appeared in the *Arbeiter-Zeitung* on November 6, 1923. Two days later, Hitler and Ludendorff launched their putsch. It was almost as if Roth, with his acute sensitivity to the perils of the time, had been able to see the future.

In 1924, Benno Reifenberg brought Roth onto the editorial board of the *Frankfurter Zeitung*. He held that position until 1933 and became one of the paper's most highly regarded contributors.

ON SEPTEMBER 23, THREE days before Ebert and Stresemann announced the end of passive resistance in the Ruhr, Franz
Kafka arrived at Berlin's Anhalter Bahnhof train station. Awaiting
him there was Dora Diamant. Kafka, the forty-year-old writer from
Prague who had been suffering from tuberculosis for several years,
had almost no popular success but did enjoy a small reputation in
literary circles. He had met Diamant, a twenty-five-year-old Eastern
European Jewish woman, at Müritzsee lake, where she was managing
a children's camp of the Jewish People's Home in Berlin. "He was
tall and thin, had a dark complexion, and took long steps when he
walked, so that I thought at first he must be a half-blood Indian and
not a European," she recalled.[99] The two were immediately attracted
to one another, and Kafka's new friends invited the bachelor to move
to Berlin and live with her. Kafka agreed, seeing it as a way of escaping
the cloistered atmosphere of his family home in Prague. But this step
wasn't easy for him. In a letter written only days after his move, he
spoke of "an act of rashness for which comparisons can only be found
if we flip back through the pages of history, for instance, to Napoleon
invading Russia."[100]

Diamant had found quarters for them on Miquelstrasse 8, in the
outer district of Steglitz well away from the bustle of the big city. "My
narrow street is the last somewhat urban one, behind it the city landscape dissolves into gardens, splendid gardens, and villas," Kafka wrote
to his friend Felix Witsch.[101]

Kafka had chosen a bad time to move to Berlin. Hyperinflation
exacerbated social conflicts, and unrest on the streets, demonstrations, and looting were everyday occurrences, reaching a tragic nadir
with the Scheunenviertel violence of early November 1923. In Steglitz, Kafka didn't directly experience the explosive mood in the German capital, but he was of course affected by inflation. Although he
received a monthly pension of 1,000 Czech crowns, he still had to
exchange them for inflationary marks, which took time and entailed

significant losses. In the letters and postcards Kafka sent to his parents during his months in Berlin, he wrote almost exclusively about prices, exchange rates, and his difficulty in procuring food. Without regular packages from Prague, the writer and his partner would have hardly survived the Berlin winter.[102]

Rents were skyrocketing along with everything else. That created tension with their landlady, who found the unmarried couple bothersome to begin with. In November, she canceled their lease. Kafka created an unflattering portrait of her in his short story "A Little Woman," written at the end of 1923: "This little woman, then, is very ill-pleased with me, she always finds something objectionable in me, I am always doing the wrong thing to her, I annoy her at every step; if a life could be cut into the smallest of small pieces and every scrap of it could be separately assessed, every scrap of my life would certainly be an offense to her."[103]

Kafka found a new home only a few streets away on Grunewaldstrasse 13, where he led a retiring existence. But word of his presence in Steglitz had spread in Berlin, and he was visited by a series of cultural luminaries, including Rudolf Kayser of the Fischer publishing house's literary journal *Neue Rundschau*, and Willy Haas, the editor in chief of the *Literarische Welt*, as well as Egon Erwin Kisch and Franz Werfel. And one of Kafka's friends from Prague, Max Brod, always stopped by when he was in the German capital.[104]

In October 1923, the publisher Kurt Wolff informed Kafka that his works weren't selling and that his royalty account would be closed. Through Brod, Kafka met Rudolf Leonhard, editor at the publishing house Die Schmiede, founded in 1921; the two men had met for negotiations the previous July. In early 1924, they arrived at an agreement for Die Schmiede to publish a volume of short stories entitled *A Hunger Artist*. Kafka's new publisher gave him a small but very welcome advance.[105]

In late January 1924, Kafka and Diamant were forced to move again, settling into a two-room apartment with stove heat and a terrace on Heidestrasse 25/26 in the wealthy district of Zehlendorf. Kafka's health had declined significantly. Running a near-constant fever and suffering from painful coughing fits, he rarely left the house. His uncle Siegfried Löwy traveled from Prague and convinced his nephew to seek treatment at a specialist clinic. On March 17, 1924, accompanied by Brod, he left the city to which he had moved with such high hopes just six months before.[106]

Kafka's end came sooner than expected. In a forest sanatorium, a one-hour train ride from Vienna, it was discovered in early April 1924 that his tuberculosis had spread to his esophagus. All hope of recovery was gone. "Terrible days of unhappiness," Brod noted in his diary.[107] Kafka spent the final weeks of his life in a private respiratory clinic in the village of Kierling near Klosterneuburg bei Wien, with Diamant and his friend Robert Klopstock taking turns staying at his bedside. Shortly before his death, Kafka was able to review the proofs for the *Hunger Artist* volume, which now also included his final finished story, "Josephine the Singer, or the Mouse Folk," which he had completed in March.

Franz Kafka died at noon on June 3, 1924, one month before his forty-first birthday. "He knew people as only a man of great, magnificent sensitivity can know them," eulogized Milena Jesenská. "He knew the world in an unusual and profound way. He himself was an unusual and profound world. He wrote books that are among the most significant in recent German literature. . . . They are so true, naked, and painful that they seem naturalistic even in those passages where things are expressed symbolically."[108]

IN THE EARLY 1920S, Berlin welcomed many Russian immigrants. Hundreds of thousands of people fled revolution, civil war, and the rule of the Bolsheviks in the former Romanov Empire, and the German capital offered them a safe haven. The high point of the mass migration came in 1922 and 1923. Some six hundred thousand Russian émigrés and refugees arrived in Germany in those two years alone, with half going to Berlin.[109] The largest group came from the educated and propertied classes: lawyers, doctors, journalists, businesspeople, bankers, civil servants in the old Russian state apparatus, officers, and aristocrats. Many were familiar with Germany from before 1914, having studied there or because they were related to German aristocratic families.[110]

Russians who managed to transfer their wealth abroad in time led carefree lives. In his "Idle Chatter" column from the German capital in December 1921, Kerr expressed his amazement at the number of Russians running around Berlin "spending sinful amounts of money." His explanation was that they had brought jewelry and precious stones with them or, before the First World War, had deposited their savings in the Bank of England since the British pound, which "had climbed to fantastic heights," offered a "permanent basis for a luxurious lifestyle."[111] Of course, not all Russian émigrés lived extravagantly. Many were forced to earn their keep as waiters, taxi drivers, street peddlers, and ballroom dancers for hire and lived in cheap hotels and boardinghouses.[112]

Russian émigrés gravitated toward western Berlin, especially the Charlottenburg district, which local wits renamed "Charlottengrad." The bus from there to Halensee became known as the "Russian slingshot" and pricey Kurfürstendamm boulevard as the "Neppsky-Prospect" (*Nepp* being the German word for "rip-off").[113] "You hear more Russian than German on Kurfürstendamm," recalled Asta Nielsen. "That's the reason for the common joke in which one Berliner says to another, 'I don't go to Kurfürstendamm. I get homesick.'"[114]

The Cuno government registered this demographic development with concern. In notes from January 1923, State Secretary Hamm complained that "Russian and other eastern immigrants" were forming "veritable colonies" in Berlin and "gradually taking over" some streets. As a countermeasure he suggested erecting barriers to keep Russians from getting permission to open businesses and cultural venues and to "make their stay here unpleasant."[115]

Nonetheless, the Russian diaspora in Berlin developed a very active social and cultural life. "Filled with a lively need for activity and a business acumen that should not be underestimated," Ossietzky wrote in March 1923, "they have rebuilt their own Petrograd, Moscow, or far-flung corner of Russia on foreign soil and feel quite comfortable there."[116] There were eighty-six Russian publishers of books and periodicals in Berlin, which between 1918 and 1924 introduced more titles than those in Moscow and Petrograd (St. Petersburg) combined. The largest publisher for exiles was Slovo (The Word), which was supported by the powerful German publisher Ullstein. A variety of Russian-language newspapers and magazines were available at kiosks, and every political and intellectual current within the diaspora had its own public organ. "When you pick up one of the Russian newspapers in Berlin and scan the classifieds, you might think you had gotten hold of a paper from the 'good old days' in Moscow or Petersburg," one observer wrote in 1922. "You see advertisements for theatrical performances, concerts, and cabarets. Numerous restaurants recommend that the esteemed readers try their national cuisine . . . and the obligatory vodka with *zakuski*. Attorneys make it known when and where they are holding consultations. . . . Only when you more closely examine the addresses of these people is it apparent that you're in Berlin, not Petersburg."[117]

The most important daily Russian newspaper—*Rul* (Rudder)—was known for its liberalism and relative objectivity. For a time, its editor in chief was Vladimir Dmitrievich Nabokov, the father of Vladimir Nabokov. In March 1922, the elder Nabokov was shot to death by two extreme right-wing Russian terrorists from Munich, after he threw himself in front of Pavel Milyukov, a former minister in the Kerensky government, at the Berliner Philharmonie.[118] His son, who had just moved from Cambridge to the German capital, began his years in Berlin under an unhappy star. Nabokov would go on to create tributes to the Russian émigré community in the city in his novels *Mary* (1925–26) and *King, Queen, Knave* (1928).[119]

The Russian diaspora and mainstream German society rarely interacted. Émigrés met in their own restaurants and cafés, for instance, the Prager Diele (Prague Parlor) in the district of Wilmersdorf and the Russische Teestube (Russian Tea Room) on Nürnberger Strasse, where "there was sugar in large bowls for liberal use on all the tables and cookies were brought in a large basket, also *á discrétion*, whenever you ordered a glass of tea."[120]

There was also a Russian cabaret, the Blaue Vogel (Blue Bird), run by the witty and inventive director and master of ceremonies, Jurij Jushnij. "The Blue Bird is a couple of thousand versts above what is known as 'cabaret' in Germany thanks to its vividness, penchant for the bizarre, invention, and spirit," effused Alfred Polgar in the *Weltbühne*. Tucholsky concurred that the troupe offered "the best sort of cabaret," writing, "With what graceful ease everything is performed! . . . Love for the Old Moscow is everywhere on the stage, leaping from one end to the other, and a murmur goes through the audience, as they recognize, 'Yes, that's how it was.'"[121]

IN THE SUMMER OF 1920, Berlin saw its First International Dada Fair. On exhibit were 174 works: photo collages, posters, paintings, and objects of various provenances. The Dada movement had grown out of an association of avant-garde artists and writers in Zürich's Cabaret Voltaire in February 1916. Berlin native Richard Huelsenbeck, who with Hugo Ball coined the term *dada*, returned to the German capital in January 1917 and assembled a group of like-minded experimenters. The Dadaists wanted to radically break with the bourgeois notion of art and were driven by a desire to provoke hostile reactions. In this spirit, their first Berlin exhibition featured a life-sized puppet called the "Prussian archangel, dressed in an officer's uniform with a pig's head." A sign dangled from it that read, "In order to understand this work of art, go on a daily twelve-hour exercise session on the Tempelhof Field with full backpack and equipped for maneuvers."[122]

Tucholsky found such attempts to outrage narrow-minded model citizens "a little forced"—with one notable exception. "There is one man among them who truly turns the exhibition on its head," he wrote. "That person, who makes a visit worthwhile, is George Grosz, a man's man and a fellow of limitless ferocity. If drawings could kill, the Prussian military would be dead.... No respectable bourgeois family table should be without his portfolio *God at Our Side*—the twisted faces of his majors and sergeants are infernal phantoms that haunt the real world today."[123]

George Grosz was born in Berlin in 1893 as Georg Ehrenfried Gross and studied at the Royal Academy of Art in Dresden and then the School of Handicrafts in Berlin. Like many members of his generation, the First World War was a formative experience. In November 1914, he volunteered to fight but was discharged in May 1915 as "unfit for duty" because of a sinus suppuration. Drafted back into the armed forces in January 1917, he suffered a nervous breakdown. He was permanently discharged as "incapable of service" and allowed to return home in April.[124]

In the summer of 1915, in painter Ludwig Meitner's studio, Grosz met Wieland Herzfeld, a budding publisher three years his junior. Herzfeld soon visited Grosz in his studio in Berlin-Südende and was immediately fascinated by his drawings. "Never has the work of any artist ever made a comparable impression on me," he recalled decades later.[125] Wieland and his brother Helmut Herzfeld, who began calling himself John Heartfield in 1916 to protest the hateful wartime songs directed against the British, became close friends with Grosz, who likely adopted his new name in imitation of Heartfield. They convinced him to submit several of his drawings as illustrations to their magazine *Neue Jugend* (New Youth). Among those works was the pen drawing *Durchhalten* (Hold Out), with which Grosz satirized the official propaganda encouraging Germans to fight until the bitter end. It depicted a horrific funeral procession led by a prostitute and a creepy figure carrying a child's coffin under his arm. Grosz's acerbic style was already at full force.[126]

In the fall of 1917, a "small Grosz portfolio" with twenty original lithographs and poems written by the artist was published by Wieland Herzfeld's Malik publishing house in a numbered edition of one hundred. In the years to come, almost all of Grosz's portfolios and anthologies would appear with Malik. They established the artist as a genius illustrator and ferocious critic of German philistines.[127] Under Herzfeld's careful guidance, Malik joined the established houses S. Fischer and Rowohlt as one of the leading publishers of left-wing literature. It introduced German audiences not only to Upton Sinclair but also the latest Soviet literature. With John Heartfield photo collages on their covers, these works had a distinctive, unmistakable look.[128]

Grosz and the Herzfeld brothers were examples of the decided left-wing tendency of the Berlin dada group. They supported the November Revolution and joined the KPD soon after it was formed in late 1918 and early 1919. Grosz leveled unsparing criticism at the SPD leadership, whom he accused of allying with the old guard against the revolutionary Left. In March 1919, on the cover of the first issue of the Malik magazine *Pleite* (Bankrupt), Grosz published a satiric illustration depicting Ebert as a tiny king sitting in an armchair and being offered a wheat beer glass full of champagne by a bold-looking officer. The caption read "By the grace of his moneybags."[129]

Count Harry Kessler, who took an early interest in Grosz's works and bought several from him, described in his diary what he had seen and heard in the artist's new studio in the Wilmersdorf district in early February 1919: "Grosz had a large political painting called *Germany, a Winter Fairy Tale*, in which he mocked the earlier aristocratic ruling classes as pillars supporting a bloated, sluggish bourgeoisie.... He said that he wanted to become a 'German Hogarth,' intentionally figurative and moral. His mission was to preach, improve, and reform. He had no interest in abstraction. He had conceived of this painting as something to be hung in schools." Kessler concluded, "In essence, Grosz is a Bolshevist of painting. He is disgusted by painting, by the senselessness of previous styles and wants to do something entirely new with the tools of painting—or perhaps more accurately he wants to return to something painting used to do ... but that was lost in the nineteenth century. Reactionary and revolutionary, a phenomenon of his time."[130]

*George Grosz*, The Pillars of Society, *oil on canvas, 1926.*
*Grosz's satiric paintings dissected the Weimar Republic's "ruling class" with unmatched incision and precision.*

A second visit by Kessler to Grosz's studio was colored by the violence in Berlin in March 1919, when government troops under Reichswehr Minister Gustav Noske had carried out multiple massacres of Communist agitators. Grosz was "deeply shaken" by these events and argued that the Left must now use violence to advance its cause. Kessler disagreed, countering that "any idea of fraternity would be discredited by violence" and that "violence invariably engenders further violence."[131]

The First International Dada Fair was simultaneously the high point and the end of the Dada movement. The Dadaists' strategy of provocation had led in some respects to an artistic dead end. But the provocation itself worked. The Reichswehr felt that its honor had been besmirched by the portfolio *God at Our Side* and sued Grosz and his publisher, the first in a series of legal actions that saw artists during the Weimar Republic, despite the abolition of censorship in Article 118 of the Constitution, put on trial. Owing to the testimony of Edwin Redslob in his capacity as "Reich art attendant" and that of the director of the Dresden city art collections, Paul Ferdinand Schmidt, the defendants came away with a relatively mild sentence: Grosz was fined 300 marks and Herzfeld 600 marks.[132]

Neither man was deterred by police harassment and lawsuits. In 1921, Malik published one of Grosz's best portfolios. *The Face of the Ruling Class* depicted those in power in Germany as still possessed by the old anti-democratic, monarchist, and militaristic spirit and showing no sense of community at all. Tucholsky praised the collection of fifty-five political illustrations as "the most masterful visual work of the postwar era" and said he didn't know of any other artist who had "captured the modern face of the powerful down to the final wine-burst vein." He added, "The way these officers, captains of industry, and uniformed nightwatchmen of public order look in every situation Grosz depicts is the way they always look their whole lives through."[133]

More than a few German artists and writers made their way in the early 1920s to the Soviet Union, which they regarded, despite all of its manifest shortcomings, as the only viable model for the future. In summer 1922, Grosz, too, journeyed to postrevolutionary Russia. The trip was a huge disappointment. What shocked the artist most was the hunger he saw all around. Everywhere he looked, instead of promising signs of socialist progress, Grosz could only see signs of disintegration. He discovered "nothing significant," not even when introduced in the Kremlin to Lenin, who was battered by illness. Sobered and disillusioned, Grosz returned to Berlin after six months.[134] He tacitly renounced the KPD the following year by simply failing to pay his membership dues.[135]

In 1923, Grosz published a compilation with Malik of sixteen watercolors and eighty-four drawings under the title *Ecce Homo*. Hans Reimann wrote in the *Tage-Buch* that "all of its pages are politically charged, and it's the political charge of a fanatic moralist."[136] In a personal look back at his career in 1930, Grosz described his intentions: "It's a document of the period of inflation . . . with its vices and immorality. . . . In its effect, it's as brutal as the period that inspired me to it. . . . And if you ask about its effect . . . it is a true deterrent . . . but it doesn't encourage profligacy in the slightest." The guardians of morality in Germany took the opposite view. *Ecce Homo*, they contended, contained twenty-two "pornographic depictions" that violated the "sense of shame and morality of any person with normal sensibilities."[137]

At a trial in front of the Berlin Regional Court in February 1924, the presiding judge asked Grosz where he derived the "artistic justification" to "depict things of this nature in such unveiled fashion." It was a clear transgression of the limits of art, the judge added. Grosz replied, "For the artist, this limit doesn't exist."[138] Grosz and Wieland Herzfeld were fined 500 marks each, and the twenty-two illustrations that had been deemed unacceptable were confiscated and their printing plates destroyed.[139]

In late 1923, Malik opened a modern bookstore on Köthener Strasse, with a "Gallery Georg Grosz" attached. In the Christmas edition of the *Weltbühne*, Friedrich Sieburg—three years later the Paris correspondent for the *Frankfurter Zeitung*—called upon his readers to visit this new cultural center: "Go there! Enjoy the lovely space in the bookstore, the boldly and cleverly grouped treasures there, and then stand before the works of this master, who traces the lines and curves of his impudent semi-corpses with his left while thrusting a glowing hot poker into the syphilitic face of his age with his right."[140]


WALTER GROPIUS, THE FOUNDER of the legendary Bauhaus in Weimar, also faced hostility from the outset of his career. Born in 1883 in Berlin, he followed in the footsteps of his father, who worked as a master builder for the government, and studied architecture in Munich and Berlin, albeit without ever getting a degree. The decisive phase of his education came between 1908 and 1910, when he worked in the office of Peter Behrens, a pioneer of industrial architecture, who caused a furor with buildings like the AEG turbine factory in Berlin. In late 1910, Gropius opened his own "studio for architecture" in Berlin-Wilmersdorf. With the construction of the Fagus factory in Alfeld near Hanover and his contributions to the 1914 Werkbund Exhibition in Cologne, he made a name for himself before the First World War.[141]

When the war began, Gropius volunteered for the Wandsbek Hussars, an elite regiment from Hamburg. By November 1914, he had already been made a lieutenant, and he spent the entire war either at the front or just behind it. The 1918 revolution in Germany marked a break in his life story, one in which, as he wrote to his mother, he "was completely transformed internally and refocused around the new things that are rising to prominence with incredible vigor."[142] Soon after returning to Berlin, he joined the Work Council for Art, an association of artists and architects that had coalesced under the leadership of architect Bruno Taut. Their principal tenet was that art should no longer provide enjoyment for the few but should serve the happiness and welfare of all. The goal was to end the elite position of artists and reestablish a connection between them and the larger community by returning to craftsmanship as the original source of creative design. They took as a symbol of the unity of tradespeople, artists, and architects the Gothic cathedrals of the Middle Ages, which they considered the purest expression of large-scale communal building and a "total work of art."[143]

In October 1915, Henry van de Velde, the Belgian director of the Grand Ducal Saxon Academy of Applied Arts in Weimar, asked Gropius if he would be interested in succeeding him. Nothing came of that overture, but in January 1919, Gropius revisited the possibility with the newly created independent city-state of Saxony-Weimar. That April, Gropius was named the director of both the former academy of applied arts and the academy of fine arts, which were merged under the name State Bauhaus in Weimar.

Gropius detailed what he wanted to achieve in a manifesto that showed how much he had been influenced by the discussions within the Work Council for Art. "Architects, sculptors, painters—we all must return to craftsmanship!" he exclaimed with deep emotion. "Let us strive for, conceive, and create the new building of the future that will unite every discipline—architecture and sculpture and painting—and that will one day rise heavenward from the million hands of craftsmen as a clear symbol of a new belief to come."[144] The fitting image on the cover of the manifesto was a Lyonel Feininger woodcut of a medieval cathedral, at whose top three beams of light—representing painting, architecture, and sculpture—joined together.

Gropius declined the title of professor, signaling his distance from the usual workings of academia, just as the Bauhaus eliminated the customary distinctions between faculty and students in favor of a community of masters, journeymen, and apprentices. Gropius was able to persuade some of the leading artists of his day—the German American Feininger, the Swiss Johannes Itten and Paul Klee, the German Gerhard Marcks and Oskar Schlemmer, and the Russian Wassily Kandinsky—to teach at his new institution.

Instruction began at Bauhaus in the summer semester of 1919. In his inaugural address to students, Gropius sought to win them over to his ideas of community and challenged them not to become discouraged by failures but instead to dare to experiment as though they were in a laboratory. "Try, test, throw out, and try again," he told them.[145] Gradually, Bauhaus established individual workshops for weaving, carpentry, mural painting, printing, sculpture, forging, glass painting, and pottery. In each of them, a "master of craft" and a "master of form" shared teaching duties.[146]

One of the leading figures of the first phase of Bauhaus was Itten. Gropius had met the painter and art theorist in Vienna through his first wife, Alma Mahler (previously married to composer Gustav Mahler). Itten was a follower of the neo-Zoroastrian Mazdaznan religion, which united Persian, Indian, and Buddhist elements and prescribed vegetarianism and regular fasting. With his shaven head and his self-made garb, a kind of monk's frock, Itten immediately attracted a circle of young disciples. "For us members of the Mazdaznan clique . . . Itten possessed a special aura," one of his devotees recalled. "You could almost call it a form of holiness. We whispered

*The Bauhaus—founded in 1919 in Weimar and located as*
*of 1926 in Dessau—would become one of the most influential*
*design movements of the twentieth century. Its functionalist*
*aesthetics continue to influence contemporary design.*
*Walter Gropius (seventh from left, in front row) is*
*surrounded by other Bauhaus "masters."*

when we approached him. Our reverence was immense, and we were
always delighted and buoyed when he interacted with us in his folksy
and casual manner."[147]

Gropius initially tolerated the idiosyncratic Itten, but by the spring
of 1921, tensions had arisen, sparked by the Bauhaus director's plans
to increasingly use the workshops for commercial production as a way
of giving the institution more financial independence. Itten rejected
such profane economic considerations. His focus was teaching students to become creative, harmonious "new men." The wider context
of the two men's conflict was the Bauhaus's general shift away from
effusive enthusiasm for craftsmanship and toward a new openness to
industry and technology. One of the driving forces behind this reori-
entation was the Dutchman Theo van Doesburg, one of the found-
ers of De Stijl. In 1921 and 1922, he held a series of lectures entitled

"The Will to Style: Redesigning Life, Art, and Technology." Although Doesburg was never appointed a "master," he was crucial to the development of Bauhaus's signature functionalism.[148] Instead of trading in utopian visions, the goal was to produce new, purpose-built industrial products characterized by utility.

In April 1923, Itten left the Bauhaus and was replaced by Hungarian artist László Moholy-Nagy. Instead of the usual priestly Bauhaus outfit, he went around in what looked like a workman's jumpsuit, an expression of his connection to the aesthetics of technology.[149]

Although Gropius insisted on Bauhaus's political neutrality, he couldn't prevent his institution from getting drawn into political conflicts. It didn't take long for his enemies to coalesce. The conservative professors of the former academy of fine arts refused to accept the loss of their prestigious positions and voiced suspicions that the Bauhaus director wanted to start a political revolution. Under Gropius, the once flourishing Weimar academy had devolved into a "hotbed of Spartacus agitation and Jewry," a privy councilor from the city carped to Kessler in late August 1919.[150] Gropius's detractors achieved an initial victory in April 1921 when the State Academy for the Fine Arts was refounded in a wing of the former academy building.[151]

For well-off Weimar residents, the invasion of long-haired students represented an unwelcome intrusion of anarchy into their secure bourgeois order. They saw Bauhaus as a breeding ground of vice and excess. With a mixture of horror and curiosity, they gossiped about students throwing wild parties, skinny-dipping in city lakes and the Saale River, and practicing free love. The conservative newspaper *Weimarer Zeitung* lambasted such alleged activities as the "product of completely degenerate sensibilities" and the "outgrowth of destructive methods of teaching and instruction."[152]

When the regional state of Thuringia was constituted in May 1920, the Bauhaus became subject to the new Ministry of Popular Education under Social Democrat Max Greil. He backed Gropius against all the attacks and ensured that he had access to the financial resources he needed. Nonetheless, over the course of 1922, the Bauhaus came under increasing pressure to justify its existence by staging an exhibition that would highlight its achievements.[153]

Gropius threw himself into preparations for the event. In January 1923, he summarized the institution's work to that point in a statement entitled "Idea and Development of the State Bauhaus in Weimar," which reflected the academy's new direction: "The Bauhaus affirms and engages with the machine as the most modern means of creating form. . . . The Bauhaus doesn't aspire to be an academy of handicraft, breeding artisanal idiosyncrasy. It seeks connection to industry."[154]

On August 15, 1923, Gropius opened the First Bauhaus Exhibit with a lecture entitled "Art and Technology: A New Unity." Masters and students exhibited images in the Weimar Landesmuseum while works from Bauhaus classes and workshops were displayed in schools. Hallways and staircases were decorated with frescoes and murals. Gropius's redesigned director's office on the second floor of the academy building, in which all objects were arranged at strict right angles, attracted particular attention. "Spend three days in Weimar, and you'll never want to see another square in your entire life," quipped critic Paul Westheim in the Berlin art journal *Das Kunstblatt*.[155]

The real highlight, however, was a functionally designed model dwelling, the "Haus am Horn," which exemplified Bauhaus's ideas about future domestic living. The building featured clear, simple lines, and its individual elements were standardized so that they could be recombined like building blocks. Most critics remained unconvinced. The house's exterior drew comparisons to a "white chocolate box." In the *Weltbühne*, architecture critic Adolf Behne characterized the house as a transitional work: "It's partly luxurious, partly primitive, partly an idealistic challenge and partly a child of its time, partly handicraft and partly industry, partly category and partly idyll, but in no single point is it pure and convincing. On the contrary, this is yet another aesthetic and theoretical object for discussion." Yet despite his criticism, Behne also described the exhibition as "important and significant," writing that what Gropius had achieved in "four years of determined effort" deserved the utmost respect. He had made Bauhaus into a "place of independent work," concluded Behne, and should be thanked for his efforts.[156]

All in all, Gropius had reason to be satisfied with the public reaction. Journalists from throughout Germany and abroad covered the event. But by the time the show closed in September, the writing was already on the wall for the cultural institution whose world fame continues to this day. Mid-October saw the formation of the SPD coalition government that would end with the intervention of Reichswehr troops early the following month. Thuringian state premier August Frölich, who tried to run a minority government, resigned in mid-December. The regional parliament was dissolved, and emerging victorious in the subsequent election of February 10, 1924, was a "law-and-order alliance" of conservative parties that had long advocated shutting down Bauhaus.

Gropius fought valiantly but in vain to preserve his project. In November 1924, after a motion by ultranationalists, the budgetary committee of the Thuringian regional parliament slashed regional state support for Bauhaus in half, from 100,000 marks to 50,000 marks, and only approved a continuation of its contract with the institution for six months. In late December, the Bauhaus masters put an end to the slow strangulation, announcing that they considered their relationship with the state of Thuringia ended as of March 1925. Bauhaus would find a new home in Dessau, which is where the twentieth century's most influential academy of art and architecture would fully blossom.[157]

AT 8:00 P.M. ON October 29, 1923, the words "Attention, attention—this is Berlin on frequency 400!" came from an improvised studio on the top floor of the Vox Haus on Potsdamer Strasse. The *Berliner Radio-Stunde*, later known as the *Funk-Stunde*, was the first radio entertainment program in Germany. Only two hundred people could tune in because that was how many radio receivers there were in the city. But it was the start of a new mass medium in Germany. With hyperinflation reaching its nadir, people no doubt approved when Hans Bredow, a state secretary in the postal ministry, said in his introduction to the program that radio would "take people's minds off their difficult, everyday cares" and "inject some inspiration and joy into the lives" of listeners.[158] In keeping with this mission, the first German radio shows were dedicated to light music. There wasn't much talking, although for Christmas in 1923, there were readings of a Hans Christian Andersen fairy tale and a chapter of the Bible.

Initially, you had to be affluent to afford a radio. "It was Christmas 1923 when one of the expensive receivers appeared on a neighbor's table of presents," remembered one Berlin resident.

> The handsome device stood on a wide, gleaming white windowsill in the living room of the lady of the house. New and well taken care of, its dark polish shimmered in contrast. . . . As the headphones were passed around the circle (we listened in pairs using one ear each), we were truly surprised. We could hear human voices, then music that was somehow floating through space and had been received by the naked wire under the roof of our building. We sat respectfully in front of this gleaming brand-new appliance, as the expert hand of the owner switched, plugged, and even turned its dial.[159]

The 200 listeners who tuned into German radio's first hour became 1,025 by the start of 1924 and 120,000 by the end of that year. "Soon, people in Berlin said of this or that person, 'He has radio,'" recalled German radio pioneer Albert Braun. "A short time later, you would get asked, 'Do you have radio?' And a short time later the question became, 'What, you don't have radio?'"[160] The variety and quality of the programming increased along with the number of listeners. One could enjoy first-rate music, including concerts by the Berlin Philharmonic, as well as readings by authors, radio plays, and live broadcasts of soccer games, boxing matches, and the six-day bicycle race, the

Sechstagerennen. Braun, the moderator of the *Funk-Stunde*, became a celebrity. "In terms of popularity, he held his own with movie stars," remarked Curt Riess, sports reporter for the daily newspaper *12-Uhr-Blatt*. "With justification since he carried out the task of transporting an audience he could neither see nor hear with skill and sensitivity."[161]

In principle, German radio was politically neutral, but even in the Weimar Republic, the leanings of various programs were impossible to miss. Nonetheless, it wasn't until National Socialist rule in 1933 that the new medium would place itself completely in the service of propaganda.

# CHAPTER 9

# AFTER 1923

## *A New Period in German History?*

*Nazi Reichstag deputies show their contempt for the parliament of which they were members by attending a session wearing their uniforms. This image was taken by the well-known Jewish photographer Erich Salomon in 1931. He was murdered in Auschwitz in 1943.*

IN DECEMBER 1923, HISTORIAN ARTHUR ROSENberg remarked that critics of the Weimar Republic "wouldn't have bet five Rentenmarks on it surviving for long,"[1] but in fact the crises of that year had begun to subside when the calendar turned to 1924. Hyperinflation had been brought under control, and the Rentenmark proved astonishingly stable. "Imagine—Germany is now a country with a hard currency, and our Rentenmark is better than the pound,"

Dorothy von Moltke wrote in early 1924 to her parents, who were living in South Africa. "Isn't that crazy?"[2] Apocalyptic despair gave way
to cautious optimism. "There was a new confidence—a mood of reconstruction and 'Let's start all over again!' which gradually replaced the
hectic bustle of the past few years," recalled Klaus Mann. "The German people began to awake and to recuperate from a nightmare that
had been inflicted upon them, violently upsetting their moral standards and their bank accounts. They had no kaiser anymore, no German Alsace, no fleet, no army, no generals, no decorations, no titles, no
colonies, no illusions. But they had a future."[3]

In early February 1924, Victor Klemperer visited his bank for the
first time since the introduction of the Rentenmark. He had been given
500 marks by his brother, a Berlin lawyer, and he wanted to invest the
money in stocks. "The inside of the bank, which used to be overfull,
was entirely empty," he discovered. "The bank employees who used to
be so rude now presented themselves as though I were a billionaire. . . .
It's almost comic how things have turned on their heads since the days
of inflation and feverish speculation."[4]

Germany's growing domestic calm was preceded by a new international situation.[5] Influential political and economic circles in the
United States, where isolationism had held sway since 1919, now
demanded more engagement with the "old continent," particularly
with regard to America's vital interest in European currencies. Power
brokers in Washington increasingly came to see that economic chaos
in Germany was not only detrimental to the political stabilization of
Europe but also increasingly harmful to the global economy. Before
1914, Germany had been a lucrative market for American exports,
and as excess American capital looked for investment opportunities,
Germany—which combined a massive need for investment with a
strong, industrial base—looked particularly promising. What was
needed was a solution to the reparations issue tolerable to all sides. On
this score, US secretary of state Charles Hughes was determined to
show the Europeans a way out.[6]

Major changes were also afoot in the Soviet Union. After years of civil war, "war communism," and terrible hunger, domestic stability and economic development became priorities. On January 21, 1924, the founder of the Soviet state, Vladimir Ilyich Lenin, died after a long illness. His death elicited sympathy among not only communists all over the world but also from some bourgeois admirers. "The telegram with the news of Lenin's death has been posted all over the city," noted Thea Sternheim. "I cried when I saw it. I'll never forget how his name cropped up toward the end of the war. My delight at that etched itself on my memory in jolting fashion. . . . Someone who compelled peace has died. Suffering humanity has lost a friend."[7]

Even before Lenin's passing, a power struggle had broken out between Leon Trotsky, the charismatic war commissar and founder of the Red Army, and the "troika" of Stalin, Lev Kamenev, and Grigory Zinoviev. The rivalry involved fundamental disagreements about the path the Soviet Union should follow. While Trotsky stuck to his idea of a "permanent revolution"—the conviction that the success of the socialist experiment in the Soviet Union depended on revolutionizing the major industrial nations of the West—Stalin, the secretary general of the Communist Party and the new strongman in the Politburo, believed that attempts to export revolution had failed and that instead of placing faith in global upheaval, Soviets should concentrate on "creating socialism in one country." Stalin's doctrine didn't entail support for attempts to topple foreign governments, such as the one the Comintern had tried to launch in Germany in the fall of 1923. There would be no "German October." Instead, the primary goal of Soviet foreign policy would be to end its status as an international pariah and reestablish relations with the western powers. On February 1, 1924, the United Kingdom officially recognized the Soviet Union, and many other countries followed suit, including France in October. The United States, however, would not take this step until Franklin D. Roosevelt became president in 1933.[8]

In the elections for British Parliament on December 6, 1923, the Labour Party and the Liberals defeated the Tories. With Prime Minister Stanley Baldwin no longer commanding a parliamentary majority, for the first time a Labour leader, Ramsay MacDonald, had a mandate to form the next British government. He put together a minority cabinet tolerated by the Liberals. MacDonald would have to surrender power after an accelerated parliamentary election on October 29, 1924, with Tories reinstalling Baldwin as prime minister. But it was hugely significant for Germany that in the decisive months of 1924, when the reparations issue was being settled, the British government was more inclined to support the cause of international reconciliation.[9]

The same was true of France. There, the Poincaré-led Bloc National suffered a spectacular defeat in the general election of May 11, 1924, to a left-wing alliance known as the Cartel des Gauches. "In Paris, the Left, which is already striking up songs of victory, is hoping for Poincaré's fall," noted Kessler when the initial results of the vote were announced.[10] And in fact, Poincaré, who had refused any compromise with Germany, was forced to step down. France's new prime minister—and foreign minister—was the mayor of Lyon and chairman of the Radical Party, Édouard Herriot. The German government had reason to hope that he would not continue to stand in the way of a sensible arrangement.[11]


WITH THE FOREIGN POLICY situation having shifted in Germany's favor with the dawn of 1924, most of the national government's attention was focused on domestic political problems. The first priority was to ease the conflict between Bavaria and the Reich. As we've seen, the commander of the Seventh Reichswehr Division, General Lossow, had been suspended for failing to carry out orders in October 1923. General State Commissar Kahr immediately restored him to that position and had the Bavarian division swear an oath of loyalty to himself. The two men's ambiguous roles during the Hitler Putsch of November 8–9 left both fundamentally compromised and should have resulted in their immediate dismissal. But Bavarian state premier Eugen von Knilling, who did not want to be too conciliatory toward the national government in Berlin, initially refused to oust them. On

January 2, 1924, Lossow offered to resign in a letter to Seeckt, but only after the trial of Ludendorff and Hitler, to prevent handing the Nazis any political capital. Seeckt recommended that Ebert accept Lossow's resignation on the condition that the Bavarian division's oath of loyalty was revoked.[12]

The Bavarian government responded by demanding a federalist revision of the Weimar Constitution that would have restored the financial sovereignty of the individual regional states and stipulated that the commander of Bavarian Reichswehr troops could only be replaced in agreement with the Bavarian government. The national government wouldn't hear of such a change, which would have called the unity of the Reich supreme command into question. After some back and forth, a compromise was reached on February 14, 1924, in which the national government agreed to "consult" with the Bavarian government should it want to replace the region's Reichswehr commander and to take into account Bavarian wishes as much as possible if troops from Bavaria were deployed beyond its borders. Moreover, German soldiers in the future would swear their loyalty not just to the national Constitution but to the constitution of their respective home regional states. That superseded the oath to the Munich government required of the Seventh Reichswehr Division. On February 18, Lossow and Kahr resigned, with no fear of ever having to face criminal charges for their treasonous activities of 1923.[13] "Audible sighs of relief in the Reich Chancellery," noted civil servant Max von Stockhausen in his diary.[14]

THE NEXT STEP WAS the lifting of the military state of emergency that had been declared on September 26, 1923, and that had been enforced by Seeckt since the night of Hitler's attempted putsch. The less chaotic the domestic political situation became, the more urgently the limits on personal freedom associated with the measure were called into question. The SPD in particular pushed for an end to the official emergency with an eye toward Saxony and Thuringia, where there was friction between the Social Democratic regional governments and military commanders.[15] At a cabinet meeting on January 11, 1924, Seeckt vigorously opposed changing the status quo, arguing that it would hinder the fight against both Communists and the radical Right and increase "the danger of civil war." But one month later, on February 12, it was Seeckt himself who demanded an end to the military state of emergency, suggesting a state of "civilian emergency" could be imposed instead under the direction of the interior minister.[16] The following day, Seeckt repeated his suggestion to Ebert, saying, "The authority of state has been reinforced to the point that the reform of our governmental and economic life introduced under the state of emergency can be continued without it."[17]

It's hard to know with certainty what caused Seeckt's about-face. He probably feared that the Reichswehr's reputation might be permanently damaged by the constant skirmishes with civilian authorities not only in Saxony and Thuringia but also in Prussia. Stabilization on the domestic front no doubt helped change his mind.[18]

Ebert took up Seeckt's suggestion and promised to take action, lifting the military state of emergency via presidential decree on February 28, 1924. With that, all restrictions on personal liberties and the rights to free speech and assembly were ended, including the bans Seeckt had placed on the KPD, the Nazi Party, and the radical right-wing DVFP on November 20, 1923. At the same time, the Reich Interior Ministry was empowered to "take the necessary steps to defend against activities hostile to the Constitution." After a protest by the Bavarian government, which cited concerns about the imminent trial of Hitler and the other putschists, Bavaria was exempted from the decree "in recognition of the existing and continuing state of emergency there." The new national "civilian state of emergency" would persist until October.[19] In a proclamation on March 1, 1924, Seeckt thanked his commandants and asked them "to work on reinforcing the [mind-set among the] troops, so that the Reichswehr can remain the incisive nonpartisan instrument serving only the fatherland that it has proven to be in most recent months."[20] It was a fairly hypocritical statement considering the eagerness with which the military had gone after the left-wing regional governments in the fall of 1923—while treating rebellious Bavaria much more gently.


ON FEBRUARY 26, HITLER, Ludendorff, and the other con- spirators in the November putsch were put on trial. Because Bavaria didn't recognize the State Court for the Protection of the Consti- tution in Leipzig, the case was tried at the Munich Regional Court I. That ensured there would be no thorough investigations into the connections between the putschists and the triumvirate of Kahr, Lossow, and Seisser in the fall of 1923. "The defendants sit motion- less at small tables," reported journalist Leo Lania about the pro- ceedings in the former war academy building on Blutenburgstrasse. "Behind them are the witness benches, seats for the press, and a cou- ple of rows of observers. We are alone among ourselves. There are no barriers that could give the defendants the feeling of . . . not being heard in full. The court's brown paneling makes the space feel cozy and warm—a refreshing change from the coldly sober atmosphere of most German courts. A legal proceeding? No, more like a seminar about high treason."[21]

From the very start, Hitler acted like the master of ceremonies. In his four-hour opening statement for the defense, he took full respon- sibility for the attempted putsch: "In the final analysis, I alone wanted this matter." At the same time, he rejected the main charge against him, claiming that there could be "no such thing as high treason against the traitors to the country in 1918."[22] The presiding judge, Regional Court Director Georg Neithardt, made clear his sympathies for the defendants, allowing Hitler to use the proceedings to go on tirades and only rarely speaking mild words of censure when Hitler heaped too much contempt on the Weimar Republic and its represen- tatives. In his closing argument, Hitler theatrically turned to address the five judges directly: "You will not be the ones to speak the final judgment. The final judgment will be spoken by that goddess of the

*Hitler and his co-defendants after the verdict in*
*their trial was announced, April 1, 1924.*

Day of Judgment who will one day lift us from your and our graves as 'history.'"[23]

The trial was the talk of the town in Munich. Respected citizens followed the proceedings in extensive reports in the *Münchner Neueste Nachrichten* newspaper, in which Hitler still attracted the greatest sympathy. At an evening in the literary and musical salon of Maximilian and Else Bernstein on Briennerstrasse in late February 1924, Hedwig Pringsheim witnessed ladies from Munich society, including Else Bruckmann, the wife of publisher Hugo Bruckmann, displaying "such an enthusiasm for Hitler and [his] racism" that her heart began to race and only "calmed down somewhat" after some soothing words from her host.[24]

The verdicts were announced on April 1. Ludendorff was acquitted, while Hitler and three co-conspirators—Weber, Kriebel, and Pöhner—were given sentences of no less than five years, albeit with a possibility of parole after only six months. Five further defendants, including Frick and Röhm, received suspended sentences of a year and three months. The court found that the defendants had been directed "by a pure sense of patriotism and the most noble, selfless will." It then added, "That doesn't justify their actions, but it does provide the key to understanding their deeds."[25] The verdicts were tantamount to a moral acquittal.

Supporters of Weimar democracy were appalled by the outcome of the trial. "In Munich, judicial murder has been committed against the Republic," objected the correspondent for the *Weltbühne*, who compared the mild verdicts with the draconian severity meted out to former Saxon state premier Erich Zeigner: "We in Germany are now well and truly accustomed to differing standards of legal justice, while not at all blessed by any sort of justice between social classes."[26] The *Berliner Tageblatt* asked, "Where is the justice in any of this? How can anyone still talk about law and legal judgment? . . . As of yesterday, Bavaria stopped being a state ruled by law and order."[27] Meanwhile, the *Vossische Zeitung* objected, "The trial could have been cleansing. The nests and hiding places of subversion could have been uncovered, cleared, and smoked out. The dirt and filth should have been swept up and burned in a mighty auto-da-fé. . . . Instead with the windows and doors closed, the dust was superficially wiped away, stirring it up without removing it."[28]

The outcome of the trial reinforced in Hitler his belief that he had been charged with a historic mission. With the friendly support of a Bavarian court, he had been able to transform his fiasco of a coup into a propaganda triumph. He and his fellow inmates spent a few quite comfortable months in Landsberg prison, where he typed most of the manuscript for his screed *Mein Kampf.*[29] If the law had been upheld and justice served, Hitler would have disappeared behind bars for years, and it would have been far harder for him to launch a second political career. As things turned out, he was released from prison on December 20, 1924, and immediately started rebuilding the Nazi Party. The biggest lesson he learned from his failed uprising of November 8–9, 1923, was that if he wanted to take power, he needed to follow a different path: not that of a putsch but of ostensible legality in concert with conservative economic, military, and administrative elites.

FEBRUARY 15, 1924, SAW the expiration of the additional governmental authority Marx had succeeded in getting the Reichstag to authorize on December 8, 1923. Given the situation, there was no expectation that those powers would be extended. When the Reichstag reconvened on February 20 after a break of more than two months, the SPD, KPD, and DNVP immediately filed motions to alter and revoke edicts issued by the government. For Marx and his ministers, that put the achievements of the stabilization policies in jeopardy, and they were determined to defend those policies with all the means at their disposal. The government "would not allow itself under any circumstances to be steamrolled by the Reichstag," as Finance Minister Luther put it at a cabinet meeting on February 6.[30] In a meeting with leading deputies of the coalition on February 14, Foreign Minister Stresemann, too, insisted that the governing parties should "by no means participate in any attempt to change or reverse the orders issued under the emergency powers act." He added, "The message must be, either the preservation of the orders or new economic misery and new inflation."[31] The following day, the cabinet agreed to "initially adopt a wait-and-see attitude and only take action if threatened with attacks from the opposition."[32]

Conversations with representatives from opposition parties quickly made it clear that those parties were unwilling to back off their demands for their motions to be heard in parliament. In response to a threat by Marx to dissolve the Reichstag, DNVP spokesman Hergt responded coolly that his party didn't shy away from fights. On the contrary, he considered fresh elections "urgently desirable."[33] Apparently, the ultranationalists thought they had a good chance to pick up more votes and further mandates if Germans went back to the polls. By contrast, an accelerated new election would be inopportune for Social Democrats, but they, too, showed no inclination to withdraw their parliamentary objections, particularly on the issues of job protection and working hours, and criticized the pressure the government was applying as "dictatorial politics."[34]

On February 28, the Reichstag began debating the motions to alter the emergency decrees. Right at the start, Marx announced that he would ask Ebert to dissolve parliament should the body vote to rescind or change the substance of crucial economic and financial reform measures. After the conclusion of the debates on March 13, the moment of truth had arrived. But before the Reichstag could vote on the opposition motions, Marx read out Ebert's dissolution order. After lengthy discussions in the governing cabinet, May 4 was set as the date for new elections.[35] The four-year legislative period of the Reichstag, which had been elected in 1920, would have come to an end anyway on June 6. Nonetheless, in the words of historian Ursula Büttner, the premature dissolution of the parliament to prevent it from exercising its constitutional rights "set a fateful precedent."[36]

ON MARCH 12, 1924, a day before the dissolution of the Reichstag, a "National Liberal Alliance of the DVP" was constituted in Berlin's Esplanade Hotel. The forces behind this group were the same men who had made Stresemann's life so difficult as chancellor. All twenty people in attendance came from the Ruhr Valley iron, steel, and mining industries, including thirteen mine directors, five of them managing directors in the Stinnes conglomerate. Twelve were members of the right wing of the DVP parliamentary group in the Reichstag, among them two familiar faces: Stinnes director general Vögler and Essen Chamber of Commerce attorney Quaatz, who became the association's manager. The explicit aim of these party secessionists was to depart from Stresemann's centrism. Instead, they wanted the DVP to chart a strict nationalist, antisocialist course, which meant forming a bourgeois coalition that included the ultranationalist DNVP.[37]

Stresemann took this challenge very seriously. The founding of the National Liberal Alliance, he told a fellow party member, was "the worst stab in the back ever inflicted on a party before an election," adding that it was "of course untenable" for "two parties to exist within one."[38] On March 15, the members of the DVP board present in Berlin unanimously decided that "tolerating a special political organization within the party was impossible and unacceptable."[39]

The struggle to determine the future direction of the DVP ended at a central executive committee meeting in Hanover on March 28 and the party conference that directly followed with an overwhelming vote of confidence in Stresemann. The vast majority of delegates approved the policies of their party chairman and condemned the founding of the National Liberal Alliance, whose members were told they would be stripped of party membership should they not immediately quit this "special organization."[40]

On April 2, the board of the National Liberal Alliance urged members to "Leave the Stresemann Party!" but very few heeded that call. It was obvious that the secession movement enjoyed little support. Facing exclusion from the party and the resulting loss of their Reichstag mandates, six deputies renounced the alliance. Three, among them Vögler, left the DVP to run in the next election on the National Liberal Alliance's own ticket. The remaining three, including Quaatz, jumped ship to the DNVP, which offered them secure spots on its party list.[41] "These gentlemen have finally gone where they belong, namely, to the ultranationalists," a satisfied Stresemann remarked. Then he added with relief, "At least we've been freed of several persons in the parliamentary group who were constant causes of discord."[42]

THE NATIONAL LIBERAL ALLIANCE lost its most influential supporter with the death of Hugo Stinnes on April 10, 1924. Stresemann's most powerful rival finally succumbed to a long-term gallbladder infection after having undergone two operations in March from which he never recovered. Chancellor Marx, most of the members of his cabinet, and many high-ranking civil servants and industrial magnates attended his funeral in Berlin-Grunewald.[43] The satirical magazine *Simplicissimus* published a cartoon depicting St. Peter in heaven summoning the angels with his bell and warning them, "Stinnes is coming! Wake up, children, or in a fortnight he'll own the whole works!"[44]

As could have been expected, responses to the death of the controversial businessman were divided. His house organ, the *Deutsche Allgemeine Zeitung*, lionized him as the most important industrialist Germany had ever produced: "From the chaos of collapse his name arose, visible from a great distance as that of the great and perhaps only leader."[45] In the *Vossische Zeitung*, on the other hand, Richard Lewinsohn criticized Stinnes for having increasingly equated the welfare of society with his own private economic interests: "He didn't want to become a politician, but he considered it self-evident that the interests of Germany's business leaders should set the tone on the decisive political issues. That was a fateful mistake."[46] In the *Berliner Tageblatt*, Ernst Feder found words of the highest admiration for Stinnes's business sense: "His economic creativity recalled the imagination of an artist. He made poems out of businesses." Feder added, however, that Stinnes was completely unsuited to the political role he had desired.[47]

But questions also surrounded Stinnes's much-vaunted business acumen. His gigantic industrial empire was too much the child of inflation and hyperinflation to be able to survive in times of economic stabilization. In the words of Stockhausen, it was like a "Tower of Babel that carried with it the seed of its own destruction."[48] Only one year after Stinnes's death, the conglomerate was swamped by debt and sold off piece by piece.[49]

The dissolution of the Reichstag on March 13, 1924, immediately launched a fiercely contested election in which the reparations evaluation, presented in Paris on April 9, played a central role. Recall that on October 24, 1923, the Stresemann government had filed a motion with the Reparations Committee to have Germany's solvency reviewed by independent experts. Once Poincaré had assented, it was agreed on November 30 to employ two expert committees. The first and more important of the pair was led by American banker Charles D. Dawes and was tasked with determining the amount and the forms of German reparations payments. The second committee, under the direction of Reginald McKenna of Britain, was to examine how much German capital had been transferred abroad and how it could be brought back to Germany. Committee members came exclusively from the Entente powers; Germany was not represented.

Nonetheless, the Marx government cooperated closely from the start with the dual committees' work. When the experts visited Berlin in late January 1924, Stresemann greeted them with promises to "expedite things as much as possible and be forthright without exception."[50] The German foreign minister had high hopes for the continuing investigations. In a speech in Elberfeld on February 17, he approvingly quoted a statement made by State Secretary Carl Bergmann of the Reich Economics Ministry that "for the first time he could see a small band of silver on the otherwise gloomy horizon."[51]

It was primarily the intense interest of the United States that gave the talks in Paris the necessary drive. Never had the "psychological moment" been so favorable for "reaching a solution to the reparations issue," Secretary of State Hughes declared in a conversation with Germany's US ambassador Wiedfeldt and Kessler in late January. Dawes and his principal assistant, Owen D. Young, were "extraordinarily gifted people." The significant devaluations of the French franc and the new Labour government in Britain had improved the prospects for a compromise. Everything now hinged on the work in Paris "not being disrupted by any public controversies," since there was no telling "whether such a favorable constellation would ever come round again."[52]

On April 9, the Dawes Committee presented its findings, which didn't set a final sum for German reparations payments. Without any discussion, the British plan to extract 132 billion gold marks was thereby laid to rest. Instead, the committee recommended that payments begin at one billion gold marks annually and rise to 2.5 billion within five years. The annuities were to come from funds in the German national budget and a mandatory mortgage on German industry and the Reichsbahn. For this purpose, the German rail company was to be transformed into an independent corporation, half of whose board of directors would consist of Entente representatives. The Dawes Plan also foresaw a central bank independent of the government, also with foreign representatives on its board. The Rentenmark was to be replaced by an internationally accepted currency backed by gold and foreign currency reserves. To help it get started, Germany would receive an international loan of the equivalent of 800 million gold marks it could use toward the reparations payments.

A major advantage of the Dawes Plan from the German vantage point was that it was based on Germany's real economic capacity. To secure the transfer of German payments into the currency of its creditors, the office of "reparations agent" in Berlin was created. In case Germany was unable to meet the agreed-on demands, the agent could suspend the transfer and, if the difficulties went on for some time, propose a reduction of annuities. When the Dawes Plan was accepted, American financial expert Parker Gilbert was appointed as reparations agent. This ruled out a unilateral seizure of assets such as those the French and Belgians had undertaken with the occupation of the Ruhr in 1923. Along with this "transfer protection," the prospect of foreign, especially American, credit was the Dawes Plan's most significant advantage for Germany.[53]

EVEN AS THE EXPERTS were going about their work, the American government had begun to exert pressure on Berlin. At a meeting in late February 1924 with the ministerial director in the German Foreign Ministry, Carl Schubert, Ambassador Houghton communicated his expectation that the Germans would be "sensible enough to immediately accept the results of evaluation." If not, they would play into Poincaré's hands. Germany should recognize that in all likelihood the Dawes Plan would improve Germany's position. "We should cash this in," Schubert said, relaying Houghton's message, "and we should not be fussy about provisions that may turn out to be less pleasant."[54]

On April 11, the Reparations Commission sent the German government the experts' recommendations, asking for approval. Three days later, Marx summoned his cabinet ministers and the regional state premiers to the Chancellery. Finance Minister Luther questioned whether Germany could afford the sums demanded, but Stresemann strongly recommended accepting the Dawes Plan, which had "come about against Poincaré's will" because of the decisive advocacy of the United States, "the only power that perhaps still has influence over France." For this reason alone, a brusque refusal was out of the question. In that event, France would "be given a free hand, and Germany would be unable to find help from any country in the world."[55] Stresemann's plea made a strong impression. That very day, on April 14, the cabinet gave its basic approval and told the Reparations Commission the German government regarded the evaluation as a "practical basis for rapid resolution of the reparations issue" and was therefore prepared to "confirm their cooperation with the plans of the experts."[56]

Unsurprisingly, the Right sought to stir up opposition to the Dawes Plan, bemoaning, as they had with earlier reparations regulations, the "enslavement" of future generations of Germans. Karl Helfferich, the DNVP's foreign policy spokesman, launched a vicious attack on Stresemann in the Reichstag, pillorying the Dawes Plan as a "second Versailles." A few days later, Helfferich would die in a train accident in Switzerland.[57]

Despite his weak health, Stresemann was a major force in the election. In a key speech in Magdeburg on April 29, for instance, he defended the cabinet's decision, saying that it had not been born of fear but made "from a sense of responsibility that at this juncture, when Germany had no other alternative, we had to at least ensure several years of calm, peaceful development." One day later in Bremerhaven, he declared that Germany would have committed the "greatest act of diplomatic stupidity" had it said no to the deal. "We would have played into Poincaré's hands."[58]


"IT'S A GREAT DAY of battle for us," Stockhausen noted on Election Sunday, May 4. "The telephone is ringing incessantly, and the radio transmitter, that new innovation, is announcing the results in its scratchy voice."[59] It would be a day of major disappointment for the governing coalition. The DVP declined from 13.9 to 9.2 percent of the vote, the DDP from 8.3 to 5.7 percent, and the BVP from 4.2 to 3.2 percent. The Center Party was the most successful at minimizing its losses, from 13.6 to 13.4 percent. The clear winners were the radical Right and Left. The DNVP increased its share of the vote from 15.1 to 19.5 percent, and its right-wing competitors, the DVFP, whose election list included National Socialists, suddenly shot up to 6.5 percent. The KPD, which had polled only 2.1 percent in June 1920, improved its performance to 12.6 percent. The misadventure of the Hamburg uprising of October 1923 hadn't hurt the party as much as many people had thought. The SPD, which had reunified in 1922 with those members of the USPD who hadn't joined the KPD, declined from 21.7 percent to 20.5 percent—seemingly only a small drop. But considering that together the two Social Democratic parties had won 39.6 percent of the vote in 1920, with the USPD taking 17.9 percent, the 1924 result was still a slap in the face. Nor had the KPD been able to attract all former USPD voters.

The larger vote shares for the extremist parties clearly showed that Germans had been radicalized by the crises of 1923. Conspicuously, the ultranationalists had taken votes away from the two liberal parties, the DVP and the DDP. A large percentage of new DNVP voters came from the middle classes, which had been particularly hard hit by inflation and hyperinflation. Bourgeois splinter groups like the Economy Party and the Agrarian League, which now polled at 8.5 percent in comparison to 5.3 percent in 1920, also siphoned support away from the established center. The KPD claimed the majority of former USPD supporters to the detriment of the SPD. Many of these voters seem to have turned their backs on social democracy after the harsh treatment of the left-wing governments in Saxony and Thuringia.[60]

As disappointed as the pro-democracy camp was at the outcome of the election, some republicans still took an optimistic stance. Theodor Wolff emphasized that while the parliamentary basis for the Marx government had been "extraordinarily narrow and feeble," the ultranationalists, racists, and communists had fallen significantly short of a majority.[61] In the *Vossische Zeitung*, Julius Elbau recalled that the ultranationalists had achieved their gains with means that "were no different in spirit and essence than the criminal demagoguery of the German racists." Elbau laid considerable blame at the feet of the right-wing media empire of Alfred Hugenberg, which had "openly flown the German ultranationalist flag" in advance of the election. But despite its gigantic propaganda efforts, the Right had been unable to wrest a majority away from the parties of the bourgeois center and moderate Left: "The enemies of the Republic are still considerably outnumbered by the supporters and protectors of the Constitution, who now are truly gaining the courage and the strength to reinforce their defensive opposition and go on the counterattack."[62] Kessler, too, saw the situation after the election as by no means hopeless: "If this government can disentangle the foreign policy situation on the basis of the Dawes Plan and can get a constructive and energetic grasp on the domestic situation with social and economic measures, in three to four years, radicalism might considerably ebb and allow Germany to be solidly established on the basis of the Weimar Republic."[63]

Despite the poor performance of the governing parties, the Marx government decided at its first meeting after the May 6 election not to resign immediately but to wait for the constituent session of the Reichstag, thus avoiding a political vacuum and any threat to the Dawes Plan. A press release to this effect was presented to and approved by Ebert.[64] The Right was outraged. The DNVP, which together with the Agrarian League had earned 106 seats in the Reichstag, thereby overtaking the SPD—which now had 100 instead of its former 171 seats—as the biggest parliamentary group, demanded a leading role in the new government. "Their heads," Kessler remarked in his diary, "have swollen immensely."[65]

On May 15, the DNVP called for the resignation of the Marx government, arguing that it no longer had the legitimacy "to represent Germany decisively regarding the expert evaluation." Although Marx's cabinet reiterated its determination not to give up its governmental duties before the constituent session of the Reichstag, the ministers disagreed about the date on which they would step down and how to proceed tactically until then.[66]

The day before, on May 14, the DVP's executive committee and parliamentary group had decided at a joint meeting to join a government of cooperation between all bourgeois parties prepared to "continue the fundamentals of our previous foreign policy."[67] With that, the question of whether the DNVP would be part of the next government was back on the agenda. On May 20, as a basis for negotiations with the ultranationalists, the coalition parties agreed on a binding foreign-policy declaration characterizing the expert recommendation as a "serious attempt at a peaceful resolution of the reparations issue" and a "unified and indivisible whole," which could only be accepted as such.[68]

But the first negotiations already made it clear that the DNVP was by no means willing to back the Dawes Plan in its entirety. Moreover, the party demanded that it name the chancellor, suggesting former Imperial Grand Admiral Alfred von Tirpitz, who had just been elected a DNVP Reichstag deputy and whose name was synonymous with the lunatic buildup of the German Navy in 1914. He was completely unacceptable to the coalition parties, which knew there would be no chance of a successful conclusion to reparations negotiations with him at the helm. At a cabinet meeting, Stresemann reported that Houghton and several colleagues at the US Embassy had told him that Washington regarded a Tirpitz candidacy as a "heavy burden."[69]

The negotiations thus threatened to unravel before they had even really begun, and then the DVP parliamentary group turned on the government. On May 26, deputies passed a resolution calling for the resignation of the cabinet "to clear the way for the constitutional duty of the Reich president to bring about a government in line with the new relations of power in parliament." Chancellor Marx had no choice but to confirm the breakup of the coalition that evening and inform the president that the cabinet had stepped down.[70]

Ebert thus had to act. On May 28, after exploratory talks with DNVP chairman Hergt came to naught, he charged Marx with forming a new cabinet. In the second round of talks, the ultranationalists no longer insisted on Tirpitz as chancellor but still demanded a change of course in German foreign policy, the replacement of Stresemann as foreign minister, and a revision of the grand coalition in the Prussian regional government under State Premier Otto Braun. The DNVP knew only too well that Marx would reject their demands. That gave rise to suspicions that the party didn't really want to be part of the government but preferred to wait until the reparations issue had been resolved so as not to attract potential blame for the outcome.[71]

But the right wing of the DVP refused to give up on the idea of getting the DNVP to join the government. After a heated debate, the parliamentary group decided on May 30, over vehement opposition from Stresemann supporters, not to risk destroying the coalition over the foreign minister. "The parliamentary group is sticking to Stresemann as long as he himself desires," was the formulation announced by Parliamentary Chairman Scholz. The foreign minister reacted to this thinly veiled call for him to resign by asking Marx not to give any regard to Stresemann's own person in the coalition negotiations.[72] In conversation with D'Abernon, however, Stresemann confessed how wounded he was by the act of disloyalty, relating that "Events like this which are now going on make one realise what Bismarck meant when he said 'I hated the whole night through.'" And in his calendar Stresemann recorded Ebert saying, "It's tragic how a man like Stresemann is being treated by his own party."[73]

MARX, HOWEVER, WAS of no mind to drop his foreign minister, especially not after Germany's foreign policy outlook had again significantly improved with the results of the French national election, so on June 3, he broke off talks with the DNVP. The DVP parliamentary group wasted no time expressing its regret that "the negotiations on forming a broad bourgeois coalition have failed." It then added, "The parliamentary group does not consider the idea in and of itself dead. It hopes the greater goal can still be reached at the proper time."[74] The

Center Party, DDP, and DVP declared themselves willing to continue the existing coalition. The BVP was no longer represented in the Reichstag. Justice Minister Erich Emminger had quit the government in mid-April after a disagreement with the Center Party;[75] otherwise the ministers retained their offices.

"The comedy of errors is over, and the old Marx cabinet has resurfaced," commented Erich Dombrowski in the *Berliner Tageblatt*. "The crisis went on for more than a fortnight. You have to rub your eyes if you want to see these events for what they are. For a time, what went on in some parliamentary groups resembled an asylum. No one knew who was coming or going. Landmines were laid, and conspiracies hatched. False information was given to the press, followed by denials. . . . In short, there was during that period every reason to doubt the mental health of the participants."[76]

The parliamentary basis of the second Marx cabinet was even more tenuous than the first, commanding the support of only 138 out of 472 deputies. To govern, it needed to be at least tolerated by Social Democrats or the DNVP. On June 6, Marx survived a vote of confidence brought by the DNVP with the help of the SPD, as his governmental declaration was approved by 246 of the 429 votes cast. But a simple parliamentary majority in the Reichstag wasn't sufficient to accept the Dawes Plan and pass the necessary laws to implement it. The transformation of the Reichsbahn into a corporation, with members of the creditor nations on its supervisory board, required a constitutional amendment and thus a two-thirds majority. That could only happen if a part of the DNVP parliamentary group voted for the changes. It was entirely unclear in the summer of 1924 whether the ultranationalists could be made to change their stance on the issue. The struggle over the acceptance of the Dawes Plan would prove the decisive test of strength for the second Marx government.[77]

ON JULY 16, 1924, the negotiations among the United States, France, and Britain over the plan began in London under the chairmanship of Prime Minister MacDonald. Before the conference, Stresemann had made clear in conversations with US diplomats that without a binding declaration that France would evacuate the occupied parts of Germany, there would be no way to get the plan through the Reichstag.[78] Despite the changing of the guard in Paris, the outlook for a successful solution to the impasse wasn't particularly rosy. "The political horizon has darkened," wrote Stresemann on July 7 to his wife, who was spending time in Switzerland. "The French don't want to evacuate the Ruhr. Herriot is weak—and the position of our government precarious, if we don't improve the situation." In a letter on July 25, he was even more pessimistic: "We still don't have an invitation to London, and it has not at all been decided whether the conference will yield a positive result or come to nothing."[79]

It was only after pressure from the Americans that the French and British agreed on August 2 to invite a German delegation to London. Before the leaders of the cabinet—Marx, Stresemann, and Luther—departed Berlin two days later, Ebert instructed them to negotiate with "all their energy and extreme determination" on the issue of French withdrawal from the Ruhr.[80]

This was the German delegation's premiere on the international stage. Stresemann was initially concerned over whether he would be equal to the demands of the negotiations, but he soon reported to his wife that he had "found his way into the atmosphere of the conference" and was able to follow "almost completely" the statements of the British and French delegates.[81] In his opening speech on August 6, Marx encouraged the participants to make the issue of evacuation of the occupied German regions, which wasn't on the official agenda, part of the conference.[82] Because the question of reparations, narrowly defined, was no longer such a contentious subject, the occupation became the cardinal problem to be negotiated. The French delegation realized that it could not continue its categorical refusals, but it was unclear how far Herriot could accommodate the Germans without alienating French public opinion.

In their first face-to-face talks, Stresemann sought to convince the

French prime minister that there was no reason for France to fear the nationalist movement in Germany. The ethnic supremacists had already passed their zenith after their good performance in the May elections, Stresemann assured his colleague, and the leading organizations of German industry, despite the agitation from the Hugenberg press, had come out in favor of the expert recommendations. For the Dawes Plan to be accepted, in view of the "psychological makeup of the German people," an agreement on the occupation was essential. For his part, Herriot expressed understanding for the German desire for a quid pro quo "equivalent," without letting himself get tied down.[83]

After consulting with his cabinet, Herriot told Stresemann in a second meeting on August 11 that he could agree to French troops leaving the Ruhr within a year. Any further concessions would risk the demise of his government. Stresemann countered that a year was "definitely too long,"[84] but the French side rejected urgent German requests for shorter deadlines. Talks had reached an impasse. On August 14, a critical day, MacDonald and the American ambassador in London, Frank Kellogg, succeeded in convincing the Germans that Herriot, given his position in France, couldn't improve his offer. If the Germans refused the deal, they would bear the blame for the conference's failure.[85] After Ebert gave his approval, the German delegation agreed to the one-year deadline. As a gesture of goodwill, the French agreed to immediately begin pulling out from the Dortmund area and to extend the one-year evacuation commitment to the three cities—Düsseldorf, Duisburg, and Ruhrort—outside the Ruhr proper, which France had occupied in a punitive action in March 1921. On August 16, the various sides signed the London Agreement.

THE NEXT HURDLE FOR the German side was to get the agreement through the Reichstag. With the Reichsbahn Law requiring a two-thirds majority and thus votes from the DNVP, Germany's leading business organizations—the Reich Association of German

Industry and the Reich Agrarian League—applied pressure to the party, and the Ebert and Marx government did everything it could to convince the ultranationalists to give up their stubborn opposition to the deal. At the Germans' request, on August 20, Ambassador Houghton hosted the DNVP leadership—Hergt, Count Kuno von Westarp, and the party's foreign policy spokesman, Otto Hoetzsch—and made it clear that Germany wouldn't receive urgently needed American assistance if it rejected the agreement. In addition, Marx again threatened to ask Ebert to dissolve parliament should the Dawes Plan be defeated—an unappetizing prospect for the DNVP, which could by no means count on equaling their impressive showing in May in new elections.[86]

Nonetheless, the DNVP parliamentary group nearly unanimously rejected the Reichsbahn Law during its second reading on August 27. In a last-minute move to save the agreement, the core of his foreign policy, Stresemann decided on an extraordinary reversal of position. In a hastily called parliamentary group meeting on August 28, which may or may not have taken place with Chancellor Marx's knowledge, he persuaded his colleagues to declare in an open statement that they would advocate with "all means at their disposal" a role for the DNVP in the government if the ultranationalists were prepared to take on "the responsibility for adoption of the London pact."[87]

The cabinet as a whole also approached the DNVP. Before the third and decisive reading of the legislation, the government agreed on a declaration, long demanded by the ultranationalists, on the issue of who was to blame for the First World War. It rejected the statement in the Treaty of Versailles that Germany "had unleashed the world war" with its aggression. The declaration read, "It is a justified demand of the German people to be liberated from this false accusation."[88] The Reich government reneged, however, on its pledge to officially submit this declaration to the Entente powers after warnings from Paris and London. Such a denial of responsibility would indeed have caused discord with Germany's former enemies and undermined the politics of reconciliation, which had only just begun.[89]

THE FINAL DECISION WAS scheduled for the afternoon of August 29. Kessler wrote of the dramatic atmosphere in the Reichstag, "The air was terribly humid, warm, and stale. But everyone was holding his breath in anticipation that increased from minute to minute. You could feel something like a major turning point in world history approaching: the true end of the war or a new, more bitter continuation of it."[90] All eyes were on the DNVP parliamentary group. And it turned out that the combination of sticks and carrots had achieved the desired effect. Forty-eight DNVP deputies, almost half of the parliamentary group, voted for the Reichsbahn Law, helping give it a two-thirds majority. All told, 331 out of 441 deputies said yes to the legislation. With that, the acceptance of the results of the "London Conference on the Application of the Dawes Plan" was secure.

After the result of the vote was announced, ultranationalists and Communists vented their displeasure at deafening volume. Werner Scholem, a KPD deputy and an editor of the *Rote Fahne*, shouted, "You gang of swine!" while DVFP deputy Albrecht von Graefe raised a threatening fist in the direction of diplomats in attendance, earning applause for his gesture. "This is a disgrace," called out Ludendorff, who also represented the racist party in the Reichstag, to DVP deputy Rear Admiral Franz Brüninghaus as he exited the building. "Ten years ago, I won the Battle of Tannenberg. Today you brought about the Jewish Tannenberg."[91]

"The battle has been fought," commented Dombrowski in the *Berliner Tageblatt*. "A line had been drawn under all the days of uncertainty, trepidation, and worry about tomorrow. Now we know that things can and will look up again."[92] The *Vossische Zeitung* wrote of a "new chapter in German history," declaring, "The policies for which Walther Rathenau and Erzberger were martyred have prevailed.... That is the decisive achievement that can no longer be shaken."[93]

In fact, the London Agreement was a major triumph for Germany. While it did have to accept limitations on its sovereignty in the form of a general agent supervising the transfer of reparations payments in Berlin, this disadvantage was far outweighed by its restored creditworthiness. The Dawes loan was soon multiply oversubscribed, and foreign and particularly American capital began pouring in. As Marxist historian Arthur Rosenberg put it, a "sun of dollars" rose over Germany.[94] On August 30, when the London Agreement was signed, the provisional Rentenmark was replaced by the new Reichsmark, 40 percent of which was required by law to be covered by gold-backed foreign currencies.

Moreover, the German delegation in London had succeeded in negotiating a binding deadline for the end of the military occupation of the Ruhr Valley. The deescalation of the issues of reparations and occupation significantly calmed the overall situation in the country. The postwar era was over, and a path had been cleared for Germany to rejoin the international community as an equal member.[95]

THE YEARS 1924 TO 1929 are considered the zenith of the Weimar Republic, the epitome of the oft-cited Golden Twenties. The crises and turmoil of the immediate postwar period and the hyperinflation of 1923 were followed by economic and political consolidation. The economy recovered remarkably quickly once the currency was stabilized. By 1927 industrial production had returned to postwar levels. Real wages rose significantly while unemployment, which had topped 20 percent in the winter of 1923–24, decreased. The social welfare state was shored up, and in 1927, unemployment insurance was introduced.[96]

Germany also made further progress in the foreign-policy arena. Under Stresemann, who would remain foreign minister until his death in 1929, reconciliation with the western powers continued apace. The Locarno treaties of October 1925 saw Germany recognizing the western border set in the Treaty of Versailles and confirming the demilitarization of the Rhineland. The following September, Germany joined the League of Nations. Only eight years after the end of the

First World War, the German Reich once again occupied a respected position in the community of global powers.[97] But at no point did Stresemann's willingness to reconcile with France include recognizing Poland's western border, which would have amounted to an "Eastern Locarno." The foreign minister's goal remained the reestablishment of Germany as a major world power, and in his eyes that entailed a peaceful revision of Germany's eastern border.[98]

The phrase Golden Twenties admittedly refers less to economic recovery and foreign-policy triumphs than to "Weimar culture," whose unusual surfeit of creativity and experimentalism we examined in the preceding chapter. Expressionism, with its ecstatic pathos and revolutionary utopias, was succeeded around 1924 by the "New Objectivity," an emotionally cooler trend in literature, painting, and architecture that focused on social realities. "Nothing is more astonishing than the plain and simple truth, nothing is more exotic than the world around us, and nothing is more imaginative than objectivity," wrote Egon Erwin Kisch in the preface to the first edition of his 1924 anthology *The Roving Reporter*.[99]

New media, especially film and radio, created a modern mass culture whose offerings were no longer restricted to the privileged classes. The vibrant epicenter of the Golden Twenties remained the metropolis of Berlin with its massive entertainment industry and wealth of theaters, opera houses, palatial cinemas, variety theaters, and dance clubs. Sports continued to be extremely popular, from boxing matches and bicycle and car races to soccer games and track-and-field meets. Sebastian Haffner recalled that he and many of his peers succumbed to a veritable "sports craze" in the middle years of the Weimar Republic.[100]

Traditional class and gender roles were superseded. Women's fashion became more practical and casual. Pageboy hairstyles were a sign of emancipation, and it was no longer taboo for women to smoke in public. A freer approach to sexuality, liberated from the constraints of Wilhelmine morality, redefined relations between men and women.[101] The result was a richness of new experiences, stimuli, and entertainment whose spirit was the opposite of dogmatic political extremism.

NONETHELESS, CRACKS COULD BE seen in the otherwise comforting picture of a solidly established democracy. Even in the middle phase of the Weimar Republic, stability was illusory. In a sense, this short stretch of time was—to take an image from cultural historian Peter Gay—like the sanatorium society in Thomas Mann's *Magic Mountain*, the literary sensation of 1924, in which the ruddy cheeks of tuberculosis patients covered up the progression of their disease.[102] The post-1924 economic upsurge, financed as it was mainly by American credit, was unsustainable. Five billion dollars flooded into Germany between 1924 and 1930, more than would be pumped into the country under the Marshall Plan after the Second World War. This left the German economy at the mercy of American business cycles, a dependency that would leave Germany in a particularly dire place when Black Tuesday, October 29, 1929, on Wall Street sparked the Great Depression.[103]

The political equilibrium also remained fragile. Cabinet crises and government reshuffling were part of everyday Weimar reality. In October 1924, Ebert again dissolved the Reichstag, after the DVP, mindful of its promise, agitated for the DNVP to join the government. The subsequent national election of December 7 featured a moderate trend toward "deradicalization." The bourgeois centrist parties—the DDP, the Center Party, the DVP, and the BVP—all made slight gains, as did the DNVP. The big winners were the SPD, whose share of the vote rose from 20.5 to 26 percent. The clear losers were the radical fringes. The joint ticket of Nazis and other racist parties went from 6.5 to 3 percent, while the Communists fell from 12.9 to 9 percent. On January 15, 1925, the party-unaffiliated finance minister Hans Luther formed a new cabinet consisting of members of the DNVP, DVP, Center Party, and BVP. It was the Weimar Republic's first right-wing government. Before its formation, the DVP acceded to an old condition imposed by the DNVP and quit the grand coalition in Prussia.[104]

But less than a year later, in October 1925, the DNVP departed the national government to protest the Locarno treaties. On December 5, Luther and his cabinet stepped down, although Ebert immediately charged him with forming a new government. On January 20, 1926, he presented a new bourgeois minority coalition of the DDP, DVP, Center Party, and BVP, but it wouldn't even last as long as his first one. On May 12, the coalition fell apart over the so-called flag quarrel: Luther had given German embassies and consulates the right to fly the old black, white, and red imperial flag alongside the colors of the Weimar Republic, outraging the pro-democracy camp.[105]

The man of the hour was once again Marx, who took over the basically unchanged minority government on May 17. The third Marx cabinet was brought down on December 17, after Social Democrat Philipp Scheidemann revealed the government's illegal rearmament program in a controversial speech in the Reichstag. On January 29, 1927, Marx formed his fourth cabinet. This time there were four ultranationalist ministers, but the second right-wing coalition disintegrated in February 1928 over a new education law. The Reichstag was dissolved on March 21 and new elections called for on May 20.[106]

The SPD emerged as the victors of that vote, becoming the strongest party by a wide margin, with 29.8 percent of the vote, while the DNVP plummeted from 20.5 to 14.3 percent. Clearly, being part of two governments had failed to pay off for the ultranationalists. Centrist parties also lost support, and on the extreme fringes, the Nazis only won 2.6 percent of the vote, while the Communists improved from 9 to 10.6 percent. SPD chairman Hermann Müller, who had already served as chancellor for a few months in 1920, was charged with forming the next government. After some difficult negotiations, he was able to put together a "cabinet of personalities" from the SPD, DDP, Center Party, DVP, and BVP on June 28, 1928. It was the second grand coalition since 1923.[107]

In the four and a half years since the end of hyperinflation, six German governments had come and gone. Every one of them had carried within it the seeds of its own demise because there was no consensus among the partners on important issues and the parties were generally unwilling to compromise. "Our entire parliamentary life continues to be completely overshadowed by Wilhelmine absolutism, in which the Reichstag had a lot to say but nothing to decide, and every action, no matter how calamitous, was ordered from above," criticized Ossietzky in the *Weltbühne* on August 11, 1929, the tenth anniversary of the Weimar Constitution. "That has created a state of dissatisfaction that undermines people's belief in the Republic's potential, surrounds the arena of politics with an atmosphere of cool, somewhat contemptuous skepticism, and makes the sad impression, particularly on today's twenty-year-olds, of a system that can't possibly work."[108]

THE INSTABILITY OF GERMAN government was indeed incapable of strengthening people's trust in the democratic system. Germans quickly tired of the Weimar "state of parties," as it was contemptuously known, and many looked to the Reich president to inject order into the confusion. The more the German parliament was deadlocked, the more the presidential aspects of the Weimar Constitution came to the fore. On February 28, 1925, Ebert died at the age of fifty-four from an undiagnosed appendix infection. In a two-stage vote, ending on April 26, the former Imperial Field Marshal Paul von Hindenburg, an enormously popular "world war hero" on the Right, was elected as his successor. The triumph of an aging—already seventy-seven years old at the time—avowed monarchist over the other leading candidate, Wilhelm Marx, appalled supporters of democracy. Betty Scholem wrote to her son Gershom that she would never have thought there would be "14 million such pigheaded people among us."[109] When Thea Sternheim heard the election results, she felt "the same sensations of terror and helplessness" as in August 1914.[110] Victor Klemperer, who was in Paris at the time, was also reminded of the First World War: "I have the impression that something akin to the murder of the Austrian heir to the throne on June 28, 1914, has just happened. What will become of Germany?"[111]

Count Harry Kessler, in contrast, tried to see the positive side of the election result. After Hindenburg swore in the Reichstag on May 12, 1925, to uphold the Weimar Constitution, Kessler wrote that the Republic had now become "acceptable to the aristocracy since everything about it, including the black, red, and gold flag, will appear wherever Hindenburg does as his personal standard and colors. Some of the admiration for him will inevitably bleed over. . . . If the republicans remain vigilant and unified, Hindenburg's election can be very useful for the Republic and the cause of peace."[112]

In the near term, the pro-democracy camp's worst fears concerning Hindenburg's election failed to materialize. The new Reich president had promised to respect the democratic Constitution, and in the first years of his tenure, he seemed to want to keep his word. But any hopes that those who hated the Republic could be won over to the democratic Weimar system proved to be in vain. In October 1928, the DNVP elected the ultraconservative media mogul Hugenberg as its new chairman, and he steered the party toward uncompromising opposition.[113] Meanwhile, Hindenburg gave the old elites of heavy industry, the large estates east of the Elbe River, the military, and the civil service direct access to power. It didn't take long before men close to the former field marshal began drawing up plans for a presidential regime entirely independent of parliament.[114]

On March 27, 1930, internal tensions ripped apart Müller's grand coalition. The main point of conflict was comparatively banal: a proposed rise in unemployment contributions from 3.5 to 4 percent, supported by the SPD and opposed by the DVP. Yet advocates of authoritarian solutions to crises saw their hour at hand. The next chancellor, the Center Party's Heinrich Brüning, was allowed to govern independently of the Reichstag on the basis of Hindenburg's faith in him and Article 48 of the Reich Constitution. The next three years saw the death throes of German parliamentarianism, the erosion of the bourgeois political center, and the breakthrough of the Nazi Party as a mass movement. Those years ended—after the short intermezzi of the "presidential cabinets" under Franz von Papen and

Kurt von Schleicher—with Hitler being named German chancellor on January 30, 1933.[115]

"NOTHING EVER EMBITTERED THE German people so much—it is important to remember this—nothing made them so furious with hate and so ripe for Hitler as the inflation," Stefan Zweig would write from Brazilian exile in 1941 in his autobiography *The World of Yesterday*, which he submitted to his publisher one day before committing suicide.[116] Many of Zweig's contemporaries agreed. The "insanity of inflation" had laid "the foundation for an illness a thousand times more terrible: Hitlerism," wrote Martin Feuchtwanger, brother of best-selling author Lion Feuchtwanger, in his memoirs.[117] Sebastian Haffner concluded that "the year 1923 prepared Germany, not specifically for Nazism, but for any fantastic adventure."[118] And in his essay "Memories from the German Inflation," written in Californian exile in 1942, Thomas Mann depicted the period of hyperinflation as a prelude for what was to come: "There is a direct line between the insanity of German inflation and the insanity of the Third Reich. Just as Germany watched their monetary unit swell to millions, billions, and trillions and finally explode, they have now watched their state swell into the empire of all Germans, living space, a European order, and world domination, and they will also see it explode in the future."[119]

The experience of the crises of 1923 had etched itself profoundly on Germans' collective mentality. The devaluation of the mark took place simultaneously with the devaluation of ethical ideals and social norms, with the faith in reliability and sustainability giving way to massive insecurity. Inflation destroyed the prosperity and status of hundreds of thousands of people. The educated upper middle classes in particular suffered from the loss of their material security and the privileged place they had possessed in Wilhelmine society. People retrospectively romanticized the years before 1914 as the "good old days," a time of stability and bourgeois certainty. The trauma of inflation continued to loom long after it had ended. The fear that the currency would collapse again was one of the rationales that led Chancellor Heinrich Brüning to cling to his deflationary policies between 1930 and 1932 instead of increasing government expenditures to jump-start the economy.[120]

Only six years after the discouraging experiences of hyperinflation, the Weimar Republic underwent an infernal descent "into the abyss of an unprecedented economic depression."[121] Germany was particularly hard hit by the global economic crisis because it coincided with a dramatic loss of legitimacy for its democratic institutions and parties. The onset of a new dual economic and political crisis of unprecedented dimensions psychologically exhausted many people. Even more so than in 1923, a general apocalyptic mood of catastrophe spread, supercharging the existing resentments of the Weimar order derisively seen as more "system" than substance. More than any other politician, Hitler knew how to present himself as a national messiah and direct the longings for salvation of the populace at large to his own person.[122] The National Socialist German Workers' Party (NSDAP) won a landslide victory in the national election of September 12, 1930, increasing its share of the vote from 2.6 to 18.3 percent. In the national poll on July 31, 1932, it more than doubled its support. With 37.3 percent of the vote, the Nazis were now the most powerful party in Germany—a status the party was able to maintain, despite a slight decline, in the election of November 6, 1932.[123] Hitler had never made any secret of his intention should he come to power to dissolve all parties other than his own.

Yet despite the lingering memories of 1923, there was no direct line between the events of that year and Hitler being given power in Germany. The Weimar Republic was not fated to fail. In 1923, the first German democracy showed an astonishing resilience, and it might have been able to come through the even more difficult period of 1930 to 1932 had the head of state been someone like Ebert—that is, someone determined to defend parliamentary democracy with all the means at his disposal. But during its second existential crisis, the Republic lacked the reliable support of the Reich president. Hindenburg was a creature of precisely those forces that ultimately achieved what they had failed to in 1923: the overthrow of the democracy they so detested and establishment of an authoritarian order. In late January 1933, these forces thought they had attained their goal. Hitler's conservative coalition partners possessed a clear majority of ministries in his "cabinet of national concentration." But the notion that they could harness the Nazi leader for their own reactionary interests and control the dynamic of his movement would be revealed as a tragic illusion. Hitler needed only a few months to overcome all opposition and set up a national dictatorship whose radicalism and inhumanity went drastically beyond anything the enemies of democracy in business, politics, and the military could have ever envisioned in 1923.

# ACKNOWLEDGMENTS

My greatest gratitude goes out to Detlef Felken, the editor in chief of my German publisher C. H. Beck, for suggesting this book and for his encouragement and support while I was writing it.

I would also like to thank Dorothee Mateika from the Forschungsstelle für Zeitgeschichte in Hamburg, as well as Mirjam Zimmer and Kerstin Wilhelms from the *Zeit* newspaper for helping to procure the literature I needed.

While public libraries were closed during the coronavirus pandemic, my friend Professor Klaus Wernecke allowed me to use important works from his large personal library. He has my thanks for that.

Special thanks are due to my longtime colleague at *Zeit*, Benedikt Erenz, who read the manuscript with an eagle eye and made many suggestions that improved the whole.

This book is dedicated to my wife, Gudrun, who died in April 2022. In our more than fifty years of life together, she was a constant source of inspiration and constructive criticism for me. Without her, none of my books would have been written. Sadly, she was unable to read this last one.

Hamburg, June 2022

# NOTES

*Preface*

1. Hedwig Pringsheim, *Tagebücher*, vol. 6: *1917–1922*, ed. Christina Herbst (Göttingen, 2017), 335.

2. Sebastian Haffner, *Defying Hitler: A Memoir*, trans. Oliver Pretzel (New York, 2000), 54.

3. Stefan Zweig, *The World of Yesterday: An Autobiography* (New York, 1943), 217. See also Stefan Zweig to Romain Rolland, November 16, 1923: "What is going on in Germany exceeded the saddest expectations. Lunacy upon lunacy!" in Zweig, *Briefe 1920–1931*, ed. Knut Beck and Jeffrey B. Berlin (Frankfurt, 2000), 449.

4. Gerald D. Feldman, *The Great Disorder: Politics, Economics, and Society in the German Inflation, 1914–1924* (New York: Oxford, 1997).

5. Harry Graf Kessler, *Das Tagebuch—Siebter Band: 1919–1923*, ed. Angelika Reinthal, Janna Brechmacher, and Christoph Hilse (Stuttgart, 2007), 312 (May 25, 1920).

6. Victor Klemperer, *Leben sammeln, nicht fragen wozu und warum: Tagebücher 1918–1924*, ed. Walter Nowojski and Christian Löser (Berlin, 1996), 697 (May 27, 1923), 741 (September 6, 1923).

7. Elias Canetti, *Masse und Macht* (Frankfurt, [1960] 2006), 218.

8. Jens Bisky, *Berlin: Biographie einer großen Stadt* (Berlin, 2019), 467.

9. George Grosz, *Ein kleines Ja und ein großes Nein: Sein Leben von ihm selbst erzählt* (Reinbek bei Hamburg, 1974), 120–121.

10. Wolfgang Ruge, *Weimar: Republik auf Zeit* (Berlin, 1969), 112.

11. See Karl Dietrich Bracher, *Die Auflösung der Weimarer Republik: Eine Studie zum Problem des Machtverfalls in der Demokratie, 3. Verbesserte und ergänzte Auflage* (Villingen, 1960); Hans Mommsen, *Die verspielte Freiheit: Der Weg der Republik von Weimar in den Untergang 1918 bis 1933* (Berlin, 1989); and Heinrich-August Winkler, *Weimar 1918–1933: Die Geschichte der ersten deutschen Demokratie* (Munich, 1993).

12. See Ursula Büttner, *Weimar: Die überforderte Republik 1918–1933* (Stuttgart, 2008), 17; and Nadine Rossol and Benjamin Zieman, eds., *Aufbruch und Abgründe: Das Handbuch der Weimarer Republik* (Darmstadt, 2021), 10–11.

13. See Peter Longerich, *Deutschland, 1918–1933: Die Weimarer Republik— Handbuch zur Geschichte* (Hanover, 1995), 144.

14. Arthur Rosenberg, *Geschichte der Weimarer Republik*, ed. Kurt Kersten (Frankfurt, [1935] 1961), 129.

15. See Georg von Wallwitz, *Die große Inflation: Als Deutschland wirklich pleite war* (Berlin, 2021), 187–188, 292–293.

*Chapter 1:* THE BATTLE FOR THE RUHR VALLEY

1. See Klaus Schwabe, ed., *Die Ruhrkrise 1923: Wendepunkt der internationalen Beziehungen nach dem Ersten Weltkrieg* (Paderborn, 1985), 1–2.

2. Klemperer, *Tagebücher 1918–1924*, 650 (January 5, 1923).

3. See Gerd Meyer, "Die Reparationspolitik: Ihre außen- und innenpolitischen Rückwirkungen," in *Die Weimarer Republik 1918–1933: Politik-Wirtschaft-Gesellschaft*, ed. Karl Dietrich Bracher, Manfred Funke, and Hans-Adolf Jacobsen (Düsseldorf, 1987), 327–342 (here 327–328).

4. See Denise Artaud, "Die Hintergründe der Ruhrbesetzung 1923: Das Problem der interalliierten Schulden," *Vierteljahrshefte für Zeitgeschichte* 27 (1979): 241–259.

5. Kessler, *Tagebuch*, vol. 7, 541–542 (August 5, 1922).

6. See Meyer, "Die Reparationspolitik," 329–330; and Klaus Schwabe, "Großbritannien und die Ruhrkrise," in Schwabe, ed., *Die Ruhrkrise 1923*, 53–87.

7. See Peter Wulf, *Hugo Stinnes: Wirtschaft und Politik 1918–1924* (Stuttgart, 1979), 196–221.

8. See Meyer, "Die Reparationspolitik," 332; and Peter Krüger, *Die Außenpolitik der Republik von Weimar* (Darmstadt, 1993), 121.

9. Klemperer, *Tagebücher 1918–1924*, 410 (February 3, 1920).

10. See Walter Mühlhausen, *Friedrich Ebert 1871–1925: Reichspräsident der Weimarer Republik* (Bonn, 2006), 442–443. On the reaction in Germany, see Feldman, *Great Disorder*, 328–329.

11. See Krüger, *Außenpolitik der Republik*, 124–125; Mommsen, *Die verspielte Freiheit*, 124–125; and Christoph Stamm, "Großbritannien und die Sanktionen gegen Deutschland vom März 1921," in *Francia* 7 (1979): 340–364.

12. See Jörn Leonhard, *Der überforderte Frieden: Versailles und die Welt 1918–1923* (Munich, 2018), 1228–1229; and Büttner, *Weimar*, 156.

13. See Winkler, *Weimar*, 139–140, 155–157; and Mühlhausen, *Friedrich Ebert*, 447–453.

14. Carl von Ossietzky, "In Ludendorffs Schatten," *Berliner Volks-Zeitung*, May 14, 1921. See also Ossietzky, *Sämtliche Schriften,* vol. 1: *1911–1921*, ed. Matthias Bertram, Ute Maack, and Christoph Schottes (Reinbek bei Hamburg, 1994), 443.

15. See Wirth's speech to the Reichstag on March 28, 1922, in Longerich, *Deutschland, 1918–1933*, 122–123.

16. See Mühlhausen, *Friedrich Ebert*, 457–463; and Winkler, *Weimar*, 166.

17. See Krüger, *Außenpolitik der Republik*, 138–139; and Mommsen, *Die verspielte Freiheit*, 126.

18. See Büttner, *Weimar*, 157; Wulf, *Hugo Stinnes*, 269–288; Gerald D. Feldman, *Hugo Stinnes: Biographie eines Industriellen 1870–1924* (Munich, 1998), 717ff.; and Feldman, *Great Disorder*, 358ff.

19. See Krüger, *Außenpolitik der Republik*, 162–163, 170; Büttner, *Weimar*, 157–158; and Feldman, *Great Disorder*, 418–419, 431–434.

20. See Leonhard, *Der überforderte Frieden*, 657–662. On Poincaré's biography, see John Keiger, *Raymond Poincaré* (Cambridge, 2002).

21. See *Akten der Reichskanzlei (AdR): Weimarer Republik—Das Kabinett Cuno: 22. November 1922 bis 12. August 1923*, ed. Karl-Heinz Harbeck (Boppard am Rhein, 1968), xxvii; and Jacques Bariéty, "Die französische Politik in der Ruhrkrise," in Schwabe, ed., *Die Ruhrkrise 1923*, 11–27 (here 12).

22. See Krüger, *Außenpolitik der Republik*, 174–176; and Winkler, *Weimar*, 167–169.

23. Kessler, *Tagebuch*, vol. 7, 467 (April 19, 1922). See Morus (Richard Lewinsohn), "Das Ergebnis von Genua," *Die Weltbühne*, no. 18/21, 536 (May 25, 1921): "We came to Genoa as equals, we left as wounded … [but] we're right back where we were a year ago when Wirth became chancellor. That's the sad result of Genoa." See Mommsen, *Die verspielte Freiheit*, 135–136; and Feldman, *Great Disorder*, 436–437.

24. See Mühlhausen, *Friedrich Ebert*, 500–503; and Gustav Radbruch, *Der innere Weg: Aufriss meines Lebens* (Stuttgart, 1951), 167.

25. See Winkler, *Weimar*, 173.

26. Kessler, *Tagebuch*, vol. 7, 425 (March 20, 1922).

27. Bernd Sösemann, ed., *Theodor Wolff: Der Journalist—Berichte und Leitartikel* (Düsseldorf, 1993), 178. On the "Organisation Consul," see Martin Sabrow, *Der Rathenaumord: Rekonstruktion einer Verschwörung gegen die Republik von Weimar* (Munich, 1994), 17ff.

28. See Georges Soutou, "Vom Rhein zur Ruhr: Absichten und Planungen der französischen Regierung," in *Der Schatten des Weltkriegs: Die Ruhrbesetzung 1923*, ed. Gerd Krumeich and Joachim Schröder (Essen, 2004), 63–83 (here 64–66); Meyer, "Die Reparationspolitik," 334; and Krüger, *Außenpolitik der Republik*, 186–187.

29. Edgar Vincent D'Abernon, *An Ambassador of Peace: Pages from the Diary of Viscount D'Abernon (Berlin, 1920–1926)*, 89, https://archive.org/details/ambassadorofpeac0002dabe/page/89/mode/2up.

30. See *AdR: Das Kabinett Cuno*, xxii; and Feldman, *Great Disorder*, 488–489.

31. See Winkler, *Weimar*, 184–185; and Mühlhausen: *Friedrich Ebert*, 556–574.

32. D'Abernon, *Ambassador*, 132.

33. Kessler, *Tagebuch*, vol. 7, 574–575 (November 14, 1922).

34. Kessler, *Tagebuch*, 788 (May 16, 1923). See also Max von Stockhausen, *Sechs Jahre Reichskanzlei: Von Rapallo bis Locarno—Erinnerungen und Tagebuchnotizen 1922–1927*, ed. Walter Görlitz (Bonn, 1954), 53: "[The new chancellor] is of excellent appearance, tall, thin, the very picture of an old-school elegant man of the world."

35. See Mühlhausen, *Friedrich Ebert*, 578–580; and Winkler, *Weimar*, 185. On Cuno's biography, see Bernd Braun, *Die Weimarer Reichskanzler: Zwölf Lebensläufe in Bildern* (Düsseldorf, 2011), 237–239; and *AdR: Das Kabinett Cuno*, xix–xxi.

36. See *AdR: Das Kabinett Cuno*, xxi–xxii; Winkler, *Weimar*, 185; Mühlhausen, *Friedrich Ebert*, 588–589; and Feldman, *Great Disorder*, 490–491.

37. See *AdR: Das Kabinett Cuno*, xxvii, 17 (here 7). On the Cuno government's reparations policies, see Hermann-Josef Rupieper, *The Cuno Government and Reparations, 1922–1923: Politics and Economics* (The Hague, 1979), 11ff.

38. *AdR: Das Kabinett Cuno*, xxviii, 20 (here 5).

39. See Bariéty, "Die französische Politik," 19; and Soutou, "Vom Rhein zur Ruhr," 66.

40. D'Abernon, *Ambassador*, 139 (December 15, 1922). See also Klaus Schwabe, "Großbritannien und die Ruhrkrise 1923," in Schwabe, ed., *Die Ruhrkrise 1923*, 53–87 (here 56–57).

41. See Werner Link, *Die amerikanische Stabilisierungspolitik in Deutschland 1921–32* (Düsseldorf, 1970), 169–171; and *AdR: Das Kabinett Cuno*, xxxi, 109 (here 8).

42. Kessler, *Tagebuch*, vol. 7, 598 (January 2, 1923).

43. See *AdR: Das Kabinett Cuno*, xxxi.

44. "Note der französischen Regierung v. 10.1.1923," *Ursachen und Folgen*, ed. Herbert Michaelis and Ernst Schraepler, vol. 5, *Die Weimarer Republik: Das kritische Jahr 1923* (Berlin, 1961), doc. 998a, 16–18 (here 17).

45. "Die Besetzung Essens," *Berliner Tageblatt* 19 (January 12, 1923).

46. "Verordnung Degouttes v. 11.1.1923," *Ursachen und Folgen*, vol. 5, doc. 998b, 18–20.

47. See Conan Fisher, *The Ruhr Crisis, 1923–1924* (Oxford, 2003), 40; and Gerd Krumeich, "Der 'Ruhrkampf' als Krieg," 9–24 (here 16), and Laurence van Ypersele, "Belgien und die Ruhrbesetzung: Wagnisse und Erwartungen," 99–118 (here 101), in Krumeich and Schröder, eds., *Der Schatten des Weltkriegs*.

48. J[ulius] E[lbau], "Der Einmarsch," *Vossische Zeitung* 18 (January 11, 1923).

49. Ernst Feder, "Einmarsch 'in friedlicher Absicht,'" *Berliner Tageblatt* 17 (January 11, 1923).

50. *Deutsche Allgemeine Zeitung* 16/17 (January 12, 1923).

51. D'Abernon, *Ambassador*, 159. See Georg Bernhard, "Abwehrpolitik": "The pressure France is exerting from the Ruhr has forged together parts of population with contrary views. The quarrels concerning republic or monarchy have been silenced for the time being." *Vossische Zeitung* 47 (January 28, 1923).

52. See Christoph Cornelißen, *Gerhard Ritter: Geschichtswissenschaft und Politik im 20. Jahrhundert* (Düsseldorf, 2001), 103.

53. Erich Mühsam, *Tagebücher (1910–1924)*, ed. Chris Hirte (Munich, 1994), 319 (January 21, 1923).

54. Thea Sternheim, *Tagebücher 1903–1971*, vol. 1: *1903–1925*, ed. Thomas Ehrsam and Regula Wyss (Göttingen, 2002), 614 (January 14, 1923). See also 615 (January 24, 1923): "Otherwise a gloomy pessimism is spreading rapidly in our bourgeois newspapers."

55. Rilke to Gudi Nölke, February 12, 1923, in Rainer Maria Rilke, *Briefe zur Politik*, ed. Joachim W. Storck (Frankfurt, 1992), 418. See also Gunter Martens and Annemarie Post-Martens, *Rainer Maria Rilke* (Reinbek bei Hamburg, 2008), 139.

56. Klemperer, *Tagebücher 1918–1924*, 659 (February 9, 1923).

57. Thomas Mann, *Briefe II: 1914–1923*, ed. Thomas Sprecher, Hans R. Vaget, and Cornelia Bernini (Frankfurt, 2004), 466. Gerhart Hauptmann is even more direct in his diary entry on March 4, 1923: "The terribly savage decadence of the French attack: the absence of all reason and moderation, which knows nothing of Europe or European responsibility." See Peter Sprengel, *Gerhart Hauptmann: Bürgerlichkeit und großer Traum—Eine Biographie* (Munich, 2012), 569.

58. Heinrich Mann and Félix Bertaux, *Briefwechsel 1922–1948* (Frankfurt, 2002), 44–45 (January 30, 1923).

59. *Das Tage-Buch* 7/4 (February 17, 1923), 207.

60. Morus (Richard Lewinsohn), "Der Kohlenkrieg," *Die Weltbühne* 19/3, 61 (January 18, 1923).

61. D'Abernon, *Ambassador*, 151 (January 10, 1923). Rosenberg also told Kessler, "The occupation of the Ruhr will completely destroy Germany's economic life, paralyzing it for fifty years." Kessler, *Tagebuch*, vol. 7, 632 (January 19, 1923).

62. *AdR: Das Kabinett Cuno*, no. 37, 122–129 (here 122, 123, note 3); and Ebert's public announcement of January 9, 1923, in *Deutsche Allgemeine Zeitung* 14/15 (January 11, 1923). See also Mühlhausen, *Friedrich Ebert*, 596–597; and Feldman: *Great Disorder*, 633.

63. *Ursachen und Folgen*, vol. 5, no. 999a, 21–22.

64. *Ursachen und Folgen*, vol. 5, no. 999e, 26–28 (here 27).

65. Excerpts from Cuno's speech, in *Ursachen und Folgen*, vol. 5, no. 1000a, 28–31 (here 30). See also Cuno's speech to Germany's regional state premiers on January 12, 1923: "France's current attack is no less serious than any previous ones. Everything—the very existence of the Reich—is at stake." *AdR: Das Kabinett Cuno*, no. 42, 141.

66. See Winkler, *Weimar*, 188; and Winkler, *Von der Revolution zur Stabilisierung: Arbeiter und Arbeiterbewegung in der Weimarer Republik von 1918 bis 1924* (Berlin-Bonn, 1984), 556. On the Reichstag session, see Erich Dombrowski, "Der feierliche Akt des Reichstags gegen den Gewaltakt," *Berliner Tageblatt* 13 (January 14, 1923). The *Tage-Buch* (3/4 [January 20, 1923], 81) complained that Cuno hadn't been able to speak freely for five sentences in an article entitled "Outrage Read from Paper, but Nonetheless Outrage."

67. "Der Tag des deutschen Volkes," *Vossische Zeitung* 24 (January 15, 1923).

68. "Gegen den Feind im Land," *Deutsche Allgemeine Zeitung* 22/23 (January 16, 1923).

69. Hermann Weber, Klaus Schönhoven, and Klaus Tenfelde, eds., *Bericht der ADGB-Sekretäre Knoll und Wissell über Besprechungen anlässlich der Besetzung des Ruhrgebiets, 8.–10.1.1923, zu Quellen zur Geschichte der deutschen Gewerkschaftsbewegung im 20. Jahrhundert*, vol. 2: *Die Gewerkschaften in den Anfangsjahren der Republik: Bearbeitet von Michael Ruck* (Cologne, 1985), doc. 75,

733–744 (here 735). See also Michael Ruck, *Die Freien Gewerkschaften im Ruhrkampf 1923* (Cologne, 1986), 42–46.

70. *Korrespondenzblatt des Allgemeinen Deutschen Gewerkschaftsbundes,* 33 (1923), no. 3, 25 (reprint, Berlin-Bonn, 1985). See also Ruck, *Freien Gewerkschaften,* 58–59.

71. *Sitzung des Bundesausschusses des ADGB, 24.1.1923, zu Quellen zur Geschichte der Gewerkschaftsbewegung,* vol. 2, doc. 78, 747–763 (here 751).

72. "Mut steckt an," *Deutsche Allgemeine Zeitung* 22/23 (January 16, 1923). On the move of the Rhenish-Westphalian Coal Syndicate, see Wulf, *Hugo Stinnes,* 350–351; Feldman, *Hugo Stinnes,* 842–843; and Feldman, *Great Disorder,* 633–634.

73. See Feldman, *Hugo Stinnes,* 843.

74. Carl Duisberg to Paul Silverberg (January 12, 1923), in Werner Plumpe, *Carl Duisberg 1861–1935: Anatomie eines Industriellen* (Munich, 2016), 614. German economics minister Johann Becker noted on January 15, 1923, "The Ruhr industrialists continue to insist on an extreme form of passive resistance." See Ruck, *Freien Gewerkschaften,* 75.

75. See Peter Langer, *Macht und Verantwortung: Der Ruhrbaron Paul Reusch* (Essen, 2012), 306–308; and Christian Marx, *Paul Reusch und die Gutehoffnungshütte: Leitung eines deutschen Großunternehmens* (Göttingen, 2013), 182–183.

76. *Ursachen und Folgen,* vol. 5, no. 999d, 24–25 (here 25).

77. "Auszug aus der Rede Hermanns Müllers, 13.1.1923," *Ursachen und Folgen,* vol. 5, no. 1000c, 33–36 (here 34).

78. "Erklärung Gustav Stresemanns, 13.1.1923," *Ursachen und Folgen,* vol. 5, no. 1000b, 31–33. See also Henry von Bernhard, ed., *Gustav Stresemann: Vermächtnis—Der Nachlass in drei Bänden,* vol. 1 (Berlin, 1932), 31; and Ludwig Richter, *Die Deutsche Volkspartei, 1918–1933* (Düsseldorf, 2002), 267.

79. "Auszug aus der Rede Helfferichs, 26.1.1923," *Ursachen und Folgen,* vol. 5, no. 1015, 59–60.

80. See Volker Ullrich, *Hitler: Ascent 1889–1939,* trans. Jefferson Chase (London, 2013), 132.

81. *Berliner Tageblatt* 24 (January 15, 1923).

82. *Die Rote Fahne* 18 (January 22, 1923); and *Ursachen und Folgen,* vol. 5, no. 1006, 45–46. See also Winkler, *Von der Revolution zur Stabilisierung,* 561–562.

83. See Joachim Schröder, "Deutsche und französische Kommunisten und das Problem eines gemeinsamen Widerstands gegen die Ruhrbesetzung," in Krumeich and Schröder, eds., *Der Schatten des Weltkriegs,* 169–186 (here 171–178).

84. See Manfred Zeidler, *Reichswehr und Rote Armee 1920–1933: Wege und Stationen einer ungewöhnlichen Zusammenarbeit* (Munich, 1993), 67.

85. Georg Bernhard, "Abwehrpolitik," *Vossische Zeitung* 47 (January 28, 1923).

86. *AdR: Das Kabinett Cuno,* no. 42, 138–139.

87. Kessler, *Tagebuch,* vol. 7, 634 (January 20, 1923). See also Otto Gessler, *Reichswehrpolitik in der Weimarer Zeit* (Stuttgart, 1958), 240.

88. "Vereinbarung zwischen dem Reichswehrministerium und dem preußischen Minister des Innern, January 30, 1923," *AdR: Das Kabinett Cuno,* no. 61, 207. See also Winkler, *Weimar,* 189.

89. See Zeidler, *Reichswehr und Rote Armee*, 68–72; and Hans Meier-Welcker, *Seeckt* (Frankfurt, 1967), 353–355.

90. *AdR: Die Kabinett Cuno*, no. 45, 147 (here 4). See also *Vossische Zeitung* 29 (January 18, 1923); and "Die Anweisung des Reichskommissars für die Kohleverteilung v. 11.1.1923," *Ursachen und Folgen*, vol. 5, no. 999b, 22–23.

91. *Ursachen und Folgen*, vol. 5, no. 1003, 42, and no. 1008, 47; and *AdR: Das Kabinett Cuno*, no. 49, 176 (here 12). See also the general order issued by Reich Minister von Rosenberg on January 17, 1923: "Our policies toward the Ruhr are designed to counter the worst French and Belgian violence. Civil servants have strict orders not to follow military commands." See Winfried Becker, ed., *Frederic von Rosenberg: Korrespondenzen und Akten des deutschen Diplomaten und Außenministers, 1913–1937* (Munich, 2011), no. 132, 228.

92. *AdR: Das Kabinett Cuno*, no. 51, 183.

93. See Wulf, *Hugo Stinnes*, 354.

94. Friedrich Stampfer, "Einen Monat Ruhrkrieg," *Vorwärts* 71 (January 12, 1923); and *Ursachen und Folgen*, vol. 5, 70–73. See also *Vossische Zeitung* 77 (February 15, 1923): "The balance of the first months of occupation was a losing enterprise for the French and Belgians."

95. "Rede Cunos vor Wirtschafts- und Gewerkschaftsführern in Bochum, 4.2.1923," *Ursachen und Folgen*, vol. 5, no. 1021, 66–68 (here 68).

96. *AdR: Das Kabinett Cuno*, no. 65, 218–219. See Rosenberg, February 4, 1923: "The solidarity and determination of our resistance is only going to become greater under the pressure of France's violence which is growing more brutal by the day." In Becker, ed., *Frederic von Rosenberg*, no. 156, 250.

97. See "Bericht des Vertreters des Auswärtigen Amtes im Ruhrgebiet, Legationsrat Redlhammer, vom 7.2.1923 über die Ruhrreise Cunos," *AdR: Das Kabinett Cuno*, no. 65, 218 (here 2). On April 9, 1923, D'Abernon noted, "The government is stronger and more popular than it was." In D'Abernon, *Ambassador*, 225.

98. "Bericht des Staatssekretärs Hamm über den Besuch des Reichskanzlers in München und Stuttgart am 22. und 23.3.1923," *AdR: Das Kabinett Cuno*, no. 103, 322–326.

99. Kessler, *Tagebuch*, vol. 7, 661 (Feburary 1, 1923).

100. "Unterredung Leiparts mit Cuno, 26.2.1923," in *Quellen zur Geschichte der deutschen Gewerkschaftsbewegung*, vol. 2, doc. 80, 802–804 (here 802).

101. Eugeni Xammar, *Das Schlangenei: Berichte aus dem Deutschland der Inflationsjahre 1922–1924* (Berlin, 2007), 96–97.

102. *Ursachen und Folgen*, vol. 5, no. 1029, 78. See Schwabe, ed., *Die Ruhrkrise 1923*, 4.

103. "Note der Reparationskommission an die deutsche Regierung, 26.1.1923," *Ursachen und Folgen*, vol. 5, no. 1014, 57.

104. See Krumeich, "Der 'Ruhrkampf' als Krieg," 16.

105. See Erich Eyck, "Komödie des Rechts," *Vossische Zeitung* 41 (January 25, 1923). For the protocol of the negotiations, see Hans Spethmann, *Zwölf Jahre Ruhrbergbau*, vol. 3 (Berlin, 1929), 94–101.

106. Kessler, *Tagebuch*, vol. 7, 658 (January 31, 1923). On the unrest in Mainz, see *AdR: Das Kabinett Cuno*, no. 54, 194–195, note 3; and Ruck, *Freien Gewerk-*

*schaften*, 91. Reporter Stefan Grossmann wrote that workers in Essen, by contrast, rejected the "foolishly warlike uproar on the streets." *Das Tage-Buch* 5/4 (February 1924), 152.

107. See Stanislas Jeannesson, "Übergriff e der französischen Besatzungsmacht und deutsche Beschwerden," in Krumeich and Schröder, eds., *Der Schatten des Weltkriegs*, 207–231 (here 209).

108. "The Terror in the Ruhr Valley," *Vossische Zeitung* 49 (January 30, 1923).

109. *AdR: Die Kabinett Cuno*, no. 53, 192.

110. "Verfügung betr. Einreiseverbot v. 20.2.1923," *Ursachen und Folgen*, vol. 5, no. 1023b, 70.

111. The fake identity paper is reproduced in Stresemann, *Vermächtnis*, vol. 1, 36; for an excerpt of his Dortmund speech, see 36–38 (here 38). Prussian interior minister Carl Severing also traveled to the occupied regions with the help of fake documents made out to "Business Director Wilhelm Gerviens." See Severing, *Mein Lebensweg*, vol. 1: *Vom Schlosser zum Minister* (Cologne, 1950), 371.

112. "Die Kohlensperre," *Vossische Zeitung* 54 (February 1, 1923); "Note der französischen Regierung betr. Kohlelieferungen aus dem besetzten Gebiet, 31.1.1923," *Ursachen und Folgen*, vol. 5, no. 1016, 60–61; and *AdR: Das Kabinett Cuno*, no. 62, 209, and note 2 (January 31, 1923).

113. "Vermerk des Staatssekretärs Hamm über den Eisenbahnverkehr im Ruhrgebiet, 11.3.1923," *AdR: Das Kabinett Cuno*, no. 95, 303–304.

114. Winkler, *Weimar*, 193.

115. See Feldman, *Great Disorder*, 669ff.

116. Hagen Schulze, *Otto Braun oder Preußens demokratische Sendung* (Frankfurt, 1977), 428.

117. Xammar, *Das Schlangenei*, 91 (March 21, 1923). See also L. Lania, "An der Ruhrfront," *Die Weltbühne* 19, no. 4 (January 25, 1923): "The provcative show of force by soldiers is what upsets workers most, not national differences."

118. For the statistics, see Jeannesson, "Übergriffe der französischen Besatzungsmacht," 210.

119. See Klaus Wisotzky, "Der 'blutige Karsamstag' 1923 bei Krupp," in Krumeich and Schröder, eds., *Der Schatten des Weltkriegs*, 265–287.

120. Paul Scheffer, "Das Blutbad von Essen," *Berliner Tageblatt* 154 (April 1, 1923).

121. *Ursachen und Folgen*, vol. 5, no. 1039, 95–97.

122. Wisotzky, "Der 'blutige Karsamstag,'" 269. See also Mühlhausen, *Friedrich Ebert*, 611.

123. "An die Arbeiter der Welt!" *Korrespondenzblatt des Allgemeinen Deutschen Gewerkschaftsbundes* 33, no. 14 (April 7, 1923): 152.

124. Theodor Wolff, *Berliner Tageblatt* 156 (April 3, 1923).

125. See Schröder, "Deutsche und französische Kommunisten," 179.

126. See Wisotzky, "Der 'blutige Karsamstag,'" 277.

127. Wisotzky, 280.

128. See Langer, *Macht und Verantwortung*, 310.

129. *Vorwärts* 215 (May 9, 1923), in Wisotzky, "Der 'blutige Karsamstag,'" 282.

130. *Das Tage-Buch* 19/4 (May 12, 1923), 665.

131. *Das Tage-Buch* 19/4 (May 12, 1923), 282, note 72.

132. Xammar, *Das Schlangenei*, 64. See Jeannesson, "Übergriffe der französischen Besatzungsmacht," 216.

133. Krumeich,"Der 'Ruhrkampf' als Krieg," 22. For the caricature, see p. 23.

134. Jeannesson, "Übergriff e der französischen Besatzungsmacht," 212 (graphic), 217 (quotation).

135. See Gerd Krüger, "'Wir wachen und strafen!' Gewalt im Ruhrkampf von 1923," in Krumeich and Schröder, eds., *Der Schatten des Weltkriegs*, 233–255 (here 237–242).

136. See Manfred Franke, *Schlageter: Der erste Soldat des 3. Reiches—Die Entmythologisierung eines Helden* (Cologne, 1980), 20–28, 37–39, 44–45.

137. Franke, *Schlageter*, 50–87.

138. *Ursachen und Folgen*, vol. 5, no. 1047a, 137.

139. See "Bericht von Kriminalkommissar Weitzel über die Tätigkeit der Organisation Hauenstein im besetzten Gebiet, 25.5.1923," in *Das Krisenjahr 1923: Militär und Innenpolitik 1922–1924*, ed. Heinz Hürten (Düsseldorf, 1980), doc. 16, 34–40; *AdR: Das Kabinett Cuno*, no. 184, 550, note 2; Franke, *Schlageter*, 38–40; and Langer, *Macht und Verantwortung*, 317–318.

140. Harry Graf Kessler, *Das Tagebuch: Achter Band—1923–1926*, ed. Angela Reinthal, Günter Riederer, and Jörg Schuster, with help from Janna Brechmacher, Christoph Hilse, and Nadin Weiss (Stuttgart, 2009), 52 (July 4, 1923).

141. See Franke, *Schlageter*, 92–98; and Langer, *Macht und Verantwortung*, 318.

142. Günther Rühle, *Theater für die Republik im Spiegel der Kritik, 2. Band: 1926–1933*, (Frankfurt, 1988), 1155–1157 (here 1157).

143. For an interpretation of Schlageter's speech, see Hans Hecker, "Karl Radeks Werben um die deutsche Rechte: Die Sowjetunion und der Ruhrkampf," in Krumeich and Schröder, eds., *Der Schatten des Weltkriegs*, 187–205; Wolf-Dietrich Gutjahr, *Revolution muss sein: Karl Radek—die Biographie* (Cologne, 2012), 572–574; and Winkler, *Weimar*, 195–196.

144. *AdR: Das Kabinett Cuno*, no. 91, 292 (March 5, 1923). See also Karl Holl, *Ludwig Quidde (1858–1941): Eine Biographie* (Düsseldorf, 2007), 334–335.

145. *AdR: Das Kabinett Cuno*, no. 109, 344 (March 27, 1923). In a meeting of the Center Party parliamentary group on March 23, 1923, deputies were of the opinion "that the defensive struggle is on the down slope and that it's time to seek a path of understanding." Rudolf Morsey and Karsten Ruppert, eds., *Die Protokolle der Reichstagsfraktion der Zentrumspartei, 1920–1925* (Mainz, 1981), doc. 227, 448–449.

146. *AdR: Das Kabinett Cuno*, no. 110, 348 (March 28, 1923). See also the letter of the Miners Association to Cuno, on April 14, 1923, in no. 120, 376–377. On the growing pressure on Cuno, see Ruck, *Die Freien Gewerkschaften*, 295–307.

147. "Auszug aus der Rede Rosenbergs v. 16.4.1923," *Ursachen und Folgen*, vol. 5, no. 1041a, 103–106 (here 106).

148. Kessler, *Tagebuch*, vol. 7, 775 (April 16, 1923).

149. Stresemann, *Vermächtnis*, vol. 1, 45–55. See also *Ursachen und Folgen*, vol. 5, no. 1041d, 113–115. For an interpretation of the speech, see Karl Heinrich Pohl, *Gustav Stresemann: Biographie eines Grenzgängers* (Göttingen, 2015), 219–227.

150. Georg Bernhard, "Stresemann über Lösungs-Möglichkeiten," *Vossische Zeitung* 181 (April 18, 1923).

151. "Reichstag und Ruhr," *Die Weltbühne* 19/17 (April 26, 1923), 408. See also *Das Tage-Buch* 16/4 (April 21, 1923), 546: "Stresemann's speech was a platform and above all a demonstration of his capabilities."

152. "Auszug aus der Rede Curzons v. 20.4.1923," *Ursachen und Folgen*, vol. 5, no. 1042a, 116–117.

153. Stresemann, *Vermächtnis*, vol. 1, 55–57 (here 55); and *Ursachen und Folgen*, vol. 5, no. 1042b, 117–119. See also Georg Bernhard, "Die Vermittlung," *Vossische Zeitung*, 189 (April 22, 1923): "The parliamentary speech of Foreign Secretary Curzon fundamentally clarified the international situation."

154. Kessler, *Tagebuch*, vol. 7, 777 (April 21, 1923). In the *Berliner Volks-Zeitung*, Carl von Ossietzky wrote that "the whole world" expected of Germany "an offer demonstrating the will to end this terrible quarrel." Ossietzky, *Sämtliche Schriften*, vol. 2, 247.

155. *AdR: Das Kabinett Cuno*, no. 140, 430 (April 25, 1923).

156. *AdR: Cuno*, no. 142, 433–438, and no. 144, 440–444 (here 442).

157. D'Abernon, *Ambassador*, 204.

158. "Note der deutschen Regierung v. 2.5.1923," *Ursachen und Folgen*, vol. 5, no. 1044a, 121–124; also in Becker, ed., *Frederic von Rosenberg*, no. 188, 295–300. See also Wulf, *Hugo Stinnes*, 328; Krüger, *Außenpolitik der Republik*, 203–204; and Feldman, *Great Disorder*, 662–663.

159. Kessler, *Tagebuch*, vol. 7, 782 (May 2, 1923).

160. Georg Bernhard, "Form und Zahl," *Vossische Zeitung* 218 (May 6, 1923). See also D'Abernon, *Ambassador*, 206: "On the diplomatic side the whole tone of their offer is such that it will alienate public opinion instead of winning it."

161. Morus (Richard Lewinsohn), "Worte und Taten," *Die Weltbühne* 19/19 (May 10, 1923), 545.

162. Theodor Wolff, *Berliner Tageblatt* 207 (May 4, 1923).

163. *Ursachen und Folgen*, vol. 5, no. 1044c, 125–130.

164. "Abgelehnt!" *Deutsche Allgemeine Zeitung* (May 7, 1923), 209.

165. *Ursachen und Folgen*, vol. 5, no. 1044d, 130–132.

166. "Keine Kabinettskrise!" *Vossische Zeitung* 225 (May 14, 1923).

167. D'Abernon, *Ambassador*, 219. Rosenberg, in his instructions to Germany's ambassador in London, Sthamer, on May 27, characterized the British response to the German proposals as a "major disappointment," adding that "the German government would have expected a more just appraisal of its step since it was based on a suggestion by Lord Curzon." Becker, ed., *Frederic von Rosenberg*, no. 196, 311.

168. Kessler, *Tagebuch*, vol. 7, 795 (May 24, 1923).

169. Stresemann to his wife, May 28, 1923, and undated (probably June 3, 1923), in Wolfgang Stresemann, *Mein Vater Gustav Stresemann* (Munich, 1979), 224–225. See also Jonathan Wright, *Gustav Stresemann 1878–1929: Weimars größter Staatsmann* (Munich, 2006), 215.

170. See Richter, *Deutsche Volkspartei*, 268; and Stresemann, *Vermächtnis*, vol. 1, 65–66.

171. See Winkler, *Weimar*, 193; and Mühlhausen, *Friedrich Ebert*, 613. On May 7, 1923, SPD deputy Rudolf Breitscheid rejected any participation as "completely useless suicide," while Rudolf Hilferding asserted that the grand coalition could "no longer be delayed" since Cuno and Rosenberg were "incapable of leading negotiations, that is to say: any negotiations with the Entente ... are bound to fail because of their views and political incompetence." Kessler, *Tagebuch*, vol. 8, 785 (May 7, 1923).

172. "Denkschrift des Reichsverbands der Deutschen Industrie an den Reichskanzler, 25.5.1923," *AdR: Das Kabinett Cuno*, no. 168, 508–513. See also Wulf, *Hugo Stinnes*, 383–385; Feldman, *Hugo Stinnes*, 872–875; Feldman, *Great Disorder*, 664–667; Winkler, *Weimar*, 197–198; and Winkler, *Von der Revolution zur Stabilisierung*, 575–576.

173. Morus (Richard Lewinsohn), "Patrioten," *Die Weltbühne* 19/23 (June 7, 1923), 669.

174. "Schreiben der Gewerkschaften an den Reichskanzler, 1.6.1923," *AdR: Das Kabinett Cuno*, no. 177, 537–539 (here 538).

175. "Memorandum der deutschen Regierung v. 7.6.1923," *Ursachen und Folgen*, vol. 5, no. 1048, 145–146. See also Wulf, *Hugo Stinnes*, 386–387; Krüger, *Außenpolitik der Republik*, 204–205; and Feldman, *Great Disorder*, 668.

176. *AdR: Das Kabinett Cuno*, no. 196, 587, note 4.

177. D'Abernon, *Ambassador*, 222.

178. "Auszug aus der Rede Poincarés v. 29.6.1923," *Ursachen und Folgen*, vol. 5, no. 1051, 149.

179. Hoesch to Auswärtiges Amt, June 23, 1923, in Wulf, *Hugo Stinnes*, 389.

180. D'Abernon, *Ambassador*, 208.

181. Schubert to Hoesch, June 13, 1923, in *Akten zur deutschen auswärtigen Politik 1918–1945* (ADAP), series A, vol. 8 (Göttingen, 1990), 43. See also Mühlhausen, *Friedrich Ebert*, 612–613.

182. See Winkler, *Von der Revolution zur Stabilisierung*, 577; and Winkler, *Weimar*, 198–199.

183. Morus (Richard Lewinsohn), "Stützungsaktionen," *Die Weltbühne*, 19/27 (July 5, 1923), 22.

184. "Denkschrift Hamms v. 16.6.1923," *AdR: Das Kabinett Cuno*, no. 192, 575–577 (here 575). See also Winkler, *Weimar*, 199; Mommsen, *Die verspielte Freiheit*, 145, 147; and Feldman, *Great Disorder*, 669ff.

185. Winkler, *Von der Revolution zur Stabilisierung*, 588. See Theodor Leipart to Reichsregierung, July 4, 1923: "The urgent reports filed by our local chapter show that dull desperation is everywhere overcoming the unemployed." *Quellen zur Geschichte der Gewerkschaftsbewegung*, vol. 2, doc. 89, 865.

186. See Winkler, *Von der Revolution zur Stabilisierung*, 566, 593–594; Ruck, *Freien Gewerkschaften*, 378–379; Martin Geyer, "Teuerungsprotest und Teuerungsunruhen 1914–1923: Selbsthilfegesellschaft und Geldentwertung," in *Der Kampf um das tägliche Brot: Nahrungsmangel, Versorgungspolitik und Protest, 1770–1990*, ed. Manfred Gailus and Heinrich Volkmann (Opladen, 1994), 319–345 (here 341–343).

187. *Quellen zur Geschichte der Gewerkschaftsbewegung*, vol. 2, doc. 93, 898, note 2. See "Aufzeichnung des Staatssekretärs Hamm über die Lage im Ruhrgebiet, 20.7.1923": "A dull mood of 'We'll carry on, but the cause is lost' is descending everywhere." *AdR: Das Kabinett Cuno*, no. 221, 650.

188. See Winkler, *Von der Revolution zur Stabilisierung*, 593; and Ossip K. Flechtheim, *Die KPD in der Weimarer Republik* (Frankfurt, 1969), 179–191.

189. Rosenberg, *Geschichte der Weimarer Republik*, 136. Ossip K. Flechtheim didn't go quite that far, writing, "In 1923, at least a significant minority of organized and perhaps a majority of unorganized workers backed the KPD." *KPD in der Weimarer Republik*, 181.

190. *Die Rote Fahne* 158 (July 12, 1923), in *Ursachen und Folgen*, vol. 5, no. 1052, 150–151.

191. Werner T. Angress, *Stillborn Revolution: The Communist Bid for Power in Germany, 1921–1923* (Port Washington, NY), 392. See also Winkler, *Weimar*, 200.

192. Angress, *Stillborn Revolution*, 396–401 (here 401). See also Winkler, *Von der Revolution zur Stabilisierung*, 596–597.

193. D'Abernon, *Ambassador*, 227. See also D'Abernon to Curzon, August 11, 1923, about a meeting with Rosenberg, in which the English ambassador didn't rule out the possibility of a German civil war. Becker, ed., *Frederic von Rosenberg*, no. 244, 370–371.

194. "Tagebuch Georg Escherichs 1923," N l, Escherich 10, Bayerisches Hauptstaatsarchiv, München (hereafter BayHStA).

195. See Krüger, *Außenpolitik der Republik*, 205–206; and Klaus Schwabe, "Großbritannien und die Ruhrkrise," in Schwabe, ed., *Die Ruhrkrise 1923*, 64.

196. *Germania* 205 (August 27, 1923); and *AdR: Das Kabinett Cuno*, no. 233, 695 (here note 1). See Ulrich Hehl, *Wilhelm Marx 1863–1946: Eine politische Biographie* (Mainz, 1987), 232.

197. "Stresemann to Kempkes, July 29, 1923," *AdR: Das Kabinett Cuno*, no. 233, 695, note 1.

198. *Vossische Zeitung* 354 (July 28, 1923); and Hehl, *Wilhelm Marx*, 232. In the *Weltbühne*, Richard Lewinsohn wrote, "The attacks in the Center Party press, *Germania* and the *Kölnische Volkszeitung*, are the final warnings for the Cuno government." Quoted in Hehl, *Wilhelm Marx*, 232.

199. *Das Tage-Buch* 31/4 (August 4, 1923), 1066.

200. "Ministerrat v. 27.7.1923," *AdR: Das Kabinett Cuno*, no. 227, 672–679.

201. "Kundgebung des Reichspräsidenten und der Reichsregierung," *Vossische Zeitung* 355 (July 29, 1923).

202. Georg Bernhard, "Die Steuertäuschung," *Vossische Zeitung* 355 (July 29, 1923).

203. "Auszug aus der Rede Cunos v. 8.8.1923," *Ursachen und Folgen*, vol. 5, no. 1059a, 159–163.

204. Th[eodor] W[olff], "Kabinettswechsel," *Berliner Tageblatt* 375 (August 12, 1923). On August 8, 1923, Stresemann noted in his calendar, "Cuno's speech in the Reichsttag. Very depressing impression." Stresemann, *Vermächtnis*, vol. 1, 75. "Auszug aus der Rede Stresemann v. 9.8.1923," *Ursachen und Folgen*, vol. 5, no. 1059d, 167–168.

205. *AdR: Das Kabinett Cuno*, no. 244, 727–732 (here 727, 730).

206. See Winkler, *Von der Revolution zur Stabilisierung*, 598–599; and Wilhelm Ersil, *Aktionseinheit stürzt Cuno: Zur Geschichte des Massenkampfs gegen die Cuno-Regierung 1923 in Mitteldeutschland* (East Berlin, 1963), 244ff.

207. "Beschluss der SPD-Reichstagsfraktion v. 11.8.1923," *Ursachen und Folgen*, vol. 5, no. 1061, 170. See also "Die Bedingungen der VSPD," *Vossische Zeitung*, 376–378 (August 11, 1923).

208. Stresemann, *Vermächtnis*, vol. 1, 77.

209. Stresemann, vol. 1, 77.

210. Stresemann, vol. 1, 77–78. See also Richter, *Deutsche Volkspartei*, 271.

211. "Die Regierungskrise," *Deutsche Allgemeine Zeitung* 369 (August 12, 1923).

212. *AdR: Das Kabinett Cuno*, xxiv–xxv, and no. 246, 734 (here note 6).

213. Gessler, *Reichswehrpolitik*, 250. Cuno also made "the impression of a broken man" on Severing. Severing, *Mein Lebensweg*, vol. 1, 423.

214. *AdR: Das Kabinett Cuno*, no. 246, 733–738 (here 733); and no. 247, 738–746 (here 739).

215. Seeckt to his sister, August 19, 1923, in Meier-Welcker, *Seeckt*, 369.

216. Georg Bernhard, "An die Arbeit," *Vossische Zeitung* 379 (August 12, 1923).

217. Carl von Ossietzky, "Brandstätte," *Berliner Volks-Zeitung* (August 14, 1923), in *Sämtliche Schriften*, vol. 2, 289–290.

218. Tyrus, "Regierungsumbildung," *Die Weltbühne* 19/34 (August 23, 1923), 187.

219. Th[eodor] W[olff ], "Kabinettswechsel," *Berliner Tageblatt* 375 (August 12, 1923).

220. "Die neue Reichsregierung," *Deutsche Allgemeine Zeitung* 371 (August 14, 1923).

**Chapter 2:** FROM INFLATION TO HYPERINFLATION

1. Thea Sternheim, *Tagebücher*, vol. 1, 641 (August 12, 1923).

2. Klemperer, *Tagebücher 1918–1924*, 732 (August 13, 1923).

3. See Manfred Zeidler, "Die deutsche Kriegsfinanzierung 1914 bis 1918 und ihre Folgen," in *Der Erste Weltkrieg: Wirkung, Wahrnehmung, Analyse*, ed. Wolfgang Michalka (Munich, 1994), 415–433; and Büttner, *Weimar*, 166. For the wider context, see also Feldman, *Great Disorder*, 25ff.

4. Felix Pinner, "Entfesselte Instinkte," *Berliner Tageblatt* (December 21, 1918), cited in Wallwitz, *Die große Inflation*, 31.

5. See Büttner, *Weimar*, 166–167; and Winkler, *Weimar*, 144. On the "inflation consensus," see Charles S. Mayer, "Die deutsche Inflation als Verteilungskonflikt," in *Historische Prozesse der deutschen Inflation 1914 bis 1924*, ed. Otto Büsch and Gerald D. Feldman (Berlin, 1978), 329–342.

6. See the figures in Büttner, *Weimar*, 168. On Erzberger's finace reform, see Winkler, *Weimar*, 109–111; Frederick Taylor, *Inflation: Der Untergang des Geldes in der Weimarer Republik und die Geburt eines deutschen Traumas* (Munich, 2013), 127–131; Feldman, *Great Disorder*, 162–165; and Wallwitz, *Die große Inflation*, 118–132.

7.  "German Trade Boom and the Sinking Mark," *Manchester Guardian* (November 11, 1923), cited in Taylor, *Inflation*, 171. On unemployment, see the figures in Feldman, *Great Disorder*, 127, 218. On Germany's special economic development, see Winkler, *Von der Revolution zur Stabilisierung*, 373–377; and Hans-Ulrich Wehler, *Deutsche Gesellschaftsgeschichte*, vol. 4 (Munich, 2003), 244–245.

8.  Cited in Carl-Ludwig Holtfrerich, *Die deutsche Inflation 1914–1923* (Berlin, 1980), 207. In the *Weltbühne* (18/19 [May 11, 1922]), Richard Lewinsohn complained that for three years the German government hadn't made "the slightest attempt" to "combat growing inflation and the decline of the mark."

9.  See Taylor, *Inflation*, 141, 154, 164–165 (Tabelle), 182–183. On the phase of relative stability, see Feldman, *Great Disorder*, 211ff.

10. Georg Bernhard, "Der Kampf ums Leben," *Vossische Zeitung* (January 1, 1922). See also Taylor, *Inflation*, 185–186. On the decline of the mark between the summer and the end of 1921, see Feldman, *Great Disorder*, 385–386.

11. Klemperer, *Tagebücher 1918–1924*, 498 (September 18, 1921).

12. Klemperer, 530 (November 19, 1921).

13. Klemperer, 538 (December 23, 1921).

14. Alfred Kerr, *Berlin wird Berlin: Briefe aus der Reichshauptstadt 1897–1922*, ed. Deborah Vietor-Engländer, vol. 4: *1917–1922* (Göttingen, 2021), 444 (December 18, 1921).

15. Sling, "Mein Tipp," *Vossische Zeitung* 537 (November 17, 1921).

16. Siegfried Jacobsohn, *Briefe an Kurt Tucholsky 1915–1926*, ed. Richard von Soldenhoff (Munich, 1989), 146 (June 17, 1922). See also Taylor, *Inflation*, 191–192. On the connection between inflation and reparations, see Feldman, *Great Disorder*, 418; and Holtfrerich, *Die deutsche Inflation*, 135ff.

17. Mühsam, *Tagebücher*, 293 (May 31, 1922).

18. Sternheim, *Tagebücher*, vol. 1, 375 (April 30, 1922).

19. Morus (Richard Lewinsohn), "Von Paris bis Leipzig," *Die Weltbühne* 18/26, 661 (June 29, 1922). See also Morus, "Kapital und Kohle," *Die Weltbühne* 18/29, 67 (July 20, 1922): "Since the German currency has begun to slip, no political event has had such a direct and catastrophic effect on the value of the mark as Rathenau's murder."

20. Zweig, *World of Yesterday*, 217. On the figures, see Taylor, *Inflation*, 207; and Feldman, *Great Disorder*, 450.

21. See excerpt from August Heinrich von der Ohe's diary, http://kollektives-gedaechtnis.de/texte/weimar/ohe/inflation1923.htm. See also Klemperer, *Tagebücher 1918–1924*, 610 (August 25, 1922): "The wildest sort of currency devaluation. The dollar has jumped to 800, then 1,000, now 2,000. Butter is at 230, no-brand bread 47, etc., etc."

22. Kerr, *Berlin wird Berlin*, vol. 4, 502–503 (August 27, 1922).

23. Kessler, *Tagebuch*, vol. 7, 567 (November 7, 1922).

24. See Taylor, *Inflation*, 233; and the figures in Feldman, *Great Disorder*, 505.

25. Sternheim, *Tagebücher*, vol. 1, 605 (December 20, 1922).

26. See Winkler, *Von der Revolution zur Stabilisierung*, 391–392; Taylor, *Inflation*, 208; and Feldman, *Great Disorder*, 452.

27. Klemperer, *Tagebücher 1918–1924*, 658 (February 2, 1923).

28. Klemperer, 705 (June 29, 1923). See also Pringsheim, *Tagebücher*, vol. 7, 84 (July 5, 1923): "Gradually, the prices make you want to commit suicide." On the Reichsbank's attempt to prop up the currency, see "Sitzung des Reichsbank-Kuratoriums v. 21.3.1923," *AdR: Das Kabinett Cuno*, no. 101, 319–321. On the collapse of that effort, see "Ministerbesprechung v. 19.4.1923," *AdR: Das Kabinett Cuno*, no. 128, 402. On the figures, see Taylor, *Inflation*, 272–273; and Feldman, *Great Disorder*, 643.

29. "Aufzeichnung Hamms für die Besprechung mit Wirtschaftsführern am 31.7. und 1.8.1923," *AdR: Das Kabinett Cuno*, no. 234, 697.

30. Excerpt from Ohe's diary, August 1, 1923, http://www.kollektives-gedaechtnis .de/texte/weimar/ohe/inflation1923.htm. See also Sternheim, *Tagebücher*, vol. 1, 640 (August 5, 1923): "The five-million-mark notes have been issued. But no one is able to change them."

31. Klemperer, *Tagebücher 1918–1924*, vol. 2, 725 (August 3, 1923).

32. See Taylor, *Inflation*, 287.

33. Taylor, 272.

34. "Defizit-Wirtschaft," *Vossische Zeitung* 350 (July 26, 1923).

35. See Büttner, *Weimar*, 172–177; Ulrich Herbert, *Geschichte Deutschlands im 20. Jahrhundert* (Munich, 2014), 202; Detlev Peukert, *Die Weimarer Republik* (Berlin, 1987), 74–75; and Martin H. Geyer, "Die Zeit der Inflation 1919–1923," in Rossol and Ziemann, eds., *Aufbruch und Abgründe*, 66–89 (here 77–80).

36. Ernst Troeltsch, *Die Fehlgeburt einer Republik: Spektator in Berlin 1918 bis 1922—Zusammengestellt und mit einem Nachwort versehen von Johann Hinrich Claussen* (Frankfurt, 1994), 255–256 (March 4, 1922). See Karl Alexander von Müller, *Im Wandel einer Welt: Erinnerungen,* vol. 3 (Munich, 1966), 139–140: "It was a large stratum of society that was forced helpless into decline. Middle-class people, artisans and small retailers, intellectuals and artists, former officers and civil servant families. It was like a plague."

37. Erich Kästner, . . . *was nicht in euren Lesebüchern steht,* ed. Wilhelm Rausch (Frankfurt, 1968), 152.

38. See Taylor, *Inflation*, 219; and Büttner, *Weimar*, 173.

39. Klemperer, *Tagebücher 1918–1924*, 633 (November 12, 1922).

40. Klemperer, 642 (December 12, 1922).

41. Ohe's diary, March 31, 1923, http://www.kollektives-gedaechtnis.de/texte/ weimar/ohe/inflation1923.htm.

42. See Winkler, *Von der Revolution zur Stabilisierung*, 375–387; and Wehler, *Deutsche Gesellschaftsgeschichte*, vol. 4, 312. On the development of take-home wages, see Holtfrerich, *Die deutsche Inflation*, 224ff.

43. Dorothy von Moltke, *Ein Leben in Deutschland: Briefe aus Kreisau und Berlin, 1907–1934*, ed. Beate Ruhm von Oppen (Munich, 1999), 72 (January 6, 1922).

44. See Büttner, *Weimar*, 176–177; and Wehler, *Deutsche Gesellschaftsgeschichte*, vol. 4, 334–335.

45. Franz Eulenburg, "Die sozialen Wirkungen der Währungsverhältnisse," *Jahrbücher für Nationalökonomie und Statistik* 122 (1924): 748–794 (here 789). See

also Wehler, *Deutsche Gesellschaftsgeschichte*, vol. 4, 248; and Winkler, *Von der Revolution zur Stabilisierung*, 388–389.

46. Kessler, *Tagebuch*, vol. 7, 789 (May 16, 1923). The SPD parliamentary deputy and editor in chief of *Vorwärts* Friedrich Stampfer, who regularly encountered Stinnes in the Reichstag's foreign affairs committee, recalled, "He commanded an aura of shy respect. He spoke so softly that even in this relatively close space, everyone huddled together so as not to miss a single one of his words." Stampfer, *Erfahrungen und Erkenntnisse: Aufzeichnungen aus meinem Leben* (Cologne, 1957), 249–250. See also the contemporary portrait of Stinnes by Johannes Fischart (Erich Dombrowski), in Fischart, *Köpfe der Gegenwart: Das alte und das neue System—Dritte Folge* (Berlin, 1920), 247–256 (here 249–250).

47. See Wulf, *Hugo Stinnes*; and Feldman, *Hugo Stinnes*. See also Feldman, *Great Disorder*, 284ff.; Taylor, *Inflation*, 118–121, 179–181; and Wallwitz, *Die große Inflation*, 79–86, 109–114, 206–212.

48. Paul Ufermann, *Könige der Inflation* (Berlin, 1924), 20.

49. Frank Fassland, "Wirtschaftsführer: Hugo Stinnes," *Die Weltbühne* 18/10 (March 9, 1923), 234–237, and 11 (March 16, 1923), 261–267 (here 267). In March 1923, Stinnes was featured on the cover of *Time*, which called him the new "Kaiser" of Germany. See Wolfgang Martynkewicz, *1920: Am Nullpunkt des Sinns* (Berlin, 2019), 76.

50. Hans Ostwald, *Sittengeschichte der Inflation: Ein Kulturdokument aus den Jahren des Marksturzes* (Berlin, 1931), 99.

51. Kerr, *Berlin wird Berlin*, vol. 4, 448–449 (December 25, 1921).

52. Ernest Hemingway, "On the Low Value of the Mark," *Daily Star* (Toronto), Alpha History (website), https://alphahistory.com/weimarrepublic/ernest-hemingway-on-low-value-of-mark-1922/.

53. Joseph Roth, "Die fremden Bürger," *Vorwärts* (May 27, 1923), cited in Ruth Glatzer, *Berlin zur Weimarer Zeit: Panorama einer Metropole 1919–1933* (Berlin, 2000), 121. See also *Das Tage-Buch* 23/4 (June 9, 1923), 801: "Every drop in the mark accompanied by a wave of foreigners. . . . The hoteliers who sighed in despair yesterday are now sighing in relief, the gourmet restaurateurs are beaming, and the theater owners wear gleeful faces."

54. Malcolm Cowley, *Exile's Return: A Literary Odyssey of the 1920s* (New York, 1934), 133. See also Otto Friedrich, *Morgen ist Weltuntergang: Berlin den zwanziger Jahren* (Berlin, 1998), 161.

55. "Die Auslands-Missionen in Berlin," *Die Weltbühne* 18/48, 565–566 (November 30, 1922).

56. *Die Weltbühne* 19/11 (March 15, 1923), 318.

57. Haffner, *Defying Hitler*, 61. Also at the age of sixteen, literary scholar Hans Mayer observed a "new, deep rift" forming in his class at the Schiller Gymnasium in Cologne, in which "kids were split into the children of the have-nots and nouveau riche wheelers and dealers." See Mayer, *Ein Deutscher auf Widerruf: Erinnerungen*, vol. 1 (Frankfurt, 1982), 35.

58. Klaus Mann, *The Turning Point: Thirty-Five Years in This Century* (Lexington, MA, 2017), n.p., Kindle position 2352. The original version of Klaus Mann's autobiography appeared in English in 1942. An expanded and considerably revised German version, entitled *Der Wendepunkt*, was published in 1952. Unless otherwise noted, the English version has been used.

59. See Ulrich Linse, *Barfüßige Propheten: Erlöser der zwanziger Jahre* (Berlin, 1983).

60. Linse, 34.

61. Linse, 38.

62. See Hermann Behr, *Die Goldenen Zwanziger Jahre—das fesselnde Panorama einer entfesselten Zeit* (Hamburg, 1964), 43ff.; Ostwald, *Sittengeschichte der Inflation*, 38–40; Martin Geyer, *Verkehrte Welt: Revolution, Inflation und Moderne* ([Munich, 1914–1924] Göttingen, 1998), 312; and Martynkewicz, *1920*, 79–81.

63. Morus (Richard Lewinsohn), "System Klante," *Die Weltbühne* 18/51, 651 (December 21, 1922).

64. See the excellent translation at Walter Benjamin, "Imperial Panorama: A Tour of German Inflations," June 6, 2016, Salad of Pearls (website), https://saladofpearls .wordpress.com/2016/06/06/a-tour-of-german-inflation/. See also Jean-Michel Palmier, *Walter Benjamin* (Frankfurt, 2009), 384–386.

65. Klemperer, *Tagebücher 1918–1924*, 721 (July 28, 1923), and 731 (August 8, 1923). See also Friedrich, *Morgen ist Weltuntergang*, 170; and Taylor, *Inflation*, 207.

66. Georg Bernhard, "Der Leidensweg der Mark," *Vossische Zeitung*, no. 348 (July 22, 1923).

67. Xammar, *Das Schlangenei*, 49.

68. *Das Tage-Buch* 5/4 (February 5, 1923), 160.

69. Haffner, *Defying Hitler*, 54.

70. Hedwig Hirschbach, "Das Großstadt-Gesicht," *Die Weltbühne* 19/15, 433–434 (April 12, 1923).

71. Xammar, *Das Schlangenei*, 53.

72. Morus (Richard Lewinsohn), "Hochbetrieb," *Die Weltbühne* 18/44, 478 (November 2, 1922).

73. Ostwald, *Sittengeschichte der Inflation*, 57.

74. Haffner, *Defying Hitler*, 54–55.

75. Klemperer, *Tagebücher 1918–1924*, 697 (May 27, 1923).

76. Klemperer, 701 (June 2, 1923).

77. Klemperer, 705 (June 29, 1923), and 708 (July 5, 1923).

78. See Sternheim, *Tagebücher*, vol. 1, 616 (January 28, 1923), and 632 (June 2, 1923).

79. Theodor Heuss, *Erinnerungen 1905–1933* (Frankfurt, 1965), 188. See also Peter Merseburger, *Theodor Heuss: Der Bürger als Präsident—Biographie* (Stuttgart, 2012), 238; and *Die Weltbühne* 18/42 (October 19, 1922), 424: "If a journalist is able to write an article a week for the foreign press, he only has to work four afternoons a month and can laze around luxuriantly the rest of the time."

80. Theodor Heuss, *Bürger der Weimarer Republik: Briefe 1918–1933*, ed. Michael Dorrmann (Munich, 2008), 184 (February 1, 1923).

81. Mann, *Briefe II*, 487 (September 5, 1923). See also Donald Prater, *Thomas Mann:*

*Deutscher und Weltbürger—Eine Biographie* (Munich, 1995), 194; and Hermann Kurzke, *Thomas Mann: Das Leben als Kunstwerk* (Munich, 1999), 352–353.

82. Siegfried von Vegesack, "Das Börsenspiel," *Das Tage-Buch* 16/4 (April 21, 1923), 565.

83. Egon Erwin Kisch, *Läuse auf dem Markt: Vermischte Prosa* (Berlin-Weimar, 1985) (*Gesammelte Werke*, vol. 10), cited in Glatzer, *Berlin zur Weimarer Zeit*, 98.

84. Carl Zuckmayer, *Als wär's ein Stück von mir: Horen der Freundschaft* (Stuttgart, 1966), 307. On the stereotype of the *Schieber*, see Ostwald, *Sittengeschichte der Inflation*, 79–82; and Geyer, *Verkehrte Welt*, 243–245.

85. Haffner, *Defying Hitler*, 57.

86. Roland Schacht, "Verteidigung des Schiebers," *Die Weltbühne* 18/50, 620 (December 14, 1922).

87. Cited in Geyer, *Verkehrte Welt*, 283. See Herbert, *Geschichte Deutschlands im 20. Jahrhundert*, 205.

88. Mann, *Turning Point*, position 2535.

89. Ilja Ehrenburg, *Menschen, Jahre, Leben: Memoiren*, vol. 2, 2nd ed. (Berlin, 1982), 9. See Taylor, *Inflation*, 278.

90. Zweig, *World of Yesterday*, 218. See Robert Beachy, *Das andere Berlin: Die Erfindung der Homosexualität—Eine deutsche Geschichte 1867–1933* (Munich, 2015), 285ff.

91. See Friedrich, *Morgen ist Weltuntergang*, 163; and Taylor, *Inflation*, 280.

92. Curt Riess, *Das waren Zeiten: Eine nostalgische Autobiographie mit vielen Mitwirkenden* (Vienna, 1977), 106–107. See also Glatzer, *Berlin zur Weimarer Zeit*, 124–125.

93. Haffner, *Defying Hitler*, 56–57.

94. German original: Warum denn weinen, wenn man auseinandergeht, / Wenn an der nächsten Ecke schon ein andrer steht. Zuckmayer, *Als wär's ein Stück von mir*, 307.

95. See Geyer, *Verkehrte Welt*, 266.

96. Mann, *Turning Point*, position 2496. See also Geyer, *Verkehrte Welt*, 266.

97. Zweig, *World of Yesterday*, 239.

98. Klemperer, *Tagebücher 1918–1924*, 666 (March 2, 1923).

99. Peter Panter (Kurt Tucholsky), "Ein deutsches Volkslied," *Die Weltbühne* 18/50 (December 14, 1922), 623–624; also in Tucholsky, *Gesammelte Werke*, vol. 3: *1921–1924*, ed. Mary Gerold-Tucholsky and Fritz J. Raddatz (Reinbek bei Hamburg, 1975), 294–295. See also Ostwald, *Sittengeschichte der Inflation*, 217–219.

100. See Lother Fischer, *Anita Berber: Die Göttin der Nacht* (Berlin, 2007); and Johanna Adoria, "Das nackte Leben," www.spiegel.de (August 6, 2006). On the "strip artists," see Ostwald, *Sittengeschichte der Inflation*, 135–146.

101. Egon Erwin Kisch, "Elliptische Tretmühle," in *Der rasende Reporter: Hetzjagd durch die Zeit—Wagnisse in aller Welt, Kriminalistisches Reisebuch* (Berlin, 1978), 234–238 (here 234). On the *Sechstagerennen*, see Riess, *Das waren Zeiten*, 109–111; and Hans Ulrich Gumbrecht, *1926: Ein Jahr am Rand der Zeit*, 3rd ed. (Frankfurt, 2020), 221–225.

102. See Benjamin Maack, "Fahren, feiern, umfallen," www.spiegel.de (January 22,

2008); David Clay Large, *Berlin: Biographie einer Stadt* (Munich, 2002), 177; Curt Riess, "Weltbühne Berlin," in *Alltag in der Weimarer Republik: Erinnerungen an eine unruhige Zeit*, ed. Rudolf Pörtner (Düsseldorf, 1990), 32–56 (see 46–47).

103. See Martynkewicz, *1920*, 258–261; and Hermann von Wedderkop, "Hans Breitenstäter: 'Kein Mensch macht Halt vor dieser prachtvollen Vitalität,'" *Die Weltbühne* 17/38 (September 22, 1921), 297.

104. Trude Hesterberg, *Was ich noch sagen wollte . . . Autobiographische Aufzeichnungen* (Berlin, 1971), 89.

105. Ostwald, *Sittengeschichte der Inflation*, 126.

106. See Geyer, *Verkehrte Welt*, 249.

107. Von zu Sonntag, "Gärung," *Deutsche Allgemeine Sonntag Zeitung* 348 (July 29, 1923).

108. Friedrich Kroner, "Überreizte Nerven," *Berliner Illustrierte Zeitung* 34 (August 26, 1923); and Ostwald, *Sittengeschichte der deutschen Inflation*, 74. See also Peter Longerich, ed., *Die Erste Republik: Dokumente zur Geschichte des Weimarer Staates* (Munich, 1992), 169.

109. Haffner, *Defying Hitler*, 60.

110. "Selbsthilfe des Mittelstandes," *Niederdeutsche Zeitung* (November 26, 1922), cited in Taylor, *Inflation*, 279–280.

111. See Ostwald, *Sittengeschichte der deutschen Inflation*, 27–28; Geyer, *Verkehrte Welt*, 261–262; Large, *Berlin*, 176; and Glatzer, *Berlin zur Weimarer Zeit*, 123–124.

112. See Taylor, *Inflation*, 268; and Geyer, *Verkehrte Welt*, 185–186.

113. Hans Fallada, *Wolf among Wolves*, no translator given (New York, 1938), 16.

**Chapter 3:** An Attempt at Crisis Management: Stresemann's Grand Coalition

1. Morus (Richard Lewinsohn), "Der Wendepunkt," *Die Weltbühne* 19/35 (August 30, 1923), 222.

2. T[heodor] W[olff], "Stresemann," *Berliner Tageblatt* 376 (August 13, 1923); also in Sösemann, ed., *Theodor Wolff*, 184–186.

3. See Wright, *Gustav Stresemann*, as well as two succinct but precise biographies: Eberhard Kolb, *Gustav Stresemann* (Munich, 2003); and Manfred Berg, *Gustav Stresemann: Eine politische Karriere zwischen Reich und Republik* (Göttingen, 1992). On Stresemann's speaking talent, see Pohl, *Gustav Stresemann*, 64–67.

4. Kurt Koszyk, *Gustav Stresemann: Der kaisertreue Demokrat—Eine Biographie* (Cologne, 1989), 188.

5. The German original reads, "Jeder weiß, dass Stresemann / mal so und manchmal anders kann." Stockhausen, *Sechs Jahre Reichskanzlei*, 73.

6. "Ebert an Stresemann, 14.8.1923," *AdR: Die Kabinette Stresemann I und II*, vol. 1: *13.8. bis 6.10.1923*, ed. Karl Dietrich Erdmann and Martin Vogt (Boppard am Rhein, 1978), no. 2, 3–4. See also Mühlhausen, *Friedrich Ebert*, 619–620, 622–623.

7.   On the formation of the cabinet, see *AdR: Die Kabinette Stresemann*, vol. 1, xxvii–xxx; Wright, *Gustav Stresemann*, 218–221; John P. Birkelund, *Gustav Stresemann: Patriot und Staatsmann—Eine Biographie* (Hamburg, 2003), 283–291; Richter, *Deutsche Volkspartei*, 273–274; Mühlhausen, *Friedrich Ebert*, 620–621; and Winkler, *Weimar*, 204–205.

8.   "Dr. Peter Bergell an Stresemann, 19.8.1923," in Stresemann, *Vermächtnis*, vol. 1, 92–93. On Stresemann's health, see Koszyk, *Gustav Stresemann*, 212–217; and Pohl, *Gustav Stresemann*, 54–64.

9.   D'Abernon, *Ambassador*, 237 (August 17, 1923). See also Stresemann's letter to the Sueva fraternity of August 20, 1923: "It takes mighty optimism to take the captain's bridge on the Reich ship." Pohl, *Gustav Stresemann*, 227.

10.  Radbruch, *Der innere Weg*, 169.

11.  "Auszug aus der Regierungserklärung Stresemanns, 14.8.1923," *Ursachen und Folgen*, vol. 5, no. 1064a, 172–174; also in Stresemann, *Vermächtnis*, vol. 1, 90–91.

12.  Georg Bernhard, "Stresemanns Rede," *Vossische Zeitung* 383 (August 15, 1923).

13.  Erich Dombrowski, "Die Reichstagssitzung," *Berliner Tageblatt* 379 (August 15, 1923).

14.  See "Auszug aus der Rede Hergts," *Ursachen und Folgen*, vol. 5, no. 1064d, 176–177.

15.  *Vorwärts* 377 (August 15, 1923), in Mühlhausen, *Friedrich Ebert*, 622.

16.  On the vote, see Alfred Kastning, *Die deutsche Sozialdemokratie zwischen Koalition und Opposition 1919–1923* (Paderborn, 1970), 115–116; Winkler, *Weimar*, 205; and Richter, *Deutsche Volkspartei*, 275.

17.  See Richter, *Deutsche Volkspartei*, 276; and *AdR: Die Kabinette Stresemann*, vol. 1, xxvii.

18.  Friedrich Meinecke, *Neue Freie Presse* (Vienna) (August 26, 1923), *AdR: Die Kabinette Stresemann*, vol. 1, xxvi–xxvii.

19.  Georg Bernhard, "Der neue Kanzler," *Vossische Zeitung* 380 (August 13, 1923).

20.  Erich Dombrowski, "Die neuen Männer," *Berliner Tageblatt* 377 (August 14, 1923).

21.  *Das Tage-Buch* 34/4 (August 25, 1923), 1184.

22.  Winkler, *Von der Revolution zur Stabilisierung*, 604.

23.  Hugenberg to Stinnes (August 11, 1923), in Feldman, *Great Disorder*, 697. See also Feldman, *Hugo Stinnes*, 884.

24.  *Deutsche Allgemeine Zeitung* 373 (August 15, 1923).

25.  Georg Bernhard, "Gerade Linie," *Vossische Zeitung* 391 (August 19, 1923).

26.  "Hamm an Stresemann, 16.8.1923," *AdR: Die Kabinette Stresemann*, vol. 1, no. 6, 11–17. At the meeting of state premiers on August 17, 1923, Knilling described Stresemann as a man "who tends to go back and forth and from whom it is to be feared that he will give in all too easily to pressure from the Left." Ernst Deuerlein, ed., *Der Hitler-Putsch: Bayerische Dokumente zum 8/9 November 1923* (Stuttgart, 1962), doc. 1, 159.

27.  "Stresemann an von Knilling, 18.8.1923," *AdR: Die Kabinette Stresemann*, vol. 1, no. 11, 33–37 (here 34).

28. Stresemann, *Vermächtnis*, vol. 1, 99 (August 25, 1923); and *AdR: Die Kabinette Stresemann*, vol. 1, no. 25, 126 (August 27, 1923).

29. Kolb, *Gustav Stresemann*, 76.

30. *AdR: Die Kabinette Stresemann*, vol. 1, no. 14, 56–60 (here 58).

31. "Aufzeichnung Stresemanns über die Unterredung mit Wolff, 21.8.1923," in Stresemann, *Vermächtnis*, vol. 1, 94–95.

32. Morus (Richard Lewinsohn), "Der Wendepunkt," *Die Weltbühne* 19/35, 223 (August 30, 1923).

33. "Kabinettssitzung v. 23.8.1923," *AdR: Die Kabinette Stresemann*, vol. 1, no. 18, 75–83 (here 80).

34. "Kabinettssitzung v. 23.8.1923," 83.

35. D'Abernon, *Ambassador*, 244 (August 30, 1923).

36. "Auszug aus der Rede Stresemanns v. 2.9.1923," *Ursachen und Folgen*, vol. 5, no. 1071, 191–192. See also Stresemann, *Vermächtnis*, vol. 1, 100–101.

37. Georg Bernhard, "Bravo, Kanzler!" *Vossische Zeitung* 426 (September 3, 1923).

38. T[heodor] W[olff], "Die Rede Stresemanns in Stuttgart," *Berliner Tageblatt* 412 (September 3, 1923).

39. Stresemann, *Vermächtnis*, vol. 1, 107.

40. *AdR: Die Kabinette Stresemann*, vol. 1, no. 18, 75.

41. Stresemann, *Vermächtnis*, vol. 1, 105–106.

42. "Aufzeichnung Stresemanns über die Besprechung mit de Margerie, 4.9.1923," in Stresemann, *Vermächtnis*, vol. 1, 101–105 (here 102). See also *Ursachen und Folgen*, vol. 5, no. 1073, 193–196.

43. *AdR: Die Kabinette Stresemann*, vol. 1, no. 47, 204–213 (here 204–205).

44. *AdR: Stresemann*, vol. 1, no. 59, 273–284 (here 281).

45. *AdR: Stresemann*, vol. 1, no. 61, 290–294 (here 290).

46. *AdR: Stresemann*, vol. 1, no. 62, 294–295.

47. *AdR: Stresemann*, vol. 1, no. 64, 299–305 (here 301).

48. See Stresemann, *Vermächtnis*, vol. 1, 128.

49. "Kabinettssitzung v. 20.9.1923," *AdR: Die Kabinette Stresemann*, vol. 1, no. 71, 19–325 (here 320).

50. "Kabinettssitzung v. 20.9.1923," *AdR: Stresemann*, vol. 1, no. 76, 334–338 (here 334–335, 338).

51. *AdR: Stresemann*, vol. 1, no. 77, 339–345 (here 344). The state secretary in the Reich Chancellery, Werner von Rheinbaben, remembered Jarres calling out in Stresemann's presence, "All of nationalist Germany is covering its head." Rheinbaben, *Kaiser, Kanzler, Präsidenten: Erinnerungen* (Mainz, 1968), 217.

52. *AdR: Die Kabinette Stresemann*, vol. 1, no. 79, 349–356, and no. 80, 356–361.

53. "Der Aufruf vom 26.9.1923," *Ursachen und Folgen*, vol. 5, no. 1079, 203–204.

54. "Aufzeichnung Stresemanns v. 27.9.1923," in Stresemann, *Vermächtnis*, vol. 1, 135–137 (here 136).

55. "Die Ruhrbevölkerung zur Einstellung des passiven Widerstands," *Berliner Tageblatt* 452 (September 26, 1923).

56. *AdR: Die Kabinette Stresemann*, vol. 1, no. 60, 285.

57. See Koszyk, *Gustav Stresemann*, 262; and Berg, *Gustav Stresemann*, 74. On the

stance of the *Rheinisch-Westfälische Zeitung* in the Ruhr conflict, see Stefan Frech, *Wegbereiter Hitlers? Theodor Reismann-Grone: Ein völkischer Nationalist (1863–1949)* (Paderborn, 2009), 271–272. The Ruhr industrialist Paul Reusch also condemned Stresemann as the "chancellor of capitulation." Gerald D. Feldman and Heidrun Homburg, *Industrie und Inflation: Studien und Dokumente zur Politik der deutschen Unternehmer, 1916–1923* (Hamburg, 1977), 143.

58.  Carl von Ossietzky, "Wie der Ruhrkampf verloren ging," *Berliner Volks-Zeitung* (September 27, 1923); and Ossietzky, *Sämtliche Schriften*, vol. 2, 299.

59.  "Der Vertreter der Reichsregierung in München, Edgar von Haniel, an die Reichskanzlei, 27.9.1923," *AdR: Die Kabinette Stresemann*, vol. 1, no. 84, 387–389. See also "Aufzeichnung Stresemanns über das Telefonat mit von Knilling v. 27.9.1923," in Stresemann, *Vermächtnis*, vol. 1, 132–133.

60.  See Winkler, *Weimar*, 210. On the emergency powers act, see Mühlhausen, *Friedrich Ebert*, 625–628; and "Befehl Geßlers über die Handhabung der vollziehenden Gewalt durch die Militärbefehlshaber, 27.9.1923," in Hürten, ed., *Krisenjahr 1923*, no. 34, 71.

61.  *AdR: Die Kabinette Stresemann*, vol. 1, no. 83, 378–398 (here 383, 382).

62.  *AdR: Stresemann*, vol. 1, no. 94, 410–415 (here 411, 413).

63.  "Ministerrat v. 1.10.1923," *AdR: Stresemann*, vol. 1, no. 97, 417–421 (here 425). See Mühlhausen, *Friedrich Ebert*, 631.

64.  *AdR: Stresemann*, vol. 1, no. 94, 414.

65.  Deuerlein, ed., *Hitler-Putsch*, 74–76, note 71. See also Meier-Welcker, *Seeckt*, 378–379.

66.  Georg Bernhard, "Bayern," *Vossische Zeitung* 463 (September 30, 1923).

67.  See Winkler, *Weimar*, 211, 223; Mühlhausen, *Friedrich Ebert*, 631–632, 676–677; and Meier-Welcker, *Seeckt*, 380–384. On the conflicts surrounding the ban on the *Völkischer Beobachter*, see "Stresemann an von Knilling, 20.10.1923," in Deuerlein, ed., *Hitler-Putsch*, doc. 55, 245–249; and "Ausführungen Stresemanns und Geßlers in der Sitzung der Ministerpräsidenten und der Gesandten der Länder in der Reichskanzlei am 24.10.1923," *AdR: Die Kabinette Stresemann*, vol. 2, no. 174, 730–746.

68.  See Wright, *Gustav Stresemann*, 231; and Kolb, *Gustav Stresemann*, 82.

69.  "Stresemann an Stinnes, 12.10.1923," *AdR: Die Kabinette Stresemann*, vol. 2, no. 131, 560–562 (here 561).

70.  "Kabinettssitzung v. 10.10.1923," *AdR: Stresemann*, vol. 2, no. 125, 524–535 (here 529). On the MICUM negotiations, see Wulf, *Hugo Stinnes*, 393ff.

71.  *Ursachen und Folgen*, vol. 5, no. 1081, 206–207.

72.  Winkler, *Weimar*, 216. See also Winkler, *Von der Revolution zur Stabilisierung*, 625–626; and Feldman and Homburg, *Industrie und Inflation*, 147–148.

73.  "Ein Arbeiterführer," *Deutsche Allgemeine Zeitung* 452 (September 29, 1923).

74.  Richter, *Deutsche Volkspartei*, 281–282. See also Winkler, *Weimar*, 218.

75.  *AdR: Die Kabinette Stresemann*, vol. 1, no. 97, 429–430. See Winkler, *Weimar*, 216–217; and Winkler, *Von der Revolution zur Stabilisierung*, 626–627.

76.  *AdR: Stresemann*, vol. 1, no. 99, 436–444 (here 437, 439).

77.  Ernst Feder, "Die Streitpunkte," *Berliner Tageblatt* 464 (October 3, 1923).

78. "Worum geht's?" *Deutsche Allgemeine Zeitung* 459 (October 4, 1923).

79.· Georg Bernhard, "Die nächste Aufgabe," *Vossische Zeitung* 471 (October 5, 1923). See also "Politischer Hexensabbath," *Die Weltbühne* 19/41 (October 11, 1923), 350–351: "The attack on Stresemann himself began when he was stabbed in the back by Mr. Scholz, the parliamentary leaders of the DVP. . . . The voice was Mr. Scholz's, but the hands belonged to Stinnes and Hugenberg."

80. *Das Tage-Buch* 40/4 (October 6, 1923), 1389–1390.

81. *AdR: Die Kabinette Stresemann*, vol. 1, no. 97, 444.

82. *AdR: Stresemann*, vol. 1, no. 100, 444–445. See also "Rücktrittsschreiben von Raumers an Stresemann v. 2.10.1923," in vol. 1, no. 101, 446.

83. *AdR: Stresemann*, vol. 1, no. 102, 447–452 (here 451). See also Winkler, *Weimar*, 218–219; and Winkler, *Von der Revolution zur Stabilisierung*, 630.

84. *AdR: Stresemann*, vol. 1, no. 106, 459–462 (here 460). On the decision of the SPD parliamentary group, see vol. 1, no. 105, 458, note 6.

85. Stresemann, *Vermächtnis*, vol. 1, 145; and W. Stresemann, *Mein Vater Gustav Stresemann*, 243.

86. Erich Dombrowski, "Die Krise: Was nun?" *Berliner Tageblatt* 465 (October 4, 1923).

87. Georg Bernhard, "Wie es kam," *Vossische Zeitung* 469 (October 4, 1923).

88. See Winkler, *Weimar*, 202–203; Richter, *Deutsche Volkspartei*, 285; and Wright, *Gustav Stresemann*, 227–228.

89. "Aufzeichnung über die Besprechung der Führer der Koalitionsparteien beim Reichskanzler, 5.10.1923," *AdR: Die Kabinette Stresemann*, vol. 1, no. 113, 484–485.

90. See Winkler, *Weimar*, 221–222; and Richter, *Deutsche Volkspartei*, 286. Helfferich greeted the new finance minister with the historical words with which Martin Luther had once been received in Worms: "Little monk, it is an arduous path you are taking." Hans Luther, *Politiker ohne Partei: Erinnerungen* (Stuttgart, 1960), 120.

91. Erich Dombrowski, "Die gestrige Reichstagssitzung," *Berliner Tageblatt* 471 (October 7, 1923). On the physical stress Stresemann went through during this time, see W. Stresemann, *Mein Vater Gustav Stresemann*, 246–247.

92. "Auszug aus der Programmrede Stresemanns v. 6.10.1923," *Ursachen und Folgen*, vol. 5, no. 1085, 211–221 (here 215, 217, 221).

93. "Auszug aus der Rede von Westarps v. 8.10.1923," *Ursachen und Folgen*, vol. 5, no. 1088c, 234–236 (here 235).

94. Georg Bernhard, "Die Abfuhr," *Vossische Zeitung* 477 (October 9, 1923), which also contains the chancellor's speech under the headline "Stresemann's Final Reckoning with the Ultranationalists."

95. Stresemann, *Vermächtnis*, vol. 1, 155.

96. Houghton's diary on October 6, 1923, read, "All here agree that the Cabinet will be short-lived." Cited in Mühlhausen, *Friedrich Ebert*, 636, note 196. See also Klemperer, *Tagebücher 1918–1924*, 751 (October 9, 1923): "Stresemann's cabinet has been patched up and can only hold together for days."

97. "Vor der Abstimmung über das Ermächtigungsgesetz," *Berliner Tageblatt* 477

(October 11, 1923). See also *Vossische Zeitung* 480 (October 10, 1923): "It's a true path of thorns the Stresemann government is having to go down. Above all, the duty of the coalition parties is at least not to make things more difficult internally for their political leadership and grant it the freedom to take rapid action."

98. See "Stresemanns Ausführungen in der Kabinettssitzung v. 11.10.1923," *AdR: Die Kabinette Stresemann*, vol. 2, no. 128, 543. See also Mühlhausen, *Friedrich Ebert*, 637.

99. *Vossische Zeitung* 486 (October 13, 1923).

100. See Winkler, *Weimar*, 222; and Richter, *Deutsche Volkspartei*, 287.

101. "Entwurf des Ermächtigungsgesetzes," *AdR: Die Kabinette Stresemann*, vol. 2, no. 117, 499–500.

102. Georg Bernhard, "Die Ermächtigung," *Vossische Zeitung* 487 (October 14, 1923). See also Theodor Wolff's editorial in *Berliner Tageblatt* 484 (October 15, 1923).

103. See Taylor, *Inflation*, 293; and Winkler, *Von der Revolution zur Stabilisierung*, 609. See Erich Dombrowski, "Die Forderung der Stunde," *Berliner Tageblatt* 410 (September 1, 1923): "The decline in the currency has gotten so bad that for all intents the value of the paper can be measured as just the ever longer series of zeroes behind the first number."

104. Klemperer, *Tagebücher 1918–1924*, 740 (August 27, 1923), and 741 (September 6, 1923). See Pringsheim, *Tagebücher*, vol. 7, 91 (August 25, 1923): "Inflation races on!"

105. Klemperer, *Tagebücher*, 748 (September 30, 1923).

106. *Berliner Tageblatt* 411 (September 2, 1923; supplement).

107. "Die Gewerkschaftsverbände an die Reichsregierung, 28.9.1923," *AdR: Die Kabinette Stresemann*, vol. 1, no. 90, 401–403 (here 401, 402).

108. Klemperer, *Tagebücher 1918–1924*, 749 (October 4, 1923).

109. Taylor, *Inflation*, 291.

110. Betty Scholem and Gershom Scholem, *Mutter und Sohn im Briefwechsel 1917–1948*, ed. Itta Shedletzky with Thomas Sparr (Munich, 1989), 83 (October 9, 1923).

111. Scholem and Scholem, *Mutter und Sohn*, 84–85. (October 15, 1923).

112. "Besprechung über die Währungssanierung, 18.8.1923," *AdR: Die Kabinette Stresemann*, vol. 1, no. 9, 23–29 (here 24). "Auszug aus dem Projekt Helfferichs," *Ursachen und Folgen*, vol. 5, no. 1225, 546–549. See also William Smaldone, *Rudolf Hilferding: Tragödie eines deutschen Sozialdemokraten* (Bonn, 2000), 163–167; Claus-Dieter Krohn, "Helfferich contra Hilferding: Konservative Geldpolitik und die sozialen Folgen der Inflation 1918–1923," *Vierteljahrsschrift für Sozial- und Wirtschaftsgeschichte* 62 (1975): 62–92; and Feldman, *Great Disorder*, 708ff. For a summary, see Winkler, *Von der Revolution zur Stabilisierung*, 610–612; and *AdR: Die Kabinette Stresemann*, vol. 1, lxxvi–lxxxi.

113. See Krohn, "Helfferich contra Hilferding," 87.

114. *AdR: Die Kabinette Stresemann*, vol. 1, no. 33, 164.

115. See "Kabinettssitzungen v. 7.9.1923" and "Kabinettssitzungen v. 10.9.1923," *AdR: Die Kabinette Stresemann*, vol. 1, no. 47, 208–213, and no. 51, 224–228.

116. See Theodor Wolff's editorial, *Berliner Tageblatt* 424 (September 10, 1923).

117. See "Ausführungen Hilferdings in der Kabinettsitzung v. 13.9.1923," *AdR: Die Kabinette Stresemann*, vol. 1, no. 55, 257; "Stellungnahme der Reichsbank," vol. 1, no. 55, 257, note 20; and "Aufzeichnung des Ministerialrats Kiep v. 18.9.1923," vol. 1, no. 66, 308.

118. "Kabinettssitzung vom 13.9.1923," *AdR: Die Kabinette Stresemann*, vol. 1, no. 55, 256–261 (here 261, 258).

119. For Richter to Hilferding on September 26, 1923, see Feldman, *Great Disorder*, 732–733.

120. See "Kabinettssitzung v. 26.9.1923," *AdR: Die Kabinette Stresemann*, vol. 1, lxxx, and no. 82, 375–376; and "Die neue deutsche Goldwährung," *Vossische Zeitung* 442 (September 18, 1923).

121. Richard Lewinsohn, "Die Bodenmark," *Vossische Zeitung* 450 (September 22, 1923).

122. Luther, *Politiker ohne Partei*, 115. Prussian state premier Otto Braun claimed to have told Stresemann he considered Hilferding a "valuable expert adviser for a decisive minister" but "too clever" to be a minister himself. Braun, *Von Weimar zu Hitler* (Hamburg, 1949), 52. Leopold Schwarzschild criticized Hilferding for not believing himself in the effectiveness of the measures that bore his name. Schwarzschild wrote, "In this time of extraordinary need for action, we don't need a critical, dialectically inclined, exhausted pessimist at the head of the German financial administration, but rather a constructive, go-getting, relentless optimist. He who wants reform has to believe in it." *Das Tage-Buch* 40/4 (October 6, 1923), 1413.

123. See *AdR: Die Kabinette Stresemann*, vol. 1, 83–84; "Kabinettssitzung v. 15.10.1923," *AdR: Stresemann*, vol. 2, no. 136, 578–580; "Die Grundlagen der neuen Währung," *Vossische Zeitung* 490 (October 16, 1923); and Erich Dombrowski, "Die Rentenbank," *Berliner Tageblatt* 486 (October 16, 1923).

124. Richard Lewinsohn, "Die Rentenbank," *Vossische Zeitung* 491 (October 17, 1923).

125. *AdR: Die Kabinette Stresemann*, vol. 2, no. 136, 576. See also "Entwurf der Note an die Reparationskommission v. 4.10.1923," *AdR: Stresemann*, vol. 1, no. 110, 473.

126. D'Abernon, *Ambassador*, 268 (October 29, 1923). See also *AdR: Die Kabinette Stresemann*, vol. 1, 81–84; Winkler, *Weimar*, 232–233; and "Der 'Umschwung' in Paris," *Vossische Zeitung* 510 (October 27, 1923).

*Chapter 4:* THE GERMAN OCTOBER

1. Ludwig Quessel, "Jusqu'au bout?" *Die Weltbühne* 19/37 (September 13, 1923), 253. In late September 1923, BVP politician and forestry councilor Georg Escherich noted, "The mark and Germany are speeding rapidly downhill!" N 1, Georg Escherich 10, BayHStA.

2. Klemperer, *Tagebücher 1918–1924*, 253 (October 14, 1923). See also Pringsheim, *Tagebücher*, vol. 7, 99 (October 4, 1923): "Politics, chaos, abyss."

3.   "Stalin to Zinoviev on August 7, 1923," in *Deutscher Oktober: Ein Revolutions-plan und sein Scheitern*, ed. Bernhard H. Bayerlein et al. (Berlin, 2003), doc. 5, 99–100; and "Zinoviev to Brandler and Thalheimer on July 27, 1923," doc. 3, 95–96.

4.   Fridrich I. Firsov, "Ein Oktober, der nicht stattfand: Die revolutionären Pläne der RKP und der Komintern," in *Deutscher Oktober*, 35–58 (here 39). For an excerpt from the first draft of Zinoviev's guidelines, see doc. 7, 103–104.

5.   "Konspekt der Debatte des Politbüros des ZK der RKP über die 'deutsche Revolution,'" in *Deutscher Oktober*, doc. 10, 116–126 (here 123–124).

6.   "Beschluss des Politbüros des ZK der RKP, 22.8.1923," in *Deutscher Oktober*, doc. 12, 130–131; and "Mitteilung Josef Unschlichts über seine geheime Mission in Deutschland," doc. 16, 138. See also Firsov, "Ein Oktober," 41.

7.   See Hugo Eberlein's report to Comintern on August 15, 1923, in *Deutscher Oktober*, doc. 8, 105–110 (here 105).

8.   See Angress, *Stillborn Revolution*, 433; Winkler, *Weimar*, 214–215; and August Thalheimer, *1923: Eine verpasste Revolution? Die deutsche Oktoberlegende und die wirkliche Geschichte von 1923* (Berlin, 1931), 21: "The schema of October 1917 was transferred to Germany without the same situation existing on the ground."

9.   "Protokoll der geheimen Moskauer Konferenz der russischen Mitglieder des EKKI mit der Delegation der KPD, der KP Frankreichs und der KP der Tschechoslowakei, 25.9.1923," in *Deutscher Oktober*, doc. 22, 162–178 (here 163, 165). On Brandler's change of heart, see also Angress, *Stillborn Revolution*, 433–436; and Jens Becker, *Heinrich Brandler: Eine politische Biographie* (Hamburg, 2001), 223–227.

10.  See also "Telegramm Sinowjews an die Zentrale der KPD, 1.10.1923," in *Deutscher Oktober*, doc. 28, 187; "Protokoll der Sitzung des Politbüros des ZK der RKP, 4.10.1923," doc. 31, 195–197; and Firsov, "Ein Oktober," 47.

11.  See Karsten Rudolph, *Die sächsische Sozialdemokratie vom Kaiserreich zur Republik (1871–1923)* (Weimar, 1995), 220ff.; Winkler, *Weimar*, 191–192; and Mühlhausen, *Friedrich Ebert*, 641ff.

12.  "Richtlinien von SPD und KPD für die künftige Politik in Sachsen," *Ursachen und Folgen*, vol. 5, no. 1192, 473–475.

13.  On Zeigner's biography, see also Michael Rudloff, ed., *Erich Zeigner: Bildungsbürger und Sozialdemokrat* (Leipzig, 1999); and Rudolph, *Die sächsische Sozialdemokratie*, 344–345.

14.  *AdR: Das Kabinett Cuno*, no. 119, 375, note 18.

15.  "Meldung Müllers an das Gruppenkommando I, 12.4.1923," in Hürten, ed., *Krisenjahr 1923*, doc. 11, 26–27.

16.  *AdR: Das Kabinett Cuno*, no. 215, 638, note 6.

17.  See also Helmut Gast, "Die proletarischen Hundertschaften als Organe der Einheitsfront im Jahre 1923," *Zeitschrift für Geschichtswissenschaft* 4 (1956): 439–465; and Winkler, *Von der Revolution zur Stabilisierung*, 620–621.

18.  "Besprechung mit Vertretern des Verbandes Sächsischer Industrieller, 19.6.1923," *AdR: Das Kabinett Cuno*, no. 197, 590–592 (here 591, 592).

19.  "Besprechung mit dem sächsischen Ministerpräsidenten, 10.7.1923," *AdR: Das*

*Kabinett Cuno*, no. 215, 636–639 (here 636); and "Auszug aus der Rede Zeigners v. 16.6.1923 nach dem Bericht der Sächsischen Volkszeitung," on 637, note 4. See also Rudolph, *Die sächsische Sozialdemokratie*, 359–360.

20. "Ministerrat beim Reichspräsidenten, 10.8.1923," *AdR: Das Kabinett Cuno*, no. 244, 731. On Zeigner's speech in Leipzig, see no. 241, 725, note 7; and Hürten, ed., *Krisenjahr 1923*, doc. 28, 62, note 1. See also Mühlhausen, *Friedrich Ebert*, 644; and Rudolph, *Die sächsische Sozialdemokratie*, 370.

21. "Schreiben des Befehlshabers im Wehrkreis IV, General Müller, an Zeigner, 10.8.1923," in Hürten, ed., *Krisenjahr 1923*, doc. 28, 62.

22. Klemperer, *Tagebücher 1918–1924*, 733 (August 13, 1923). Heinrich Mann wrote to Félix Bertaux on August 16, 1923: "With conditions the way they are, it's difficult to speak ceremoniously. I did the opposite of that. I only satisfied the Saxon government, which was my intent since I wanted to support it." Mann and Bertaux, *Briefwechsel*, 68.

23. "Auszug aus der Rede Heinrich Manns," in Hürten, ed., *Krisenjahr 1923*, doc. 31, 66–67, note 2. See also Rudolph, *Die sächsische Sozialdemokratie*, 344. Reichswehr Minister Gessler composed a written complaint about Mann's speech, saying that it was only by refusing to take part in the celebrations of the Constitution that the armed forces and its representatives had been spared having to listen to "the highest institutions of the Reich, the Reichstag and the constitutional government at the time being defamed." *Krisenjahr 1923*, doc. 31, 66–67.

24. "Kommuniqué über die Aussprache zwischen Stresemann und Zeigner, 17.8.1923," *AdR: Die Kabinette Stresemann*, vol. 1, no. 7, 17–18. See also Rudolph, *Die sächsische Sozialdemokratie*, 373–374.

25. Stresemann reported about his second meeting with Zeigner in a letter to SPD chairman Otto Wels on August 27, 1923. See *AdR: Die Kabinette Stresemann*, vol. 1, no. 26, 130–132.

26. "Generalsekretär Johannes Dieckmann an Stresemann, 24.8.1923," *AdR: Stresemann*, vol. 1, no. 23, 98–101 (here 100).

27. "Geßler an Stresemann, 22.8.1923, mit anliegender Denkschrift," *AdR: Stresemann*, vol. 1, no. 17, 68–74 (here 69). Justice Minister Radbruch saw nothing prosecutable about Zeigner's speech. See "Radbruch and Stresemann, 27.8.1923," vol. 1, no. 17, 68–74. See also Mühlhausen, *Friedrich Ebert*, 646, note 237.

28. *AdR: Stresemann*, vol. 1, no. 51, 223. See also Mühlhausen, *Friedrich Ebert*, 647.

29. See Mühlhausen, *Friedrich Ebert*, 647–648. On the situation in Thuringia in 1923, see Erhard Wörfel, *Die Arbeiterregierung in Thüringen im Jahre 1923* (Erfurt, 1974).

30. "Besprechung mit Sachsen, 11.9.1923," *AdR: Die Kabinette Stresemann*, vol. 1, no. 53, 238–243. See Rudolph, *Die sächsische Sozialdemokratie*, 377.

31. Reproduced in *Ursachen und Folgen*, vol. 5, no. 1195a, 478–479.

32. Stresemann, *Vermächtnis*, vol. 1, 117–118. In a letter to Stresemann on September 22, 1923, Willi Brüninghaus warned that "if nothing happens immediately, the rule of the street, alias communism, will spread." *AdR: Die Kabinette Stresemann*, vol. 1, no. 75, 332–333.

33. "Reinhardt an das thüringische Staatsministerium, 28.9.1923," in Hürten, ed.,

*Krisenjahr 1923*, doc. 36, 81. On Müller's decree of September 27, 1923, see doc. 36, 81, note 2.

34.  *AdR: Die Kabinette Stresemann*, vol. 2, no. 115, 489–492 (here 492).

35.  *AdR: Stresemann*, vol. 2, no. 117, 494–498 (here 497).

36.  Cited in Heinrich Weiler, *Die Reichsexekution gegen den Freistaat Sachsen unter Reichskanzler Stresemann im Oktober 1923: Historisch-politischer Hintergrund, Verlauf und staatsrechtliche Beurteilung* (Frankfurt, 1987), 22–23. On the formation of the Rudolph government, see Rudolph, *Die sächsische Sozialdemokratie*, 389–390; and Becker, *Heinrich Brandler*, 228–229.

37.  "Auszug aus der Regierungserklärung Zeigners, 12.10.1923," *Ursachen und Folgen*, vol. 5, no. 1199b, 484–485.

38.  "Erklärung der thüringischen Landesregierung, 17.10.1923," *Ursachen und Folgen*, vol. 5, no. 1200, 487–488; and "Das Regierungsprogramm von SPD und KPD in Thüringen v. 13.10.1923," no. 1199c, 485–486.

39.  "Der Reichskommissar für die Überwachung der öffentlichen Ordnung an den Reichswehrminister, 19.10.1923," *AdR: Die Kabinette Stresemann*, vol. 2, no. 152, 640–650 (here 644, 647). See also Winkler, *Von der Revolution zur Stabilisierung*, 649.

40.  "General Müller an die sächsische Regierung, 13.10.1923," *Ursachen und Folgen*, vol. 5, no. 1199d, 486. Reinhardt had issued a similar prohibition in Thuringia on October 6, 1923. Hürten, ed., *Krisenjahr 1923*, doc. 42, 88–89.

41.  "General Müller an die sächsische Regierung, 15.10.1923," in Hürten, ed., *Krisenjahr 1923*, doc. 46, 93.

42.  "General Müller an Zeigner, 17.10.1923," *Ursachen und Folgen*, vol. 5, no. 1201, 468–469.

43.  "Sächsische Regierung an die Reichsregierung, 17.10.1923," *AdR: Die Kabinette Stresemann*, vol. 2, no. 147, 621–627.

44.  "Auszug aus der Rede Zeigners vom 18.10.1923," *Ursachen und Folgen*, vol. 5, no. 1201a, 490–492. On the reaction of the military, see "Materialsammlung des Generalleutnants Lieber vom September bis November 1923," *AdR: Die Kabinette Stresemann*, vol. 2, suppl. no. 1, 1187. See also Mühlhausen, *Friedrich Ebert*, 654; and Rudolph, *Die sächsische Sozialdemokratie*, 393.

45.  *AdR: Die Kabinette Stresemann*, vol. 2, no. 144, 612–614.

46.  *AdR: Stresemann*, vol. 2, no. 151, 639.

47.  Thalheimer, *1923*, 26. On the Chemnitz conference, see Angress, *Stillborn Revolution*, 476–477; Winkler, *Von der Revolution zur Stabilisierung*, 652; Rudolph, *Die sächsische Sozialdemokratie*, 396–398; and Becker, *Heinrich Brandler*, 234–236.

48.  See Angress, *Stillborn Revolution*, 478–479; and Winkler, *Von der Revolution zur Stabilisierung*, 652–653.

49.  Radek, "Erster Bericht an das Politbüro des ZK der RKP, 26.10.1923," in *Deutscher Oktober*, doc. 47, 253–257 (here 255). See Gutjahr, *Karl Radek*, 587–588.

50.  On the various possible explanations, see Eva Hubert, "Der 'Hamburger Aufstand' von 1923," in *Arbeiter in Hamburg*, ed. Arno Herzig, Dieter Langewiesche,

and Arnold Sywottek (Hamburg, 1983), 483–491 (here 487); and Winkler, *Von der Revolution zur Stabilisierung*, 653.

51. On the plans for the rebellion, see Heinz Habedank, *Zur Geschichte des Hamburger Aufstands 1923* (East Berlin, 1958), 101–104; and various authors, *Ernst Thälmann: Eine Biographie* (East Berlin, 1980), 181–182.

52. See Habedank, *Zur Geschichte des Hamburger Aufstands*, 117–130; Hubert, "Der 'Hamburger Aufstand,'" 487–488; and Lothar Danner, *Ordnungspolizei Hamburg: Betrachtungen zu ihrer Geschichte 1918 bis 1933* (Hamburg, 1958), 74–79.

53. Larissa Reissner, *Hamburg auf den Barrikaden: Erlebtes und Erhörtes aus dem Hamburger Aufstand 1923* (Berlin, 1925), 33. See also Habedank, *Zur Geschichte des Hamburger Aufstands*, 132–133; and Hubert, "Der 'Hamburger Aufstand,'" 488.

54. See also Habedank, *Zur Geschichte des Hamburger Aufstands*, 155–158; and Hubert, "Der 'Hamburger Aufstand,'" 488.

55. "Bericht Roses über den Hamburger Aufstand, 26.10.1923," in *Deutscher Oktober*, doc. 46, 248–250. Hamburg's legation in Berlin reported on October 23, 1923, "All is calm in the center of the city. Nor is the situation at the harbor cause for concern." *AdR: Die Kabinette Stresemann*, vol. 2, no. 168, 701.

56. See also Danner, *Ordnungspolizei Hamburg*, 104–105; and Hubert, "Der 'Hamburger Aufstand,'" 489.

57. "'Geschlossener Brief' des EKKI an die Zentrale der KPD, 5.11.1923," in *Deutscher Oktober*, doc. 64, 319–325 (here 320).

58. See, for example, Habedank, *Zur Geschichte des Hamburger Aufstands*, 133. For an example of the glorification of Thälmann in East German historiography, see various authors, *Ernst Thälmann*, 183.

59. Sternheim, *Tagebücher*, vol. 1, 652 (October 23, 1923).

60. See Walter Fabian, *Klassenkampf in Sachsen: Ein Stück Geschichte 1918–1930* (Löbau, 1930), 171–172.

61. Hermann Windschild, "Sachsen und die Folgen," *Die Weltbühne* 19/45 (November 8, 1923), 464–465.

62. "Kabinettssitzung v. 27.10.1923," *AdR: Die Kabinette Stresemann*, vol. 2, no. 186, 854–859. See also Winkler, *Von der Revolution zur Stabilisierung*, 655–656; and Mühlhausen, *Friedrich Ebert*, 658–660.

63. "Stresemann an Zeigner, 27.10.1923," *AdR: Die Kabinette Stresemann*, vol. 2, no. 188, 860–862. Also reproduced in Stresemann, *Vermächtnis*, vol. 1, 186–187.

64. "Zeigner an Stresemann, 28.10.1923," *AdR: Die Kabinette Stresemann*, vol. 2, no. 191, 868–869. On the negotiations in Dresden, see Wilhelm Dittmann, *Erinnerungen*, ed. Jürgen Rojahn, vol. 2 (Frankfurt, 1995), 867; and Mühlhausen, *Friedrich Ebert*, 661–662.

65. "Vermerk des Reichskanzlers über seine Unterredung mit den SPD-Vertretern, 28.1.1923," *AdR: Die Kabinette Stresemann*, vol. 2, no. 192, 869–870; and "Tagesnotiz Stresemann, 28.10.1923," in Stresemann, *Vermächtnis*, vol. 1, 187.

66. *Vossische Zeitung* 512 (October 29, 1923); also in *Ursachen und Folgen*, vol. 5, no. 1204e, 500.

67.  See Mühlhausen, *Friedrich Ebert*, 664–665; and "Tagesnotiz Stresemanns v. 29.10.1923," in Stresemann, *Vermächtnis*, vol. 1, 187: "R[eich] P[resident] very agitated." On Heinze's appointment, see also "Dr. Heinze Reichskommissar in Sachsen," *Vossische Zeitung* 512 (October 29, 1923). Wolfgang Stresemann recalled his father quickly coming to regret Heinze's appointment since he soon proved a clear enemy of both the chancellor and the grand coalition. See W. Stresemann, *Mein Vater Gustav Stresemann*, 271.

68.  "Parteiführerbesprechung, 29.10.1923, 11 Uhr," *AdR: Die Kabinette Stresemann*, vol. 2, no. 193, 870–874 (here 871, 873).

69.  "Kabinettssitzung, 29.10.1923, 13 Uhr," *AdR: Stresemann*, vol. 2, no. 194, 876–879.

70.  "Der Sturz der sächsischen Regierung," *Vossische Zeitung* 513 (October 30, 1923). See also Rudolph, *Die sächsische Sozialdemokratie*, 406–407.

71.  "Ministerbesprechung, 29.10.1923, 21 Uhr," *AdR: Die Kabinette Stresemann*, vol. 2, no. 195, 879–882.

72.  "Dr. Heinzes Versuche zur Regierungsbildung," *Berliner Tageblatt* 510 (October 30, 1923).

73.  On Heinze's instructions, see "Aufzeichnung Stresemann v. 29.10.1923," in Stresemann, *Vermächtnis*, vol. 1, 189–190.

74.  "Fellisch an Stresemann, 31.10.1923, 12.35 Uhr," *AdR: Die Kabinette Stresemann*, vol. 2, no. 206, 911–912. See also Winkler, *Von der Revolution zur Stabilisierung*, 657–658; Dittmann, *Erinnerungen*, vol. 2, 868–871; "Die neue Regierung in Sachsen," *Berliner Tageblatt* 511 (October 31, 1923); and "Bildung eines Übergangskabinetts Fellisch," *Vossische Zeitung* 515 (October 31, 1923).

75.  See Karsten Rudolph, "Linke Republikaner als streitbare Demokraten—Gedanken zur mitteldeutschen Geschichte: Erich Zeigner, die SPD und der 'deutsche Oktober,'" in *Deutscher Oktober*, 65–78 (here 68).

76.  "Meldung des Befehlshabers im Wehrkreis IV, General Müller, über die politische Lage in Sachsen, 6.11.1923," in Hürten, ed., *Krisenjahr 1923*, doc. 67, 115–117. See also "Zusammenfassung der vom Truppenamt vorgetragenen Beurteilung der inneren Lage, 7.12.1923," doc. 133, 193: "The consistent execution of the intended plans failed because of the vacillations of the chancellor at the time, Stresemann."

77.  "Fellisch an den Staatsgerichtshof, 6.11.1923," *AdR: Die Kabinette Stresemann*, vol. 2, no. 226, 978–983. On the constitutional considerations, see Weiler, *Die Reichsexekution*, 63ff.

78.  See Mühlhausen, *Friedrich Ebert*, 670–671.

79.  Georg Bernhard, "Recht und Macht," *Vossische Zeitung* 512 (October 29, 1923).

80.  "Ministerpräsident Frölich an Stresemann, 30.10.1923," *AdR: Die Kabinette Stresemann*, vol. 2, no. 204, 908–909.

81.  See Winkler, *Weimar*, 236; and Mühlhausen, *Friedrich Ebert*, 671–672.

82.  Stresemann, *Vermächtnis*, vol. 1, 191.

83.  See Winkler, *Weimar*, 228; and Mühlhausen, *Friedrich Ebert*, 676.

84.  On the conflicts within the SPD parliamentary group, see Kastning, *Die deutsche Sozialdemokratie*, 122–125; and Winkler, *Von der Revolution zur Stabilisierung*,

660–662. For the wording of the parliamentary group's conditions, see Stresemann, *Vermächtnis*, vol. 1, 191–192; and *Ursachen und Folgen*, vol. 5, no. 1204i, 501.

85. "Die Bedingungen der Sozialdemokratie," *Vossische Zeitung* 517 (November 1, 1923).

86. "Kabinettssitzung v. 1.11.1923," *AdR: Die Kabinette Stresemann*, vol. 2, no. 212, 935–938.

87. Winkler, *Von der Revolution zur Stabilisierung*, 663.

88. "Besprechung der bürgerlichen Kabinettsmitglieder, 2.11.1923, 11 Uhr," *AdR: Die Kabinette Stresemann*, vol. 2, no. 214, 944–947.

89. "Ministerbesprechung, 2.11.1923, 13 Uhr," *AdR: Stresemann*, vol. 2, no. 215, 948–952.

90. See *AdR: Stresemann*, vol. 2, no. 216, 954; Stresemann, *Vermächtnis*, vol. 1, 193; and "Rücktritt der sozialdemokratischen Reichsminister," *Vossische Zeitung* 521 (November 3, 1923).

91. Bernd Braun and Joachim Eichler, eds., *Arbeiterführer, Parlamentarier, Parteiveteran: Die Tagebücher des Sozialdemokraten Hermann Molkenbuhr 1905 bis 1927* (Munich, 2000), 378 (November 2, 1923). See also Robert Schmidt's notes from the parliamentary group meeting on November 2, 1923: "The damage to the party won't be that bad. The political consequences are serious. History will blame us." *AdR: Die Kabinette Stresemann*, vol. 2, no. 216, 954, note 3.

92. Erich Dombrowski, "Die Krise," *Berliner Tageblatt* 517 (November 3, 1923).

93. Georg Bernhard, "November-Verbrechen," *Vossische Zeitung* 523 (November 4, 1923).

94. "Das Ende der Großen Koalition," *Deutsche Allgemeine Zeitung* 515 (November 3, 1923).

95. *AdR: Die Kabinette Stresemann*, vol. 2, no. 212, 936.

96. "Ministerbesprechung, 5.11.1923," *AdR: Die Kabinette Stresemann*, vol. 2, no. 222, 967–968.

97. See "DDP-Abgeordnete Carl Petersen an Stresemann betr. Stellung der DDP-Fraktion zum Rumpfkabinett, 7.11.1923," *AdR: Stresemann*, vol. 2, no. 228, 990–992 (here 992).

98. *AdR: Stresemann*, vol. 2, no. 214, 947. On pressure on Stresemann from the right wing of the party, see Stresemann, *Vermächtnis*, vol. 1, 195; and Richter, *Deutsche Volkspartei*, 291–292.

*Chapter 5:* THE CALL FOR A DICTATORSHIP

1. "Botschafter Houghton an Außenminister Hughes, 23.9.1923," in George W. F. Hallgarten, *Hitler, Reichswehr und Industrie: Zur Geschichte der Jahre 1918–1933* (Frankfurt, 1955), 67–68 (the source mistakenly gives the date as September 21). See also Wulf, *Hugo Stinnes*, 456–457; Feldman, *Hugo Stinnes*, 887–888; Feldman, *Great Disorder*, 742; and Mühlhausen, *Friedrich Ebert*, 682, note

408. Escherich wrote in his diary at the end of September 1923, "We can only be saved if we succeed in increasing production with dictatorial means. Parliamentarianism will never achieve this." N 1, Escherich 10, BayHStA. On the history of the years 1918 to 1933, see Luther, *Politiker ohne Partei* (Politicians without a Party) (Stuttgart: Deutsche Verlagsanstalt, 1960), 113.

2. Kurt Sontheimer, *Antidemokratisches Denken in der Weimarer Republik: Die politischen Ideen des deutschen Nationalismus zwischen 1918 und 1933* (Munich, 1968), 214–222; and Klaus Schreiner, " 'Wann kommt der Retter Deutschlands?' Formen und Funktionen von politischem Messianismus in der Weimarer Republik," *Saeculum* 49 (1998): 107–160.

3. Cited in Geyer, *Verkehrte Welt*, 309–310.

4. See Wolfram Wette, *Gustav Noske: Eine politische Biographie* (Düsseldorf, 1987), 627ff.; and Volker Ullrich, "Marsch auf Berlin," *Die Zeit* 11 (March 11, 2010).

5. Johannes Leicht, *Heinrich Class 1868–1953: Die politische Biographie eines Alldeutschen* (Paderborn, 2012), 298–304.

6. "Georg Escherich an Hugo Stinnes, o. D., Ende 1922 (Entwurf)," N 1, Escherich 47, BayHStA.

7. Müller, *Im Wandel einer Welt*, 154. See also Matthias Berg, *Karl Alexander von Müller: Historiker für den Nationalsozialismus* (Göttingen, 2014), 89–91.

8. "Aufzeichnung Hanfstaengls: 'Der Ruf nach dem Borgia-Typ,'" NL Hanfstaengl Ana 405, carton 25, Bayerische Staatsbibliothek, München (hereafter BSB). Hanfstaengl, who later became the Nazi Party's foreign press spokesman, got his doctorate under Müller in the 1927–28 winter semester. See Berg, *Karl Alexander von Müller*, 92.

9. *AdR: Das Kabinett Cuno*, no. 233, 695, note 1.

10. *Das Tage-Buch* 32/33, vol. 4 (August 11/18, 1923), 1147–1149.

11. Cited in Heimo Schwilk, *Ernst Jünger: Ein Jahrhundertleben—Die Biographie* (Munich, 2007), 263.

12. Arthur Moeller van den Bruck, *Das dritte Reich* (Berlin, 1923), 228. See also André Schlüter, *Moeller van den Bruck: Leben und Werk* (Cologne, 2010), 347–365; and Sontheimer, *Antidemokratisches Denken*, 237–241.

13. *AdR: Die Kabinette Stresemann*, vol. 1, no. 18, 82 (August 23, 1923), and no. 94, 414 (September 30, 1923). See also Winkler, *Weimar*, 212–213.

14. "Materialsammlung Lieber v. 19. und 20.9.1923," *AdR: Die Kabinette Stresemann*, vol. 2, no. 1, 1127. See also Wulf, *Hugo Stinnes*, 453–454; and Meier-Welcker, *Seeckt*, 374. In the spring of 1924, Seeckt told Stresemann's former state secretary in the Reich Chancellery, Baron Werner von Rheinbaben, about how he was pressured and practically beseeched from on high to employ the Reichswehr to get rid of the parliamentary system, which was allegedly in its death throes, and to take a position of leadership himself. Rheinbaben, *Kaiser, Kanzler, Präsidenten*, 182–183.

15. "Materialsammlung Lieber v. 20.9., 23.9. und 24.9.1923," *AdR: Die Kabinette Stresemann*, vol. 2, suppl. no. 1, 1177–1179. See also Wulf, *Hugo Stinnes*, 454; and Meier-Welcker, *Seeckt*, 374.

16. The German original "Schildhalter Eberts" refers to the animals who hold up

a crest of arms in heraldry. See Leicht, *Heinrich Class*, 316–317, 318, 323; and Meier-Welcker, *Seeckt*, 374–375.

17. Langer, *Macht und Verantwortung*, 295–296; and Meier-Welcker, *Seeckt*, 373. See also Spengler's letter to Stresemann of October 20, 1923, in which he demanded that a cabinet be immediately formed "exclusively of men trusted by the parties of the Right" because otherwise the "demise of the economy, the Reichswehr, and the Reich" would be unavoidable. *AdR: Die Kabinette Stresemann*, vol. 2, no. 158, 674–678 (here 677).

18. "Materialsammlung Lieber v. 25.9.1923," *AdR: Die Kabinette Stresemann*, vol. 2, suppl. no. 1, 1179. On the contracts between Seeckt and Ludendorff, see Meier-Welcker, *Seeckt*, 359–360. On Minoux and his break with Stinnes in early October 1923, see Feldman, *Hugo Stinnes*, 890–893.

19. *AdR: Die Kabinette Stresemann*, vol. 2, suppl. no. 2 and 3, 1203–1206. See also Eberhard Kessel, "Seeckts politisches Programm von 1923," in *Spiegel der Geschichte: Festgabe für Max Braubach zum 10. April 1964*, ed. Konrad Repgen and Stephan Kalweit (Münster, 1964), 887–914; Wulf, *Hugo Stinnes*, 460–461; and Meier-Welcker, *Seeckt*, 391–393.

20. See Meier-Welcker, *Seeckt*, 390; and Ernst Schröder, *Otto Wiedfeldt: Eine Biographie*, 2d ed. (Neustadt, 1981), 142.

21. "Materialsammlung Lieber v. 1.10.1923," *AdR: Die Kabinette Stresemann*, vol. 2, suppl. no. 1, 1183.

22. "Überrumpelungsversuch gegen Küstrin," *Berliner Tageblatt* 460 (October 1, 1923). See also Meier-Welcker, *Seeckt*, 377–378.

23. Carl von Ossietzky, "Der Weg ins Freie," *Berliner Volks-Zeitung* (October 5, 1923); and Ossietzky, *Sämtliche Schriften*, vol. 2, 299–301 (here 299).

24. Deuerlein, ed., *Hitler-Putsch*, doc. 3, 164. See also Ullrich, *Hitler: Ascent*, 131ff.

25. "Ein Abend bei Adolf Hitler," *Kölnische Volkszeitung* 780 (November 8, 1922), NS 26/1223, Bundesarchiv (BA), Berlin-Lichterfelde.

26. Stefan Grossmann, "Die Hitlerei," *Das Tage-Buch* 16/4 (April 21, 1923), 550–554 (here 552). Hitler wanted to sue Grossmann for libel for asserting that the Nazi movement was financed with foreign, including French, money. But the lawsuit was dropped. Carl Zuckmayer, who attended several Hitler events in Munich wrote that Hitler's rhetoric developed into a "terrible, barbarically primitive effectiveness." Zuckmayer added, "He's able to put people in a trance like the medicine man of an uncivilized tribe." Zuckmayer, *Als wär's ein Stück von mir*, 377.

27. "Margarete Vollerthun an Hitler, 27.2.1923," N 1128/5, BA, Koblenz.

28. Adolf Hitler, *Sämtliche Aufzeichnungen, 1905–1924*, ed. Eberhard Jäckel with Axel Kuhn (Stuttgart, 1980), no. 436, 754 (December 4, 1922). See also Albrecht Tyrell, *Vom "Trommler" zum "Führer": Der Wandel von Hitlers Selbstverständnis zwischen 1919 und 1924 und die Entwicklung der NSDAP* (Munich, 1975).

29. *Völkischer Beobachter* (November 8, 1922), cited in Peter Longerich, *Hitler: Biographie* (Munich, 2015), 113.

30. "Rudolf Hess an Karl Alexander von Müller, 23.2.1923," N1, K. A. v. Müller 19/1, BayHStA. For the text of the prize-winning essay, see Bruno Hipler, *Hitlers Lehrmeister Karl Haushofer als Vater der NS-Ideologie* (St. Ottilien, 1996), 221–225.

31.   See Margarete Plewnia, *Auf dem Weg zu Hitler: Der völkische Publizist Dietrich Eckart* (Bremen, 1970), 90.

32.   See Wolfgang Horn, *Der Marsch zur Machtergreifung: Die NSDAP bis 1933* (Königstein, 1980), 104. A similar tone was struck in Hitler's volume of biography and speeches, *Adolf Hitler: Sein Leben, seine Reden*: "Before our gleaming eyes, the Führer is growing taller, larger, more mature and more delightful from day to day. This man, who has raised hundreds of thousands from the filth of the new German 'freedom,' is helping legions of desperate people back to their feet." *Adolf Hitler*, ed. Adolf-Victor von Koerber (Munich, 1923), 9. Winfried Meyer has convincingly disproved Thomas Weber's thesis that Hitler himself wrote the biographical sketch at the beginning of this volume. See Meyer, "Eine Autobiographie Hitlers aus dem Jahr 1923? Kritische Sichtung einer vermeintlichen Entdeckung," *Zeitschrift für Geschichtswissenschaft* 68 (2017): 213–235.

33.   "Postsekretär J. Teuber an Hitler, 16.4.1923," along with other congratulations by letter and telegram, in N 1128/7, BA, Koblenz.

34.   "Kriegskamerad Wackerl an Hitler, 19.4.1923," N 1128/7, BA, Koblenz.

35.   *Die Weltbühne* 13/47 (November 23, 1923), 558.

36.   See "Aufzeichnung des Staatssekretärs in der Reichskanzlei Hamm über die innere Lage, 15.4.1923": "The National Socialist Workers Party is especially strong in Munich and Bavaria.... Their leader, Adolf Hitler, whose personal influence extends to highly educated circles, particularly the officers' corps and the business world, is the most celebrated speaker in Munich." *AdR: Das Kabinett Cuno*, no. 121, 379.

37.   See Dirk Walter, *Antisemitische Kriminalität und Gewalt: Judenfeindschaft in der Weimarer Republik* (Bonn, 1999), 97–110.

38.   "Buchhändler Hans Goltz an Hitler, 2.5.1923," N 1128/8, BA, Koblenz.

39.   "Dr. med. Paula Wack an Hitler, 29.4.1923," N 1128/7, BA, Koblenz. Hitler wasn't particularly impressed. In a speech in Zirkus Krone on May 4, 1923, he declared, "The lectures I hold here are my intellectual property, and I forbid anyone who doesn't suit me from taking notes." Hitler, *Sämtliche Aufzeichnungen*, no. 525, 921.

40.   "Kaufmann Walter Frömel an Hitler, 21.5.1923," N 1128/8, BA, Koblenz.

41.   "Ein treuer Anhänger an Hitler, 4.11.1923," N 1128/14, BA, Koblenz.

42.   Hitler, *Sämtliche Aufzeichnungen*, no. 525, 924 (May 4, 1923).

43.   Hitler, no. 533, 933 (June 1, 1923).

44.   Hitler, no. 544, 946 (July 6, 1923).

45.   Hitler, no. 561, 984 (August 21, 1923).

46.   "L. Schubert an Hitler, 28.8.1923," N 1128/11, BA, Koblenz.

47.   See Alexis Schwarzenbach, "'Zur Lage in Deutschland': Hitlers Zürcher Rede vom 30. August 1923," in *Traverse*, no. 1 (2006), 176–189. It contains a facsimile of Hitler's notes for the speech, which began with the words, "A Bavarian politician, who may be called in the near future to play a greater role, told me the following in a conversation on August 30, 1923."

48.   See Brigitte Hamann, *Winifred Wagner oder Hitlers Bayreuth* (Munich, 2002), 75.

49. Deuerlein, ed., *Hitler-Putsch*, doc. 2, 161–162.

50. Deuerlein, ed., doc. 6, 170.

51. See Bruno Thoss, *Der Ludendorff-Kreis 1919–1923: München als Zentrum der mitteleuropäischen Gegenrevolution zwischen Revolution und Hitler-Putsch* (Munich, 1978).

52. "Houston Stewart Chamberlain an Hitler, 7.10.1923," N 1128/16, BA, Koblenz. On Hitler's visit to Bayreuth, see Hamann, *Winifred Wagner*, 82–85.

53. Cited in Harold J. Gordon Jr., *Hitlerputsch 1923: Machtkampf in Bayern, 1923–1924* (Frankfurt, 1971), 193–194.

54. "Hauptmann d. R. Fischer an Hitler, 7.9.1923," N 1128/12, BA, Koblenz.

55. "Ein Deutscher aus Elberfeld an Hitler, 12.9.1923," "Dr. Ernst Bergmann, Leipzig, an Hitler, 7.10.1923," and "L. Schubert, München, an Hitler, 28.9.1923," N 1128/12 and 1128/14, BA, Koblenz. Further letters in N 1128/12 and 1128/14, BA, Koblenz; and NS 26/1, 26/2, 26/2a, and 26/3, BA, Berlin Lichterfelde.

56. "Felix Lippold in Firma Lippold & Geyer G.m.b.H an Hitler, 5.10.1923," N 1128/15, BA, Koblenz.

57. Hitler, *Sämtliche Aufzeichnungen*, no. 566, 1002, 1004.

58. Hitler, no. 568, 1013.

59. "R. Hess an Ilse Pröhl, 16.9.1923," in Rudolf Hess, *Briefe 1908–1933*, ed. Wolf Rüdiger Hess (Munich, 1987), 304.

60. "Plan für die 14 Massenversammlungen," in Hitler, *Sämtliche Aufzeichnungen*, no. 571, 1015–1016. See Horn, *Marsch zur Machtergreifung*, 121.

61. See the Nazi pamphlet making demands on Kahr: "Was von Kahr gefordert werden muss," Deuerlein, ed., *Hitler-Putsch*, doc. 13, 185.

62. "Hitler an Kahr, 27.9.1923," in Hitler, *Sämtliche Aufzeichnungen*, no. 573, 1017.

63. Richard Huldschiner, "Hitlers Rückzug," *Vossische Zeitung* 460 (September 28, 1923). See also *Berliner Tageblatt* 455 (September 28, 1923): "The Hitler camp is now speaking a lot more softly."

64. "Bericht eines Augenzeugen über die Ausweisungsmaßnahmen gegen Juden in München, 31.10.1923," *AdR: Die Kabinette Stresemann*, vol. 2, no. 211, 926–933 (here 927). See also Rainer Pommerin, "Die Ausweisung von 'Ostjuden' aus Bayern 1923: Ein Beitrag zum Krisenjahr der Weimarer Republik," *Vierteljahrshefte für Zeitgeschichte* 34 (1986): 311–340; and Trude Maurer, *Ostjuden in Deutschland, 1918–1933* (Hamburg, 1986), 406ff.

65. See Gordon, *Hitlerputsch 1923*, 209–210.

66. Hitler, *Sämtliche Aufzeichnungen*, no. 581, 1028–1029.

67. Hitler, no. 583, 1032.

68. Deuerlein, ed., *Hitler-Putsch*, 74.

69. Stockhausen, *Sechs Jahre Reichskanzlei*, 81.

70. "Niederschrift über die Besprechung im Wehrkreiskommando VII, 24.10.1923," in Deuerlein, ed., *Hitler-Putsch*, doc. 61, 258.

71. Adolf Hitler, *Der Hitler-Prozess 1924: Wortlaut der Hauptverhandlung vor dem Volksgericht München I*, ed. Lothar Gruchmann and Reinhard Weber with Otto Gritschneder (Munich, 1998), part 3, 788.

72. "Aufzeichnung Kahrs für eine Pressebesprechung, 1.10.1923," in Deuerlein, ed., *Hitler-Putsch*, doc. 16, 186–187.

73. Hitler, *Sämtliche Aufzeichnungen*, no. 589, 1043.

74. Hitler, no. 592, 1049–1050.

75. Hitler, *Hitler-Prozess*, part 1, 38; see also part 4, 1587.

76. "Katholischer Pfarrer Dr. Haeuser an Hitler, 14.10.1923," NS 26/1242, BA, Berlin Lichterfelde.

77. Hamann, *Winifred Wagner*, 86.

78. "Eine Münchnerin (Name unleserlich) an Hitler, 3.11.1923," N 1128/2, BA, Koblenz.

79. Hitler, *Hitler-Prozess*, part 3, 859 (Seisser's testimony), and part 1, 78 (Friedrich Weber's testimony).

80. "Niederschrift Seißers über Besprechungen in Berlin, 3.11.1923," in Deuerlein, ed., *Hitler-Putsch*, doc. 79, 301–304. See Meier-Welcker, *Seeckt*, 397–398: Gordon, *Hitlerputsch 1923*, 224–225; and Feldman, *Great Disorder*, 775–776. On October 30, 1923, the rural association (Landbund) of Mecklenburg-Strelitz had already asked Seeckt to use all his power to end the conflict with Bavaria: "An alliance between Seeckt and Kahr is the most burning desire of all German patriots!" Hürten, ed., *Krisenjahr 1923*, no. 60, 105.

81. "General von Seeckt an Generalstaatskommissar von Kahr, Entwurf, 2.11.1923 (abgesandt mit Kürzungen am 5.11.1923)," *AdR: Die Kabinette Stresemann*, vol. 2, suppl. no. 4, 1211–1215. See also Meier-Welcker, *Seeckt*, 395–396; Winkler, *Weimar*, 230–231; and "Materialsammlung Lieber v. 1.11.1923," *AdR: Stresemann*, vol. 2, suppl. no. 1, 1196: "Seeckt favors the rapid formation of a government without the Social Democrats."

82. "Materialsammlung Lieber v. 3.11.1923," *AdR: Die Kabinette Stresemann*, vol. 2, suppl. no. 1, 1192. In conversation with Seisser that same day, Seeckt assured him that he would "under no circumstances" move against Bavaria with the Reichstag. Deuerlein, ed., *Hitler-Putsch*, doc. 79, 303.

83. Gessler, *Reichswehrpolitik*, 299. See also Mühlhausen, *Friedrich Ebert*, 687–688; and Meier-Welcker, *Seeckt*, 396.

84. See Wette, *Gustav Noske*, 639.

85. "Materialsammlung Lieber v. 4.11.1923," *AdR: Die Kabinette Stresemann*, vol. 2, suppl. no. 1, 1197.

86. "General von Seeckt an Botschafter Wiedfeldt, 4.11.1923," *AdR: Die Kabinette Stresemann*, vol. 2, suppl. no. 5, 1215. See also Schröder, *Otto Wiedfeldt*, 143–144.

87. "Materialsammlung Lieber v. 4.11.1923," *AdR: Die Kabinette Stresemann*, vol. 2, suppl. no. 1, 1197. On Ebert's motives, see Mühlhausen, *Friedrich Ebert*, 684–685; and Winkler, *Weimar*, 231.

88. "Materialsammlung Lieber v. 5.11.1923," *AdR: Die Kabinette Stresemann*, vol. 2, suppl. no. 1, 1198. See also Wright, *Gustav Stresemann*, 246–247; and Meier-Welcker, *Seeckt*, 401–402.

89. See Wright, *Gustav Stresemann*, 247; Mühlhausen, *Friedrich Ebert*, 688–689; and "Tagebuch von Oberstleutnant von Selchow, Seeckts Adjutant, v. 5.11.1923," *AdR: Das Kabinett Stresemann*, vol. 2, suppl. no. 1, 1198, note 103.

90. Gessler, *Reichswehrpolitik*, 299. See Wright, *Gustav Stresemann*, 247; and Winkler, *Weimar*, 231.

91. "Fraktionssitzung der DVP, 5.11.1923," in Stresemann, *Vermächtnis*, vol. 1, 195–197 (here 196). See also Richter, *Deutsche Volkspartei*, 293–294; and Wright, *Gustav Stresemann*, 248–249.

92. "Fraktionssitzung der DVP, 6.11.1923," in Stresemann, *Vermächtnis*, vol. 1, 198–200. See also Richter, *Deutsche Volkspartei*, 294–295; and Wright, *Gustav Stresemann*, 247, 249–250.

93. "Generalstaatskommissar v. Kahr an Ministerpräsident v. Knilling, 12.12.1923," in Deuerlein, ed., *Hitler-Putsch*, doc. 182, 493. See also Hitler, *Hitler-Prozess*, part 1, 78 (Friedrich Weber's testimony); 209, 211 (Kriebel's testimony); and part 3, 790–791 (Kahr's testimony).

94. Hitler, *Hitler-Prozess*, part 2, 772 (Aussage v. Lossow). See part 1, 211 (Aussage Kriebel).

95. Hitler, part 1, 44 (Hitler's testimony).

96. Hitler, part 1, 212 (Hitler's testimony). See also Hitler, part 1, 47–48 (Hitler's testimony).

97. Theodor Schwindl, "Erlebnisbericht über die Vorgänge am 8./9. November 1923 in München," NS 26/100, BA, Berlin-Lichterfelde.

98. "Polizeidirektion München an Generalstaatskommissar v. Kahr, 7.12.1923," in Deuerlein, ed., *Hitler-Putsch*, doc. 174, 471. Hitler himself testified during the trial: "Only a very few people were in the know, and the entire organization was designed so that the leaders, especially the military leaders, didn't know why they were mobilizing the troops." Hitler, *Hitler-Prozess*, part 1, 47–48.

99. See "Protokoll eines Verhörs Dietrich Eckarts in der Münchner Polizeidirektion, 15.11.1923," NS 26/2180, BA, Berlin-Lichterfelde.

100. Hitler, *Hitler-Prozess*, part 1, 112–113 (Pöhner's testimony).

101. "R. Hess und K. Haushofer, 6.10.1923," N 1122/15, BA, Koblenz. See also "R. Hess an I. Pröhl, 1.10.1923": "Perhaps I will suddenly be there. I wondered why they haven't called yet." Nl R. Heß, J1.211–1989/148, vol. 31, BA, Bern.

102. "R. Hess an seine Eltern, 8.11.1923 (1. Fortsetzung: 16.11.1923; 2. Fortsetzung: 4.12.1923)," in Hess, *Briefe*, 310.

103. "Manuskript der Erinnerungen Hanfstaengls," Typoskript, 93, N l, Hanfstaengl, Ana 405, carton 47, BSB, München. A slightly different version of this scene can be found in Ernst Hanfstaengl, *Zwischen Weißem und Braunem Haus: Erinnerungen eines Außenseiters* (Munich, 1970), 129.

104. "R. Hess an I. Pröhl, 28.2.1924," Nl R. Heß, J1.211–1989 /148, vol. 33, BA, Bern.

105. Müller, *Im Wandel einer Welt*, 161. See Ullrich, *Hitler: Ascent*, vol. 1, 170–178. See also Gordon, *Hitlerputsch 1923*, 254ff.; Hubert Hofmann, *Der Hitlerputsch: Krisenjahre deutscher Geschichte 1920–1924* (Munich, 1961), 160ff; and Hitler, *Hitler-Prozess*, part 1, 49ff. (Hitler's testimony), and 309ff. (prosecution charges of January 8, 1924).

106. Konrad Heiden, *Adolf Hitler: Das Zeitalter der Verantwortungslosigkeit—Eine Biographie* (Zürich, 1936), 156. See also Hanfstaengl, *Zwischen Weißem und Braunem Haus*, 131; and Hitler, *Hitler-Prozess*, part 1, 49–50 (Hitler's testimony).

107. See Hess, *Briefe*, 311; and Hanfstaengl, *Zwischen Weißem und Braunen Haus*, 132.

108. Hitler, *Hitler-Prozess*, part 1, 50 (Hitler's testimony). See also Hitler, part 3, 1166 (Ulrich Graf's testimony).

109. Hitler, part 1, 309 (prosecution charges of January 8, 1924).

110. Hitler, part 2, 749 (Lossow's testimony), and part 3, 867 (Seisser's testimony). See also Kahr's unpublished memoirs, manuscript, 1355: "Lossow whispered, 'Play along,' and the three of us exchanged glances of agreement." N l, Kahr 51, BayHStA.

111. Hitler, *Hitler-Prozess*, part 1, 310 (prosecution charges of January 8, 1924). See Hitler, part 2, 750 (Lossow's testimony), and part 3, 795 (Kahr's testimony).

112. Müller, *Im Wandel einer Welt*, 162. See also Hitler, *Hitler-Prozess*, part 2, 597 (K. A. von Müller's testimony).

113. On Göring, see Hitler, *Hitler-Prozess*, part 2, 594 (Max Ritter von Gruber's testimony), 620 (Hans Ritter von Hemmer's testimony), 631 (Gustav von Müller's testimony), and 634 (August Ritter von Kleinhenz's testimony).

114. Müller, *Im Wandel einer Welt*, 162–163. See also Hitler, *Hitler-Prozess*, part 1, 52 (Hitler's testimony): "In the court, there was an unheard-of storm of applause."

115. Hitler, *Hitler-Prozess*, part 1, 311 (prosecution charges of January 8, 1924).

116. See Hitler, part 1, 277 (Ludendorff's testimony).

117. Kahr, unpublished memoir, 1345, N l, Kahr 51, BayHStA.

118. Hitler, *Hitler-Prozess*, part 1, 311 (prosecution charges of January 8, 1924).

119. Hitler, part 3, 796 (Kahr's testimony). See also Hitler, part 2, 752 (Lossow's testimony).

120. Hitler, part 1, 53 (Hitler's testimony). See Hitler, part 1, 117 (Pöhner's testimony).

121. Hitler, part 3, 797 (Kahr's testimony).

122. Hitler, part 1, 312 (prosecution charges of January 8, 1924).

123. Müller, *Im Wandel einer Welt*, 164. See also Deuerlein, ed., *Hitler-Putsch*, part 2, 598 (K. A. von Müller's testimony).

124. Hitler, *Hitler-Prozess*, part 1, 311–312 (prosecution charges of January 8, 1924). Hitler would arrive at almost the same conclusion, including the "Amen" in an address to the German nation from the Sportpalast in Berlin on February 10, 1933, a few days after he had become chancellor. See Ullrich, *Hitler: Ascent*, 418.

125. Hitler, *Hitler-Prozess*, part 1, 312 (prosecution charges of January 8, 1924). See Hitler, part 2, 598 (K. A. von Müller's testimony): "Both his appearance and his words definitely gave the impression of someone who knows he's facing a matter of life and death."

126. Hitler, part 2, 595 (Grüber's testimony), and 598 (K. A. von Müller's testimony). See Müller, *Im Wandel einer Welt*, 165.

127. Müller, *Im Wandel einer Welt*, 165. See also Hitler, *Hitler-Prozess*, part 2, 598–599 (K. A. von Müller's testimony), and part 3, 1060 (Prof. Doeberl's testimony).

128. See Hess, *Briefe*, 311–312; and Gordon, *Hitlerputsch 1923*, 261.

129. See Hitler, *Hitler-Prozess*, part 1, 86 (Weber's testimony), and 279 (Ludendorff's testimony).

130. "Generalstaatskommissar v. Kahr an Ministerpräsident v. Knilling, 12.12.1923," in Deuerlein, ed., *Hitler-Putsch*, doc. 182, 501.

131. See Deuerlein, ed., vol. 1, 321–323 (prosecution charges of January 8, 1924), and part 2, 382–384 (E. Röhm's testimony); and Gordon, *Hitlerputsch 1923*, 264–266.

132. Hitler, *Hitler-Prozess*, part 2, 756 (Lossow's testimony)

133. Deuerlein, ed., *Hitler-Putsch*, doc. 86, 310, note 166.

134. Hitler, *Hitler-Prozess*, part 2, 662–663 (Major Alexander Siry's testimony). See Hitler, part 2, 758 (Lossow's testimony).

135. Lion Feuchtwanger, *Erfolg: Drei Jahre Geschichte einer Provinz* (Frankfurt, [1930] 1975), 697ff. See also Eugeni Xammar, "Der Putsch als Spektakel," *Das Schlangenei*, 134–138.

136. See Walter, *Antisemitische Kriminalität und Gewalt*, 119–136.

137. Text in Hitler, *Sämtliche Aufzeichnungen*, 597, 1056.

138. *Völkischer Beobachter* 230 (November 9, 1923). The morning edition of the *Münchener Neueste Nachrichten* (no. 304 [November 9, 1923]) reported that "a national directorate had been installed." See this and other morning newspaper editions in N l, K. A. v. Müller 19/2, BayHStA.

139. Hitler, *Hitler-Prozess*, part 1, 282 (Ludendorff's testimony), and 57 (Hitler's testimony). See Hitler, part 1, 228 (Kriebel's testimony).

140. Hitler, part 1, 58 (Hitler's testimony), 230 (Kriebel's testimony), and part 2, 400–401 (Wilhelm Brückner's testimony).

141. See Hanfstaengl, *Zwischen Weißem und Braunem Haus*, 143. The printing of Kahr's statement began at 8:00 a.m. The morning edition of the *Münchener Zeitung* (no. 309 [November 9, 1923]) led with the proclamation, "The declarations extracted from me, General von Lossow, and Colonel Seisser at gunpoint are null and void. Had this senseless and pointless attempt at a coup succeeded, it would have led Germany and Bavaria to the edge of the abyss."

142. See "Bericht von Polizeioberleutnant v. Godin, 10.11.1923," in Deuerlein, ed., *Hitler-Putsch*, doc. 97, 330–331.

143. Ian Kershaw, *Hitler 1889–1936* (London, 2002), 211.

144. A participant in the march who encountered Hitler received no answer when he asked repeatedly whether Hitler was hurt. The man later testified that Hitler had looked entirely "confused" and was visibly in shock. See "Aufzeichnung eines Zeugen A. über die Ereignisse am 8./9.11.1923," München 13.11.1923, N l, K. A. v. Müller 19/1, BayHStA.

145. Franz Hemmrich, "Adolf Hitler in der Festung Landsberg," unpublished manuscript, 4, Institut für Zeitgeschichte, München, ED 153. On Hitler's time in Uffing, see Anna Maria Sigmund, "Als Hitler auf der Flucht war," *Süddeutsche Zeitung* (November 8–9, 2008) (which includes previously unpublished recollections of Helene Hanfstaengl); and Hanfstaengl, *Zwischen Weißem und Braunem Haus*, 5–6, 146–149. On Hitler's arrest, see "Bericht der Regierung von Oberbayern an das Generalstaatskommissariat, 13.11.1923," in Deuerlein, ed., *Hitler-Putsch*, doc. 118, 371–373.

146. See Gordon, *Hitlerputsch 1923*, 416–423.

147. Pringsheim, *Tagebücher*, vol. 7, 105 (November 10, 1923).

148. In his unpublished memoirs (1177), Kahr wrote of becoming the "most hated man" overnight, BayHStA München, Nl Kahr 51. See also Georg Escherich's diary entry of November 10, 1923: "In Munich, the mood of hostility against the 'traitor Kahr' has begun to simmer." N l, Escherich 10, BayHStA.

149. See "Bericht über den Verlauf der Versammlung in der Universität, 12.11.1923," in Deuerlein, ed., *Hitler-Putsch*, doc. 113, 357–358; and Müller, *Im Wandel der Welt*, 172–173.

150. Otto Gritschneder, *Bewährungsfrist für den Terroristen Adolf H.: Der Hitler-Putsch und die bayerische Justiz* (Munich, 1990), 35.

151. "Angela Raubal an ihren Bruder Alois Hitler, 14.12.1923," in John Toland, *Adolf Hitler*, vol. 1 (Bergisch-Gladbach, 1981), 253.

152. See David Jablonsky, *The Nazi Party in Dissolution: Hitler and the Verbotszeit, 1923–1925* (London, 1989), 28ff. Before the police could search Hitler's apartment on Thierschstrasse 41, his longtime party comrades and the parents of his then private secretary, Theodor and Dora Laaböck, took away his papers. In April 1937, the two handed over this material to the Nazi Party's main archive. See NS 26 /1242, BA, Berlin-Lichterfelde.

153. Cited in David Clay Large, *Where Ghosts Walked: Munich's Road to the Third Reich* (New York, 1997), 189.

154. *Frankfurter Zeitung* on November 10, 1923, cited in Philipp W. Fabry, *Mutmaßungen über Hitler: Urteile von Zeitgenossen* (Königstein, 1979), 25. Never had an action that began with such "loud boasting" come to a "more pathetic end," wrote Ernst Feder in "Das Ende der Hanswurstiade," *Berliner Tageblatt* 529 (November 10, 1923).

155. "R. Hess an seine Eltern, 21.12.1923," Nl Heß J1.211–1989/148, vol. 31, BA, Bern.

156. D'Abernon, *Ambassador*, 270 (November 9, 1923).

157. See W. Stresemann, *Mein Vater Gustav Stresemann*, 274; and Stresemann, *Vermächtnis*, vol. 1, 204.

158. *AdR: Die Kabinette Stresemann*, vol. 2, 231, 997, note 1. Stresemann's private secretary Henry Bernhard recalled Stresemann declaring during the night of November 8–9 that Hitler's putsch, if successful, would be a "Finis Germaniae." Bernhard, *Finis Germaniae: Aufzeichnungen und Betrachtungen* (Stuttgart, 1947), 7.

159. Stockhausen, *Sechs Jahre Reichskanzlei*, 89. Severing recalled Seeckt answering the question of how the Berlin garrison would behave with the same words he had used at the start of the Kapp Putsch: "The Reichswehr doesn't fire on the Reichswehr!" Severing, *Mein Lebensweg*, vol. 1, 447. See also Braun, *Von Weimar zu Hitler*, 59.

160. W. Stresemann, *Mein Vater Gustav Stresemann*, 275.

161. "Verordnung Eberts v. 9.11.1923," *Berliner Tageblatt* 527 (November 9, 1923).

162. Gessler, *Reichswehrpolitik*, 274; and Luther, *Politiker ohne Partei*, 173.

163. *AdR: Die Kabinette Stresemann*, vol. 2, no. 231, 997, note 1.

164. Gessler, *Reichswehrpolitik*, 275. See also Mühlhausen, *Friedrich Ebert*, 690–691; and Winkler, *Weimar*, 235.

165. Printed, among other places, in the *Berliner Tageblatt* 527 (November 9, 1923); and *Ursachen und Folgen*, vol. 5, no. 1175b, 439 (here falsely signed only by Ebert).

166. *AdR: Die Kabinette Stresemann*, vol. 2, no. 231, 997–998.

167. W. Stresemann, *Mein Vater Gustav Stresemann*, 276. That very evening the members of the government decided, unlike the government during the Kapp Putsch, not "to flee to Stuttgart." See Selchow's diary on November 9, 1923, in *AdR: Die Kabinette Stresemann*, vol. 2, no. 231, 997, note 1.

168. D'Abernon, *Ambassador*, 270 (November 9, 1923).

169. Kessler, *Tagebuch*, vol. 8, 138 (November 9, 1923).

170. "Kabinettssitzung, 9.11.1923, 12 Uhr," *AdR: Die Kabinette Stresemann*, vol. 2, no. 232, 998–999.

171. "Gesandtschaftsrat Gustaf Braun von Stumm an Reichskanzlei, 9.11.1923," *AdR: Die Kabinette Stresemann*, vol. 2, no. 235, 1011–1013.

172. "Aufzeichnung Stresemanns über die Unterredung mit de Margerie, 9.11.1923," in Stresemann, *Vermächtnis*, vol. 1, 205–207; and "Gustaf Braun von Stumm an Reichskanzlei, 9.11.1923," Stresemann, vol. 2, no. 235, 1011–1013.

173. See Richter, *Deutsche Volkspartei*, 297–299; and Wright, *Gustav Stresemann*, 251–252.

174. Stresemann, *Vermächtnis*, vol. 1, 207–211 (here 208–209).

175. Stresemann, vol. 1, 207. See also W. Stresemann, *Mein Vater Gustav Stresemann*, 277–278: "My father came back stronger from Halle. After the preceding storms and conflicts, the jubilant welcome and huge applause during his speech provided relief and gave him new power."

176. "Materialsammlung Lieber v. 10.11.1923," *AdR: Die Kabinette Stresemann*, vol. 2, suppl. no. 1, 1199; and Meier-Welcker, *Seeckt*, 408–409.

177. "Botschafter Wiedfeldt an General von Seeckt, 24.11.1923," *AdR: Die Kabinette Stresemann*, vol. 2, suppl no. 6, 1216–1217. See also Schröder, *Otto Wiedfeldt*, 144–145.

178. Cited in Meier-Welcker, *Seeckt*, 411. See also "Materialsammlung Lieber v. 18.11.1923": "Haase and Seeckt are racking their brains for another man, but they aren't finding anyone!" *AdR: Die Kabinette Stresemann*, vol. 2, suppl. no. 1, 1200.

179. Ernst Feder, "Das Ende der Hanswurstiade," *Berliner Tageblatt* 529 (November 10, 1923).

180. *Deutsche Allgemeine Zeitung* 521 (November 9, 1923), and 522 (November 9, 1923).

181. *Vossische Zeitung* 533 (November 10, 1923).

182. Georg Bernhard, "Die Masken herunter," *Vossische Zeitung* 532 (November 9, 1923). See also Bernhard, "Ludendorff," *Vossische Zeitung*, no. 534–544 (November 16, 1923).

183. Carl von Ossietzky, "Götzendämmerung," *Berliner Volks-Zeitung* (November 10, 1923), in Ossietzky, *Sämtliche Schriften*, vol. 2, 311–312.

184. Moltke, *Ein Leben in Deutschland*, 81 (November 15, 1923).

*Chapter 6:* "Freedom from Berlin": Separatist Movements in Rhineland-Pfalz

1. Theodor Wolff, *Berliner Tageblatt* 496 (October 22, 1923).

2. Friedrich Meinecke, *Werke*, ed. Hans Herzfeld, Carl Hinrichs, and Walther Hofer, vol. 2: *Politische Schriften und Reden* (Darmstadt, 1958), 284, 301. See also Erwin Bischof, *Rheinischer Separatismus 1918–1924: Hans Adam Dortens Rheinstaatsbestrebungen* (Bern, 1969), 7–32.

3. See Bischof, *Rheinischer Separatismus*, 20–21; and Leonhard, *Der überforderte Frieden*, 383–384, 779–780.

4. See Karl-Dietrich Erdmann, *Adenauer in der Rheinlandpolitik nach dem Ersten Weltkrieg* (Stuttgart, 1966), 29–30; and Hans-Peter Schwarz, *Adenauer*, vol. 1: *Der Aufstieg 1876–1952* (Stuttgart, 1986), 210–212.

5. *Kölnische Volkszeitung* 597 (December 5, 1918), cited in Bischof, *Rheinischer Separatismus*, 35.

6. "Denkschrift Adenauers über sein Verhältnis zu den Rheinstaatsbestrebungen, 9.11.1918 bis 17.3.1919," in Erdmann, *Adenauer in der Rheinlandpolitik*, doc. 4, 238–253 (here 239).

7. "Protokoll der Versammlung v. 1.2.1919," in Erdmann, *Adenauer in der Rheinlandpolitik*, doc. 1, 212–234 (here 221, 222, 226). See also Erdmann, 41–48; and Schwarz, *Adenauer*, vol. 1, 218–221.

8. Erdmann, *Adenauer in der Rheinlandpolitik*, doc. 1, 229.

9. On Dorten's biography, see Bischof, *Rheinischer Separatismus*, 39–44; and Martin Schlemmer, *"Los von Berlin": Die Rheinstaatsbestrebungen nach dem Ersten Weltkrieg* (Cologne, 2007), 116–117.

10. "Denkschrift Adenauers über sein Verhältnis zu den Rheinstaatsbestrebungen, 9.11.1918 bis 17.3.1919," in Erdmann, *Adenauer in der Rheinlandpolitik*, doc. 4, 245.

11. "Dorten an Adenauer, 5.2.1919," in Erdmann, doc. 2, 235–236.

12. Bischof, *Rheinischer Separatismus*, 56.

13. Bischof, 59–60. See also Erdmann, *Adenauer in der Rheinlandpolitik*, 52.

14. See Bischof, *Rheinischer Separatismus*, 34, 64–65; Erdmann, *Adenauer in der Rheinlandpolitik*, 24–53; and Schwarz, *Adenauer*, vol. 1, 203.

15. See Bischof, *Rheinischer Separatismus*, 70–81; and Erdmann, *Adenauer in der Rheinlandpolitik*, 53–55.

16. See "Bericht des Redakteurs der 'Kölnischen Volkszeitung,' Froberger, über eine Unterredung mit General Mangin in Mainz am 17.5.1919," in Erdmann, *Adenauer in der Rheinlandpolitik*, doc. 6, 289.

17. "Aufruf 'An das rheinische Volk!'" in Schlemmer, *"Los von Berlin,"* doc. 7, 752–753.

18. On the putsch, see Bischof, *Rheinischer Separatismus*, 85–93; and Schlemmer, *"Los von Berlin,"* 118–123.

19. See Leonhard, *Der überforderte Frieden*, 783–784, 861; and Eberhard Kolb, *Der Frieden von Versailles* (Munich, 2005), 59–60.

20. "Artikel 18 der Reichsverfassung," in Schlemmer, *"Los von Berlin,"* doc. 11, 756–757.

21. See Erdmann, *Adenauer in der Rheinlandpolitik*, 70; and Schwarz, *Adenauer*, vol. 1, 227.

22. See Bischof, *Rheinischer Separatismus*, 103–107, 119–121; and Schlemmer, *"Los von Berlin,"* 152–154, 160–161.

23. *AdR: Die Kabinette Stresemann*, vol. 1, no. 89, 399–400, note 7. See also Bischof, *Rheinischer Separatismus*, 122.

24. See Angelika Schnorrenberger, "Der Düsseldorfer 'Blutsonntag,' 30. September 1923," in Krumeich and Schröder, eds., *Der Schatten des Weltkriegs*, 289–303 (293, facsimile of the flyer).

25. "Regierungspräsident Grützner an Oberbürgermeister Köttgen, 27.9.1923," in Krumeich and Schröder, eds., 295–296.

26. See in Krumeich and Schröder, eds., 297–302.

27. Cited in Gerhard Gräber and Matthias Spindler, *Revolverrepublik am Rhein: Die Pfalz und ihre Separatisten*, vol. 1: *November 1918–November 1923* (Landau, 1992), 252.

28. See "Bericht der Nachrichtenagentur W. T. B. v. 21.10.1923," *Ursachen und Folgen*, vol. 5, no. 1119, 303; and "Separatistenputsch am Rhein," *Vossische Zeitung* 500 (October 22, 1923).

29. "Die Ereignisse von Aachen: Der erste deutsche Bericht," *Vossische Zeitung* 501 (October 23, 1923).

30. "Der Kampf um Aachen," *Vossische Zeitung* 503 (October 24, 1923).

31. See "Die Separatistenbewegung im Rheinland: Weitere Gewaltstreiche," *Berliner Tageblatt* 497 (October 23, 1923); "Die Putschbewegung im Rheinland," 498 (October 23, 1923); "Erfolgreiche Abwehraktion im Rheinland," 499 (October 24, 1923); and "Die Separatisten fast überall vertrieben," 500 (October 24, 1923).

32. *Die Tagebücher von Joseph Goebbels*, ed. Elke Fröhlich, vol. 1, part 1, *Oktober 1923–November 1925* (Munich, 2004), 36 (October 23, 1923).

33. "Aide-Mémoire der deutschen Botschaft in Paris, 24.10.1923, und Antwortnote der französischen Regierung, 29.10.1923," *Ursachen und Folgen*, vol. 5, no. 1119d and 1119e, 305–307. On the stance of the occupation authorities, see Schlemmer, *"Los von Berlin,"* 170–172.

34. "Mangin an Dorten, 22.10.1923," cited in Schlemmer, *"Los von Berlin,"* 165.

35. "Der 23. Oktober 1923: Die Separatisten in Koblenz an der Macht," https://dewiki.de/Lexikon/Rheinische_Republik#cite_note-15. See also Gräber and Spindler, *Revolverrepublik am Rhein*, vol. 1, 542–543; and Bischof, *Rheinischer Separatismus*, 125.

36. See "Der 23. Oktober 1923: Die Separatisten in Koblenz an der Macht." On the attitudes of the populace, see Schlemmer, *"Los von Berlin,"* 381–382. To the Spanish reporter Eugeni Xammar, the provisional government of the Rhenish Republic presented "when viewed up close, a quite grotesque sight." Xammar, "Koblenzer Maskerade," in *Das Schlangenei*, 130–133 (here 131).

37. "Preußische Innenminister an das Auswärtige Amt, 29.10.1923," *AdR: Die Kabinette Stresemann*, vol. 2, no. 202, 898–905 (here 904).

38. See Schlemmer, *"Los von Berlin,"* 210–212; and Johannes Thomassen, "Arbeiter-

schaft und rheinischer Separatismus im Krisenjahr 1923," *Geschichte im Westen*, vol. 1 (1992), 53–61 (here 58–59).

39. "Befehl der Exekutive der Vorläufigen Regierung v. 3.11.1923," *Ursachen und Folgen*, vol. 5, no. 1120, 309.

40. See "Die 'Schlacht' bei Aegidienberg," *Ursachen und Folgen*, vol. 5, no. 1122, 11; and "Rheinische Republik," Wikipedia, https://de.wikipedia.org./wiki/Rheinische_Republik.

41. See "Separatisten untereinander," *Vossische Zeitung* 567 (November 30, 1923) (includes Matthes's letter to Tirard of November 27, 1923).

42. See Bischof, *Rheinischer Separatismus*, 126–127.

43. "Separatisten untereinander," *Vossische Zeitung* 567 (November 30, 1923).

44. See Gräber and Spindler, *Revolverrepublik am Rhein*, vol. 1, 31–32, 39–50.

45. Wilhelm Michel, "Pfalz, Bayern, Deutschland," *Die Weltbühne* 19/46 (November 15, 1923), 470–474 (here 473).

46. See Diethard Hennig, *Johannes Hoffmann: Sozialdemokrat und Bayerischer Ministerpräsident—Biographie* (Munich, 1990), 479–481.

47. See Hennig, 481; and Gräber and Spindler, *Revolverrepublik am Rhein*, vol. 1, 396–397.

48. "Erklärung von Mitgliedern der Pfälzer Sozialdemokratie, 23.10.1923," *Ursachen und Folgen*, vol. 5, no. 1124, 313. See "Vermerk des Ministerialrats Kiep über die Ausrufung der autonomen Republik Pfalz, 24.10.1923," *AdR: Die Kabinette Stresemann*, vol. 2, no. 171, 705.

49. Hennig, *Johannes Hoffmann*, 482. See also Gräber and Spindler, *Revolverrepublik am Rhein*, vol. 1, 452–453, 455.

50. "Telegramm Hoffmanns an Hermann Müller, 24.10.1923, und Antworttelegramm Müllers, 25.10.1923," *AdR: Die Kabinette Stresemann*, vol. 2, no. 171, 706, note 6. See also the slightly differently worded version in Hennig, *Johannes Hoffmann*, 482–483.

51. "Die Vorgänge in der Pfalz," *Vossische Zeitung* 505 (October 25, 1923); and "Lösungsversuche in der Pfalz," *Berliner Tageblatt* 501 (October 25, 1923). See also Hennig, *Johannes Hoffmann*, 483.

52. Gräber and Spindler, *Revolverrepublik am Rhein*, vol. 1, 476.

53. "Das französische Manöver in der Pfalz," *Berliner Tageblatt* 501 (October 25, 1923).

54. See Hennig, *Johannes Hoffmann*, 483–484; and Gräber and Spindler, *Revolverrepublik am Rhein*, vol. 1, 516–517.

55. "Erklärung des SPD-Parteivorstands der Pfalz, 26.10.1923," *Ursachen und Folgen*, vol. 5, no. 1124b, 313–314.

56. Hennig, *Johannes Hoffmann*, 486. See also Mühlhausen, *Friedrich Ebert*, 678, note 390.

57. "Aufzeichnung von Pregers v. 25.10.1923," *AdR: Die Kabinette Stresemann*, vol. 2, no. 180, 837.

58. Hennig, *Johannes Hoffmann*, 486.

59. Hennig, 491–493.

60. "Proklamation der separatistischen Regierung in der Pfalz v. 12.11.1923," *Ursachen*

*und Folgen*, vol. 5, no. 1124d, 315. See also Gerhard Gräber, "Pfälzischer Separatismus," Historisches Lexikon Bayerns, https://www.historisches-lexikon-bayerns.de/Lexikon/Pfälzischer_Separatismus.

61. On the biographies of Heinz, Bley, and Kunz, see Gerhard Gräber and Matthias Spindler, "Friedensrepublik Heinz und Kunz," *Die Zeit* 14 (March 29, 1991); and Gräber and Spindler, *Revolverrepublik am Rhein*, vol. 1, 126–127, 581–585.

62. "Die Autonome Pfalz und die soziale Fürsorge," Eine Spurensuche (website), https://www.viktorskopf.de/autonome-pfalz/.

63. See Gräber and Spindler, "Friedensrepublik Heinz und Kunz"; and Gräber and Spindler, *Die Pfalzbefreier: Volkes Zorn und Staatsgewalt im Kampf gegen den pfälzischen Separatismus 1923–24* (Ludwigshafen, 2005).

64. See Erdmann, *Adenauer in der Rheinlandpolitik*, 70; and Schwarz, *Adenauer*, vol. 1, 260.

65. See Winkler, *Von der Revolution zur Stabilisierung*, 641; Schwarz, *Adenauer*, vol. 1, 263–266; and Erdmann, *Adenauer in der Rheinlandpolitik*, 90–91. On Jarres's position, see his memo "Denkschrift an Stresemann v. 31.10.1923," *AdR: Die Kabinette Stresemann*, vol. 2, no. 210, 920–926.

66. "Besprechung mit den Vertretern der besetzten Gebiete in Hagen, 25.10.1923," *AdR: Die Kabinette Stresemann*, vol. 2, no. 179, 761–836 (here 763–764).

67. *AdR: Stresemann*, vol. 2, no. 179, 770, 776, 778, 781, 782.

68. *AdR: Stresemann*, vol. 2, no. 179, 783, 784, 785, 786. On the negotiations in Hagen, see Erdmann, *Adenauer in der Rheinlandpolitik*, 94–103; and Schwarz, *Adenauer*, vol. 1, 268–273.

69. "Interview Adenauers mit *Le Peuple* v. 31.10.1923," in Erdmann, *Adenauer in der Rheinlandpolitik*, doc. 9, 303–304.

70. Erdmann, doc. 9, 107.

71. "Aufzeichnung des Erzbischofs Schulte über seine Unterredung mit Tirad, 29.11.1923," Erdmann, doc. 8, 298–303 (here 300, 301). See also *AdR: Die Kabinette Stresemann*, vol. 2, no. 198, 887, note 6; and no. 199, 891, note 7.

72. See Erdmann, *Adenauer in der Rheinlandpolitik*, 116–118.

73. "Niederschrift Louis Hagens über seine Besprechung mit Tirard am 3.11.1923," in Erdmann, *Adenauer in der Rheinlandpolitik*, doc. 11, 305–308 (here 306).

74. "Kabinettssitzung v. 9.11.1923," *AdR: Die Kabinette Stresemann*, vol. 2, no. 233, 1000–1007 (here 1001, 1003, 1005).

*Chapter 7:* STABILIZATION: FROM STRESEMANN TO MARX

1. Sternheim, *Tagebücher*, vol. 1, 653 (October 31, 1923). See also Klemperer, *Tagebücher 1918–1924*, 754 (October 27, 1923): "Day after day the most beautiful, abnormally warm fall weather."

2. *Die Tagebücher von Joseph Goebbels*, vol. 1, part 1, 29, 32 (October 17, 1923).

3. Klemperer, *Tagebücher 1918–1924*, 753 (October 22, 1923). See also Pringsheim, *Tagebücher*, vol. 7, 103 (October 26 and 29, 1923): "Billions are flying around. The prices are enough to drive you crazy." Moltke, *Ein Leben in*

*Deutschland*, 78 (October 25, 1923): "The prices are fabulous. A billion is already pocket change."

4.  See Feldman, *Great Disorder*, 782.

5.  *Berliner Börsen-Courier* (November 6, 1923), cited in Glatzer, *Berlin zur Weimarer Zeit*, 112.

6.  Kessler, *Tagebuch*, vol. 8, 122 (October 22, 1923).

7.  Kessler, vol. 8, 139 (November 10, 1923).

8.  Erich Wolf, "Stätten des Berliner Elends," *Berliner Tageblatt* 542 (November 24, 1923).

9.  Scholem and Scholem, *Mutter und Sohn*, 88 (October 23, 1923). See *Tagebücher von Joseph Goebbels*, vol. 1, part 1, 47 (November 7, 1923): "It's a wonder that unrest doesn't spread throughout the country like an all-consuming wildfire."

10. "Krawalle im Berliner Zentrum," *Vossische Zeitung* 525 (November 6, 1923); and "Die gestrigen Unruhen," *Vossische Zeitung* 527 (November 7, 1923). On the Scheunenviertel violence, see also Maurer, *Ostjuden in Deutschland*, 329–338; Walter, *Antisemitische Kriminalität und Gewalt*, 151–153; and Robert Scholz, "Ein unruhiges Jahrzehnt: Lebensmittelunruhen, Massenstreiks und Arbeitslosenkrawalle in Berlin 1914–1923," in *Pöbelexzesse und Volkstumulte in Berlin. Zur Sozialgeschichte der Straße (1830-1980)*, ed. Manfred Gailus (Berlin, 1984), 115–118.

11. Arthur Crispien, "Arme Betrogene," *Vorwärts* (November 8, 1923), cited in Walter, *Antisemitische Kriminalität und Gewalt*, 151.

12. "Krawalle im Berliner Zentrum," *Vossische Zeitung* 525 (November 6, 1923).

13. Sternheim, *Tagebücher*, vol. 1, 654 (November 8, 1923).

14. Scholem and Scholem, *Mutter und Sohn*, 95 (November 20, 1923).

15. Bernhard Reich, *Im Wettlauf mit der Zeit: Erinnerungen aus fünf Jahrzehnten deutscher Theatergeschichte* (Berlin, 1970), 240.

16. See Feldman, *Great Disorder*, 782.

17. *AdR: Die Kabinette Stresemann*, vol. 2, no. 227, 986–990 (November 7, 1923), and no. 233, 1005 (November 9, 1923).

18. Luther, *Politiker ohne Partei*, 181. See also *AdR: Die Kabinette Stresemann*, vol. 2, no. 242, 1032–1037, 1034–1035, note 15.

19. *AdR: Die Kabinette Stresemann*, vol. 2, no. 242, 1038 (November 12, 1923). See also Luther, *Politiker ohne Partei*, 150–151; and Feldman, *Great Disorder*, 792–793. See, despite his tendency to highlight his own role in the stabilization of the mark, Hjalmar Schacht, *76 Jahre meines Lebens* (Bad Wörishofen, 1953), 226ff. On Havenstein, see Wallwitz, *Die große Inflation*, 135–150, 262–263.

20. See Luther, *Politiker ohne Partei*, 143; and Feldman, *Great Disorder*, 795.

21. "Unser neues Geld," *Vossische Zeitung* 546 (November 17, 1923). See also Feldman, *Great Disorder*, 793.

22. Haffner, *Defying Hitler*, 65.

23. Klemperer, *Tagebücher 1918–1924*, 759 (November 22, 1923), and 761 (December 4, 1923).

24. Luther, *Politiker ohne Partei*, 215.

25. Kessler, *Tagebuch*, vol. 8, 167 (December 4, 1923). See also *Berliner Tageblatt* 580

(December 16, 1923): "The fever is receding, and people's fears about tomorrow have given way to a calmer, more confident disposition."

26. "New Confidence in Germany: A Stable Currency," *Manchester Guardian* (December 13, 1923), cited in Frederick Taylor, *The Downfall of Money: Germany's Hyperinflation and the Destruction of the Middle Class* (London, 2014), 333–334. See also Moltke, *Ein Leben in Deutschland*, 86 (December 29, 1923): "It's a great relief for everyone to again have small sums and stable prices. At least you know where you stand."

27. D'Abernon, *Ambassador*, 283.

28. Luther, *Politiker ohne Partei*, 192. On the conclusion of the MICUM negotiations, see Wulf, *Hugo Stinnes*, 410–418; and Feldman and Homburg, *Industrie und Inflation*, 150. See also the wording of the agreement itself, in *Ursachen und Folgen*, vol. 5, no. 1102, 268–273.

29. See Mühlhausen, *Friedrich Ebert*, 700.

30. D'Abernon, *Ambassador*, 282. See also Luther, *Politiker ohne Partei*, 203: "Stresemann's immediate intention was to hold out come what may, and he was supported by his colleagues in the cabinet."

31. See Jonathan Wright, *Gustav Stresemann: Weimar's Greatest Statesmen* (Oxford, 2002), 250.

32. Eberhard Kolb and Ludwig Richter, *Nationalliberalismus in der Weimarer Republik: Die Führungsgremien der Deutschen Volkspartei, 1918–1933*, vol. 1: *1918–1925* (Düsseldorf, 1999), no. 53, 476–485 (here 476, 484–485).

33. Kolb and Richter, vol. 1, 487. See also Richter, *Deutsche Volkspartei*, 301; and W. Stresemann, *Mein Vater Gustav Stresemann*, 278–279.

34. Georg Bernhard, "Stresemanns neuer Sieg," *Vossische Zeitung* 548 (November 19, 1923).

35. "Vor der Entscheidung," *Berliner Tageblatt* 538 (November 22, 1923).

36. See Winkler, *Weimar*, 240. For the wording of the vote of no confidence, see Kastning, *Die deutsche Sozialdemokratie*, 129.

37. *AdR: Die Kabinette Stresemann*, vol. 2, no. 268, 1130–1135.

38. See D'Abernon, *Ambassador*, 273–274 (November 24, 1923).

39. See Mühlhausen, *Friedrich Ebert*, 702.

40. "Drei Misstrauensanträge gegen Stresemann," *Vossische Zeitung* 549 (November 20, 1923).

41. Erich Dombrowski, "Unterbrechung der Verhandlungen: Der Kommunist Remmele als Störenfried," *Berliner Tageblatt* 537 (November 21, 1923). See also "Die Kanzlerrede auf Donnerstag verschoben," *Vossische Zeitung* 551 (November 21, 1923); and Luther, *Politiker ohne Partei*, 200–201.

42. *AdR: Die Kabinette Stresemann*, vol. 2, no. 278, 1162.

43. On Stresemann's motivations, see Wright, *Gustav Stresemann*, 256–257. Quotation from Stresemann, *Vermächtnis*, vol. 1, 244.

44. See "Keine Störung der Sitzung," *Vossische Zeitung* 553 (November 22, 1923).

45. See E[rich] D[ombrowski], "Die gestrige Reichstagssitzung," *Berliner Tageblatt* 540 (November 23, 1923).

46. See W. Stresemann, *Mein Vater Gustav Stresemann*, 281. Seeckt to his wife on

November 22, 1923: "Today [Stresemann] is said to have spoken marvelously." *AdR: Die Kabinette Stresemann*, vol. 2, appendix no. 1, note 122; and "Stresemanns Rede," *Vossische Zeitung* 554 (November 23, 1923). Erich Dombrowski was less impressed: "The chancellor's speech was in a minor key. More defense than offense. More a look back than a look ahead. More a justification than statement of intent." *Berliner Tageblatt* 540 (November 23, 1923).

47. Georg Bernhard, "Vor der Entscheidung," *Vossische Zeitung* 554 (November 23, 1923).

48. Gustav Stresemann, *Reichstagsreden*, ed. Gerhard Zwoch (Bonn, 1972), 155–206. For more details on the content of the speech, see Wright, *Gustav Stresemann*, 257–260.

49. Stresemann, *Vermächtnis*, vol. 1, 244.

50. "Seeckt verbietet die Putschparteien," *Vossische Zeitung* 555 (November 23, 1923). See also "Aufzeichnung über das vom Chef der Heeresleitung eingeleitete Verbotsverfahren gegen KPD, DVFP, und NSDAP, 20.11.1923," *AdR: Die Kabinette Stresemann*, vol. 2, no. 273, 1153; and "Verordnung Seeckts v. 23.11.1923," *Ursachen und Folgen*, vol. 5, no. 1206, 502–503.

51. "Das Kabinett Stresemann zurückgetreten," *Vossische Zeitung* 556 (November 24, 1923).

52. "Kabinettssitzung v. 23.11.1923, 19.45 Uhr," *AdR: Die Kabinette Stresemann*, vol. 2, no. 279, 1163.

53. "Tagesnotiz v. 23.11.1923," in Stresemann, *Vermächtnis*, vol. 1, 245. State Secretary Meissner recalled Ebert being "quite vexed about the behavior of his party colleagues" and criticizing the parliamentary group's decision with "a sharpness that was unusual for him." See Meissner, *Staatssekretär unter Ebert-Hindenburg-Hitler* (Hamburg, 1950), 133–134.

54. W. Stresemann, *Mein Vater Gustav Stresemann*, 283; and Stresemann, *Vermächtnis*, vol. 1, 245.

55. "Drei Monate," *Deutsche Allgemeine Zeitung* 546 (November 24, 1923).

56. Erich Dombrowski, "Stresemann," *Berliner Tageblatt* 542 (November 24, 1923).

57. Georg Bernhard, "Der Endkampf," *Vossische Zeitung* 547 (November 18, 1923).

58. Klaus Römer, "Abschied von Stresemann," *Die Weltbühne* 19/48, 521 (November 29, 1923).

59. *Das Tage-Buch* 48/4 (December 1, 1923), 1644.

60. See Kolb, *Gustav Stresemann*, 92–93; Berg, *Gustav Stresemann*, 82–83; Wright, *Gustav Stresemann*, 261; and Winkler, *Weimar*, 241–242.

61. See Koszyk, *Gustav Stresemann*, 227–228.

62. See Wright, *Gustav Stresemann*, 235.

63. "Stresemann an Kronprinz Wilhelm, 23.7.1923," in Stresemann, *Vermächtnis*, vol. 1, 215–219 (here 215). On the stance of the Cuno government, see *AdR: Das Kabinett Cuno*, no. 206, 617–619.

64. "Kronprinz Wilhelm an Stresemann, 29.9.1923," in Stresemann, *Vermächtnis*, vol. 1, 219–220.

65. "Kabinettssitzung v. 23.10.1923," *AdR: Die Kabinette Stresemann*, vol. 2, no. 167, 698–699.

66. "Stresemann an Kronprinz Wilhelm, 24.10.1923," in Stresemann, *Vermächtnis*, vol. 1, 221–222.

67. See John C. G. Röhl, *Wilhelm II: Der Weg in den Abgrund 1900–1941* (Munich, 2008), 1300. See also the diary entry by Wing Adjutant Sigurd von Ilsemann on November 12, 1923: "The right-wing circles who had no time for Stresemann will be infuriated that my young fellow has achieved his return thanks to the grace of this gentleman." Cited in Koszyk, *Gustav Stresemann*, 267.

68. See *AdR: Die Kabinette Stresemann*, vol. 2, no. 167, 699, note 8; Wright, *Gustav Stresemann*, 236; and Stresemann, *Vermächtnis*, vol. 1, 215.

69. Kessler, *Tagebuch*, vol. 8, 140 (November 13, 1923), and 143 (November 14, 1923). Thomas Wehrlin (Stefan Grossmann) also vigorously criticized Wilhelm II's return to Germany in his article "Der heimgekehrte Kronprinz," *Das Tage-Buch* 46/4 (November 17, 1923), 1591: "If one were to hand out sober grades on statesmanship, the chancellor's report card would contain a 'completely unsatisfactory' in 'political psychology.'" On November 16, 1923, Stefan Zweig wrote to Romain Rolland, "It was the stupidest gesture imaginable to summon the crown prince back." Zweig, *Briefe 1920–1931*, 449.

70. D'Abernon, *Ambassador*, 269 (November 11, 1923).

71. See Stephan Malinowski, *Die Hohenzollern und die Nazis: Geschichte einer Kollaboration* (Berlin, 2021), 213ff., 241ff.

72. Cited in Rudolf Morsey, *Die Deutsche Zentrumspartei 1917–1923* (Düsseldorf, 1966), 550. See also Erich Dombrowski, "Stresemann," *Vossische Zeitung* 542 (November 24, 1923): "What now? That's the big question everything will revolve around in the next few days."

73. Kessler, *Tagebuch*, vol. 8, 155 (November 24, 1923).

74. D'Abernon, *Ambassador*, 275 (November 25, 1923).

75. Seeckt to his sister on November 18, 1923, in Meier-Welcker, *Seeckt*, 411.

76. See Mühlhausen, *Friedrich Ebert*, 691–697; and Meier-Welcker, *Seeckt*, 414.

77. "Materialsammlung Lieber v. 17., 18., 20.11.1923," *AdR: Die Kabinette Stresemann*, vol. 2, appendix no. 1, 1200–1201.

78. Seeckt to his wife on November 22, 1923, in Mühlhausen, *Friedrich Ebert*, 699. See also Meier-Welcker, *Seeckt*, 412.

79. See Hehl, *Wilhelm Marx*, 250–251; Mühlhausen, *Friedrich Ebert*, 703–704; and "Kardorff als Reichskanzler vorgeschlagen," *Vossische Zeitung* 557 (November 24, 1923).

80. See Mühlhausen, *Friedrich Ebert*, 704–707; "Die Kombination Kardorff gescheitert," *Vossische Zeitung* 559 (November 25, 1923); and "Kardorff s Mission gescheitert," *Berliner Tageblatt* 544 (November 25, 1923).

81. Ebert to Albert on November 25, 1923, published in *Vossische Zeitung* 559 (November 26, 1923).

82. See Mühlhausen, *Friedrich Ebert*, 708–711; and "Materialsammlung Lieber v. 26.11.1923," *AdR: Die Kabinette Stresemann*, vol. 2, appendix no. 1, 1202.

83. Erich Dombrowski, "Die ungelöste Kabinettskrise," *Berliner Tageblatt* 546 (November 27, 1923; and Stresemann, *Vermächtnis*, vol. 1, 255.

84. See *Akten der Reichskanzlei (AdR): Die Kabinette Marx I und II*, vol. 1: *Novem-*

*ber 1923 bis Juni 1924*, ed. Günter Abramowski (Boppard am Rhein, 1973), viii; Mühlhausen, *Friedrich Ebert*, 711–712; "Der Kampf um die preußische Koalition," *Vossische Zeitung* 564 (November 29, 1923); and "Stegerwalds endgültiger Verzicht," *Berliner Tageblatt* 551 (November 29, 1923).

85. "Die Parteiverhandlungen gescheitert," *Deutsche Allgemeine Zeitung* 554 (November 29, 1923).

86. See *AdR: Die Kabinette Marx*, vol. 1, viii; Hehl, *Wilhelm Marx*, 252–253; and Mühlhausen, *Friedrich Ebert*, 712–713.

87. Luther, *Politiker ohne Partei*, 209–211. The letter was published in the *Berliner Tageblatt* 551 (November 29, 1923).

88. See *AdR: Die Kabinette Marx*, vol. 1, ix; Braun, *Weimarer Reichskanzler*, 305–307; and Hehl, *Wilhelm Marx*, 254–255.

89. "Marx an Stresemann, 24.11.1923" and "Stresemann an Marx, 28.11.1923," in Stresemann, *Vermächtnis*, vol. 1, 247–248. See also W. Stresemann, *Mein Vater Gustav Stresemann*, 287, which has Stresemann saying of Marx, "He's an upstanding man with whom I can work."

90. See *AdR: Die Kabinette Marx*, vol. 1, x; and Hehl, *Wilhelm Marx*, 249ff.

91. Georg Bernhard, "Nothelfer," *Vossische Zeitung* 570 (December 2, 1923).

92. *AdR: Die Kabinette Marx*, vol. 1, xi (Einleitung); no. 1, 1–3 (Kabinettssitzung v. 1.12.1923); and no. 2, 7–10 (Kabinettssitzung v. 2.12.1923). See also Winkler, *Weimar*, 246.

93. *AdR: Die Kabinette Marx*, vol. 1, no. 2, 8 (Kabinettssitzung v. 2.12.1923). See also Winkler, *Von der Revolution zur Stabilisierung*, 679; and Mühlhausen, *Friedrich Ebert*, 714–715.

94. "Ministerbesprechung v. 4.12.1923," *AdR: Die Kabinette Marx*, vol. 1, no. 7, 35. See also Kastning, *Die deutsche Sozialdemokratie*, 134–135; Winkler, *Von der Revolution zur Stabilisierung*, 679–680; and Mühlhausen, *Friedrich Ebert*, 715.

95. Erich Dombrowski, "Die gestrige Reichstagssitzung," *Berliner Tageblatt* 560 (December 5, 1923).

96. "Programmatische Erklärung des Reichskanzlers Marx im Reichstag, 4.12.1923," *Ursachen und Folgen*, vol. 5, no. 1104, 75–277 (here 276). See also Hehl, *Wilhelm Marx*, 257–258.

97. See "Die Entscheidung im Reichstag vertagt," *Berliner Tageblatt* 564 (December 7, 1923); "Das Ermächtigungsgesetz angenommen," *Berliner Tageblatt* 568 (December 9, 1923); and Winkler, *Von der Revolution zur Stabilisierung*, 680.

98. *Ursachen und Folgen*, vol. 5, no. 1106, 283.

99. *AdR: Die Kabinette Marx*, vol. 1, xxv–xxvi.

100. "Kabinettssitzung v. 10.12.1923," *AdR: Die Kabinette Marx*, vol. 1, no. 15, 72–75. See also *AdR: Marx*, vol. 1, xxv; Luther, *Politiker ohne Partei*, 219; and Winkler, *Weimar*, 249.

101. Klemperer, *Tagebücher 1918–1924*, 762 (December 10, 1923).

102. See *AdR: Die Kabinette Marx*, vol. 1, xxvii–xxviii; Luther, *Politiker ohne Partei*, 220–225; Winkler, *Von der Revolution zur Stabilisierung*, 694–695; and Longerich, *Deutschland, 1918–1933*, 149–150.

103. *AdR: Die Kabinette Marx*, vol. 1, no. 23, 105 (Kabinettssitzung v. 14.12.1923);

and no. 25, 113–114 (Sitzung des Wirtschaftsausschusses des Kabinetts v. 15.12.1923). See also Gerald D. Feldman and Irmgard Steinisch, "Die Weimarer Republik zwischen Sozial- und Wirtschaftsstaat: Die Entscheidung gegen den Achtstundentag," *Archiv für Sozialgeschichte* 18 (1978): 353–439 (here 411–412); Winkler, *Weimar*, 248–249; and Ruck, *Freien Gewerkschaften*, 527–529.

104. Winkler, *Von der Revolution zur Stabilisierung*, 713.

105. "Bericht des Justizrats Hugo Mönnig in der Sitzung des Reichskabinetts und des Fünfzehnerausschusses, 17.11.1923," *AdR: Die Kabinette Stresemann*, vol. 2, no. 267, 1110–1111.

106. "Denkschrift Tirards v. 29.11.1923," in Erdmann, *Adenauer in der Rheinlandpolitik*, doc. 17, 322–323. See also Erdmann, 150–151; and Schwarz, *Adenauer*, vol. 1, 278.

107. "Gegenvorschlag Adenauers zur Denkschrift Tirards v. 12.12.1923," in Erdmann, *Adenauer in der Rheinlandpolitik*, doc. 20, 327–331.

108. "Aufzeichnung Adenauers über seine Unterredung mit Marx, 14.12.1923," Erdmann, doc. 23, 35–36. See also Erdmann, 163.

109. "Niederschrift über eine Besprechung mit Vertretern der besetzten Gebiete, 9.1.1924," *AdR: Die Kabinette Marx*, vol. 1, no. 53, 211–215 (here 212, 215).

110. "Stresemann an Marx, 16.1.1924," in Erdmann, *Adenauer in der Rheinlandpolitik*, doc. 32, 361–365 (362, 365). See also Erdmann, 177–178; and Schwarz, *Adenauer*, vol. 1, 285–286.

111. "Adenauer an Marx, 23.1.1924," in Erdmann, *Adenauer in der Rheinlandpolitik*, doc. 35, 369–370.

112. See *AdR: Die Kabinette Marx*, vol. 1, xxxiii; and Winkler, *Weimar*, 251.

113. Pringsheim, *Tagebücher*, vol. 7, 114 (December 31, 1923). See also Erich Dombrowski, "Silvester," *Berliner Tageblatt* 602 (December 31, 1923): "When one looks back upon the year that ends tonight, one finds oneself standing before a glimmering pile of wrecked hopes."

114. Kessler, *Tagebuch*, vol. 8, 187 (December 31, 1923).

115. Haffner, *Defying Hitler*, 66.

116. Alfred Döblin, "Berliner Weihnachten," *Prager Tagblatt* (December 30, 1923), cited in Glatzer, *Berlin zur Weimarer Zeit*, 131.

117. *Das Tage-Buch* 52/4 (December 19, 1923), 1767.

118. D'Abernon, *Ambassador*, 290 (December 31, 1923).

119. "Oberstleutnant Erfurth an Oberstleutnant Joachim von Stülpnagel, Leiter der Heeresabteilung (T I) im Truppenamt der Heeresleitung, 1.1.1924," in Hürten, ed., *Krisenjahr 1923*, no. 152, 223.

*Chapter 8:* CULTURE IN A TIME OF CRISIS

1. *Gewerkschafts-Zeitung* 34/1 (January 5, 1924), 1.

2. See Sabina Becker, *Experiment Weimar: Eine Kulturgeschichte Deutschlands, 1918–1933* (Darmstadt, 2018), 17–19; and Becker, "Zu neuen Ufern," *Zeit-Geschichte* 1 (2020): 16–19.

3. See Peukert, *Die Weimarer Republik*, 169–174; Büttner, *Weimar*, 331–334; and Jochen Hung, "Massenkulturen," in Rossol and Ziemann, eds., *Aufbruch und Abgründe*, 699–721.

4. Kerr, *Berlin wird Berlin* 4, 438 (December 11, 1921).

5. See Kolb, *Die Weimarer Republik*, 92–93; Büttner, *Weimar*, 298–299; and Becker, *Experiment Weimar*, 26–27.

6. Klaus Kreimeier, *Die Ufa-Story: Geschichte eines Filmkonzerns* (Munich, 1992), 77. See also Becker, *Experiment Weimar*, 275.

7. *Das Tage-Buch* 40/6 (October 3, 1925), 1504. See also Kreimeier, *Ufa-Story*, 136.

8. Kreimeier, *Ufa-Story*, 120.

9. Hans Siemsen, "Die Filmerei," *Die Weltbühne* 17/4 (January 27, 1921), 101–105 (here 101).

10. Kerr, *Berlin wird Berlin*, vol. 4, 187 (October 12, 1919), and 276 (September 12, 1920): "Film is an artistic genre like all others, with a certain future, and deserves for people to devote attention to it."

11. Klemperer, *Tagebücher 1918–1924*, 626–627 (October 22, 1922).

12. Klemperer, 767 (December 30, 1923).

13. Peter Panter (Kurt Tucholsky), "Dr. Caligari," *Die Weltbühne* 16/11 (March 11, 1920), 347–348; and Tucholsky, *Gesammelte Werke*, vol. 2: *1919–1920* (Reinbek bei Hamburg, 1985), 292–293. See also Peter Gay, *Weimar Culture: The Outsider as Insider* (New York, 1968), 102ff; and Becker, *Experiment Weimar*, 279. On Erich Pommer, see Kreimeier, *Ufa-Story*, 146–147.

14. Siegfried Kracauer, *From Caligari to Hitler: A Psychological History of the German Film* (Princeton, 1846), 32ff. See also Momme Brodersen, *Siegfried Kracauer* (Reinbek bei Hamburg, 2001), 120–122; and Jörg Später, *Siegfried Kracauer: Eine Biographie* (Berlin, 2016), 448ff.

15. See Martynkewicz, *1920*, 69–70; and Kreimeier, *Ufa-Story*, 61–62, 104–106.

16. "Nosferatu," *Vossische Zeitung* 111 (March 7, 1922).

17. Barbara Beuys, *Asta Nielsen: Filmgenie und Neue Frau* (Berlin, 2020), 193.

18. Beuys, 199.

19. Klemperer, *Tagebücher 1918–1924*, 662 (February 18, 1923). See also Kurt Pinthus, "Die Tänzerin Navarro," *Das Tage-Buch* 4/14 (April 7, 1923), 502.

20. *Das Tage-Buch* 4/21 (May 26, 1923), 759. Roland Schacht was likewise enthusiastic in *Die Weltbühne* 19/23 (June 7, 1923), 675–676.

21. Klemperer, *Tagebücher 1918–1924*, 761–762 (December 4, 1923). See also Beuys, *Asta Nielsen*, 220–222; and Hanna Vollmer-Heitmann, *Wir sind von Kopf bis Fuß auf Liebe eingestellt: Die Zwanziger Jahre* (Hamburg, 1993), 140–141.

22. See Beuys, *Asta Nielsen*, 224; and Vollmer-Heitmann, *Wir sind von Kopf*, 131–132.

23. Hans Siemsen, "Kino-Elend," *Die Weltbühne* 18/33 (August 17, 1922), 169.

24. *Das Tage-Buch* 4/52 (December 29, 1923), 1790. See also Beuys, *Asta Nielsen*, 224–225; and Kreimeier, *Ufa-Story*, 119–120.

25. Peter Panter (Kurt Tucholsky), "Tragödie der Liebe," *Die Weltbühne* 19/43 (October 25, 1923), 406–408; also in Tucholsky, *Gesammelte Werke*, vol. 3, 355–358. See also Kurt Pinthus, "Tragödie der Liebe," *Das Tage-Buch* 4/41 (October

13, 1923), 1457: "What we have here is simply the best contemporarily set film that has ever been made."

26. Kurt Pinthus, "Alles für Geld," *Das Tage-Buch* 4/47 (November 24, 1923), 1638.

27. Ossietzky, *Sämtliche Schriften*, vol. 2, 222–223.

28. Rudolf Geldern, "Der historische Film," *Die Weltbühne* 19/38 (September 20, 1923), 297–298.

29. Theobald Tiger (Kurt Tucholsky), "Fridericus Rex," *Die Weltbühne* 18/8 (February 23, 1922), 194; also in Tucholsky, *Gesammelte Werke*, vol. 3, 132.

30. Curt Rosenberg, "Fridericus Rex," *Die Weltbühne* 19/27 (July 5, 1923), 13–14.

31. Kreimeier, *Ufa-Story*, 113.

32. Hanfstaengl, *Zwischen Weißem und Braunem Haus*, 104.

33. Klemperer, *Tagebücher 1918–1924*, 564–565 (March 14, 1922).

34. Klemperer, 695–696 (May 20, 1923).

35. Tucholsky, *Gesammelte Werke*, vol. 3, 230–232 (here 232). Alfred Kerr was less enthusiastic: "After ten minutes I could no longer watch the little fellow with his thick, narrow mustache—all I took with me were the wonderful moments of surprise provided by his truly zoological adroitness." *Berlin wird Berlin*, vol. 4, 509 (September 3, 1922).

36. Hans Siemsen, "Chaplin," *Die Weltbühne* 18/42 (October 19, 1922), 415.

37. *Die Weltbühne* 17/40 (October 5, 1922), 367–368; 17/41 (October 12, 1922), 385–387; 17/42 (October 19, 1923), 415–416; 17/43 (October 26, 1922), 447–448; and 17/44 (November 2, 1922), 473–474 (here 474).

38. Kurt Pinthus, "Filme aus Amerika," *Das Tage-Buch* 4/49 (December 8, 1923), 1702. See also Kurt Tucholsky, "The Kid," *Die Weltbühne* 19/49 (December 9, 1923), 564–566; also in Tucholsky, *Gesammelte Werke*, vol. 3, 358–361.

39. Klemperer, *Tagebücher 1918–1924*, 766–767 (December 30, 1923).

40. See Reinhard Mehring, *Carl Schmitt: Aufstieg und Fall—Eine Biographie* (Munich, 2009), 163.

41. Ludwig Marcuse, *Mein Zwanzigstes Jahrhundert: Auf dem Weg zu einer Autobiographie* (Frankfurt, 1968), 58–59.

42. See Glatzer, *Berlin zur Weimarer Zeit*, 270–271, 253, 263. See also Becker, *Experiment Weimar*, 470; and Kolb, *Die Weimarer Republik*, 96–97.

43. See Becker, *Experiment Weimar*, 437–438; Rühle, *Theater für die Republik*, vol. 1, 170; and Büttner, *Weimar*, 305.

44. Fritz Engel in *Berliner Tageblatt* (November 29, 1919). See also Rühle, *Theater für die Republik*, vol. 1, 174; and Glatzer, *Berlin zur Weimarer Zeit*, 265.

45. See Rühle, *Theater für die Republik*, vol. 1, 203, 425; Glatzer, *Berlin zur Weimarer Zeit*, 266; and Becker, *Experiment Weimar*, 439.

46. Fritz Kortner, *Aller Tage Abend: Autobiographie* (Munich, 1959), 350–362. On the performance of *Wilhelm Tell*, see Gay, *Weimar Culture*, 111–112; Rühle, *Theater für die Republik*, vol. 1, 190–196; Becker, *Experiment Weimar*, 442–443; and Rainer Metzger, *Die Zwanziger Jahre: Kunst und Kultur 1918–1933* (Munich, 2007), 126–127.

47. Rühle, *Theater für die Republik*, vol. 1, 210.

48. Rühle, 201.

49. Rühle, 201.

50. See Becker, *Experiment Weimar*, 464–465; and Glatzer, *Berlin zur Weimarer Zeit*, 277–280.

51. Hans Sahl, *Memoiren eines Moralisten* (Zürich, 1983). See also Glatzer, *Berlin zur Weimarer Zeit*, 264–265; Peter Hoeres, *Die Kultur von Weimar: Durchbruch der Moderne* (Berlin-Brandenburg, 2008), 146–147; and Zuckmayer, *Als wär's ein Stück von mir*, 315: "The two men existed and wrote their reviews in the most intimate enmity, tearing apart the other's favorite until the feathers flew."

52. Rühle, *Theater für die Republik*, vol. 1, 255.

53. Rühle, 421.

54. Kurt Tucholsky, "Bergner! Bergner!" *Die Weltbühne* 19/19 (May 10, 1923), 553–554; also in Tucholsky, *Gesammelte Werke*, vol. 3, 320–322.

55. Georg Hensel, *Der Spielplan: Der Schauspielführer von der Antike bis zur Gegenwart*, vol. 2, 4th ed. (Munich, 1992), 940. On the two plays, see Hensel, 944–947; and Rühle, *Theater für die Republik*, vol. 1, 53–57, 57–61.

56. Georg Kaiser, *Stücke, Erzählungen, Aufsätze, Gedichte* (Cologne, 1966), 168.

57. Kaiser, 254. On the *Gas* trilogy, see Hensel, *Spielplan*, vol. 2, 947–949; and Rühle, *Theater für die Republik*, vol. 1, 79–86, 124–131, 183–189.

58. See Kaiser, *Stücke*, 797–798; and Hensel, *Spielplan*, vol. 2, 940.

59. Milena Jesenská, "Der Fall Georg Kaiser," in *"Alles ist Leben": Feuilletons und Reportagen, 1919–1939*," ed. Dorothea Rein (Frankfurt, 1984), 38–41 (here 39).

60. Kaiser, *Stücke*, 323.

61. Rühle, *Theater für die Republik*, vol. 1, 483.

62. Siegfried Jacobsohn, "Nebeneinander," *Die Weltbühne* 19/46 (November 15, 1923), 482–483. See also Alfred Polgar, "Nebeneinander," *Die Weltbühne* 20/23 (June 5, 1924), 780–782.

63. Ernst Toller, *Prosa, Briefe, Dramen, Gedichte* (Reinbek bei Hamburg, 1961), 285. On Toller's life, see Wolfgang Rothe, *Toller* (Reinbek bei Hamburg, 1983); and Richard Dove, *Ernst Toller: Ein Leben in Deutschland* (Göttingen, 1993).

64. Rühle, *Theater für die Republik*, vol. 1, 157, 163.

65. See Dove, *Ernst Toller*, 131–138; Rothe, *Toller*, 64–68; and Hensel, *Spielplan*, vol. 2, 1570. On Toller's reception, see Rühle, *Theater für die Republik*, vol. 1, 320–326.

66. See Dove, *Ernst Toller*, 143–144; and Rühle, *Theater für die Republik*, vol. 1, 383–389.

67. Toller, *Prosa*, 433.

68. Rühle, *Theater für die Republik*, vol. 1, 486–487. See also Carl von Ossietzky, "Hinkemann und Hakenkreuz: Der organisierte Theaterskandal," in *Sämtliche Schriften*, vol. 2, 322–324 (here 323): "The entire racist army was sent into the field for the premier of 'Hinkemann' in Dresden."

69. Dove, *Ernst Toller*, 152–153.

70. Dove, 152–157.

71. Kurt Tucholsky, "An Ernst Toller," *Gesammelte Werke*, vol. 3, 443.

72. Zuckmayer, *Als wär's ein Stück von mir*, 305. See also Bisky, *Berlin*, 489–490.

73. Bertolt Brecht, *Briefe 1: 1913–1936; Werke: Große kommentierte Berliner und*

*Frankfurter Ausgabe*, ed. Werner Hecht, Jan Knopf, Werner Mittenzwei, and Klaus-Detlef Müller, vol. 28 (Frankfurt, 1998), 101, 102.

74.  See Werner Hecht, *Brecht Chronik, 1898–1956* (Frankfurt, 1997), 87.

75.  See Jan Knopf, *Bertolt Brecht: Lebenskunst in finsteren Zeiten—Biografie* (Munich, 2012), 122–124; and Reinhold Jaretzky, *Bertolt Brecht* (Reinbek bei Hamburg, 2006), 31–32.

76.  See Glatzer, *Berlin zur Weimarer Zeit*, 338–340; and Michael Bienert, *Brechts Berlin: Literarische Schauplätze* (Berlin, 2018), 51.

77.  Hesterberg, *Was ich noch sagen wollte*, 108–109.

78.  See Hesterberg, 126–127; and Bienert, *Brechts Berlin*, 52.

79.  Arnolt Bronnen, *Tage mit Bertolt Brecht: Die Geschichte einer unvollendeten Freundschaft* (Vienna, 1960), 14.

80.  See Rühle, *Theater für die Republik*, vol. 1, 106; and Gay, *Weimar Culture*, 114.

81.  Bronnen, *Tage mit Bertolt Brecht*, 41–43 (here 43). See also Hecht, *Brecht Chronik*, 139; and Knopf, *Bertolt Brecht*, 105.

82.  Rühle, *Theater für die Republik*, vol. 1, 377. See also Rühle, 375–376; and Jaretzky, *Bertolt Brecht*, 33.

83.  Bertolt Brecht, *Gesammelte Werke*, vol. 1: *Stücke 1* (Frankfurt, 1967), 123.

84.  Brecht, 70.

85.  Hecht, *Brecht Chronik*, 144. See also Knopf, *Bertolt Brecht*, 105–106; and John Fuegi, *Brecht & Co. Biographie* (Hamburg, 1997), 161–162.

86.  Rühle, *Theater für die Republik*, vol. 1, 406–408 (here 406). See also Ihering's response to Kerr's criticism, in Rühle, 408–410.

87.  Rühle, *Theater für die Republik*, vol. 1, 452–453. See also Rühle, 446; Hecht, *Brecht Chronik*, 157; and Knopf, *Bertolt Brecht*, 107–108.

88.  Hecht, *Brecht Chronik*, 158.

89.  Bronnen, *Tage mit Bertolt Brecht*, 140–142. See also Klaus Völker, *Bertolt Brecht: Eine Biographie* (Munich, 1976), 75–76.

90.  Hecht, *Brecht Chronik*, 165. On the reception of the premier of *Baal*, see Rühle, *Theater für die Republik*, vol. 1, 486–493.

91.  See Zuckmayer, *Als wär's ein Stück von mir*, 393–404; Becker, *Experiment Weimar*, 448; and Gay, *Weimar Culture*, 121.

92.  Wilhelm von Sternburg, *Joseph Roth: Eine Biographie* (Cologne, 2009), 203.

93.  Heinz Lunzer and Victoria Lunzer-Talos, *Joseph Roth: Leben in Werk und Bildern* (Cologne, 1994), 90.

94.  Herbert Günther, *Drehbühne der Zeit: Freundschaften, Begegnungen, Schicksale* (Hamburg, 1957). See also Glatzer, *Berlin zur Weimarer Zeit*, 260; Large, *Berlin*, 190f.; and Bienert, *Brechts Berlin*, 23–24.

95.  Joseph Roth, *Werke*, ed. Fritz Hackert and Klaus Westermann, vol. 1 (Cologne, 1989), 876. See also Sternburg, *Joseph Roth*, 259–261.

96.  The announcement is reproduced in Lunzer and Lunzer-Talos, *Joseph Roth*, 118.

97.  Joseph Roth, *The Spider's Web and Zipper and His Father*, trans. John Hoare (Woodstock, NY: Overlook, 1989), 5.

98.  Roth, 40.

99.  Dora Diamant, "Mein Leben mit Franz Kafka," in *"Als Kafka mir entgegen-*

*kam...": Erinnerungen an Franz Kafka*, ed. Hans-Gerd Koch (Berlin, 1995), 174. See also Reiner Stach, *Kafka: Die Jahre der Erkenntnis* (Frankfurt, 2008), 542ff.; and Peter-André Alt, *Franz Kafka: Der ewige Sohn—Eine Biographie* (Munich, 2005), 640–643, 667ff.

100. Franz Kafka, *Briefe, 1902–1924*, ed. Max Brod and Klaus Wagenbach (Frankfurt, [1958] 1975), 447. See also Alt, *Franz Kafka*, 667.

101. Kafka, *Briefe, 1902–1924*, 451. See also Klaus Wagenbach, *Franz Kafka in Selbstzeugnissen und Bilddokumenten* (Reinbek bei Hamburg, 1964), 133; and Stach, *Kafka*, 557–558.

102. See Stach, *Kafka*, 562–564; and Alt, *Franz Kafka*, 677.

103. Franz Kafka, *The Complete Stories*, trans. Nahum Norbert Glatzer (New York, 1971), 347.

104. See Stach, *Kafka*, 569; and Alt, *Franz Kafka*, 675.

105. See Stach, *Kafka*, 574–577; and Alt, *Franz Kafka*, 680. On the publishing house Die Schmiede, see Alt, 639–640.

106. See Stach, *Kafka*, 580–585; and Alt, *Franz Kafka*, 681–682.

107. See Alt, *Franz Kafka*, 683.

108. Jesenská, *"Alles ist Leben,"* 96–97.

109. See Karl Schlögel, "Berlin: 'Stiefmutter unter den russischen Städten,'" in *Der große Exodus: Die russische Emigration und ihre Zentren 1917 bis 1941*, ed. Schlögel (Munich, 1994), 235–259 (here 237).

110. Schlögel, 240.

111. Kerr, *Berlin wird Berlin*, vol. 4, 436–437 (December 4, 1921).

112. See Glatzer, *Berlin zur Weimarer Zeit*, 256; and Schlögel, "Berlin," 241.

113. See Large, *Berlin*, 186ff.; Glatzer, *Berlin zur Weimarer Zeit*, 256; and Schlögel, "Berlin," 257.

114. See Beuys, *Asta Nielsen*, 209.

115. "Aufzeichnung von Staatssekretär Hamm, 17.1.1923," *AdR: Das Kabinett Cuno*, no. 48, 159–162.

116. Ossietzky, *Sämtliche Schriften*, vol. 2, 219.

117. Schlögel, "Berlin," 244–246 (here 246).

118. See Dieter E. Zimmer, *Nabokovs Berlin* (Berlin, 2001), 120, 130; and Large, *Berlin*, 186.

119. Zimmer, *Nabokovs Berlin*, 8ff.

120. Zuckmayer, *Als wär's ein Stück von mir*, 328. See also Glatzer, *Berlin zur Weimarer Zeit*, 257–258.

121. Alfred Polgar, "Der blaue Vogel," *Die Weltbühne* 19/2 (January 11, 1923), 44–45; Peter Panter (Kurt Tucholsky), "Der blaue Vogel," *Die Weltbühne* 18/12 (March 23, 1922), 305–306; also in Tucholsky, *Gesammelte Werke*, vol. 3, 149–151.

122. Large, *Berlin*, 200. See also Martynkewicz, *1920*, 27–29.

123. Kurt Tucholsky, "Dada," *Gesammelte Werke*, vol. 2, 382–383.

124. Lothar Fischer, *George Grosz: Vollständig überarbeitete Neuausgabe* (Reinbek bei Hamburg, 1993).

125. Wieland Herzfeld, *Immergrün: Merkwürdige Erlebnisse eines fröhlichen Waisenknaben* (Berlin, 1969), 178.

126. See Fischer, *George Grosz*, 36; Roland März, "Metropolis-Krawall der Irren: Der apokalyptische Grosz der Kriegsjahre 1914 bis 1918," in *George Grosz: Berlin/New York*, ed. Peter-Klaus Schuster (Berlin, 1994), 126. On Grosz's friendship with the Herzfeld brothers, see Ulrich Faure, *Im Knotenpunkt des Weltverkehrs: Herzfelde, Heartfield, Grosz, und der Malik-Verlag, 1916–1947* (Berlin, 1992), 31ff.

127. See Uwe M. Schneede, "Infernalischer Wirklichkeitsspuk," in Serge Sabarsky, *George Grosz: Die Berliner Jahre* (Hamburg, 1985), 27–33.

128. See Faure, *Im Knotenpunkt des Weltverkehrs*, 140ff.; and Glatzer, *Berlin zur Weimarer Zeit*, 292–293.

129. See Fischer, *George Grosz*, 61. Reproduction in Faure, *Im Knotenpunkt des Weltverkehrs*, 88.

130. Kessler, Uwe M. Schneede, "Infernalischer Wirklichkeitsspuk," in Sabarsky, *George Grosz*, vol. 7, 123 (February 5, 1919).

131. Kessler, 189 (March 16, 1919).

132. Rosamunde Neugebauer, "Der Satire wird der Prozess gemacht—der Fall Grosz," in Schuster, ed., *George Grosz*, 167–174 (here 168–169); and Fischer, *George Grosz*, 77.

133. Ignaz Wrobel (Kurt Tucholsky), "Fratzen von Grosz," *Die Weltbühne* 17/33 (August 18, 1921), 184–185; also in Tucholsky, *Gesammelte Werke*, vol. 3, 41–43.

134. Grosz, *Ein kleines Ja*, 153–176 (here 173).

135. See Fischer, *George Grosz*, 81.

136. Hans Reimann, "George Grosz," *Das Tage-Buch* 31/4 (August 4, 1923), 1115.

137. See Neugebauer, "Der Satire wird," 169.

138. Fischer, *George Grosz*, 83–84.

139. See Neugebauer, "Der Satire wird," 170–171.

140. Friedrich Sieburg, "Galerie George Grosz," *Die Weltbühne* 19/52 (December 27, 1923), 668–669. On the Malik bookstore, see Faure, *Im Knotenpunkt des Weltverkehrs*, 179–180.

141. See Wilfried Nerdinger, *Walter Gropius: Architekt der Moderne, 1883–1969* (Munich, 2019), 18–93.

142. Nerdinger, 100–101.

143. Nerdinger, 100–103.

144. "Program of the Staatliche Bauhaus in Weimar," Design Museum of Chicago (website), https://bauhausmanifesto.com.

145. Nerdinger, *Walter Gropius*, 117.

146. On the workshops, see Magdalena Droste and Bauhaus-Archiv, *Bauhaus, 1919–1933* (Berlin, 1998), 34–36.

147. Droste, 32–33. See also Nerdinger, *Walter Gropius*, 134–135; and Peter Merseburger, *Mythos Weimar: Zwischen Geist und Macht* (Stuttgart, 1998), 297–298.

148. See Nerdinger, *Walter Gropius*, 136–142; Droste, *Bauhaus, 1919–1933*, 54–57; and Merseburger, *Mythos Weimar*, 298.

149. See Nerdinger, *Walter Gropius*, 154; and Droste, *Bauhaus, 1919–1933*, 60–61.

150. Kessler, *Tagebuch*, vol. 7, 268 (August 19, 1919).

151. See Nerdinger, *Walter Gropius*, 120; and Droste, *Bauhaus, 1919–1933*, 48.

152. Merseburger, *Mythos Weimar*, 294. See also Merseburger, 293–294; Nerdinger, *Walter Gropius*, 134; and Friedrich, *Morgen ist Weltuntergang*, 194–195.

153. See Nerdinger, *Walter Gropius*, 122, 149; Droste, *Bauhaus, 1919–1933*, 46–47, 105; and Merseburger, *Mythos Weimar*, 304.

154. Nerdinger, *Walter Gropius*, 155.

155. Nerdinger, 169. See also Droste, *Bauhaus, 1919–1933*, 106.

156. Adolf Behne, "Das Bauhaus Weimar," *Die Weltbühne* 19/38 (September 20, 1923), 289–292. On the model house, see Nerdinger, *Walter Gropius*, 304; Droste, *Bauhaus, 1919–1933*, 105; and Merseburger, *Mythos Weimar*, 304–305.

157. See Nerdinger, *Walter Gropius*, 170ff.; and Droste, *Bauhaus, 1919–1933*, 113ff.

158. Glatzer, *Berlin zur Weimarer Zeit*, 361–362 (here 362).

159. See Glatzer, *Berlin zur Weimarer Zeit*, 363.

160. Alfred Braun, *Achtung, Achtung: Hier ist Berlin! Aus der Geschichte des Deutschen Rundfunks in Berlin, 1923–1932* (Berlin, 1968). See also Glatzer, *Berlin zur Weimarer Zeit*, 364.

161. Riess, "Weltbühne Berlin," 46.


*Chapter 9:* AFTER 1923: A NEW PERIOD IN GERMAN HISTORY?

1.  Rosenberg, *Geschichte der Weimarer Republik*, 184.

2.  Moltke, *Ein Leben in Deutschland*, 87 (January 9, 1924). See also Moltke, 87 (January 17, 1924): "Our Rentenmark has brought about an unbelievable upsurge in every political, economic, social, and moral sense."

3.  Mann, *Turning Point*, 103.

4.  Klemperer, *Tagebücher 1918–1924*, 784–785 (February 9, 1924).

5.  Winkler, *Weimar*, 259.

6.  See Link, *Die amerikanische Stabilisierungspolitik in Deutschland*, 203–204; Winkler, *Weimar*, 258–259; and Mommsen, *Die verspielte Freiheit*, 184–185.

7.  Sternheim, *Tagebücher*, vol. 1, 664 (January 24, 1924).

8.  See Dietmar Neutatz, *Träume und Alpträume: Eine Geschichte Russlands im 20. Jahrhundert* (Munich, 2013), 183–187, 191–192; Manfred Hildermeier, *Geschichte der Sowjetunion, 1917–1991: Entstehung und Niedergang des ersten sozialistischen Staates* (Munich, 1998), 168–182, 352–363; and Winkler, *Weimar*, 259–260.

9.  See Heinrich August Winkler, *Geschichte des Westens*, vol. 2: *Die Zeit der Weltkriege, 1914–1945* (Munich, 2011), 256–258, 321; and Franz Josef Brüggemeier, *Geschichte Großbritanniens im 20. Jahrhundert* (Munich, 2010), 137–138.

10. Kessler, *Tagebuch*, vol. 8, 331 (May 12, 1924).

11. See Jacques Bariéty, "Die französische Politik in der Ruhrkrise," in Schwabe, ed., *Die Ruhrkrise 1923*, 25; and Winkler, *Geschichte des Westens*, vol. 2, 21.

12. See *AdR: Die Kabinette Marx*, vol. 1, xiv–xv; "Haniel, Vertreter der Reichsregierung in München, an Reichskanzlei, 13.12., 15.12, 26.12.1923," no. 22, 26, 38, 103–104, 115 f, 162–163; and "Chef des Truppenamts an Staatssekretär Bracht, 14.1.1924 (mit Anlagen: Lossow an Seeckt, 12.1.1924, und Seeckt an

Ebert, 13.1.1924)," no. 60, 236–238. See also Meier-Welcker, *Seeckt*, 425–426; and Winkler, *Von der Revolution zur Stabilisierung*, 690–691.

13. *AdR: Die Kabinette Marx*, vol. 1, xv; "Ministerbesprechung v. 17.1.1924," no. 63, 243–248; "Haniel an Reichskanzlei, 28.1.1924," no. 75, 286–287; "Ministerbesprechung v. 29.1.1924," no. 79, 297–298; "Knilling an Marx, 12.2.1924," no. 101, 353–357; and "Bayerischer Gesandter v. Preger an Staatssekretär Bracht, 19.2.1924 (mit Anlage: Vereinbarung zwischen dem Reich und Bayern)," no. 109, 377–379. See also Meier-Welcker, *Seeckt*, 427–429; and Winkler, *Von der Revolution zur Stabilisierung*, 691.

14. Stockhausen, *Sechs Jahre Reichskanzlei*, 107 (February 17, 1924).

15. See "Hermann Müller an Marx, 18.12.1923," *AdR: Die Kabinette Marx*, vol. 1, no. 32, 133–135.

16. "Ministerbesprechung v. 11.1.1924," *AdR: Marx*, vol. 1, no. 58, 230, and "Ministerbesprechung v. 12.2.1924," no. 99, 348.

17. "Seeckt an Ebert, 13.2.1924," *AdR: Marx*, vol. 1, no. 99, 349, note 6.

18. See *AdR: Marx*, vol. 1, xiii; and Winkler, *Weimar*, 253.

19. "Verordnung Eberts v. 28.2.1924," *AdR: Marx*, vol. 1, no. 122, 409, note 7. See also p. xiv; and Winkler, *Von der Revolution zur Stabilisierung*, 693.

20. Meier-Welcker, *Seeckt*, 435.

21. Leo Lania, "Hitler-Prozess," *Die Weltbühne* 20/10 (March 6, 1924), 298–301 (here 298). See also Lania, "Der Hitler-Ludendorff-Prozess," *Schreibheft: Zeitschrift für Literatur* 87 (2016 reprint), 170–198.

22. Hitler, *Hitler-Prozess*, part 1, 60–61. See also Ullrich, *Hitler: Ascent*, 160ff.

23. Hitler, *Hitler-Prozess*, part 4, 1591.

24. Pringsheim, *Tagebücher*, vol. 7, 123 (February 28, 1924). See in the appendix on pp. 547 to 585, the trial reports in the *Münchner Neueste Nachrichten*. On Elsa Bruckmann's attitudes, see Wolfgang Martynkewicz, *Salon Deutschland: Geist und Macht 1900–1945* (Berlin, 2009), 391–392.

25. Gritschneder, *Bewährungsfrist für den Terroristen Adolf H.*, 67–94 (here 92). In an article in the *Münchener Zeitung* (no. 100 [April 10, 1923]), Karl Alexander von Müller described Hitler and Ludendorff as "German men who acted out of passionate love for Germany." Cited in Berg, *Karl Alexander von Müller*, 97.

26. Jacob Altmaier, "Zeigner und Hitler," *Die Weltbühne* 20/15 (April 10, 1924), 463–467 (here 466, 463).

27. "Nach dem Münchener Urteil: Das erschütterte Rechtsempfinden," *Berliner Tageblatt* 158 (April 2, 1924).

28. "Der schwarzweißrote Wimpel," *Vossische Zeitung* 157 (April 1, 1924).

29. See Ullrich, *Hitler: Ascent*, 165–184.

30. "Ministerbesprechung v. 6.2.1924," *AdR: Die Kabinette Marx*, vol. 1, no. 90, 322–325 (324). See also p. xvi–xvii; Winkler, *Weimar*, 253; Hehl, *Wilhelm Marx*, 275–276; and Mühlhausen, *Friedrich Ebert*, 719–720.

31. *AdR: Die Kabinette Marx*, vol. 1, no. 104, 362–364 (here 363).

32. See "Ministerbesprechung v. 15.2.1924," *AdR: Marx*, vol. 1, no. 105, 365–367 (here 367).

33.  "Besprechung mit führenden Reichstagsabgeordneten der DNVP v. 19.2.1924,"
     *AdR: Marx*, vol. 1, no. 113, 384.

34.  "Besprechung mit führenden Reichstagsabgeordneten der SPD v. 19.2.1923,"
     *AdR: Marx*, vol. 1, no. 111, 380–381.

35.  "Kabinettssitzung v. 14.3.1924," *AdR: Marx*, vol. 1, no. 144, 462. See also Stock-
     hausen, *Sechs Jahre Reichskanzlei*, 112 (March 13, 1924); Hehl, *Wilhelm Marx*,
     277–278; and Mühlhausen, *Friedrich Ebert*, 720.

36.  Büttner, *Weimar*, 338.

37.  See Wulf, *Hugo Stinnes*, 524–525; and Richter, *Deutsche Volkspartei*, 312–313.

38.  "Stresemann an Georg Wache (Glatz), 17.3.1924," in Stresemann, *Vermächtnis*,
     vol. 1, 355. Wolfgang Stresemann recalled his father returning home in an equally
     dark and angry mood: "He talked on the phone the whole evening, dictating a
     long editorial to his Berlin press outlet *Die Zeit*." *Mein Vater Gustav Stresemann*,
     298.

39.  Stresemann, *Vermächtnis*, vol. 1, 354.

40.  See Kolb and Richter, eds., *Nationalliberalismus in der Weimarer Republik*, doc.
     55, 489–491; Stresemann, *Vermächtnis*, vol. 1, 372–373; and Richter, *Deutsche
     Volkspartei*, 316–319.

41.  See Richter, *Deutsche Volkspartei*, 319–320.

42.  Richter, 21.

43.  See Feldman, *Hugo Stinnes*, 928, 931–935; and Wallwitz, *Die große Inflation*,
     278–282.

44.  Gordon A. Craig, *Germany, 1866–1945* (Oxford, 1980), 452.

45.  *Deutsche Allgemeine Zeitung* 173 (April 11, 1924).

46.  Richard Lewinsohn, *Vossische Zeitung* 174 (April 11, 1924).

47.  Ernst Feder, *Berliner Tageblatt* 174 (April 11, 1924).

48.  Stockhausen, *Sechs Jahre Reichskanzlei*, 115. See also Morus (Richard Lewin-
     sohn), "Hugo Stinnes," *Die Weltbühne* 20/16 (April 17, 1924), 518: "His time was
     done, not just because inflation was over, but also because he had taken the princi-
     ple by which he accumulated his wealth as far as it would go."

49.  See Feldman, *Hugo Stinnes*, 936ff.

50.  Stresemann, *Vermächtnis*, vol. 1, 289.

51.  Stresemann, 300. See also W. Stresemann, *Mein Vater Gustav Stresemann*, 297.

52.  Kessler, *Tagebuch*, vol. 8, 206 (January 21, 1924). Hughes's quotes appear here as
     recorded in German: his actual wording may have differed.

53.  See Winkler, *Weimar*, 258; Büttner, *Weimar*, 351; Longerich, *Deutschland, 1918–
     1933*, 153–154; and Mommsen, *Die verspielte Freiheit*, 186–187.

54.  Link, *Die amerikanische Stabilisierungspolitik in Deutschland*, 272–273.

55.  "Besprechung mit den Ministerpräsidenten der Länder v. 14.4.1924," *AdR: Die
     Kabinette Marx*, vol. 1, 175, 555–565 (here 556–557).

56.  "Ministerbesprechung v. 14.4.1924," *AdR: Marx*, vol. 1, no. 177, 567–568; and
     "Die deutschen Note v. 14.4.1924," 568, note 6.

57.  See Werner Liebe, *Die Deutschnationale Volkspartei, 1918–1924* (Düsseldorf,
     1956), 76; and John G. Williamson, *Karl Helfferich, 1872–1924: Economist,
     Financier, Politician* (Princeton, 1971), 395–400.

58. Stresemann, *Vermächtnis*, vol. 1, 397, 400.

59. Stockhausen, *Sechs Jahre Reichskanzlei*, 117 (May 4, 1924).

60. See Heinrich August Winkler, *Der Schein der Normalität: Arbeiter und Arbeiterbewegung in der Weimarer Republik, 1924 bis 1930* (Berlin, 1985), 177–188. See also Büttner, *Weimar*, 338–339; Longerich, *Deutschland, 1918–1933*, 156; and Richter, *Deutsche Volkspartei*, 330–331.

61. *Berliner Tageblatt* 213 (May 5, 1924).

62. Julius Elbau, "Die Sieger," *Vossische Zeitung* 213 (May 5, 1924).

63. Kessler, *Tagebuch*, vol. 8, 324–325 (May 6, 1924).

64. See *AdR: Die Kabinette Marx*, vol. 1, xviii, and "Ministerbesprechung v. 6.5.1924," no. 193, 613–614. See also Hehl, *Wilhelm Marx*, 283.

65. Kessler, *Tagebuch*, vol. 8, 326 (May 9, 1924).

66. See *AdR: Die Kabinette Marx*, vol. 1, xviii–xix, and "Ministerbesprechung v. 15.5.1924," no. 199, 633–638. On the DNVP parliamentary group's decision, see 636, note 13.

67. Richter, *Deutsche Volkspartei*, 336.

68. "Abdruck der Erklärung v. 20.5.1924," *AdR: Die Kabinette Marx*, vol. 1, no. 206, 659, note 1.

69. "Ministerbesprechung v. 24.5.1924," *AdR: Marx*, vol. 1, no. 206, 660. See Hehl, *Wilhelm Marx*, 285. D'Abernon noted, "If the Germans want to bring about a concentration hostile to them I do not think they could take a step more appropriate than putting Tirpitz in as Chancellor." D'Abernon, *Ambassador*, 66 (May 25, 1924).

70. "Ministerbesprechung v. 26.5.1924," *AdR: Die Kabinette Marx*, vol. 1, no. 209, 666. See also note 2: "Beschluss der DVP-Reichstagsfraktion v. 26.5.1924."

71. See *AdR: Marx*, vol. 1, xix, and "Ministerbesprechung v. 31.5.1924," no. 212, 6171–6172; Mühlhausen, *Friedrich Ebert*, 875–878; Richter, *Deutsche Volkspartei*, 338; Winkler, *Weimar*, 262–263; and Hehl, *Wilhelm Marx*, 286–287.

72. Stresemann, *Vermächtnis*, vol. 1, 412 ("Tagesnotiz v. 30.5.1924"), and 413 ("Brief Stresemanns an Marx, 2.6.1924"). See also Richter, *Deutsche Volkspartei*, 338.

73. D'Abernon, *Ambassador*, 69 (May 30, 1924); Stresemann, *Vermächtnis*, vol. 1, 413. See W. Stresemann, *Mein Vater Gustav Stresemann*, 302.

74. Stresemann, *Vermächtnis*, vol. 1, 413.

75. See "Rücktrittschreiben Emmingers an Marx v. 14.4.1924," *AdR: Die Kabinette Marx*, vol. 1, no. 176, 565–566.

76. Erich Dombrowski, "'Unser Banner hat nie geschwankt': Die Rolle der Deutschnationalen," *Berliner Tageblatt* 263 (April 4, 1924).

77. See Winkler, *Weimar*, 264; and Mühlhausen, *Friedrich Ebert*, 879–880.

78. See Stresemann, *Vermächtnis*, vol. 1, 407, 416.

79. W. Stresemann, *Mein Vater Gustav Stresemann*, 309–310. See Stockhausen, *Sechs Jahre Reichskanzlei*, 123 (July 8, 1924): "Low mood in the Reich Chancellery, where people fear the French standpoint will win out."

80. "Ministerbesprechung v. 2.8.1924," *AdR: Die Kabinette Marx*, vol. 2, no. 269, 937.

81. W. Stresemann, *Mein Vater Gustav Stresemann*, 311.

82. Stresemann, *Vermächtnis*, vol. 1, 470–471. On the course of the London confer-

ence, see Stresemann, 468–501; Link, *Die amerikanische Stabilisierungspolitik in Deutschland*, 296–306; Hehl, *Wilhelm Marx*, 294–303; Wright, *Gustav Stresemann*, 290–291; and W. Stresemann, *Mein Vater Gustav Stresemann*, 311–316.

83. Stresemann, *Vermächtnis*, vol. 1, 480–481.

84. Stresemann, 485.

85. Stresemann, 493.

86. See Mühlhausen, *Friedrich Ebert*, 884–885; and Link, *Die amerikanische Stabilisierungspolitik in Deutschland*, 312–313.

87. Richter, *Deutsche Volkspartei*, 344 and note 42.

88. "Kundgebung zur Kriegsschuldfrage v. 29.8.1924," *AdR: Die Kabinette Marx*, vol. 2, no. 290, 1006–1007. The declarations were published in the press on August 30, 1924.

89. See "Aufzeichnung des Auswärtigen Amtes v. 10.9.1924," *AdR: Die Kabinette Marx*, vol. 2, no. 298, 1020–1031, and "Ministerbesprechung v. 15.9. 1924," vol. 2, no. 301, 1038–1042.

90. Kessler, *Tagebuch*, vol. 8, 411 (April 29, 1929).

91. Kessler, 412 (August 29, 1924); and *Berliner Tageblatt* 412 (August 30, 1924).

92. Erich Dombrowski, "Die gestrige Reichstagssitzung," *Berliner Tageblatt* 412 (August 30, 1924).

93. *Vossische Zeitung* 412 (August 30, 1924).

94. Rosenberg, *Geschichte der Weimarer Republik*, 169.

95. See Winkler, *Weimar*, 264–265; Büttner, *Weimar*, 357–358; and Wright, *Gustav Stresemann*, 291–292.

96. See Longerich, *Deutschland, 1918–1933*, 159–176; and Winkler, *Der Schein der Normalität*, 26ff., 46ff.

97. See Wright, *Gustav Stresemann*, 322ff.; Berg, *Gustav Stresemann*, 84ff.; and Kolb, *Gustav Stresemann*, 94–98, 108–111.

98. See Klaus Hildebrand's critical account *Das vergangene Reich: Deutsche Außenpolitik von Bismarck zu Hitler 1871–1945* (Stuttgart, 1995), 400ff.; and Pohl, *Gustav Stresemann*, 261ff.

99. Kisch, *Der rasende Reporter*, 660.

100. Haffner, *Defying Hitler*, 75. See also Bisky, *Berlin*, 487, 502ff.

101. See Vollmer-Heitmann, *Wir sind von Kopf*, 22ff., 61ff.; and Ute Planert, "Körper, Sexualität und Geschlechterordnung in der Weimarer Republik," in Rossol and Ziemann, eds., *Aufbruch und Abgründe*, 595–618.

102. Gay, *Weimar Culture*, 133–134.

103. See Winkler, *Der Schein der Normalität*, 727–728.

104. See Winkler, 267–268, 271–274; Büttner, *Weimar*, 340; and Mühlhausen, *Friedrich Ebert*, 894, 897–899.

105. See Winkler, *Weimar*, 309–312; Büttner, *Weimar*, 341; and Longerich, *Deutschland, 1918–1933*, 237–238.

106. See Winkler, *Weimar*, 320–321; and Büttner, *Weimar*, 341–342.

107. See Winkler, *Weimar*, 334–338; and Büttner, *Weimar*, 383–384.

108. Carl von Ossietzky, "Zum Geburtstag der Verfassung," *Die Weltbühne* 25/32 (August 6, 1929), 189–191 (here 191); also in Ossietzky, *Sämtliche Schriften*, vol.

5: *1929–1930*, ed. Bärbel Boldt, Ute Maack, and Günther Nickel (Reinbek bei Hamburg, 1994), 161–164 (here 164).

109. "Scholem an Gershom Scholem, 28.4.1925," in Scholem and Scholem, *Mutter und Sohn*, 130. On Hindenburg's election, see Wolfram Pyta, *Hindenburg: Herrschaft zwischen Hohenzollern und Hitler* (Berlin, 2007), 461–476.

110. Sternheim, *Tagebücher*, vol. 1, 722 (April 28, 1925).

111. Victor Klemperer, *Leben sammeln und nicht fragen wozu und warum: Tagebücher, 1925–1932*, ed. Walter Nowojski (Berlin, 1996), 49 (April 27, 1925).

112. Kessler, *Tagebuch*, vol. 8, 685–686 (May 12, 1925).

113. See Klaus Wernecke, *Der vergessene Führer: Alfred Hugenberg—Pressemacht und Nationalsozialismus* (Hamburg, 1982), 142ff.

114. See Winkler, *Weimar*, 283–284; Büttner, *Weimar*, 348–349; and Mommsen, *Die verspielte Freiheit*, 253.

115. See the canonical study by Karl Dietrich Bracher, *Die Auflösung der Weimarer Republik*, 3rd rev. ed. (Villingen, 1960).

116. Zweig, *World of Yesterday*, 315.

117. Martin Feuchtwanger, *Zukunft ist ein blindes Spiel: Erinnerungen* (Munich, 1989), 136. In the words of Hans Mayer, inflation has opened an "abyss...that would never be closed off again." Mayer, *Ein Deutscher auf Widerruf*, vol. 1, 35.

118. Haffner, *Defying Hitler*, 53.

119. Kurzke, *Thomas Mann*, 353.

120. See Taylor, *Inflation*, 344, 348–349.

121. Wehler, *Deutsche Gesellschaftsgeschichte*, vol. 4, 259.

122. Ullrich, *Hitler: Ascent*, 223.

123. See Winkler, *Weimar*, 388, 505, 535.

# INDEX

Page numbers in italics indicate a figure on the corresponding page.